DATE DUE

JA 28 '94			
NO 18 '94			
MY 10 '96			
DE 0 '97			

DEMCO 38-296

Pitt Series in Policy and Institutional Studies

The
Political Failure of
Employment Policy
1945–1982

Gary Mucciaroni

University of Pittsburgh Press

Published by the University of Pittsburgh Press, Pittsburgh, Pa. 15260
Copyright © 1990, University of Pittsburgh Press
All rights reserved
Baker & Taylor International, London
Manufactured in the United States of America

Library of Congress Cataloging-in-Publication Data

Mucciaroni, Gary.
   The political failure of employment policy, 1945–1982 / Gary
Mucciaroni.
      p.   cm. — (Pitt series in policy and institutional studies)
      ISBN 0-8229-3648-8
      1. Manpower policy—United States.   2. United States—Politics and
government—1945–   1. Title.   II. Series.
      HD5724.M78   1990
      331.11'0973—dc20   90-31987
                                                                              CIP

To my parents, Al and Joan,
who sparked my interest in politics
and in the plight of labor

Contents

III   INTERESTS

IV   THE POLITICAL FAILURE OF EMPLOYMENT POLICY

List of Acronyms

AFL	American Federation of Labor
AFL-CIO	American Federation of Labor–Congress of Industrial Organizations
AFSCME	American Federation of State, County, and Municipal Employees
BAT	Bureau of Apprenticeship and Training
BES	Bureau of Economic Security
BLS	Bureau of Labor Statistics
BWP	Bureau of Work Programs
BWTP	Bureau of Work and Training Programs
CAAs	community action agencies
CAMPS	Cooperative Area Manpower Planning System
CBO	Congressional Budget Office
CEA	Council of Economic Advisers: the council
CED	Committee for Economic Development
CEP	Concentrated Employment Program
CETA	Comprehensive Employment and Training Act (1973)
CMPS	Center for Manpower Policy Studies
DOL	Department of Labor: Labor Department
EEA	Emergency Employment Act (1971)
EOA	Economic Opportunity Act (1964)
EOP	Executive Office of the President
GAO	General Accounting Office
HEW	Department of Health, Education, and Welfare
ICESA	Interstate Conference of Employment Security Agencies
JEC	Joint Economic Committee
JOBS	Job Opportunities in the Business Sector
JTPA	Job Training Partnership Act (1982)
LO	Swedish Labor Federation
MDTA	Manpower Development and Training Act (1962)

MTA	Manpower Training Act
NAB	National Alliance of Business
NMAC	National Manpower Advisory Committee
NMPTF	National Manpower Policy Task Force
NRPB	National Resources Planning Board
NUC	National Urban Coalition
NYC	Neighborhood Youth Corps
OEO	Office of Economic Opportunity
OICs	opportunity industrial centers
OMAT	Office of Manpower, Automation, and Training
OMB	Office of Management and Budget
OPEC	Organization of Petroleum Exporting Countries
PCOM	President's Commission on Manpower
PIC	private industry council
PSE	public service employment
SAP	Swedish Social Democratic party
TUC	Trades Union Congress
UI	unemployment insurance
USES	United States Employment Service
VISTA	Volunteers in Service to America
WIN	Work Incentive Program

Acknowledgments

I WISH to express my appreciation for the assistance that I received from many people during the course of my research and writing. In providing the intellectual stimulation for launching the project, and his helpful comments at the dissertation-writing stage, I thank Leon Lindberg. Peter Eisinger provided guidance and support throughout and I am forever grateful to him. As friend and colleague, Paul Brace encouraged me to transform a very lengthy dissertation into a publishable manuscript. I received helpful comments and sound advice from a number of other colleagues who read the manuscript in various stages of its development, including Bert Rockman, William Gormley, Lawrence Mead, and above all, Tom Anton. Whatever the shortcomings of the work, they are my responsibility.

Generous financial support came from the Governmental Studies Program of the Brookings Institution where I served as a research fellow for one year and a visiting scholar for another. I thank Martha Derthick, director of the program, in particular for creating a climate conducive to fruitful research activity. I also wish to acknowledge the support of the United States Department of Labor which awarded me a Fellowship in Employment and Training, administered through the Social Science Research Council. For helping me obtain access to Labor Department documents, I thank the librarians and archivists in the Historian's Office of the department and those in the National Archives.

Robert Lehrmann, Patricia Moynagh, and Norberto Terrizas provided competent research assistance. Jane Flanders and Diane Hammond of the University of Pittsburgh Press rendered competent and prompt editorial assistance.

The Political Failure of Employment Policy
1945–1982

1

Employment Policy and Liberal Failure

WITH HIGH HOPES in the early 1960s the federal government began a modest program to retrain unemployed adults. The program was called the Manpower Development and Training Act (MDTA). Two decades and almost $77 billion later, a similar program was enacted by Congress entitled the Job Training Partnership Act (JTPA). The MDTA is now long forgotten, and the JTPA is hardly a household word even though it is a current federal program. In certain respects, the JTPA brought us full circle from where we were two decades earlier. Once again a modestly funded effort to employ some of the unemployed was launched at a time of renewed concerns about international competition, adjusting the skills of the workforce to economic change, and expanding economic opportunity.

These similarities notwithstanding, the atmosphere in which the JTPA was debated in the early 1980s was in marked contrast with the 1960s. It was characterized by greater contentiousness and uncertainty, reflecting the sobering experience of the preceding twenty-year period. The MDTA was forged during a period of growing liberal confidence, the JTPA in the midst of a dispirited liberalism. Gone was the faith in the capacity of the federal government to solve major social and economic problems, which had inspired the authors of the 1960s legislation. Diminished, though by no means vanished, was the broad bipartisan consensus that had supported as legitimate and desirable a federal role in employment and training. The administration in power did not share the consensus. It was only the persistence of Congress, and a 1982 unemployment rate in double digits, that kept the federal role alive.

Between MDTA and JTPA were two more memorable initiatives— the Economic Opportunity Act (EOA), better known as the poverty program, and the Comprehensive Employment and Training Act (CETA). These two programs remain key parts of the liberal domestic policy legacy of the postwar era. Under the EOA, a haphazard profusion

3

of specific categorical measures were created to provide training and work experience, with the objective of promoting the employability of the poor population. Two issues came to dominate the agenda of employment policy in the wake of the legislative outpouring of the Kennedy-Johnson years. At the federal and local levels, administrative chaos reigned. A consensus among experts and administrators emerged calling for "consolidation, decentralization, and decategorization" of the programs. Second, there was concern about the actual impact the programs were having on the population they were intended to help. Disenchanted with training and work experience programs, liberals turned to directly creating jobs as a way both to reduce poverty and to meet the growing demand for public services in fiscally strapped cities. Both issues turned out to be a source of serious ideological and institutional conflict between President Nixon and the Democratic-led Congress. In the midst of a recession, Nixon reluctantly gave into the pressures for a jobs program. The Emergency Employment Act of 1971 was the first effort to directly create jobs since the Great Depression. Administrative reform, however, was not accomplished until Nixon, beleaguered by Watergate, capitulated to liberal demands for a continuation of the public employment program under CETA.

During the high unemployment and urban fiscal crises of the 1970s, CETA's budget and objectives grew substantially, so that by late in the decade it had dwarfed the entire poverty program of the 1960s.[1] As CETA expanded, so did its troubles. Federal officials found themselves confronted with a new set of administrative problems arising out of the devolution of authority to local governments. Much of the decade was spent trying to reform the reforms that CETA had put in place. The basic problem was that CETA was called upon to perform several conflicting tasks. The local governments that were authorized to run the programs had objectives that were not congruent with those deemed most important in Washington. As local officials used CETA to meet local needs, and as mismanagement and abuse took a toll on the reputation of the program, Washington was compelled to recentralize authority. The program's poor public image and the recentralization of control after 1978 spelled the end for CETA, depriving it both of credibility and of a constituency that valued the fiscal assistance it could provide. CETA's fate was sealed with the coming to power of the Reagan administration, which quickly liquidated the program.

The passage of JTPA confirmed that, even in the heyday of the Reagan Revolution and despite the CETA debacle, a broad bipartisan consensus in favor of a federal role in employment policy endures. Yet it also confirmed the narrowness of vision and commitment upon which that agreement rests. Everyone, or almost everyone, could agree that positive intervention to address unemployment was desirable and needed—but only if it was confined to training (rather than direct job creation), only if it was hedged with conditions that made it possible for only the most disadvantaged Americans to participate, and only if its budgetary commitment was so meager as to assist only a fraction of the eligible population.

This study recounts the story of employment policy in the United States during the post–World War II decades of liberal activism. It seeks to understand why employment policy has remained of peripheral importance to the labor market and why its history is one of such disappointment. What accounts for the inability to create and sustain a consensus in support of a significant role for employment policy in managing the economic affairs of the nation? And why has the consensus that exists for what is a comparatively limited mission for employment policy been strained and overshadowed by a troubled legacy? Why, in short, did a key response to unemployment by liberal reformers end largely in political failure?

To adequately address these questions, we must understand not only what happened but also what failed to happen. We need to look not only at the policy options that were chosen and carried out but, as well, at those issues that never reached the political agenda and those options that were never adopted. What did not happen is important because, by looking only at what programs existed and how they performed, we risk construing the reasons for the failure too narrowly. It is plausible to argue that a different kind of employment policy would have developed greater political support within government and outside of it.

It is also necessary that we conceptualize employment policy sufficiently broadly to encompass those activities that address unemployment as a principal goal, yet not so broadly as to make the study unwieldy and lacking focus. Virtually every government activity has an impact on unemployment—from environmental regulation to the Peace Corps, and from the Pentagon's procurement policies to the incentives for economic investment in the tax code. Two sets of policy instruments have as their sole purpose (or at least as a central one) the prevention or amelioration of joblessness. One set consists of employment and training programs. These are micropolicy measures that are intended to affect both the demand for and supply of labor. These include directly creating jobs in the public or private sectors, training, retraining, counseling, and placement. The other is macroeconomic policy—the manipulation of fiscal and monetary aggregates—that influences overall economic activity and, consequently, demand for labor.[2]

A central focus of this study is the formulation of employment and training programs, which takes place in what we shall call the employment policy subsystem. The subsystem is concerned primarily with programmatic issues—eligibility criteria for participants, the mix of services and benefits to be provided, administrative and service delivery arrangements, and the level of annual appropriations. We shall also examine a set of broader issues and policies that fall outside the subsystem but that critically impinge upon it. These include struggles to adopt full-employment legislation, major initiatives in macroeconomic management, and other developments in economic policy that have had a direct impact on the mission and scale of employment and training programs. Whether employment policy will play a central role in economic management and planning or, alternatively, whether it will be relegated to a residual social welfare mission depends in great measure on developments outside the employment policy subsystem.

Although there is an important relationship between employment programs and these broader issues and policies, the two arenas are politically quite distinct. Each is characterized by different kinds of conflict, constellations of institutional actors, and coalitions of organized interests. Because the issues that fall outside the subsystem raise basic issues about the role of government in the economy and have the potential for redistributing substantial economic power and resources between labor and business, they tend to be more visible and conflictual than those issues that occupy the agenda of the subsystem. Because the issues in the subsystem are more narrow and specific, the scope, visibility, and intensity of conflict is usually reduced.[3] Subsystem participants include the congressional labor committees and subcommittees, the Labor Department and other operating agencies, interest groups, labor economists, and program specialists. In the nonsubsystem arena, the main institutional actors are political parties, top leaders of the executive branch, and Congress as a whole. Political interests form encompassing coalitions around class and ideological divisions, with labor and liberal activists on one side and business and conservative groups on the other.

In examining the broader issues that fall outside the employment policy subsystem, we begin with the defeat of the Full Employment Bill of 1945, a watershed event that had critical implications for the development of employment policy. Its rejection testified to the profound obstacles in the United States to the establishment of a "right to employment" and to an economic policy based upon large spending deficits and public planning of investment. Absent the legal mandate to pursue full employment, the numerous employment programs eventually enacted in the 1960s and 1970s were left without any overarching purpose and devoid of a rationale for budgets sufficiently large to have an appreciable effect on unemployment and poverty. In the wake of the full-employment defeat, a vacuum was created, setting the stage for the formulation and adoption of a much more conservative brand of Keynesianism, stressing tax cuts and automatic stabilizers rather than increased spending. (A similar outcome emerged with the defeat of the Humphrey-Hawkins full-employment proposal in the late 1970s and, subsequently, the tax cuts of 1981.)

These developments, along with the insistence of influential Keynesian economists that unemployment was strictly a problem of demand deficiency rather than structural problems in the labor market, left employment policy with little in the way of a positive role to play in economic policy. With the coming of the poverty program, employment policy was placed on a trajectory that defined its mission in terms of social policy objectives and that prevented it from becoming utilized as a tool of economic management. Employment and training programs were left outside the realm of economic intervention, given no meaningful role in maintaining economic stability or growth. Their purpose became merely to offset and ameliorate some of the undesirable impacts of private economic activity. Thus, the enduring feature of American employment policy has been its overwhelming emphasis upon residual social welfare or "relief" objectives, broadly conceived. These have taken a variety of forms—addressing the intractable problems of the "disadvantaged" and long-term unemployed, assisting those left jobless by cyclical downturns, and subsidizing local governments in fiscal crisis. All of these have been ad hoc reactions to economic and social crises, that were intended as—or evolved into—relief programs rather than economic recovery strategies. Cross-national comparison is especially useful in examining the question of why the United States adopted a less-than-full-employment, social-welfare-oriented policy. In chapter 10 we explore why other countries developed more positive employment policies, policies committed to the goal of full employment, and assigned them a critical role in economic intervention.

Only when we understand the actors and forces that shaped and constrained employment policy can we diagnose the reasons for political failure. The argument of this book is that employment policy is rooted in the *ideas, institutions,* and *interests* that operate in the policy-making arena. *Ideas* refer to the ideological and intellectual premises of employment policy. Here we will consider the cognitions, beliefs, and values that affect policy makers' understanding of problems and their crafting of policies. These ideas may be found in ideology, in economic doctrines and prescriptions, and in the causal maps that policy makers bring to specific problems. *Institutions* refer to the organizations and capacities of the American state; that is, the decision-making processes, rules, norms and incentives that structure policy makers' behavior. *Interests* concern the needs, demands, and preferences arising out of groups and classes in society, as they influence or fail to influence policy makers. Relevant here are the level and scope of mobilization of constituencies and patterns of coalition building. We shall also see that public policy is an important determinant in its own right, because previous policy choices shape future ones. In particular, policy trajectories are difficult to redirect once established, making certain future choices more likely and others less so. The three factors, along with antecedent policy commitments, circumscribed the mission and scale of employment programs, negatively affected their design and performance, and in turn, undercut their potential and actual political support.

Each of the these analytic tools guides the search for patterns of behavior in the policy arena. Each provides an alternative perspective on the evolution of employment policy and what may account for its political failure in the United States. The impact of each is traced separately in parts 1, 2, and 3. No pretense is made to find a single cause or elegant explanation of the political failure of employment policy. An adequate explanation requires all of the causes. It is precisely the combination of factors that would have made overcoming the political failure so difficult and that presents such a formidable challenge to those who might seek to rebuild employment policy in the future. All of them are interrelated and mutually reinforcing. The concluding chapter assesses the relative importance of each factor, elucidates the linkages between them, and distinguishes those aspects of the policy record that are better explained by certain of the factors than by others.

However, to view employment policy as determined by cultural values and intellectual paradigms, institutional structure, and powerful interests is not enough. We must be careful not to view policy as exclusively shaped by constraints. To simply present and synthesize the three interpretations of the policy record is to leave the analysis overdetermined but not to tell us very much about how policy was constructed. In employment policy, choices were not so constricted that they kept alternative options off the agenda, dictated the particular content of policy at key historical junctures, or guaranteed results. Rather than see policy choices as automatic, we should view them as contingent outcomes. They are adaptive responses at particular historical junctures. Whether policy changes or fails to change, the content and direction of policy change, its timing, and its political ramifications all turn on defining and diagnosing the problem, figuring out why it

exists, and developing feasible courses of action to address it. Hugh
Heclo calls this engaging in "collective puzzlement" or "*political learning*"—altering behavior in light of experience.[4] Policy making is intrinsically a creative, problem-solving process in which information gathering, analysis, deliberation, and innovation play a crucial part. In this
context, institutions and interest organizations do not just structure
conflict, distribute authority, and bring to bear power on decisions, but
also serve as vehicles through which learning takes place or fails to
occur.

Political learning shapes policy indirectly as well, by reinforcing,
diminishing, or otherwise altering the constraints on choice. How policies are designed and implemented and whether they succeed or fail
contribute to building constituencies, thus potentially altering the balance of power among interests. The choice of policy objectives, instruments, and administrative arrangements also helps determine which
institutional actors will manage policy and the configuration of the
arena in which future choices will be made. Over time, such choices
may even affect the continued relevance and resonance of values and
ideology for policy.

It is plausible that the reason, or reasons, for the political failure of
employment policy are far more obvious than the ones advanced in this
book. If the American people do not support such programs, or if the
programs have failed to have a positive impact on the problems they
were intended to address, then it would be no surprise that it has been
difficult to sustain a broad consensus for these programs. Neither of
these explanations—that Americans do not want the programs or that
they "don't work"—is very persuasive. But because both have gained
a degree of popular acceptance, let us deal with each of them.

First, one must be very careful in attempting to make causal connections between public opinion and public policy. Even if it could be
shown that a majority (or a large segment) of the American public
rejected most government programs to address unemployment, this
would not necessarily mean that the political failure of employment
policy is the result of public opinion. And it obviously would not explain
the existence of the programs and the billions of dollars that have
been spent over the postwar period, in the first place. The relationship
between mass opinion and policy varies widely across policy areas and
over time periods. There are many cases of the public's lack of awareness of, indifference toward, and outright opposition to many programs
and policies. A majority of the public opposes the busing of school
children to achieve racial integration, spending on foreign aid programs, and under Reagan, many of the cutbacks in spending and

regulatory programs. And in many cases where there is public support for existing policies, such support was absent or unclear until they were adopted.[5]

Second, there is scant evidence to indicate that most Americans consider it inappropriate or undesirable for government to take actions intended to reduce unemployment. In an opinion poll conducted in the mid-1970s, 77 percent of the respondents agreed that "the government should be making considerable efforts to end unemployment."[6] There is also clear support for specific kinds of government programs. Eighty-nine percent agreed when they were asked, "when people can't find any jobs, would you be in favor of the government putting them on the payroll and finding work for them" in various public services?[7] Another poll found that 74 percent supported a jobs program even if it meant increasing the size of the federal deficit.[8] Although no poll data are available on attitudes toward training programs, there is abundant evidence that Americans not only support public spending on education (an activity very similar to training) by wide majorities, but that they want government to increase spending.[9] These responses are consistent with the literature on public opinion as a whole, which characterizes Americans over the past generation as "programmatically liberal" in their support of an interventionist government and specific domestic programs.[10]

This is not to say that the public has supported the entire liberal agenda as it relates to unemployment. As we shall see in chapter 5, a majority of the public does not appear to support "guaranteed full employment"—that is, a mandate that government provide jobs for everyone who is either unable or unwilling to find work in the private sector—even though they may have done so earlier in the postwar period. But the efforts of the 1960s and 1970s never amounted to a full-employment policy anyway. There is no reason to believe that Americans were, or are now, opposed to the level of government activity and spending that existed in those years.

Third, while the attitudes of a majority of Americans reveal programmatic liberalism, they have long been described as ideologically conservative in that they respond favorably to the values and beliefs related to competitive capitalism and negatively to "big government" and "socialism."[11] Policy makers, experts, interest group spokesmen, and other opinion leaders are exposed to these dominant values and beliefs through socialization processes, the mass media, and their various contacts with the public. By examining the role of ideas in how issues are defined, in the formulation of policy options, and in levels of mobilization of coalitions representing the ideological and material interests of classes in society, this study takes into account the influence of values and beliefs that are widely shared in society.

There are several reasons for rejecting any simplistic explanation of political failure based upon the programs' impacts upon individuals or the economy. First, it is not necessarily clear what results were intended or, to the extent that clear objectives can be discerned, which among several (sometimes competing) objectives were most important. If policy makers cannot agree substantially upon objectives, then any attempt to measure results is likely to be arbitrary. This problem is compounded by the fact that we are looking across several years at a number of programs that came and went and whose priorities shifted. One program, the Comprehensive Employment and Training Act, was actually a complex of programs, which varied in their impact. The resulting mix of results made generalizations about success or failure difficult. There has been a lack of agreement on how to measure results and at what level a program should be deemed a "success" or a "failure." More sophisticated evaluation studies came only late in the period under study.[12]

These caveats aside, the best evaluative evidence suggests that, on the whole, training and job creation programs have produced positive results. The MDTA program placed about 70 percent of its participants in jobs for which they had been trained, the overall dropout rate was less than that of the nation's high schools, and the taxes paid by employed graduates replaced the costs of their training within five years. Cost-benefit studies estimated that total benefits exceeded total costs in almost every case, sometimes by over 100 percent.[13] The most extensive nationwide study of CETA, conducted by the National Academy of Sciences, found mixed results. The report concluded, however, that the overall results were favorable and recommended that CETA be reauthorized. Most participants experienced increases in employment stability and earnings (albeit often modest ones) in relation to the experiences of comparison groups.[14] Some programs with a major training component were often quite successful. The Job Corps, for instance, has a highly favorable reputation, with well over 90 percent of its enrollees placed.[15] CETA's impacts clearly varied from locality to locality. The most intense study of CETA's long-term effects was done in and around Baltimore. Over one thousand participants were examined for five years, 1973–1978, most were from disadvantaged backgrounds, and 60 percent were black. The results were highly favorable. Participants' employment rates rose significantly upon terminating the program, and their employment status persisted. After five years, only 6 percent were looking for jobs. Real wages went up significantly over the period, as well.[16]

One of the most important reasons for rejecting the notion that political failure is due to a lack of results is simply the fact that the ability or inability of employment and training programs to achieve results had little appreciable, discernible impact on policy decisions. Even when reliable data on results were available, they often came late—after the program had been abandoned or significantly modified or had changed objectives. To the extent that evaluative data was used by policy makers, they usually followed a predictable political pattern: those who were negatively (or positively) disposed toward the program, for other reasons, interpreted the data to support their positions. Moreover, many programs in other policy areas (e.g., agriculture, income maintenance for the poor) have retained considerable political support and large budgets despite widespread reputations as programs having dubious records of accomplishment and having produced negative, unintended consequences. For these reasons alone it is unlikely that program results were of decisive importance.

This is not to deny that political support for employment and training programs has suffered from both real and perceived failures of performance. Indeed, this is the major proximate cause for their decline. But both the reality and perception of failure have had more to do with program design, administration, and service delivery than they have with the substantive impacts on the targeted populations. Thus, performance is important in understanding the political failure of employment policy, but performance mainly in the sense of how employment policy was conducted rather than what it accomplished.[17] Poor performance regarding the conduct of employment policy refers to multiple, ambiguous, and conflicting goals, uncertain funding, and seemingly endless administrative and service delivery problems. Policy has shifted from social to economic goals, from training to job creation, from efforts to assist the long-term unemployed living in the nation's cities to the cyclically unemployed and those displaced by structural economic change. Administrative arrangements have alternated from centralization, to decentralization, to a reassertion of centralization, before giving way most recently to another attempt at decentralization. Funding has risen and fallen less in response to any policy rationale than in reaction to economic crises and shifting political winds. If lack of political support is partly the result of shortcomings in design and poor performance (real and perceived), then we must ask: what accounts for them? The argument of this book is that program design and performance problems are symptomatic of a more profound set of constraints, and political failure is its result.

In showing how the failure of employment policy is rooted in long-standing political, institutional, and intellectual problems of the policy-making arena, this book can contribute to the broader debate over the exhaustion of the liberal policy agenda. Obviously, we cannot provide any definitive answer to the question of why the positive government intervention championed by liberals reached its limits in the 1970s and 1980s. For one thing, the decline of liberalism reflects a complex interaction of factors at many levels—demographic changes, changes in party organization and patterns of electoral behavior, the rise of cultural and foreign policy issues, and liberal politicians' responses to them that have placed reform liberalism at a distinct disadvantage.[18] Not everyone would even agree that liberalism has declined in certain aspects of political life. For another, many initiatives launched by liberals in this century *have* become political success stories—Social Security, Medicare, and Head Start among the most notable—and remain a permanent part of the American landscape. Employment policy is a single case with particular characteristics that may or may not be generalizable to other cases of policy formation. Any investigation of why certain liberal initiatives failed and why the liberal agenda has reached an impasse would need to compare the successes with the failures, a task that is beyond the scope of this study. My objective here is more modest and preliminary, yet one that is indispensable before moving on to the more general question of liberal decline. It is to point in three analytically separate, though interrelated, directions that might be worth pursuing using a broader set of cases.

This study is meant to caution liberal revisionists, and those who seek to reconstruct the liberal agenda, that in assessing the past and prospects for the future we must confront the fundamental constraints and limitations on positive government action in American politics. In response to conservative critics' interpretations of the postwar record, many of which interpretations became popular by the 1980s, liberals have sought refuge in two directions. One has been to question as naive the faith in positive government intervention to solve major social problems, to call for abandoning electoral strategies based upon appeals to "special interests," and to advocate a rightward shift in politics and policy.[19] The problem with this position is that it is based on a series of assumptions—that positive government intervention on behalf of groups like the poor and unemployed have failed; that these interventions account for the economic difficulties of the 1970s; that the public has grown more conservative and rejects government intervention to solve major problems in society; that political success will come only by abandoning liberal principles, programs, and appeals to traditional constituencies—that are easier to assert than to confirm.

Others have defended the record of the past and offered reinterpretations that place the liberal legacy in a more favorable light. According to John Schwarz, for instance, liberal decline is due to a misunderstanding of recent history, a misunderstanding that has become popularized.

Government programs were much more successful than the critics of "big government" want to admit, and the economic and other difficulties that the nation faced in the 1970s were mistakenly attributed to the growth of government.[20] The problem with this kind of vindication of the liberal record is simply that it fails to appreciate many of the real challenges that proponents of positive government intervention faced, and will continue to face, and that led to liberalism's enervation as a political force. Programs such as CETA become powerful symbols of the failure of positive government intervention not primarily because they were misunderstood and made into scapegoats, but because their design and performance assured that they would lose political credibility. The problems were real, not imagined, and their sources deserve a full investigation.

Part I

Ideas

2

Constrained Origins:
Ideology, Economic Doctrine, and the
Debate over Postwar Unemployment

WHILE MANY specific features of employment policy have changed over the years, there has been an underlying continuity that has persisted from the start. This continuity lies at the heart of its mission, though it is rarely ever explicitly acknowledged by policy makers. It is a social welfare mission, intended to offset undesired social and economic trends. This is a narrow mission that constitutes not so much an employment policy as it does a policy for the unemployed, and for only a minority of the total unemployed population, at that. Employment programs have been a series of emergency measures, undertaken in a post hoc fashion to deal with the victims of social dislocation and deprivation, rather than any deliberate effort to deal with the systemic problems of the labor market itself. The programs always have been targeted on people—usually those on the periphery of the economy— or on communities in search of a federal subsidy. Whether directed at dislocations induced by automation or international competition, at economically disadvantaged and undereducated poverty dwellers, or at distressed central cities, employment measures have been used to offset the impact of social and economic changes, rather than to promote adaptation to them.[1]

An alternative to the social welfare mission is positive intervention in the labor market. By positive intervention, I mean that public policy attempts to promote desirable economic outcomes, rather than simply trying to pick up the pieces when undesirable outcomes occur. Positive intervention is proactive rather than reactive, it requires public authorities to anticipate problems of economic adjustment and prevent them from occurring in the first place, or if that cannot be accomplished, to respond to unemployment in a fashion that does not impede the adjustment process itself. Positive labor market intervention is undertaken with the primary objective of increasing economic growth and productivity. Individuals and communities experiencing employment

difficulties are assisted, but only as a by-product of the primary objective.[2]

Although the social welfare orientation is so thoroughly embedded
in the assumptions and practice of employment policy that it is taken
for granted, there have been occasional criticisms of it. In the 1960s,
E. Wight Bakke expressed his "uneasiness about the limited mission
which has emerged for what has been labeled 'manpower policy and
practice' in the United States."[3] Bakke was among a handful of American experts that had closely studied other nations' experience with labor
market intervention. He concluded that the United States had settled on
a policy whose purpose was unduly limited and narrow. The American
brand of manpower (i.e., employment) policy had developed as an
instrument of social policy. At best, it sought to provide remedial education and training to individuals on the margins of American society. At
its worst, it served as a glorified form of relief. Rather than concern
itself with the needs of an advanced industrial economy, it served
the needs of categories of socially disadvantaged individuals. Bakke's
alternative model was Europe, where the very same programs had
been designed and utilized to promote economic stability and growth.
"Unless the recent direction of legislative and administrative thinking
and action is changed," Bakke warned, "the manpower function of
government will remain what it is actually becoming—a sophisticated
form of public assistance."[4] In 1979, ten years after Bakke's admonition,
and almost two decades since employment programs were launched in
the United States, another labor economist made essentially the same
argument: "As a nation, we have always chosen to react to, and defend
against, structural [economic] change rather than to promote it. Our
employment policy has been used to cushion the impact of structural
changes in labor demand."[5]

The political implications of the social welfare mission are critical. If
the policy is designed and used as a strategy for assisting the disadvantaged and unemployed, then the coalition in support of the programs
will be limited. Crucial economic interests like organized labor and
business will have little incentive for getting behind them. What is
worse, it invites a backlash from middle-class taxpayers, who feel they
are footing the bill but getting none of the benefits. The great redeeming
feature of the positive, economic mission is that the benefits from the
program are spread diffusely throughout society, or at the very least it
is perceived as such to a greater degree than in the social welfare
approach.

To understand why this mission emerged and took hold, and why
a positive labor market policy never did, we must turn back to the first

two decades after World War II. The policy choices made in the period from 1945 to 1965 imposed a set of constraints on the federal government's response to unemployment. These choices had long-lasting effects on what kind of employment policy would develop, with what objectives, the scope of its activities, and the level of resources devoted to it. They put employment policy upon a distinctive social policy trajectory.

This chapter examines three critical developments and the impact on them of ideological predispositions, economic doctrines, and the interplay between the two: (1) the ill-fated struggle over full employment legislation, (2) the subsequent development of a commercial Keynesian strategy of economic management, and (3) the Keynesian-structuralist controversy over the nature of unemployment.

The Full Employment Bill of 1945 embodied a brand of Keynesian analysis labeled *secular stagnation,* which assumed that the regenerative capacities of capitalism had been permanently dissipated, and which prescribed that the federal government undertake a massive program of ever increasing public investment and budgetary deficits. The bill ignited intense ideological debate over the appropriate role of the state in the economy, and full employment fell victim to a determined conservative opposition.

In the wake of the bill's defeat, American Keynesianism developed in a direction that diverged dramatically from that which informed the authors of the Full Employment Bill. The notion that the economy was in the throes of secular stagnation was discarded in favor of one that stressed fluctuations in the business cycle as the problem of economic policy and one that could be adequately addressed merely by offsetting such fluctuations through timely and temporary adjustments in aggregate demand policies. Moreover, there was a shift in the expert consensus on the preferred choice among policy instruments for stimulating the economy during stagnant periods. Instead of reliance upon the spending side of the budget and discretionary expenditures, tax cuts and automatic stabilizers were presented as more attractive means for economic management. These changes in economic thinking accommodated Keynes to conservative values, retaining the growth-producing potential of the new economic tools without seriously threatening business's basic prerogatives. For the development of employment policy there was a world of difference between creating deficits through higher spending as opposed to lower tax rates. The first course was compatible with an expanding budget for the programs, the second was a prescription for keeping them small.

We then turn to the split among economists in their diagnosis of unemployment during the Eisenhower years, which pitted job training programs against macroeconomic policies as alternative means for combating joblessness. The Keynesians, who argued that unemployment was due to an insufficiency in aggregate demand, rejected the argument of those who posited a structural imbalance in the labor market due to technological advances. The first group defined the problem in macroterms and argued for the sufficiency of aggregate measures, while the second maintained the need for micropolicy interventions in the form of manpower training and labor market planning. The debate between the two camps presented policy makers with the misleading and ersatz choice of attacking unemployment either through the management of aggregate demand or by supply-side efforts to retrain the jobless. While Congress was persuaded by the argument for the need for retraining, the Keynesians held the high ground in the economics profession and in the economic policy-making machinery of the executive branch and were able to define economic policy in purely macroeconomic terms. The result was that employment programs remained outside the sphere of economic policy, under the auspices of the Department of Labor.

THE STRUGGLE FOR FULL EMPLOYMENT AND THE TRIUMPH OF COMMERCIAL KEYNESIANISM

The most visible and painful consequence of the Great Depression of the 1930s was mass unemployment. At one point, joblessness reached one in every four workers. It took a cataclysm of such proportions to usher in a period of unprecedented innovation in American economic and social policy.[6] On the eve of the Depression the United States was one of the few nations in the industrialized world with neither an unemployment insurance scheme nor a system of labor exchanges (i.e., employment offices). Both had been pushed earlier in the century by Progressive reformers, but to no avail. It was the New Deal that secured passage of the Wagner-Peyser Act (1933) and the Social Security Act (1935), setting up the United States Employment Service and the federal-state system of unemployment insurance, respectively.[7] Roosevelt's most memorable method of addressing joblessness, though, was the provision of work relief through a tangle of New Deal programs: in order of appearance, these were the Federal Emergency Relief Administration (FERA), the Civil Works Administration (CWA), the Public Works Administration (PWA), the Works Progress Administration (WPA), the Civilian Conservation Corps (CCC), the National Youth Administration (NYA), and the Farm Security Administration (FSA). This alphabet soup of initiatives was the main mechanism through which the government spent in order to create and support incomes.

These programs and the deficits that were created to finance them, no matter how dramatic by American standards, did not constitute an economic recovery program. The New Deal's relief programs were just that—humanitarian efforts undertaken in an emergency to ameliorate the plight of the unemployed. The expenditures were segregated into an "emergency budget," while the president clung to the belief that the regular budget should be balanced. Despite correspondence and a personal meeting with John Maynard Keynes, Roosevelt did not perceive deficit spending as an economic stimulant for ending the Depression, but rather as a social palliative or, as one observer put it, "more as a condition to be overcome in the course of recovery than as a theoretical prescription to be followed."[8] Once Depression-level rates of unemployment began to recede during his second term of office, Roosevelt immediately took steps to bring the budget into balance. The New Deal was a cacophony of advice on what to do about the Depression, amplified by Roosevelt's preference for an informal, ad hoc process of intellectual competition among his circle of advisers, and his refusal to institute more formal and structured lines of communication and consensus building. There was wide recognition of the basic fact that the state's role in economic affairs was expanding, but there was no consensus on what the substance of that role should be.[9] It was not until the late 1930s that the New Deal developed a Keynesian recovery program.

In providing a compelling intellectual justification for government intervention, Keynes overturned the prevailing notion that economic behavior was governed by the hidden hand of the price mechanism, which was thought to bring the economy to full employment automatically. In the *General Theory*, Keynes argued that during the Depression investment and savings decisions fell out of step, and that the interest rate failed to bring the two into line, as posited by orthodox economic theory. Once savings persistently outran investment, economic activity declined, and mass unemployment resulted. By creating a deficit, the government could play the critical role of bringing savings back into the economy, thus redressing the shortfall in the level of investment. Keynes's decisive contribution to policy was not in planting the idea that deficit spending could reduce unemployment but in demonstrating how fiscal policy could be used in a positive and aggressive fashion to prevent an economic slump. Unemployment ceased to be a problem during World War II, prompting William Beveridge to ask, "Why does war solve the problem of unemployment which is so unsoluble in peace?"[10] Keynes had found the answer and had given a basis in economic theory. Once governments were forced to create huge deficits to finance production during World War II, the Keynesian analysis and prescription appeared irrefutable. The beginnings of an intellectual conversion that had begun in the late 1930s had taken over most of the profession.

While Keynes's prescription seemed at first glance straightforward, it nevertheless produced a spectrum of views within the United States as to just how interventionist economic management ought to be. "Keynesianism . . . offered policy formulations which differed significantly in their ideological, political, and economic potentials."[11] At one end were the "pump primers," who believed a dose of heavy deficit spending was sufficient for getting the economy back to normal. Further to the left were the "compensatory spenders," who thought that government spending would be a recurrent necessity between short periods in which the private economy was able to achieve stability on its own. Furthest to the left were the "secular stagnationists," who believed that the existing structure of capitalism was completely incapable of achieving or sustaining economic growth and who called for ongoing government intervention, primarily in the form of spending deficits.

Stagnationist analysis emerged from the pack as especially persuasive in the wake of the 1937/38 recession, when the New Deal's pump priming was shown to be inadequate. A group of young Harvard and Tufts economists, led by Alvin Hansen, were the main expounders of stagnationist ideas. Stagnationist analysis had been implied by Keynes, but economists like Hansen stressed the notion and explained why it existed. According to some adherents to the analysis, including Hansen, America had reached a stage of economic maturity in which population increases had slowed, territorial expansion had come to an end, and technological innovation had not produced an industrial boom for decades. The result was stagnation, and the cure was government investment to take up the slack, which was now a natural condition of the system. Others, such as Alan Sweezy, did not argue that innovation or productivity had ceased but that, in a developed economy, the attempt to accumulate capital might outrun the development of opportunities for its profitable employment.[12] With the economy sliding back into the Depression in 1937/38, Roosevelt proposed boosting expenditures by $7 billion. This was the first indication that the president had begun to see spending as a tool of economic recovery. A few years later the United States entered World War II, compelling the federal government to create much larger deficits. It was the war, not the New Deal, that got the nation out of the Depression.

Full Employment Lost

After the war there was considerable fear that the United States and the rest of the industrialized world would return to the stagnation of the 1930s. Scores of economists in and out of government served as intellectual middlemen in translating Keynes's diagnosis into a set of concrete policy proposals and in educating policy makers in the new economic doctrine. Many worked through the National Planning Association, the Bureau of the Budget, and the National Resource Planning Board (NRPB), where Hansen served as an adviser. By the end of the war, the National Resource Planning Board developed an elaborate set of policies, which rested on a "new Bill of Rights" that included a "right to work," endorsed by President Roosevelt in 1944. Shortly after the war, Congress cut off appropriations to the NRPB, but up until that time it had become a center of Keynesian, and specifically stagnationist, policy advice.

The culmination of the stagnationist victory came in 1945, when proposals for sustained levels of high public spending and investment became the underpinning of the Full Employment Bill. Both the Democratic and Republican platforms of 1944 endorsed the idea of full employment—that anyone willing and able to work would have a job—and their presidential candidates gave it unequivocal support. According to Bailey, "Positive federal action in the field of postwar employment planning seemed to come as close to a bipartisan mandate as any issue in the 1944 campaign."[13] Likewise, public opinion polls revealed a healthy majority of the American people agreed that "government should provide jobs for everyone able and willing to work but who cannot get a job in private employment." When asked in October 1944, 68 percent agreed, 25 percent disagreed, and 7 percent had no opinion.[14] In short, all the prerequisites existed for launching Keynesian-style economic planning in the United States by the war's end. The only question that remained was whether sufficient political skill and commitment existed to adopt such a far-reaching and, by U.S. standards, radical innovation.

The Full Employment Bill was authored by Senator James Murray, a liberal Democrat from Montana, and Murray's staff assistant Bertram Gross, who assembled a group of committed Keynesians from various agencies of the federal government. It guaranteed a job to any who wanted one by declaring that "all Americans able to work and seeking work" had the right to useful and remunerative employment. It also provided a mechanism through which government would be obligated to achieve this goal. The president was required to submit annually to Congress a National Production and Employment Budget, which would estimate the size of the labor force, the total national production needed to provide jobs for that labor force, and the total investment needed to meet such a level of production. If the anticipated level of private investment was insufficient to absorb the entire labor force, the federal government would provide such additional investment and spending needed to reach full employment.

The Full Employment Bill was considered in a highly charged ideological atmosphere. According to Bailey, "the overwhelming conservatism of the House of Representatives," where ultimately the bill was defeated, "was the underlying condition" that led to the outcome.[15] Even before debate began, its liberal authors sought to avoid conservative objections by altering the language of the original draft. The opening policy declaration of the bill stated, "It is the policy of the United States to foster free competitive enterprise." Similar terms and phrases giving reassurance that the bill was consistent with capitalist principles, and others toning down language that would incite fears of expanding federal control over the economy, were sprinkled throughout the bill. Opposition to the bill, particularly in the House, was waged by raising fears of impending "state socialism" and the decline of "free enterprise," and "the American way of life." Bailey stressed that conservative and business influence in defeating the bill was due less to direct pressure and arguments based on short-term economic interest than to the more subtle but pervasive transmission of cultural values:

In general, the analysis which the conservative pressures presented to the public and Congress was that S. 380 was totalitarian and un-American in implication, destructive of free enterprise, and dangerous or impractical in its underlying economic theories. . . .

Through the considered use of word-symbols over a couple of generations . . . through the concerted drive of business organizations to convince the public-at-large that "What is good for business is good for America," the conservative pressures helped to shape the prepossessions which a majority of our national legislators brought with them to the 79th Congress.[16]

The House version of the Murray bill was discarded and a substitute was written by southern conservative Will Whittington. Whittington solicited advice from the business community, including the Chamber of Commerce, the Committee for Economic Development, and most importantly, Dr. George Terborgh, who was a vocal critic of stagnationist analysis. What emerged in the final legislation was essentially the House substitute—an emasculated version of the original bill: the Employment Act of 1946. The word *full* was dropped from the bill's title and the much vaguer term *maximum employment* was used in the bill's declaration. Full employment was no longer the top priority of economic policy. Government was only to use "practical" means of attaining the act's goals, and these had to be "consistent with the needs and obligations of national policy" (e.g., price stability). Finally, the provisions for long-range forecasting of economic trends and for a National Production and Employment Budget, the explicit pledge to use spending measures, and the original bill's call for an investigation into monopoly and the distribution of national income were all removed from the final version of the legislation.

The Employment Act became an important symbol, however. For the first time, Congress gave formal recognition to the federal government's responsibility for maintaining economic prosperity. The act came to embody the spirit of the original bill, providing a powerful reminder of the unfulfilled hopes for full employment and a rallying point for those who favored federal employment programs. Second, the act introduced several institutional innovations, namely the annual *Economic Report of the President*, the Council of Economic Advisers, and the Joint Economic Committee of Congress, which helped systematize the making of economic policy in the federal government and, more importantly perhaps, provided mechanisms through which professional economists were brought into the highest levels of economic policy making in the executive branch.

Still, the overriding significance of the Employment Act of 1946 is what it failed to accomplish. Throughout the 1950s, the act's promise to provide "maximum employment" was honored more often than not in the breach. A recessionary climate plagued much of the decade, as the Eisenhower administration held firm to the pre-Keynesian stricture against deficit spending and as fears of inflation kept both the Congress and the president from using the fiscal tools at their disposal to stimulate the economy. The failure to commit the country to full employment and an extension of the state's role in the economy altered the entire course of postwar economic policy. In the wake of the full-employment debacle was left a vacuum into which stepped the architects of a form of Keynesianism that had very different political ramifications from that which informed the authors of the Full Employment Bill.

The Evolution of American Keynesianism: From Secular Stagnation to Cyclical Fluctuations

The failure of the Full Employment Bill coincided with the demise of the stagnationist brand of Keynesianism. Even before the war ended, stagnationist analysis had begun to fall out of favor within the economics discipline. This was partly due to the accumulation of "scientific" rebuttals from other economists, who questioned the entire assumption of secular stagnation. Intellectual arguments were reinforced by events. Stagnation analysis came to be seen as an overreaction to the abysmal performance of the economy during the Depression years. The economy's proven ability to reach high levels of production during the war, and predictions of a great pent-up demand for consumer goods during peacetime, indicated to many economists that there would be no question about the resumption of economic growth and, consequently, a high demand for labor.

As stagnationist theories faded, a new rationale for an active fiscal policy came to the fore: economic fluctuations. According to this notion, the demand for labor periodically fluctuates, being sometimes excessive and inflationary and at other times deficient. This shift in opinion meant a rejection of the much more pessimistic view that the market economy was fundamentally disabled and unable to regenerate growth. Moreover, if the problem were only temporary and aberrant fluctuations in economic activity, the economy would not require persistent deficits and ever rising levels of public investment. Once the problem of stabilization came to be viewed as one of moderating fluctuations rather than getting out of a deep hole or dealing with secular stagnation, then the role for fiscal policy would be simply to offset, from time to time and on a temporary but timely basis, the excess swings of the business cycle.

This new diagnosis made Keynesianism more palatable to conservatives. Those who, up until now, were hostile to an active fiscal policy now found it much less threatening. As conservatives entered into the development of economic management and gave up traditional calls for balanced budgets, a new set of values were introduced. They sought to "use fiscal policy to maintain high employment, but they were more concerned about restraining the growth of the budget and about avoiding inflation than the earlier Keynesians had been."[17]

Tax Cuts and the Ascendance of Commercial Keynesianism

The shift from secular stagnation to cyclical fluctuations in economic analysis was accompanied by an equally significant shift in economic prescription—from spending deficits to tax cuts. For virtually all economists until the late 1940s, including Keynes himself, using fiscal policy to regulate the economy meant using the spending side of the budget. Manipulating levels of tax revenue was rarely invoked as a desirable alternative. The reasons for this were several. Most stagnationists were liberals who thought increased government spending was desirable for its own sake. John Kenneth Galbraith had yet to come along to argue that the public sector had been badly neglected in the United States, but this position had been clearly taken by the stagnationists.[18] "I am convinced," Alvin Hansen once wrote, "that economists have been grossly negligent in not really examining the deficiencies in our society. We could have full employment through private enterprise for a hundred years and it would not solve the gross deficiencies which we have in education and public health or in the slums and blighted areas of our cities."[19] Thus the early Keynesians' agenda extended beyond full employment to embrace what we call today a welfare state—generous levels of spending on social services and public infrastructure and income redistribution through progressive taxation and transfer payments. Second, it was also apparent that if, as the theory of secular stagnation posited, stagnation was an ongoing problem, there was a limit to how far taxes could be cut, whereas government spending could rise indefinitely. There were other problems with the tax cut option that also precluded it from becoming a viable alternative early on. A tax cut was regarded as providing benefits mainly for the rich. This would not only be a roundabout method of eliminating excess unemployment compared to spending directly for jobs, but it would also be less stimulative, since part of the tax cut would be saved rather than spent.[20]

Why was there a shift in the consensus among experts in favor of tax cuts and automatic stabilizers? Some reasons were technical, having to do with the fact that in the postwar period the federal income tax had become a more efficient and practical policy tool than it had been previously. The need to raise large amounts of revenue to finance the war effort led to a great broadening of the tax base to encompass the middle class, and a steep rise in tax rates. By the war's end a reliable revenue instrument existed for raising consumption through the manipulation of tax rates. In addition, collection of the income tax was made more efficient with the introduction of the "system of current payment," which allowed the government to withhold income and collect it in the same year it was earned.

Second, the shift from secular stagnation to fluctuations led to the search for measures that could be used flexibly and quickly. In dealing with economic fluctuations on a timely and prompt basis, tax policy was superior to spending. Where public works projects needed long lead times to plan, fund, and construct, a tax cut could speedily put billions of dollars into consumers' pockets. The tax system was also an automatic stabilizer, because it took income out of the spending stream as personal income expanded during boom times and left it in during downturns in the economy, when stimulus was needed. No discretionary action on the part of the government was involved, as was the case with spending programs, which had to gain approval from the president and Congress.

The most important reason for the shift from discretionary spending to tax cuts and automatic stabilizers was the coming together of conservative political philosophy, business interests, and intellectual ingenuity on the question of economic management. The business community, under the leadership of the Committee for Economic Development (CED), calculated that policy makers would eventually be persuaded to abandon their belief in the balanced budget doctrine and that the "new economics" of Keynes would sooner or later find its way into public policy. Simply maintaining business opposition to the idea of deficits would be a losing strategy in the long run. Business had important stakes in the specific techniques that would be used in implementing Keynesianism. It was better to be at the forefront of efforts to shape the policy debate in a direction that was congruent with the values and interests of the private sector, so this argument ran, than be put in the position of fighting against an unwanted alternative, as had been the case with the Full Employment Bill.

Economists might argue that how a deficit is created, whether through spending increases or tax cuts, was of little importance as long as the desired stimulus was produced. But for the business community there were clear arguments in support of the latter method rather than the former. Business had long complained of burdensome taxation, and the heavy hand of "big government" that went with it. Furthermore, a stimulative tax cut had the advantage of increasing private consumption and, therefore, demand for what the private sector produced. Spending, on the other hand, obviously meant spending on public goods and services, with less resources left over for private consumption and a shift in decisions over the allocation of resources from the private to the public sector.

These arguments about the superiority of tax cuts over spending were appealing, but there remained the more basic problem of convincing the business community to abandon its balanced budget orthodoxy. Business did not come to the position of supporting tax cuts quickly or easily. It had to be educated on the potential benefits of deficits to the private sector, and this meant, above all, getting businessmen to break with their beliefs in the sanctity and wisdom of the balanced budget. It was this critical educative and persuasive role that the the CED played. The CED is no ordinary business lobby. It does not have an atavistic, principled hostility to government involvement in the economy. Nor does it seek to exert political power in the conventional manner of most lobby groups—by promising to reward or threatening to punish elected officials who do or do not protect business's interests. The CED is something of a public policy institute for the business community, seeking to influence through its research and education activities the ways in which the rest of the business community and policy makers think about and puzzle through problems. The organization's mission has been to "achieve an integration of public and private interests," while playing down the importance of just whose interests (the public's or that of business) are being served at the expense of the other. It is self-styled as a "merchant of ideas," and has been responsible for popularizing many of them among economists and laymen alike.[21]

The concepts *automatic stabilizer* and *built-in flexibility* can be traced to the CED's 1946 study, *Jobs and Markets*, and the pioneering work of staff economist Albert Hart. But the most influential of the CED's policy intellectuals in the postwar years was Beardsley Ruml. Ruml was the intellectual middleman between the business community and the economics profession. His task was not to "sell" the new economic wisdom of an active fiscal policy to businessmen but to combine "what was essential and valid in the analysis of economists as he saw it with the values of businessmen to produce a new synthesis."[22] As the CED's most fertile idea man, Ruml paved the way for shifting the emphasis from the expenditure side of the budget to the revenue side in the use of fiscal policy.

Ruml was responsible for the high-employment (or stabilizing) budget, which provided for the automatic generation of deficits in hard times and surpluses in good. He called for a reduction of tax rates "to the point where they will balance the budget at some agreed level of high employment."[23] Automatic stabilizers, the most important of which were taxes, would provide built-in flexibility by injecting or withdrawing income into the spending stream to cushion minor fluctuations in the economy. Discretionary tax reduction, rather than increased spending, would stimulate the economy in recessionary periods. "In providing for the automatic generation of deficits in hard times and surpluses in good, the CED's stabilizing budget offered a middle ground between the position of those who would balance the budget annually regardless of economic fortunes and those who would vest in the federal government the power to alter rates and expenditures to fit the conditions at hand or those predicted for the future."[24]

Ruml foresaw that none of this would be practical until the income tax were revamped. He recommended establishing the system of current payment, in which the tax on income was withheld and collected in the same year in which the income was earned. This would avoid collecting higher taxes during periods of lower business activity and collecting lower taxes during periods in which the economy was expanding. Ruml almost single-handedly pushed the proposal through Congress through his publicity campaign.

In sum, the prescriptions put forward by CED economists recast American Keynesianism in three important ways: (1) by changing the definition of the problem from one of a permanent, secular economic stagnation to one of periodic fluctuations in economic activity; (2) by replacing spending increases with tax cuts in prescribing deficit creation; and (3) by shifting from discretionary to automatic fiscal management. Working with like-minded reformers in the Chamber of Commerce, the CED helped win over other important segments of the business community to the tenets of what Robert Lekachman has

dubbed *commercial Keynesianism*—tax cuts and automatic stabilizers—
and to the abandonment of balanced budget orthodoxy. Thus, by the
time an activist president was elected in 1960, a new generation of
business leaders had been educated in the use of Keynesian fiscal policy
and weaned away from the balanced budget that their forebears had
so passionately defended against Roosevelt's fiscal program and the
Full Employment Bill. It might be added that the CED economists were
helped in their efforts at conversion by the dissatisfying performance
of the economy during the Eisenhower years, when the balanced budget was still adhered to.

Adoption of the Tax Cut

Despite pronouncements that he intended to "get the country moving again," President Kennedy was not a rabid Keynesian when he
first entered office. Like virtually all other public officials at the time,
Kennedy emphasized the virtues of fiscal orthodoxy and sacrifice during his election campaign. He opposed the idea of tax cuts because he
did not feel it fit in well with his call for sacrifice—exhorting his fellow
citizens to ask what they could do for their country, rather than the
reverse. Besides, Kennedy, like members of the business community,
was untrained in the new economics.

Kennedy did have close connections to the academic community,
however. The new administration brought to Washington a group of
economists, led by Walter Heller, all of whom were committed Keynesians, and appointed them to the Council of Economic Advisers.
Throughout the 1950s the new economics had little influence in the
high councils of government, and according to the Keynesians, the
economy's tendency to fall into repeated recessions showed it. Now
that the Keynesians occupied positions of power, they were in a much
better position to influence economic policy. "What followed was a
vigorous, unremitting campaign by the Kennedy economists to make
economics, rather than politics, the decisive influence in the fiscal policy
of the government. Beaten at first, they were wholly successful two
years later."[25]

Kennedy's economic advisers understood that, given the shifts in
opinion in the business community, a tax cut was immeasurably more
politically feasible than a spending deficit. Paul Samuelson, whom
Kennedy had commissioned to draft a set of economic policy recommendations before the inauguration, stressed the need for tax cuts over
sharp rises in federal spending. Only the more committed liberals, a
minority among the economists from whom the new president solicited
advice, insisted on the spending course instead of the tax cut. The most

vocal among them was Galbraith, who as Hansen's heir among the now virtually defunct stagnationists, argued that a tax cut could not eliminate the "public squalor" in an otherwise "affluent society." But while Heller could agree that "the cities needed to be rebuilt," there simply was not the ideological commitment within the Kennedy administration to support massive public investment and an abandonment of the politically tempting tax cut option.

During the first year and a half of his term, Heller and the CEA kept up a steady flow of information to Kennedy on the state of the economy and the benefits that would accrue from a tax cut. In the spring of 1962 the recovery from the 1960/61 recession slowed, and on May 28 occurred the "Kennedy crash" in the stock market. This event convinced Kennedy that his economic advisers were probably correct in their call for a stimulus, and he accepted the idea of an across-the-board cut in personal and corporate income tax rates.

Once converted to the idea, however, Kennedy balked at immediately sending a proposal to Congress. The commitment had been made, but the size, nature, and timing of the tax cut remained in limbo. The president's fear was that there was insufficient support among the public and on Capitol Hill. Key members of Congress, such as Ways and Means Committee Chairman Wilbur Mills, had not been tutored in Keynesian economics in the way Kennedy had been. There was no reason to believe that Mills was anything other than steadfast in his opposition to creating a deficit and using tax policy to manipulate the economy.

A key factor in Kennedy's decision to finally take the plunge in sending a proposal to Congress was the business community's receptivity to the idea and, specifically, the recommendation for it that he had received from the CED and the Chamber of Commerce.[26] Heller capitalized on the political significance of business support by keeping the president apprised of the support of the CED and the chamber. By the time the Ways and Means Committee held hearings on the plan in 1963, virtually the entire business community, including the National Association of Manufacturers, the American Bankers Association, the New York Stock Exchange, and an array of trade associations, were lined up to testify in its favor.[27] The CED's and chamber's endorsements of deficit financing had given the idea a respectability it would have otherwise lacked. As Galbraith put it, "In our tradition of economic debate, a proposition can often be more economically destroyed by association than by evidence. . . . The charge that an idea is radical, impractical, or long-haired is met by showing that a prominent businessman has favored it. Businessmen—successful ones at least—are by definition never radical, impractical, or long-haired."[28] In a speech before businessmen at the Economic Club in New York, Kennedy couched the new economics in terms that were reassuring to business:

The final and best means of strengthening demand among consumers and business is to reduce the burden on private income and the deterrents to private initiative which are imposed by our present tax system.

The present tax system . . . siphons out of the private economy too large a share of personal and business purchasing power.[29]

Once Mills was aware of the surprising popularity of the tax cut idea within business circles, and after he had been assiduously courted by Kennedy, he got behind the proposal. Mills's support helped allay the concerns of other conservatives in Congress, and on the floor of the House the Arkansas Democrat explicitly pointed out the desirability of tax cuts over spending increases. Of the "two roads to economic prosperity," Mills argued that:

One is the tax reduction road. The other is the road of Government expenditure increases. There is a big difference—a vital difference—between them. The route of Government expenditure increase . . . leads to big Government, especially big Central Government. . . . The route I prefer is the tax reduction road, which gives us a higher level of economic activity and a bigger and more prosperous and more efficient economy with a larger and larger share of the enlarged activity initiating in the private sector of the economy.[30]

Hence, in 1965 the proponents of a commercial brand of Keynesianism had triumphed two decades after the proponents of a radically different Keynesian program had been defeated.

STRUCTURALISTS VERSUS KEYNESIANS

We have seen how the rejection of the Full Employment Bill in 1946 signified the unwillingness of American policy makers to commit the government to a full-employment policy. The Eisenhower administration entered office in 1952 dedicated to ending "Democratic inflation," to a reduction in spending and taxation, and to a balanced budget. Congress, untutored in Keynesian fiscal management and ill equipped institutionally to take the necessary prompt actions that such management demands, was hardly a bastion of the new economics.[31] Not surprisingly, inflation remained low throughout most of the 1950s, and "creeping unemployment" became the main preoccupation of the economics profession. In 1957/58 the economy experienced its third, and worst, recession since World War II; the economy slowly recovered only to experience another recession in 1960/61.

The question became one of trying to explain the nature of the unemployment that existed and prescribing policies appropriate for a renewed effort to reach full employment. Keynesians, who constituted the mainstream of the economics profession, were convinced that the unemployment of the late 1950s and early 1960s reflected a slack economy that resulted from the failure to maintain a sufficiently expansionary fiscal policy. The Council of Economic Advisers, which as we have seen had become the bastion of the Keynesian demand-deficient school under Kennedy, argued that a general stimulation of demand through a tax cut was both necessary and sufficient to move the economy from the rates that prevailed during much of the 1950s to an "interim target" of 4 percent.

A tiny minority of economists (joined by a larger body of journalists and other laymen) disagreed with this diagnosis. They argued that the unemployment was structural, having to do with the nature of technological progress, in particular, automation:

Automation is different from earlier technological changes. When automation is introduced during the early growth stages of an industry it results in price reductions, which result in very large increases in demand, thus causing increases in employment, even though employment per unit of output is falling. Once an industry had reached maturity, automation allows it to keep up with its growth in demand while reducing employment.

In spite of new industries, typical mass-production industries producing consumption goods are in the mature stage, and therefore automation is destroying rather than creating jobs.

Currently, the increment in demand is shifting from durable consumption goods to services, but it is very difficult to move labor from production jobs to service jobs.[32]

To summarize the structural thesis: (1) automation, especially at its current pace, destroys more job opportunities than it creates, and (2) it results in a mismatch of specific labor skill demands and supplies, because there are limitations in the transferability and substitutability of skills from declining to expanding industries. Attempts to cut unemployment to 4 percent through an expansion of the demand for employment will encounter serious bottlenecks. The prescriptions that followed from this analysis were the provision of retraining and better labor market information, counseling, and placement services.

Roots of the Debate

The structural demand-deficiency controversy can ultimately be traced to a schism within the discipline of economics. Those who advanced the structural explanation were institutionalists, whose intellectual forebears were John R. Commons and Thorstein Veblen. Institutionalists "look at the world, then theorize," and conduct inquiry through inductive rather than deductive reasoning.[33] Institutional labor market analysis proceeds on the basis of how markets actually work. The labor market is not a market as that term is understood in orthodox economics. It has no market-clearing mechanism that can equate supply with demand for labor in any way that assures a zero surplus for labor. Instead, it is governed by a variety of institutional forces that include union politics, custom, technology, training, workplace socialization, demographics, and other sociocultural factors.[34] The ideal competitive market is seen as only as one possible set of institutional relations embedded in a cultural and historical context.

In sharp contrast to this is the orthodox, neoclassical school, which proceeds epistemologically on the basis of a set of untestable, a priori assumptions and reasons deductively about economic behavior. Neoclassical assumptions are universalist, applied across cultures and historical time periods. Economic agents are assumed to be rational, self-interested maximizers. Perhaps the central concept is that of equilibrium. The macroeconomy is inherently stable because it is guided by supply and demand, which are equilibrated through the price mechanism. With regard to labor, changes in the supply of and demand for labor reflect changes in relative wages.

Ever since Keynes wrote *The General Theory* there has been a hotly contested debate among economists as to whether or not Keynes in fact marked a break with the past by rejecting orthodox assumptions. Most professional economists in the United States adopted Keynes in the form of the "neoclassical synthesis." This was an attempt to absorb Keynes's specific response to the Great Depression within the established orthodoxy. The chief interpreter of Keynes in the neoclassical tradition was Paul A. Samuelson, probably the most influential economist in the United States during the postwar years. It was Samuelson's *Foundations of Economic Analysis* that recast Keynes in neoclassical terms, essentially grafting Keynes's policy prescription onto an economy assumed to be operating according to orthodox principles.[35] Samuelson's *Foundations,* one of the most technically formidable treatments in economics, won him the Nobel Prize in economics. But it was his economics textbook that trained a whole generation of American Keynesians in the neoclassical synthesis paradigm.[36] Under conditions like those existing during the Depression, government can expand the overall flows of investment and spending in the economy by creating a deficit. If private investment and spending are excessive, the alternative course is called for. No other government action is necessary other that the management of these aggregate flows. One economist characterized this form of intervention as "hydraulic" Keynesianism.[37]

Critics, including institutionalists, have claimed that the synthesis involved a basic contradiction. It attempted to reconcile the key theoretical assumption of orthodox microeconomics—that variation in prices was the principal mechanism for the allocation of resources among various markets—with Keynes's understanding of the macroeconomy, which explained unemployment and inflation in terms of rigidities in certain prices (particularly wages and interest rates).[38] American Keynesians adopted Keynes's conception of the macroeconomy as a set of expenditure and income flows and grafted it onto the supply and demand theories of orthodox microanalysis. In this scheme, government remained outside the market mechanism itself and influenced economic activity only exogenously, by managing aggregate demand.

We can now begin to see why the debate between the structuralists and Keynesians was so difficult to resolve, and even perhaps why it existed at all. The structural thesis controverted a basic tenet of the neoclassical paradigm, which states that when labor is economized by technological change, there is an automatic mechanism (the wage rate) that will retain (or restore) a full-employment equilibrium. The question turned on whether one treated the labor factor as a homogeneous composite. Neoclassical Keynesians assumed infinite divisibility and homogeneity of both labor and capital inputs, which permit relative prices of factors to determine the quantities that will be employed. In brief, they assumed that the market mechanism itself would iron out imbalances in supply and demand. Structuralists, by contrast, assumed that labor skills were nontransferable and nonsubstitutable in a modern economy with highly specialized and segmented markets. Consequently, greater problems of labor market adjustment existed than earlier. The Council of Economic Advisers' "insistence that structural problems had not contributed to recent increases in unemployment rates," Killingsworth asserted, "rested squarely on the view of the labor market which was most frequently stated in economic theory textbooks."[39] It was a view that the institutionalists clearly rejected, but one to which the Keynesians adhered.

Indeed, the council itself stated this view clearly in testimony before Congress throughout the 1960s:

[Structural analysis fails] to make any allowance for *the proven capacity of a free labor market* . . . to reconcile discrepancies between particular labor supplies and particular labor demands. If relative shortages of particular skills develop, the price system and the market will moderate them, as they have always done in the past. Employers will be prompted to step up their in-service training programs, as more jobs become available, poorly skilled and poorly educated workers will be more strongly motivated to avail themselves of training, retraining, and adult education opportunities.[40]

In 1966, the CEA reiterated:

It is the proper function of a market to allocate resources, and in this respect *the labor market does not function differently from any others*. If the available resources are of high quality, the market will adjust to the use of high quality resources; if the quality it low, methods will be developed to use such resources. The total number of employed and unemployed depends primarily on the general state of economic activity. The employed tend to be those near the beginning and the unemployed those near the end of the (hiring) line. Only as demand rises will employers reach further down the line in their search for employees.[41]

The Politics of Competing Economic Theories

The Keynesians in the CEA saw the structural unemployment argument, quite correctly as it turned out, as a potentially serious threat to their ability to convince policy makers that what was really needed was a fiscal stimulus. (It took the CEA from 1961 to 1964 to educate and persuade the administration and the Congress, before both went along with the tax cut.) As James Tobin, the celebrated Keynesian who served on the CEA, recalled: "One of the first tasks we set for ourselves at the Council was to refute this [structural] diagnosis."[42] It would have been perfectly reasonable for both sides in the debate to recognize the probability that both kinds of unemployment existed and that both a demand stimulus and a manpower policy were in order. But instead, both sides found it politically advantageous to polarize the debate by discrediting the other's position. As one observer sympathetic with arguments for the need for a manpower policy put it, the Keynesians felt required to defend the need for aggregate demand policies from some "over-enthusiastic proponents of manpower policies."[43]

For their part, the Keynesians portrayed the structuralists' position as more dogmatic than it turned out to be. The CEA placed the structural argument in its most extreme version, by maintaining that the structuralists assumed "that unemployment has remained at relatively high levels since mid-1957 in the face of adequate overall demand forces and despite the availability of a sufficient number of jobs." This assumption put the structuralists in the difficult position of having first to demonstrate that there existed no deficiency in aggregate demand, in order to prove that joblessness due to structural causes existed. Every major study that attempted to test the structural hypothesis during the early 1960s was done by Keynesians, who dominated the economics profession, and each one began with this assumption. Again, the structuralists themselves were partly to blame for this. According to one observer, "Many structuralists have not stated their own position clearly and have allowed themselves to be backed into a box in which they must prove the adequacy of over-all demand in order to make their case."[44]

Not surprisingly, most of the studies conducted by the Keynesians concluded that structural changes accounted for "little of the net increase in unemployment" from the mid-1950s to the mid-1960s.[45] Despite the claims and counterclaims of both sides, the structural thesis proved extremely difficult, if not impossible, to either confirm or deny. Unemployment rates and labor force participation statistics were ambiguous and inconclusive. There being no direct measure of those who were actually structurally unemployed, indirect measures had to be used that indicated symptoms of what could be structural unemployment. The only way to distinguish between a rise in unemployment due to technological causes and one due to a deficiency in demand was if the economy was operating at full capacity. This test could not be performed, of course, because during the hotly contested debate the nation's economy was not at full capacity. Otherwise, once any demand deficiency was removed, one could have looked at the structure of characteristics of the demand for labor to see if it had changed. If unemployment was simply due to a deficiency in demand, there should be no change in the characteristics of the demand for labor.[46]

A less extreme, and in retrospect more plausible, version of the structural thesis was that both structural and demand-deficient unemployment were occurring simultaneously, and even with the economy at full capacity, some structural unemployment would exist. It was not until 1963 that the structuralists made their position clear. At that time, Killingsworth testified in support of the less extreme version:

The Council [of Economic Advisers] is the victim of a half truth . . . the lagging growth rate is only part of the problem. . . . [The CEA's economic] program is seriously incomplete. . . . I cannot pinpoint the level at which the bottleneck would begin seriously to impede expansion but . . . we could not get very far below a five percent overall unemployment level without hitting that bottleneck.[47]

Due to their visibility in the CEA and their numerical superiority among economists, the Keynesians tended to dominate the "scientific" side of the debate. But this did not translate easily into the political dominance of their ideas in the policy process. Although very few in the economics profession embraced the structuralists' thesis, almost everyone outside it did, including one of the most powerful actors in economic policy making—William McChesney Martin, the chairman of the Federal Reserve Board. With the Council of Economic Advisers leading a vocal campaign in 1961 for the tax cut, Martin brandished the structural thesis as a weapon against the Keynesians. "The Martin-CEA clash," according to James Sundquist, "did more than any previous event to dramatize the importance of structural unemployment."[48] The Federal Reserve argued that no shortfall in demand existed and that large budget deficits would simply stimulate inflation. The Federal Reserve realized that it would be called upon to accommodate any deficit that the CEA was successful in getting Congress and the president to create. In order for the deficit to produce a stimulus, the Federal Reserve would have to pursue an "easier" money policy, which it feared could make its task of managing inflationary pressures in the economy more difficult.

The Keynesians countered that a fiscal stimulus could get the economy to full employment without running into inflation. Both the Keynesians and the Federal Reserve chairman subscribed to the notion that there existed a Phillips curve, which purported to show a negative statistical relationship between inflation and unemployment. Although the relationship was only statistical (and one that was later called into question), the Keynesians interpreted it as causally relating unemployment and inflation. Low unemployment rates were believed to lead automatically to high inflation. For policy, the implications of this "tragic trade-off" were obvious. Attempts to drive the unemployment rate down below some minimum entailed the cost of higher inflation. The Keynesians argued that the trade-off was not a problem, because the terms of the trade-off were favorable. Expansions of demand could drive the jobless rate to very low levels before incurring unacceptably high levels of inflation. But if the structuralists were correct—that ever higher unemployment rates were due to structural causes—then the effect of fiscal stimulation would only be to set off inflation at higher rates of unemployment than originally expected. In other words, "many demand theorists fear admitting the structuralists' diagnosis because to them it implies inflation at ever higher unemployment levels."[49]

Much to the consternation of the structuralists, their position was identified with a concern with inflation, and the Federal Reserve Board was the chief culprit in this respect. By endorsing the notion of structural unemployment and coupling it with the Phillips curve, the Federal Reserve's strategy was to quash demands for an expansionary fiscal policy. The impact of the Federal Reserve's efforts to combine their concern over inflation with support for the notion of structural unemployment was to force the structuralists into an awkward position by identifying their position with "nonliberal views."[50]

Following the lead of the Federal Reserve chairman, conservatives in Congress began embracing manpower training as an acceptable policy alternative to the Keynesian prescription. Legislators who remained opposed to deficits saw training as a way to deflect pressures that were building in the administration in favor of demand expansion. According to Sundquist, "those who opposed strong fiscal measures tended to seize upon retraining as a substitute." Stimulating the economy through fiscal measures, as the Keynesians had advocated, was an admission that the private economy was incapable of providing a sufficient supply of jobs by itself. "If the economy did not need stimulation to absorb the unemployed," this argument ran, "then jobs for all must in fact exist or would exist if only the unemployed were competent to fill them. If the shortcomings were not in the economy, they could only be in the people."[51]

So the House Republican Policy Committee set out on a study to find alternatives to what it labeled the Democratic "spending spree." The report, produced by twenty-four economists and forty-nine congressmen, stressed the need to upgrade skills throughout the population, without increasing federal spending. A bill embodying the report's major proposal—a tax incentive scheme to get employers to train unemployed workers—was introduced by Representative Thomas Curtis of Missouri. Upon introducing his bill, Curtis contended that "there is a high incidence of people not working in our society, not working because of lack of incentive or lack of skills, not because of lack of jobs."[52] One reporter made the following observation about the conservative cast lent to the structural argument:

As an approach to what the economists call structural unemployment, retraining seemed to have all of the prerequisites for speedy bureaucratic and Congressional approval. It fitted in perfectly with the conservative view that nothing is basically wrong with the economy that cannot be solved by getting capital and labor to the right place at the right time.[53]

Although the structural economists never conceived their position with such a conservative twist, this is exactly what was happening to it in conservative quarters. Given the way in which the structural thesis was argued (or at least interpreted) as an alternative to the Keynesian position, and given the way in which the structuralists never made it clear that in fact they saw this as an inherent problem of the economic structure and only incidentally as one of individuals, it is hardly surprising that conservatives would find it appealing.

The endorsement of manpower training by conservatives reinforced the notion that aggregate demand policies and training were somehow irreconcilable responses to the problem of unemployment. Second, by viewing manpower training as an acceptable conservative response to unemployment, the rationale for a manpower policy put forward by Killingsworth and other structuralists was subtly transformed. The heart of the structuralists' argument was that imbalances in the supply and demand for labor were due to inherent defects in the market mechanism itself. That is, the wage rate was incapable of bringing the supply and demand for labor into balance. That individuals were untrained for the jobs available was simply the visible result of the market's inability to adjust on its own. But if the problem is simply viewed as one of unemployed people without the right skills, then manpower policy is likely to be limited simply to retraining those people who are in trouble, rather than anticipating problems in the market's adjustment and promoting the readjustment process through stronger labor market intervention.

Implications of the Controversy

The Keynesian-structuralist controversy ultimately did not stand in the way of either a demand stimulus or a manpower policy being enacted. "The academic and journalistic debate between demand and structural strategies to deal with unemployment," according to Henry Aaron, "was made moot by the political pursuit of both."[54] The structuralist position was reflected in the Manpower Development and Training Act of 1962, and the Keynesians succeeded in seeing Congress enact a sizable tax cut three years later. What difference, then, did the controversy make? According to one observer:

The structural-demand controversy has been founded on a false dichotomy and has hindered the development of a sound full employment policy. . . . Until the interdependence of the causes of structural and demand unemployment are seen, the co-ordination of the two approaches will not be seriously undertaken. *Fiscal and selective measures will develop in isolation and with little attention to getting an integrated, adequate manpower policy of appropriate scale.*[55]

The academic debate between the two schools of unemployment structured the options that were presented to policy makers. The experts "presented manpower policies and general economic policies as alternative roads to full employment."[56] Framing the issue in terms of competing explanations and prescriptions of the problem helped to divorce macroeconomic policy from employment (manpower) programs in the minds of most policy makers.

Manpower programs were introduced to the United States as a remedy for a diagnosis of unemployment that was, if not totally rejected, certainly not adopted by the dominant voices in the field of economic policy. According to the assistant secretary for manpower at the time, this division was reflected in the executive branch between the Labor Department, which saw the need for both structural measures and stimulating demand, and the president's economic advisers, who believed that all that was necessary was the latter:

I think it is safer to say that in . . . 1961, '62, '63, '64, it was [Labor secretaries] Goldberg's and Wirtz's commitment to training that was far more significant within the Administration than the commitment of Walter Heller and the [other] economists, because there was going on, at that point in time, this overall fight between aggregate demand versus structural. . . . Those who believed in aggregate demand like Goldberg did . . . [but] who felt structural couldn't be ignored [believed] you had to do things with it simultaneously. There were others like Walter Heller and Gardner Ackley and Charlie Schultz of the Council [of Economic Advisers] who felt aggregate demand was solely and exclusively the objective.[57]

Manpower and demand management policies were in place by the middle of the decade, but institutionally they had little relationship. The separation of macroeconomic measures from manpower measures concerned a few observers who thought it necessary to forge a close relationship between the two:

Those agencies dealing with the demand side tended to think in aggregate terms and to assume that sufficient over-all demand will largely iron out particular imbalances in demand and supply through the working of market forces. Agencies concerned chiefly with the supply side dealt primarily with the development and placement of individuals at the local level. They were, therefore, more conscious of the institutional and other barriers to rapid adjustment of supply to changing demand, the human problems of adaptation to innovations, and the limits of market forces alone as means of overcoming labor shortages or oversupply in particular occupations and areas.

One result of this dualism in approach and responsibility has been that little connection has existed each year between the President's *Economic Report* . . . and the President's *Manpower Report*. . . . The same is true of the Council of Economic Advisers' report dealing with general employment policy under the Employment Act of 1946 and the Secretary of Labor's report on manpower requirements, resources, utilization, and training, which is required under the Manpower Development and Training Act of 1962. Different Congressional committees receive and discuss the *Economic* and *Manpower* reports. Thus, at the Executive and Congressional levels, the demand side and the supply side are not well integrated. That constitutes a serious defect in both employment and manpower planning in the United States.[58]

Not only had manpower policy been left out of the economic policy arena in the executive branch, it was in an institutionally inferior position. As we shall see in chapter 5, economic policy, as it is today, was planned at the highest level of the executive establishment between the Council of Economic Advisers and the Bureau of the Budget; employment programs, on the other hand, come under the authority of a second-echelon agency, the Labor Department. Not only did manpower authorities have little to say about economic issues, but their ability to garner sufficient budget resources to affect the economy is also impaired. The image of the Labor Department is that of a "constituency department," with its own specific clientele, programs, and budgets that it is expected to lobby for. Its claim on the budget is viewed as one among many other claims made by other agencies.

CONCLUSION

Of the events recounted in this chapter, none had more profound impact on postwar employment policy than the defeat of the Full Employment Bill. An unwavering commitment to full employment and to increased public planning and investment in the economy would have probably precluded the conservative brand of economic management that developed instead. With the bill's defeat, the door was left open for the proponents of commercial Keynesianism, who sought to introduce Keynesian techniques of demand management without at the same time increasing public control over private economic actors.

Clearly the stagnationist analysis and prescription that informed the Full Employment Bill was less congruent with traditional American beliefs about the role of government in the economy than was commercial Keynesianism. The Full Employment Bill's defeat ultimately was due to the belief among House members that it threatened "free enterprise" and was a major step on the road to "state socialism." By guaranteeing a right to employment for all, the bill, according to its powerful conservative opposition, exceeded the boundary of acceptable state intervention. It went beyond efforts to further equality of opportunity to insure equality of condition, and raised the specter of an all-powerful

national government curtailing economic liberty by shifting the allocation of resources from the private to the public sector. Though the
adoption of commercial Keynesianism required abandoning the belief
in the virtue of a balanced budget, it was more consistent with core
beliefs. Tax cuts and automatic stabilizers increased private rather than
public consumption and control over resources, lowered tax burdens,
and provided government with less discretion. For all the expansion of
the public sector from the Progressive period through the New Deal,
Americans continued to cling to deep-seated antistatist beliefs, which
take it for granted that the private sector is naturally superior to the
public, and that, except during a manifest emergency, "the state has
very few—and should have very few—direct operating responsibilities."[59]

Just as there would have been no Full Employment Bill of 1945 or
Employment Act of 1946 if not for Keynes's compelling intellectual
justification for using fiscal policy as a tool of economic management,
there would have been no Manpower Development and Training Act of
1962 without the discovery of structural unemployment. Yet manpower
policy, too, was tamed by conservative beliefs among those in power.
In theory, the structural analysis of unemployment contemplated more
extensive intervention in the market than did American Keynesianism.
The former posited the failure of the price mechanism to completely or
quickly bring the supply and demand for labor into equilibrium, while
the latter assumed that relative wages were an effective market-clearing
mechanism and called for simply regulating aggregate expenditure and
income flows. For the structuralists, extensive manpower planning,
relocation, and training were needed to overcome institutional barriers
that led to imbalances in the supply and demand for labor. Yet, as the
two prescriptions were debated in government, conservatives were able
to portray demand management as the liberal option, because it called
for expanding the demand for employment through deficit creation.
Manpower policy was considered the preferred option because it implied no need to expand the demand for employment, but only to
retrain individuals for jobs that already existed.

The kinds of economic and employment policies that emerged reflected more than simply the pervasiveness of conservative beliefs,
however. It was necessary to develop a concrete, practical alternative
to the Full Employment Bill. The possibility of another collapse of
capitalism as had occurred in the 1930s, and of a renewed attempt by
liberals to extend the state's role in the economy, led elements of the
business community to search for an alternative that would exploit the
enormous growth-producing potential of Keynesian techniques, while
at the same time minimizing an erosion of corporate discretion and the

expansion of positive state action. Thus, professional economists in the CED and elsewhere recast Keynesian analysis and prescription and translated the latter into a less interventionist policy. Offsetting fluctuations in aggregate demand replaced secular stagnation as an understanding of the macroeconomic problem, and tax cuts and automatic stabilizers supplanted spending programs as the solution.

Adoption of the Full Employment Bill in its original form would also have made less likely the debate between Keynesians and structuralists that emerged in the early 1960s and that had the effect of divorcing macroeconomic policy from microemployment and training programs. Had the commitment to full employment through a powerfully expansionist fiscal policy been established in 1946 and implemented throughout the succeeding decade, the confusion as to the causes of unemployment between those who argued for a demand stimulus and those who called for manpower retraining could have been avoided. The sufficiency of simply using macroeconomic policies would have then been tested. Whatever level of unemployment that remained could be attributed to structural causes. Instead, the postwar debate over unemployment became ensnarled in an unproductive controversy over whether unemployment was due to structural or demand deficiency causes, impeding the learning process. The different explanations for unemployment put forward reflected institutionalist versus neoclassical conceptions of the operation of labor markets. This was reproduced in the split within government between those who advocated demand expansion and those in favor of manpower policy. The Keynesians' rejection of the structural thesis was hardened by the need to defend their policy prescription against powerful actors like the Federal Reserve Board, which capitalized upon the conflict among the economic experts.

The defeat of stagnationist analysis, the rise of commercial Keynesiansim, and the split between Keynesians and structuralists all served to divorce economic policy from employment policy. Economic policy developed exclusively as the management of macroeconomic measures, while micropolicy tools like manpower training came to be viewed as alternative (and rival) means of addressing joblessness. The belief among economic policy makers in the 1960s was that unemployment was purely a problem of insufficient aggregate demand, which could be remedied solely by using the macro approach. Employment and training programs (adopted in the 1960s and 1970s) were left without a legally mandated, overarching goal. The Manpower Development and Training Act and the programs that followed it became ad hoc, largely isolated efforts untethered to an overall economic policy strategy. In addition, the evolution of fiscal management to embrace tax cuts and automatic stabilizers, rather than spending increases, made it more difficult to justify large expenditures for programs designed to train the unskilled and employ the unemployed. In sum, employment programs were effectively eliminated from any constructive role in economic policy.

3

Manpower Training, the War on Poverty, and Administrative Reform

EMPLOYMENT PROGRAMS were outside the orbit of economic policy, and it remained unclear what their role would be. One possibility was that a positive labor market policy would still emerge alongside conventional macroeconomic management policies, which would include an ambitious effort at manpower planning, training, relocation, placement, and direct job creation. National employment goals would be formulated, aided by forecasting trends in labor supply and demand, and pursued through high levels of spending on training, relocation, and public employment programs.

Two issues in the formative years of employment policy presented key opportunities for developing such a broad and far-reaching mission for employment policy. The first was manpower development and utilization, and the second was poverty. Both issues might have led to greatly increasing the scale and scope of training and job creation programs. The debate over manpower culminated in the adoption of the Manpower Development and Training Act (MDTA), and the poverty debate led to the Economic Opportunity Act (EOA). Manpower policy began as an ambitious idea to reform American institutions in ways that would lead to better development and utilization of human resources. It was envisioned that the federal government would make a major commitment to planning and investment in training and education. What was produced, instead, was the MDTA, a modest effort to retrain a fraction of technologically displaced, adult, experienced workers. Just as the MDTA was being implemented, poverty became a salient issue. Structural unemployment was redefined as a problem of mostly the young and disadvantaged who lived in urban areas and who had little employment experience, a shift away from the earlier concern with technologically displaced blue collar workers. Although Labor Department officials and liberals in Congress envisioned a massive public employment creation strategy as the centerpiece of the War on Poverty, the decision in 1964 to enact a large tax cut stymied those efforts. The Council of Economic Advisers, the Budget Bureau, and others close to the president argued instead for a novel and untested idea—community action—and they prevailed. The employment component of the poverty program consisted of a grab bag of small, underfunded programs to provide a variety of services, included training and work experience for poor youth. A public employment strategy had neither the ideological appeal nor the intellectual allure of community action and tax cuts.

Thus, instead of a comprehensive and positive labor market policy, the 1960s saw the creation of remedial training programs for the disadvantaged, programs that were puny in relation to the problem they were intended to address. Some measures were never adopted, such as worker relocation. Whatever labor market forecasting that was done did not contribute to policy making. The exclusive focus of employment policy was on the supply side—on training or retraining in an effort to develop or restore the employability of individuals. A strategy for the demand side, creating jobs in the public sector, was finally adopted in the 1970s, but only as an emergency measure and only after a prolonged ideological conflict over make-work. It was eventually eliminated in the 1980s.

HUMAN RESOURCES AS A POSTWAR ISSUE

The idea of a manpower policy during peacetime emerged in the 1950s. Those who originated the idea and began urging its adoption were a small group of economists and labor experts on the periphery of the economics profession. "As much, and perhaps more than most other innovative policy areas of the 1960s," wrote one observer, "manpower had a community of scholars and policy-makers who defined the conceptual arena within which programs were discussed."[1] For most of them, structural unemployment was not the chief reason for adopting a manpower policy. Structural unemployment was merely the most visible malady of a society that paid insufficient attention to the development and utilization of its "human resources." As they envisioned it, manpower policy would be more than simply providing retraining for already displaced workers. It involved institutional reform, labor market planning, and investment on a broad scale. Such a policy was necessary not only to help those who fell victim to change, but to maintain a highly productive, dynamic economy.

Most economists had little more than a passing interest in the question of human resources. Eli Ginzberg and others who were trailblazers in the human resource field were outside the mainstream of the economics profession. They were mainly institutional labor economists or industrial relations experts who had turned their attention away from traditional concerns with wage determination, income security, and collective bargaining. Ginzberg's interest in human resources, long neglected by the neoclassical school, signified a return to a theme stressed by classical economists like Adam Smith. Smith emphasized the strategic importance of human resources in economic development. Ginzberg's book *Human Resources* bore the subtitle *The Wealth of a Nation*, underscoring Smith's belief that the key to a nation's wealth lies in "the skill, dexterity and judgment with which its labour is generally applied."[2]

The central argument of the burgeoning group of human resource experts was that the United States was in the midst of a "manpower revolution." The country was faced with a number of challenges—international, demographic, sociological, and technological—that were assumed to be profoundly affecting the labor market. To maintain America's status as the preeminent economic and military power, it was necessary for the nation's major institutions (schools, businesses, and public agencies) to address problems in the development and utilization of human resources. World War II accelerated a series of changes in American life, and established institutional patterns were coming to be viewed as barriers to progress in a highly mobile and technologically complex society. Institutions needed to adapt to the changes brought by progress. The funding and quality of education, the organizational structure and management practices of industry, the recruitment policies of the military, and the functioning of labor markets were all called into question. The experts began urging "society as a whole . . . to invest more purposefully and liberally in the people of the United States—in their health, their education and training, their capacities and skills."[3] Purposeful investment implied high levels of public provision and some form of labor market planning.

The new awareness of the importance of human resources was put forth in no less grandiloquent terms than the preservation of national security, the fulfillment of democratic aspirations, and the expansion of material affluence. Freedom could be defended only through preparedness that recognized the vital necessity of a supply of well-trained military personnel. Only if individuals had access to education and training and the employment opportunities to utilize them could their dignity and their ability to shape their destiny be enhanced, and only then could they develop a sense of belonging to their community. Finally, economic expansion could continue only if investment in technology and other factors of production went hand in hand with improvements in the quality and utilization of human resources.

The cheerful amalgam of democratic ideals with the conscious planning and development of manpower inspired books with titles like *Manpower Policies for a Democratic Society* and *Manpower Planning in a Free Society*.[4] "The current concern with manpower underscores the fact that the ideals and values of a free and democratic society impose obligations upon government and private individuals and organizations alike to discover and help create conditions of life under which the potentialities of all men may be realized."[5]

Concern with the ideals of democracy, of course, is never keener than when these are threatened. World War II, the Korean conflict, and the cold war atmosphere were important events in the emergence of the manpower issue. Labor Secretary James Mitchell linked manpower with national security when he warned that "the United States' margin of advantage in the Cold War world is slipping. To prevent this, we must develop and use our skills."[6] Improvements in the preparedness and utilization of manpower were viewed as imperative in a precarious world where the United States had assumed the major responsibility for checking Communist expansion. Mitchell created the Office of Manpower Administration in 1954, headed by an assistant secretary for employment and manpower, to plan programs to meet the needs of civil defense and war mobilization, should the need arise.

The connection between American democracy, national security, and the need for a manpower policy were neatly capsulized in the favorite term of Senator Joseph Clark, manpower policy's most prominent advocate on Capitol Hill: "staffing freedom." Like many of the manpower economists, Clark's experience during the war as a manpower planner in the Air Force sensitized him to the problems of military preparedness, recruiting high-talented manpower, and allocating staff. American attitudes toward government planning during peacetime have never been terribly congenial. Planning raised fears of regimentation, bureaucratic domination, and centralized control. Manpower advocates were quick to point out that Soviet-style coercive planning was not what they had in mind, and turned the argument around by warning that the United States would have to adopt some form of manpower planning if it hoped to check the Soviets. According to Clark:

Unlike the Russians, we have no national personnel policy. There, little Ivan is set to doing what seems to the Politburo best for the state. Such a system is repulsive to our concepts of democracy and freedom. Yet it gives our Communist opponents a measurable advantage in the Cold War.

In nearly every other field of activity in America complete laissez-faire is a thing of the past. Yet we make little effort to mitigate the rigors of the amoral law of supply and demand when it comes to the selection of a

career. . . Has the time come to attempt through persuasion to channel
American ability into places where it is most needed? . . . For myself I believe the question should be answered in the affirmative. Yet no policy, no
plan, no program, no procedures are presently in existence for achieving the
desired result.[7]

The heightened interest in the nation's manpower also began in a
period of self-confidence, a period when "the illusion of triumphant
rationality" was ascendant in America.[8] The amorphous group of human resource specialists reflected this in their quintessential faith in
rational intervention by government on society's behalf. Today, the
tone of this technocratic faith appears overly sanguine, if not naive. As
the linkages between government and centers of intellectual life became
stronger, a new professionalism in the public service emerged that grew
out of the natural and social sciences. This change "gave to technically
and scientifically trained people in government service a great and
growing influence on the initiation and formation of public policy." The
"professionalization of reform," brought with it increasing efforts "to
change the American social system for the better . . . by persons whose
profession was to do just that."[9] With the G.I. Bill, educational opportunities expanded for the middle class, and the number of professionals
and professions expanded, as well. New methods of statistical measure-
ment helped to identify social problems and to measure their scope.
"By the 1960s," stated Daniel Moynihan, "the monthly employment
data had become a vital, sensitive, and increasingly reliable source of
information about American society, and that information increasingly
insisted that although the majority of Americans were prosperous indeed, a significant minority were not."[10] Finally, private philanthropy
was becoming more and more supportive of advancing an active use of
research to bring about social change. The Ford Foundation, in particular, became a major source of support for innovative applications of
social and behavioral knowledge to society's problems.

World War II greatly enhanced the perception of the federal government as an agent for accomplishing good. Only Washington possessed
the capacity to harness the nation's ingenuity and energy to direct a
nationwide effort to defeat a common enemy. The war pointed up
problems, as well. War mobilization required manpower planning and
control. As these efforts were undertaken, a number of problems were
discovered in the ways in which America's manpower had been developed and utilized. Millions of young people were rejected or discharged
from military service because of mental and emotional defects. Others
were found to be illiterate.

After the war, and upon becoming president of Columbia University, General Eisenhower made the nation's manpower one of his chief concerns. He established the Conservation of Human Resources Project at Columbia and appointed as its director Eli Ginzberg. Ginzberg, charged with developing a research agenda to investigate manpower deficiencies, had been involved with the Army Services Forces on manpower problems. Other economists who would go on to become leading proponents of the adoption of a manpower policy also had gained experience in wartime planning bodies. Charles Killingsworth had been a hearing officer for the War Labor Board, Frederick Harbison had been a manpower consultant, and Clark Kerr served as the board's vice-chairman.

The Conservation Project and the National Manpower Council, which was formed as an adjunct to it, served not only to publicize the need to improve manpower but also helped give rise to the cadre of professionals in the new human resources field. The project was charged with studying manpower problems associated with the war and postwar years: the inadequate performance of some young Americans called up for military service, the superior performance of others, and the "transformations under way in the role of work in American life."[11]

Shortly after the project was launched, the Ford Foundation began taking a great interest in it. Ford was attracted by research, such as that planned by the project, that was interdisciplinary and that sought to apply the knowledge of the social and behavioral sciences to public problems. The foundation asked General Eisenhower whether Columbia would be willing to sponsor a national council that would make use of the Conservation Project's staff but that would be concerned with assessing and reporting on manpower issues for the guidance of the government, rather than with research. The university accepted the offer, and the National Manpower Council was formed, composed of distinguished Americans from all walks of life. Both undertakings were directed toward developing "a new and deeper understanding about the individual and social factors . . . which influence the way in which the human resource potential of the American population is developed and the extent to which people are in a position to make use of their potential to their own advantage and to the advantage of the society of which they are a part."[12]

The council saw improvement and utilization of manpower as beyond the capacity of industry. Once it met its immediate needs, private industry could not be relied on to make major investments in long-range skill development and upgrading. Industry, moreover, was blamed for luring skilled technicians from the armed forces, handicapping the nation's military preparedness. The council called upon state and local governments to increase spending on vocational education and upon the federal government to supply statistical analyses and research to insure these efforts would be sufficient. It exhorted Congress to scrutinize existing legislation in the area of education, apprenticeship, and training to ascertain whether new legislation was required.[13]

When the Eighty-fifth Congress convened in 1957, the Democrats managed to regain control of the Senate by one seat. The slim margin was provided by Clark's upset victory over his Republican opponent in Pennsylvania, which had an unemployment rate just under 10 percent and the largest number of depressed areas in the nation. Clark had made this issue the keystone of his campaign. Two years later, Democrats made major gains in congressional elections. Labor leaders and liberal politicians grew impatient after the election when no action was taken on unemployment. A Republican was still in the White House, and although Democrats held a majority in Congress, no liberals were in control of the crucial committee chairmanships that handled unemployment legislation. The defeat of a bill calling for an emergency extension of unemployment compensation sparked a revolt in the Senate among northern and eastern Democrats. The object of their frustration was Senate Majority Leader Lyndon Johnson. The AFL-CIO launched a march on Washington to protest the inaction. Johnson responded by proposing to set up a joint House-Senate study commission. The idea was roundly condemned as a sop to the unemployed, and the House refused to go along. But five months later, Johnson set up the Special Committee on Unemployment Problems, with Eugene McCarthy of Minnesota as its chairman and Clark among the nine members.

The committee conducted field hearings around the country, receiving testimony from a variety of individuals in each community. "The evidence pointed to a deafening demand for legislation dealing with structural changes rather than aggregate demand."[14] The hearings produced nine volumes of testimony demanding action on behalf of the structurally unemployed. For the first time impressive evidence was collected on the need for a training program. "In field hearings, employers complained of job vacancies and no skilled help, while the unemployed, as often as not, attributed their hardships to technological displacement."[15] In its final report to the Senate in March 1960, the Special Committee recommended a broad program that amounted to a blueprint for the New Frontier and Great Society initiatives.[16] Among the recommendations was one for a nationwide training program. The Democratic platform of that year endorsed the panoply of measures

contained in the McCarthy committee report, including area redevelopment and a training program. Senator Clark would become the chairman of a new subcommittee on employment and manpower after the
election, a permanent body to legislate on the recommendations of
McCarthy's committee. Before the 1960 election, Clark introduced his
first manpower bill. A freshman senator who had won a narrow victory
four years earlier, Clark began pushing his proposal in earnest.[17] His
efforts culminated two years later in the Manpower Development and
Training Act (MTDA).

Clark and the human resource economists with whom he was associated envisioned an employment policy that included three elements:
(1) manpower planning—undertaking research and forecasting trends
in the demand and supply of labor due to structural changes in the
market, (2) substantial long-term public investments in education and
training, and (3) institutional reforms to enhance manpower development and utilization. The text of the MDTA sounded as if it had been
lifted from the publications of the National Manpower Council and the
structural economists. The declaration rings with the litany of challenges and urgent needs that faced the nation in the postwar world and
the role of manpower policy in addressing them.[18] Yet, neither planning
nor institutional reform got very far. Nor was any sizable federal investment made in either education or training. The lofty objectives they
attached to manpower policy appear wildly ambitious compared to the
limited objectives that were pursued. They did however, popularize
the idea of a manpower policy, and they inspired Senator Clark, whose
efforts were largely responsible for the MDTA.

EMPLOYMENT POLICY IN THE WAR ON POVERTY

Midway through his term, John Kennedy took stock of his domestic
policy achievements. The MDTA had been approved by Congress, and
the president had sent to Capitol Hill his tax cut proposal. An activist
in orientation, Kennedy was not satisfied. At the year-end review of
economic conditions, Kennedy is said to have turned to Walter Heller,
his chairman of the Council of Economic Advisers, and declared: "Now
look, I want to go beyond the things that have already been accomplished. Give me facts and figures on the things we still have to do. For
example, what about the poverty problem in the United States?"[19]
Kennedy's interest in poverty had been stimulated by Michael Harrington's *The Other America*, by a study of poverty done by Leon Keyserling,
and perhaps also by John Kenneth Galbraith's *The Affluent Society*.[20]

According to Arthur Schlesinger, reading these books "helped crystallize his determination in 1963 to accompany the tax cut by a poverty program." The president "was reaching the conclusion that tax reduction required a comprehensive structural counterpart, taking the form, not of piecemeal programs, but of a broad war against poverty itself. Here perhaps was the unifying theme which would pull a host of social programs together and rally the nation behind a generous cause."[21]

Kennedy's pronouncement immediately set in motion staff work that would eventually culminate in the War on Poverty. Heller assigned one of his CEA staffers, Robert J. Lampman, to assemble all of the available data on poverty in the nation. Lampman, one of the few economists during the 1950s who had studied the problem, wrote a memo that eventually reached the president showing that from 1956 to 1961 there had been a slowdown in the rate of eliminating poverty.

Poverty was the overarching issue that the Kennedy administration had searched for, because it went to the root cause of a variety of social evils: urban decay, illiteracy, unemployment, inadequate housing, and juvenile delinquency. The last problem—delinquency—was one that the administration had already been hard at work on. Congress passed the Youth Offenses Control Act in 1961, and the President's Committee on Juvenile Delinquency actively engaged social scientists and social workers to come up with answers to the problem. The committee concluded that delinquency was part of the much larger problem of poverty. A common view took hold in the administration, reflecting the views of the experts, that delinquency and poverty were not the result of deviance among individuals or subcultures but were the product of the social system.

The less visible activities of the Labor Department mirrored these developments. Juvenile delinquency was thought to be closely linked to youth unemployment. Unemployment among teenagers rose to 17 percent during 1963, at a time when the overall unemployment rate was falling. Senator Hubert Humphrey's Youth Employment Act failed in 1961 but in 1963 was given pride of place as Senate Bill 1. Again it failed in the House, when the southern-dominated Rules Committee killed the legislation. The committee was opposed to "welfare legislation" and feared that the program would be used for the purpose of promoting racial integration. Still, alarm about joblessness among youth persisted and was addressed in the 1963 amendments to MDTA and in the Vocational Education Act of that year. The amendments added basic education for youth to prepare them for skilled training.

Full Employment Lost—A Second Time

A year before the policy intellectuals in the Kennedy administration assembled to formulate a strategy to attack poverty, the Labor Department began a campaign for the federal government to start directly creating jobs for the unemployed. The department was afraid that the Keynesians in the CEA, who clung to the argument that aggregate demand expansion was all that was needed to bring down unemployment, would overlook the need for direct job creation in order to bring the economy to full employment. Labor Secretary Willard Wirtz and his assistant Stanley Ruttenberg proposed a program of labor intensive public works. Creating jobs in the public sector for the unemployed was also becoming a popular idea among liberals in Congress. Senator Clark's Committee on Automation and Technology in 1963 issued a report stressing the need for job creation. Nevertheless, the Budget Bureau and Council of Economic Advisers argued successfully against the idea on the grounds that it would cost too much, and that the anticipated tax cut should be able to work its magic unhindered by extraneous employment programs. This episode served as a harbinger of things to come.

The employment creation idea reappeared in the poverty debate a year later, when the Budget Bureau and CEA solicited ideas for the poverty program from various departments and agencies in the executive branch. The Labor Department argued that the most important and effective strategy for fighting poverty would be a massive jobs program. "Poverty was, by definition, lack of income. Income came from jobs. To have impact among the poor, the war on poverty must begin with immediate, priority emphasis on employment."[22]

But the Budget Bureau and the CEA were firmly behind an alternative idea—community action. The community action concept had been developed by social reformers at the Ford Foundation and in New York social work circles who had close contacts with the administration through the work of the Committee on Juvenile Delinquency. It called for creating and funding in each local community an agency that would launch a comprehensive program to focus federal, state, and local resources and services (health, housing, welfare, etc.) on the problem of poverty.

The idea struck a responsive chord, particularly with the Budget Bureau and the CEA. It would not cost nearly the amount of money that a large-scale employment program would. For the cost conscious Budget Bureau, this was reason enough to favor the idea. Scarce budgetary resources could be targeted to the nation's pockets of poverty, rather than spread thinly across the country. For the CEA, cost was important as well. Any large spending increases would make it more difficult to convince Congress to enact the tax cut stimulus. Second, the Budget Bureau had a special affinity for management tools that promised to bring better coordination to federal programs. Community action agencies would provide an effective umbrella for the plethora of federal grant programs operating in local areas. Third, community action was a novel concept, popular among experts and reformers in the poverty field, and appealing to an administration searching for new approaches to social problems. Employment creation, on the other hand, was an old, tired remnant of the New Deal and smacked too much of work relief. Finally, community action relieved the president's advisers of the difficult political task of having to choose among the competing proposals advocated by the various agencies in Washington. Instead, each community action agency in each local setting would decide what mix of programs and services it needed most to address its particular problems.

The community action instrument quickly became the entire poverty program as envisioned by Budget and the CEA. With the push coming from the Ford Foundation and the Committee on Juvenile Delinquency, community action was sold to CEA chairman Heller and Budget Director Kermit Gordon, who in turn sold it to President Johnson. The original proposal called for spending $500 million for a series of demonstration programs that would set up community action agencies in a number of cities.

The plan drew a vigorous protest from the Labor Department. Wirtz and his assistant, Daniel P. Moynihan, complained that the community action plan called for little in the way of subsidizing employment. They argued that the poverty program should be focused on jobs for the poor and that it should be lodged in the Labor Department, where the manpower machinery existed. The protests of Labor and other departments forced the president to bring in Sargent Shriver to head a poverty task force that would impose some order on the situation. Shriver proceeded to join the protesters, effectively leaving the whole matter up in the air. Each time community action advocates presented their proposal, the debate ended in deadlock when Wirtz and Wilbur Cohen, secretary of Health, Education and Welfare (HEW), pressed the need for jobs and education instead.

Many of Kennedy's advisers, who remained on the job after his assassination, viewed antipoverty legislation as a symbol of the slain leader's legacy. Johnson, who was running for election in 1964, wanted a major domestic policy breakthrough with the imprimatur of his presidency. Shriver decided that the most expedient course was to piece together a proposal that incorporated something for everyone. Community action remained, but only as one title in a bill with several other components. The Job Corps and Neighborhood Youth Corps were taken from Senator Humphrey's 1963 Youth Employment Act, which never passed in Congress. The Jobs Corps, what Humphrey had called the Youth Conservation Corps, was patterned after the New Deal's

Civilian Conservation Corps. Disadvantaged young people who had dropped out of school would be relocated to Job Corps training centers in rural areas. The Neighborhood Youth Corps would provide part-time work experience for disadvantaged youth still in school. There was also a scattering of other small programs—work-study programs for college students, a training program for unemployed fathers with dependent children, loans for farmers and rural businessmen, loans for low-income businessmen, and VISTA (Volunteers in Service to America). To help dispel conservative fears that these programs were handouts to the poor, the bill was given the title Economic Opportunity Act, and it designated an Office of Economic Opportunity to administer it.

As Shriver worked on his composite proposal, pressures grew steadier for a massive employment program. The Job Corps and Neighborhood Youth Corps would provide training and work experience for poor youth, but no jobs for unemployed adults were to be provided. Three members of Shriver's task force, Michael Harrington, Frank Mankiewicz, and Paul Jacobs, wrote Shriver a memorandum stating the priority of job creation: "If there is any single dominant problem of poverty in the U.S.," they proclaimed "it is that of unemployment."[23] Shriver was persuaded, and when the task force's proposals were presented to the cabinet for approval, included among them was a proposed five-cent tax on cigarettes expected to yield $1.25 billion per year to be earmarked for employment programs for the adult unemployed. Secretary Wirtz spoke in favor, but the president dismissed the idea immediately. The reason for the rejection was the tax cut he was seeking that year. There was no possibility of funding such a program with a tax increase while at the same time asking Congress to enact an income tax reduction. It is difficult to overestimate the importance of this decision in terms of its implications for the War on Poverty and its contribution to the goal of full employment. According to Moynihan, "Had Shriver's employment proposal succeeded, the character of the antipoverty program would have changed. . . . It would have dwarfed the other items. . . . The energies and attention of the administration would have been turned to the vital task of reforming and restructuring the job market. In a word, an 'employment strategy' would have become central to the war on poverty. But this did not happen."[24]

In terms of the commitment of resources, the War on Poverty amounted to merely a skirmish. Despite Johnson's lofty declaration of an "unconditional war," the effort proved to be highly conditional. The first year's appropriation of barely $1 billion (the lion's share going to the community action program) was far below what was believed necessary to eliminate poverty. A conservative estimate of the annual amount needed was $15 billion, and some observers determined the amount to be $30–$40 billion.[25] Appropriations remained low throughout the decade. An ambitious long-term budget for the Office of Economic Opportunity was presented to the president by Shriver in 1966. But the escalating war in Vietnam, plus Johnson's refusal to raise taxes in an election year, killed the idea.[26]

Fighting Poverty by Investing in Human Capital

While the poverty warriors disagreed about whether to create jobs for the unemployed, there was general agreement that education and training were key elements in any strategy to break the cycle of poverty that was thought to plague generations of the disadvantaged. There was a great degree of enthusiasm in academic circles for education and training as methods of fighting poverty, much as there had been for the novel concept of community action. By the time deliberations over the poverty program had gotten under way, a cadre of economists had come to the conclusion that at the center of the problem of poverty were the inadequate levels of "investment" in "human capital" undertaken by (or on behalf of) the poor. It is not easy to identify the influence of the human capital economists directly, but there is little doubt that their conclusions had permeated official thinking. Everyone in Washington involved with poverty in the early and mid-1960s "knew" that poverty could be successfully overcome if only the poor were given the basic education and occupational skills needed to compete in the mainstream labor market.

As pointed out earlier, the study of manpower received little attention from neoclassical economists. This changed, however, by the early 1960s, when a group of economists emerged who began to apply neoclassical assumptions about the rational maximizing behavior of individual economic agents to the issue of human resources. The focus of the human capital school was on the relation between education and training, on the one hand, and earnings, on the other. By investing in education and training, poverty could "be eliminated by raising everyone's marginal product to the level where [the worker] would be able to earn an acceptable income."[27] As one member of the human capital school put it, "A major presumption of the war on poverty is that education and training are especially effective ways to bring people out of poverty."[28] The theory blossomed in the work of three economists—Theodore Schultz, Jacob Mincer, and Gary Becker—and was subsequently refined and elaborated by many other economists.[29]

By the middle of the decade, human capital theory had superseded the earlier human resource school in the academic world and became more influential as an intellectual justification for training programs.

Human capital theory was recognized as more powerful and precise than the "soft" analyses done by Ginzberg and others in the human resource school. The centerpiece of human capital analysis consisted of a collection of estimates of the return on investments in human capital, especially from education, but from training as well. "However the question was put," according to Henry Aaron, "education seemed a very good investment indeed, with rates of return equal to or exceeding those yielded by ordinary investments and repaying more than the cost of education plus the interest at prevailing rates."[30] Second, human capital spoke more directly to the problem of poverty, defining it as a problem of "disadvantaged" persons who lacked the educational and technical skills demanded by the market. The institutional human resource school, in contrast, was concerned more broadly with how to better develop and utilize the human resources of Americans generally and tended to locate the problem at the institutional rather than individual level. Human capital theory clearly resonated better with the notion that the problem of poverty lay with a particular population of individuals with deficiencies, who no longer would have a problem if only they possessed the skills that the market demanded. "By likening education to investment in durable structures or machines, the theory of human capital created a powerful metaphor in which to express the view, widespread among the general public and held quite independently of any academic analysis, that education was a means to self-improvement and social advancement."[31]

MDTA Becomes a Poverty Program

When the MDTA was originally proposed in Congress, it limited eligibility to unemployed workers over thirty years of age who had families and work experience. An alternative proposed by the Kennedy administration, on the other hand, stipulated that anyone could participate in training and that the labor secretary could determine the composition of the program's participants, depending on the state of the labor market. In addition, the bill expanded the number of workers eligible for training allowances to include the underemployed, part-time workers, those who had exhausted their unemployment insurance benefits, and those without prior work experience. According to one observer, "The flexibility of [the administration's bill] in its projects and clientele elevated manpower policy to a position nearly equal with fiscal and monetary policy, as both a response to and reflection of changing economic conditions."[32] The final legislation failed to include the provision for universal eligibility and expanded benefits, thus establishing the practice that employment programs be made available only to a limited clientele.

When the MDTA was implemented, poverty was becoming the hot domestic policy issue. It was only a short step to shift eligibility from one category of individuals to another category. The program's original aim to retrain technologically displaced adults was almost immediately abandoned, as the department jumped on the poverty bandwagon. By late 1962 the unemployment rate had fallen to 5.7 percent, 3.7 percent for married men, and by July of 1963 the rate was down to 3.2 percent. There was no decrease in the overall level of unemployment, because teenage joblessness rose to offset the overall decline.[33] When the expected rise in unemployment among adult men never materialized, the Labor Department was left with a solution in search of a problem. Officials concluded that, faced with an increasingly tight labor market, industry had apparently found no difficulty in absorbing whatever training was necessary to give already skilled workers the new skills made necessary by the changes forced by technological progress. According to Assistant Secretary Ruttenberg:

It became increasingly evident that it was not the skilled workers, the family men with long-time work experience, who were left behind . . . in 1963; it was already evident that we were working on the wrong woodpile. . . . It was the disadvantaged who filled the ranks of the unemployed—those who were discriminated against or were never equipped in the first place to function successfully in the free labor market. The problem was the bottom of the labor barrel, not the top.[34]

Implications of the Poverty Program for Employment Policy

The absorption of MDTA into the poverty program, and the proliferation of similar programs under the EOA, effectively dispelled any remaining notion that manpower policy had much of any relationship to the larger concerns of the economy. The MDTA mandated that the secretary of labor evaluate the impacts of structural change in the economy, appraise the adequacy of manpower development efforts, and engage in the dissemination of information pertaining to the labor market. The secretary was to annually submit a manpower report of the president "pertaining to manpower requirements, resources, utilization, and training." Each year the report was sent to Congress, but little in the way of planning has stemmed from it. "MDTA data," according to Mangum, "have suffered from disuse rather than misuse."[35] The reason for this was that the report, while it contained the raw materials for a plan, contained no policy save for the descriptions of various programs, each designed to deliver its own services. Manpower planning makes sense only in the context of an overall strategy for promoting economic growth and stability. Yet it was clear that the economic policy being developed by the economic advisers in the Kennedy administration did not include any substantial role for manpower. The MDTA was simply a recognition of the acceptance by the federal government "of a social responsibility for the retraining of technologically unemployed individuals so that they and their families would not be hurt by progressive economic developments that were producing benefits for the economy as a whole."[36]

By the end of the 1960s, the view that employment programs should be used almost exclusively for purposes of social policy was taken for granted as well by the most influential manpower policy experts. Sar Levitan, one the leading authorities, rejected the idea that manpower should serve any purpose other than "relief" and "compassion for those in need":

Members of my own trade have tried to sell training as a new snake oil, good for all ailments. Expansion of manpower programs, according to these enthusiastic proponents, will cure the economy from inflation and unemployment, ease the trade-off between the two, and improve the environment to boot. . . .

Relief is given to the destitute not because it necessarily improves the efficiency of the economy, but out of compassion for those in need. So, too, training programs should be offered to those who have difficulty competing in the free labor market because they need help and not because of the impact of these expenditures on the national economy.[37]

Those who took the other side, who advocated a manpower policy oriented toward economic rather than social policy objectives, were disconcerted with the antipoverty focus. Europeans, whose policies placed primary emphasis on manpower policy as a set of instruments for promoting economic growth and productivity, were particularly critical. The architect of Sweden's employment policy, Gosta Rehn, argued that "this emphasis must work to the disadvantage of both the disadvantaged and the advantaged."[38] By concentrating only on the disadvantaged, argued Rehn, the impact of manpower training would be simply to squeeze more people onto the lower levels in the job hierarchy. It would do nothing to help the already employed and more advanced workers to climb to higher steps in the job ladder, leaving vacancies for those below. The result would be that poor people in the programs would simply displace other poor or low-income people, while preserving precisely those jobs in secondary labor markets that offered the least stable, least economically productive opportunities for employment. Rehn further argued that concentrating on the lowest rungs of the skill ladder would also fail to help relieve skill shortages in expanding sectors of the economy, especially important in higher wage sectors that are prone to set off inflation.[39]

The restriction of manpower training and work experience to the most disadvantaged members of society had other consequences as well. The structure of education and training can be viewed as a series of strata, with upper-middle-class parents sending their children to the best private and public universities, whose graduates are most sought by prestigious graduate and professional schools and by employers seeking to fill higher executive positions. Then there is a middle range of state universities and colleges, filled largely by children from the middle majority of families, which train for occupations in teaching, accounting, commerce, and industry. Next come the community colleges and the best vocational schools, which feed local economies with bank tellers, clerks, health technicians, barbers, and other service or paraprofessional workers. Finally, there are the least effective and lowest ranking vocational schools and training programs, whose graduates have a difficult time acquiring and maintaining employment in the kinds of occupations listed above.

According to Harold Wilensky, despite the distributive effects of how education is financed and where the money is spent, "there is an unmistakable process of self-selection and recruitment by social background into the [multitiered] system, with occupational prospects appropriately linked to quality [of education] levels."[40] The training and work experience offered by MDTA and EOA programs tended to be for individuals and occupations at the very bottom of the economic ladder. The result, then, was to segregate the least educated, poorest, often minority clientele from the more attractive trainees serviced by the regular vocational schools. But it is these schools that usually have the best reputations in the local community and have established relationships with private industry.[41] In short, the manpower training programs set up in the 1960s (and those existing today) most likely have reinforced and reproduced socioeconomic segmentation and inequality, rather than transcending it.

Finally, and perhaps most important, restricting the programs to the least influential groups in society greatly constricted the political constituency supporting them and, it ought to be added, contributed to resentment among many white, middle-class and working-class individuals, who believed that other groups were receiving special treatment.

DESIGNING AN ADMINISTRATIVE STRUCTURE

The pastiche of programs created during the 1960s did not constitute a comprehensive and integrated manpower policy. The period was one of experimentation, and it reflected the penchant among New Frontier and Great Society activists to respond to social problems without paying much attention to administrative matters. By late in the decade, the administrative problems had grown to nightmarish proportions. The programs themselves had come to be much of the problem of employment policy. Officials in Washington were burdened with the daunting task of approving thousands of contracts and monitoring the activities of countless service providers. The inflexibility of categorical grants compounded administrative difficulties. Despite marked variations in employment and training problems across communities, program administrators applied rigid conditions and requirements for the receipt of aid. Having its own legislative authorization, each program diverged in terms of its clients, services, funding arrangements, and administrative requirements. At the same time, there existed considerable overlap and duplication among the various programs. Many sought to serve identical groups and delivered the same or related services. The secretary of labor had considerable authority to alter the distribution of funding and administrative requirements. When viewed from the local level, these appeared capricious and contributed to frustration with the programs.

At the top, the tangle of programs came under the authority of three federal agencies: the Department of Labor (DOL), the Office of Education in the Department of Health Education and Welfare (HEW), and the Office of Economic Opportunity (OEO). There were jurisdictional rivalries among all three. The confusing pattern of administration at the federal level was mirrored below. The MDTA programs relied on established institutions like the Employment Service and the public schools' system of vocational education. The EOA programs were deliberately designed to supplant these old-line bureaucracies, which were seen as hidebound and out of touch with the objectives of the poverty program. Some programs drew funds through DOL's regional offices, whereas others were funded directly from Washington. Sometimes federal agencies contracted directly with a broad array of service providers. In addition to the Employment Service and the schools, this included community colleges, labor unions, opportunity industrial centers (OICs), and other community-based organizations. At other times, they delegated contractual authority to quasi-public bodies, such as community action agencies. Inevitably, competition among providers became intense. Public vocational schools, which had been designated under MDTA as the provider of classroom training, found their role partially eclipsed when EOA programs like the Job Corps and Neighborhood Youth Corps were begun and contracts were awarded to voc ed's competitors. The U.S. Employment Service, designated by the Labor Department as the "presumptive provider" of manpower services under MDTA, found itself competing with community action agencies.

Another effect of these labyrinthine arrangements was to circumvent the authority of locally elected officials (generalists) and to enhance the influence of functional specialists within state and local bureaucracies and community action agencies, who were not directly accountable to the electorate. Local officials found themselves held accountable for the operation of programs over which they held little control.

At the forefront of efforts to diagnose these problems and prescribe a remedy were manpower experts. The consensus that emerged in the manpower community was facilitated through several formal mechanisms for studying the programs. The most important of these were the National Manpower Policy Task Force (NMPTF) and the Center for Manpower Policy Studies (CMPS) at George Washington University, both nonprofit organizations, as well as the National Manpower Advisory Committee (NMAC), a government-sponsored body of experts established under the MDTA. The membership of the NMPTF included every prominent academic expert on the subject, with the leading roles taken by Garth Mangum and Sar Levitan. Both had been involved in launching manpower programs in the early 1960s. Mangum served as the staff director for Senator Joseph Clark's Subcommittee on Employment and Manpower, and Levitan drafted the Area Redevelopment Act, a precursor to MDTA, when he served as a staff economist in the Library of Congress. Both were immersed in an ongoing evaluation of all manpower and antipoverty programs at the CMPS.[42]

Disillusionment with the manpower programs was part of a broader reaction against federal management that was manifest throughout Washington and much of the academic community. "By the close of the decade," notes Martha Derthick, "it was the conventional wisdom in Washington that categorical grant programs had become too complicated in the course of their recent haphazard growth."[43] Not only had the federal government fallen short of expectations that it would solve major social problems, but in the process, it had created an unmanageable plethora of programs, inefficiently operated under rigid bureaucratic mandates.[44] Several noted liberal intellectuals, some like Daniel Moynihan and Richard Goodwin who themselves had been architects of the Great Society, and others with equally impressive liberal credentials like James Sundquist, grew ardently opposed to centralization. Manpower policy drew particularly sharp criticism, as Sundquist's vivid description of the administrative maladies of MDTA attests:

Our field interview notes are filled with assertions by local officials that federal decisions are being made on matters that should be wholly within the competence of communities. . . . Six years after the enactment of the Manpower Development and Training Act, every individual training course still had to be submitted for federal approval; one training center was operating on thirty-two budgets at the time of our visit—one for each course—and a request that these be consolidated into a single budget had been rejected by the Department of Labor. And the division of funds between on-the-job and institutional training was made each year in Washington, with that division applied uniformly to each of the fifty states regardless of differences in need among the states.[45]

Mangum leveled a similar criticism in testimony before Congress:

We have the Federal agency dealing with something like 10,000 sponsors of 30,000 separate contracts. The Federal agency has the authority, but it doesn't know what is going on out in the field because it is just not administratively possible to have the span of control to know what is going on in each community, what the performance is, and then enforce accountability in the system.[46]

The consensus that developed focused on three principal recommendations: *consolidation* of all programs under one roof; *decategorization,* which would increase flexibility by eliminating diverse eligibility criteria and conditions; and *decentralization* of authority to local officials held accountable to the electorate.[47] One of the more influential statements of the consensus view was contained in a seminar paper that Mangum delivered before the National Governors Conference in 1968.[48] The rationale for these changes was summarized in the 1969 and 1970 position papers of the NMPTF:

A new modesty born of experience admits the limits of Federal administrative capability. . . . The separate programs must be fused into a single comprehensive federal manpower program—providing a variety of services in varying mixes depending upon national conditions and local need, preferably funded by a single federal source . . . the first lesson [of the sixties experience] is that at the local level . . . available manpower services should be provided on the basis of need, not impeded by diverse eligibility requirements, varying administrative practices or competing agencies. Experience has clearly demonstrated that there are definite limits to the number of grants and contracts the Department of Labor can negotiate, fund, monitor, and evaluate. What is needed . . . is an orderly commitment of resources to allow states and communities to plan and implement manpower programs according to their own needs.[49]

We are convinced . . . that it is time to place responsibility for performance in the hands of elected officials who must answer to the voters they serve."[50]

Although the need for loosening federal control was widely recognized, appeals for vesting discretion with state and local governments were tempered by the recognition, first, that local decisions might run counter to national policy goals. "Communities differ, and programs must be adapted to local needs, but there is no assurance that local decisions will be in accord with national goals," admonished Levitan and Mangum. "The new clients of the federal manpower programs tend to be socially and politically, as well as economically, handicapped. The tendency of local agencies in the absence of federal pressure has been to expend their limited resources on persons easiest to serve."[51] The dilemma of incompatible goals presupposed that policy makers at each level of government were able to clearly identify what the goals of manpower policy were in the first place. "As a first step," Levitan and Mangum stated, "communities can accommodate federal and local goals only if both are clearly articulated, and neither have been."[52]

Second, it was also acknowledged that the administrative capacity to administer manpower programs was largely lacking at the subnational level. State and local officials had little experience with running manpower programs. Unlike other federally supported public services, like elementary and secondary education, there was no preexisting, well-developed service delivery structure at the local level. Hence the call for state and local governments to assume the major administrative responsibilities owed less to a firm faith in state and local political commitment and administrative capability than to a realization that the existing structure was grossly inadequate: "We share the concern over the competence and commitment of many state and local governments and agencies. On the other hand, we are not persuaded of the all-sufficiency of the federal government's wisdom. . . . It is a tough trade-off. It is very risky to decentralize authority, but on the other hand, having authority you can't exercise isn't much help either."[53]

The answer to the shortcomings of the existing system seemed to be in striking a balance of control between the different levels of government. The federal government would set broad policy goals and monitor the states and localities as they pursued the goals through means most appropriate to the community environment. This, however, was easier to conceptualize than it was to write into legislation or, most of all, to translate into reality.[54] As we shall see in chapter 7, the experts' fears that local goals might clash with those established by Congress and that local officials lacked the administrative capacity and experience necessary turned out to be well founded.

The Happy Marriage of Ideology and Expert Opinion

The election of President Nixon provided added impetus to the already sizable group of influential people favoring reform. The consensus view among manpower insiders dovetailed nicely with the Nixon administration's New Federalism initiative. The importance of New Federalism for the president lay beyond what it promised in narrow terms of efficiency and good administrative practice. The doctrine expressed more fundamental political beliefs. "Government can be made more responsive to the people only by bringing government closer to the people."[55] Nixon linked manpower reform with the possibilities for democratic control and a return of faith in government.[56] The unpruned growth of manpower programs had taken place under the auspices of two Democratic administrations and Democratic majorities in Congress. The New Federalism was a reaction against Lyndon Johnson's Creative Federalism, which was marked by a massive increase in categorical grants stressing narrow program objectives, strict eligibility criteria, and the administrative regulation of grantee behavior. This placed discretion for awarding aid in the hands of bureaucrats in Washington. It established direct federal linkages with a melange of local recipients, including both public and private agencies, thus bypassing the traditional grant-in-aid arrangements with state governments.[57]

Like almost everyone else, Nixon accepted the idea of federal training programs. His proposed reforms were intended merely "to make good on a good idea." Where he found fault with the record of his predecessors was not in what government was expected to do but in how it went about doing it: "One of the great lessons of the dramatic Federal Government growth in the 1960s is that even a good idea like this can fall short of its promise if the way in which it is carried out runs against the grain of the Federal system."[58] Of his predecessors' policies, Nixon later wrote, "The problems were real and the intention worthy," but the heavy reliance on Washington bureaucracies "had undermined fundamental relationships within our federal system, created confusion about our national values, and corroded American belief in ourselves as a people and as a nation."[59]

Just prior to taking office, Nixon appointed George Shultz to head an ad hoc task force on manpower and labor-management decisions. Mangum, who was a member of the task force, introduced the concepts decentralization and decategorization. The report of the task force faithfully reflected the consensus view, drawing heavily on the paper Mangum had prepared for the governors. The administration's proposal, the Manpower Training Act (MTA), embodied the essential reforms recommended by the manpower experts and reflected the principles espoused in the president's inchoate New Federalism doctrine. As Roger Davidson put it, "MTA was a happy marriage of traditional Republican philosophy and expert opinion within the manpower policy community."[60] The bill consolidated all existing manpower programs under MDTA, EOA, and the U.S. Employment Service. State and local

officials, acting as prime sponsors, were permitted to use their allocations in accordance with their own determination of needs and priorities. Prime sponsors could develop their own mix of programs from a
broad range of eligible training and employment activities. While the
bill made great strides toward a decentralized manpower system, the
Labor Department would need to approve local plans, provide technical
assistance, and monitor the performance of the prime sponsors. Reform
did not come until 1973 with the Comprehensive Employment and
Training Act, but it embodied the decentralized, decategorized, and
consolidated features contained in the original proposal.

CONCLUSION

In the formative years of employment policy three basic assumptions
were established: (1) that unemployment was a problem of individuals
rather than the market or other institutions; (2) that eligibility for employment programs should be limited to discrete categories of individuals, such as those living in poverty, rather than to workers generally;
and (3) that enough jobs existed paying wages above the poverty level,
and therefore employment policy should be directed toward training
people for jobs rather than creating jobs for people. If the economic
structure itself were not part of the problem, if most people in the labor
market and all of its job opportunities could be left to market forces, then
neither direct job creation nor any serious commitment to manpower
planning and development were necessary. The primary task for public
policy, through aggregate fiscal and monetary manipulations, was to
maintain a sufficient level of demand for employment. Employment
policy was assigned the residual task of providing training for those
unable to find employment who were deemed disadvantaged and de-
serving.

Because it stopped short of guaranteeing a result, providing only
the chance to better compete in the labor market, giving the poor and
unemployed training and education was consistent with equality of
opportunity. Equality of opportunity, a liberal principle that was central
to legitimating postwar employment policy, steered a middle course
between formal legal equality and equality of condition. In a social order
that stresses social equality and the possibilities for upward mobility,
on the one hand, and individual freedom and responsibility, on the
other, equal opportunity through training was a form of positive government action that could reconcile both values. Other values underpinned other elements of the poverty program. A seemingly novel idea
like community action captured the imagination of policy makers in
part because it was consistent with a traditional faith in decentralization

and local control. It was assumed that, if poverty dwellers could gain "empowerment" and mobilize resources in their own communities, they could improve their lot.

What made the meshing of policy with values possible were changing definitions of the problem and policy prescriptions put forward by reformers and experts in and out of government. First, the discovery of poverty and the successful effort to make it a salient issue resulted in redefining structural unemployment as a problem of a disadvantaged underclass rather than of experienced, mainstream workers displaced by technological advance. Second, that community action became the centerpiece of the poverty program owed much to the consensus that developed between social work professionals who championed the concept and the policy intellectuals in the executive branch who seized upon it as a plausible and superior alternative to public job creation. Third, the initial rationale for a manpower policy was to improve the development and utilization of the nation's human resources, broadly conceived. Human resource experts and labor economists saw the problem as institutional in nature—such as the market mechanism's failure to adequately adjust supply and demand in a technologically changing and segmented economic structure. They urged reforms in schools, business, government, and other institutions that would enhance how human resources were developed and utilized. The federal government was called upon to engage in labor market planning and to heavily invest in education and training. While these experts played an important role in getting the issue on the agenda by raising the consciousness of policy makers (particularly Senator Clark and Labor Department officials), their specific definition of the problem and their policy prescriptions were reshaped by the human capital theorists. Human capital theory subtly yet significantly transformed the rationale for a manpower policy. The source of poverty and joblessness shifted from institutions and the economic structure to a particular population of individuals who were deficient in education and skills. If these individuals were able to invest in education and skill training, they would be capable of taking jobs in the private sector that paid sufficiently to get them out of poverty. Finally, the decisions about what kind of poverty program to adopt were constrained by the commitment to a macroeconomic strategy based on cutting taxes. The embrace of commercial Keynesianism effectively thwarted efforts to launch a large-scale job creation program, which would have required raising taxes to pay for it.

By the end of the 1960s, the agenda had partly shifted from substantive to administrative issues. Once again, policy innovation represented a return to longstanding American values. Decentralization and decategorization of employment programs were one component of the

Nixon administration's New Federalism doctrine, a broad plan to reorder intergovernmental relations that went beyond manpower reform. There was little actually "new" in this initiative, however. It harked back to the "dual federalism" of the nineteenth century, where the different levels of government operated in largely separate spheres and were responsible for separate functions. It reflected the traditional American belief that equates local autonomy with democracy, and centralization with an overbearing government.[61]

Yet, the reassertion of a belief in decentralization would have fallen on deaf ears in Congress without the support for reform among those most intimately connected with manpower programs—the community of manpower experts. It is significant that manpower was one of only two of the Nixon administration's six block grant proposals that passed in Congress. Studies of the pattern of response to all of Nixon's New Federalism proposals point out that Congress approved those proposals that had the backing of the relevant experts and rejected those that did not.[62] Judged against the canons of good administrative practice, manpower experts deemed the existing arrangements a failure. Administrative units were uncoordinated, program components lacked integration, clear lines of accountability and an appropriate span of control were absent. Categorical programs did not consider the differences in labor markets from locality to locality and failed to recognize that the particular mixes of services needed could be decided only by those closest to the problems. The idea of reorganization spent a long gestation period, during which the general direction of change that reform should take emerged. Experience had demonstrated the limits to centralization and categorical programs and led to the search for a new administrative arrangement. There was a substantial intellectual commitment to the principles of decategorization, consolidation, and local control, which antedated Nixon's involvement. These opinions gave proponents of reform in government an authoritativeness that was denied those who sought to defend the status quo. They provided justifications for reform based on the merits of the issues, rather than simply on a traditional attachment to local control.

4

Public Job Creation and
Full Employment Revisited

EMPLOYMENT POLICY enjoyed a significant measure of bipartisan support in the early to mid-1960s, because it did not call into question the private economy's capacity to supply sufficient jobs once an appropriate fiscal stimulus was provided. The War on Poverty included training, compensatory education, and work experience.[1] The Johnson administration's aim was "not more jobs, but a more equitable distribution of the nation's 3.5 percent unemployment."[2] Employment policy meant manpower training. Training was unambiguously consistent with expanding equality of opportunity. The notion was one of helping others to help themselves, so that the disadvantaged would become better able to compete successfully in the mainstream labor market. Liberals, mostly Democrats, could support training, for the reason that government had an obligation to help the unemployed and develop the nation's manpower. Most Republicans, and conservatives generally, could justify government spending for training programs because it was compatible with the functioning of the private market. Training prepared individuals for permanent jobs, most of which were in the private sector.

It was a growing insistence by liberals in Congress for the government to create jobs for the poor and unemployed that disrupted the consensual atmosphere. The jobs issue evoked the kind of classic partisan hostility between conservatives and liberals that harked back to the New Deal. For conservatives, there were several serious objections to public employment. First, providing individuals with training gave them the opportunity to work and compete for jobs and income, but providing them with jobs was giving them a reward that they had not "earned." It was also perceived as pitting government against private enterprise. Public employment of the unemployed, especially at competitive wages, raised the specter of draining labor and other resources from the private sector. If government acted as the employer of last resort, it could easily become the employer of first resort. "Dead-end," "make-work" jobs would be substituted for "productive" employment. Public employment was an explicit admission that the private sector, on its own, was incapable of creating enough jobs for all who needed them. Finally, many conservatives believed that providing the unemployed with publicly subsidized jobs did not expand, but limited, their economic opportunity. It would create or maintain a stigmatized class of persons, who would have little incentive to compete for the more rewarding "regular" jobs that the private sector offered.

THE LIBERAL CRITIQUE OF THE POVERTY PROGRAM AND THE "NEW" PUBLIC SERVICE EMPLOYMENT

Throughout the 1960s, liberals gradually mobilized around public employment, and by the end of the decade they got the issue on the agenda. The first step was taken in amendments made to the Economic Opportunity Act (EOA). Congress approved a modest program providing conservation jobs for older workers located in rural areas. The program was known as Operation Mainstream and was sponsored by Senator Gaylord Nelson of Wisconsin, Joseph Clark's successor as chairman of the Manpower Subcommittee. New Careers, an EOA program instituted shortly afterward, was intended to create a limited number of paraprofessional jobs for the most able of the poor. These were small programs, not designed to provide massive unemployment relief or dramatically increase federal aid for local public services. They fit into the manpower development objectives of the existing MDTA and EOA programs. They were intended to prepare the disadvantaged for jobs that were already in demand in the public sector, much as the regular training programs were designed to prepare participants for private sector employment. These programs often failed to lead to permanent public employment, however. New Careers trainees, for instance, often found themselves laid off after their training period was completed, because local agencies did not have the funds to continue to employ them.[3] And often, local civil service requirements were blamed for blocking the disadvantaged from starting up the public service career ladder.

More important than these efforts was a series of studies conducted by various task forces, blue ribbon panels, and congressional committees that appeared during these years. Taken together, they argued that (1) there was a shortage of jobs, particularly in urban areas; (2) there was a tremendous growth in demand for local public services, which required a substantial expansion of local government payrolls; and (3) neither training nor macroeconomic policies were sufficient tools for attacking unemployment. Therefore, public employment creation was necessary. For liberals in and out of government, the authoritative opinions in these studies provided ammunition to maintain a drumbeat of support for a public jobs program throughout the decade.[4]

The first to appear was a ten-volume study on the nation's "manpower revolution," produced by the Senate Manpower Subcommittee. Its only controversial recommendation was that "federal, state, and local governments should undertake a joint program to directly employ the hard-core unemployed in poverty-stricken areas, both rural and urban, in an attack on the deficiencies of their own environments. Financial support should be provided by the Federal government."[5] Recognizing that such a proposal would engender criticism of make-work, the subcommittee argued that in the slums "there is more to do than rake leaves."

Pressure from the subcommittee prompted the Office of Economic Opportunity to commission a study to determine the potential for job creation. The preliminary findings were published as part of the report of the National Commission on Technology, Automation, and Economic Progress entitled *Technology and the American Economy*. The report indicated that there were 5.3 million additional jobs needed in the public sector and recommended a permanent, long-term program of public employment, with an initial appropriation of $2 billion.[6] The report also neatly summarized the argument that neither fiscal and monetary policies, nor education and training, alone or combined, could be expected to bring the economy to full employment:

In terms of our image of the labor market as a queue, fiscal and monetary policies begin at the front of the queue and work toward the rear. Education and training and labor market policies affect not only relative places in the line, but the depth to which general economic policies can reach without generating inflation. Yet when all that is done, there remains another possibility—to begin at the rear of the line and create employment opportunities tailored to the abilities of those with serious competitive disadvantages.[7]

In June 1966, President Johnson directed the Department of Labor (DOL) to make a detailed survey of unemployment in urban ghettos. The president wanted to know why, in the sixth year of uninterrupted economic expansion and tight labor markets, there were still people out of work. The survey was conducted in ten major cities and produced two reports. It showed that the low national unemployment rate of 3.7 percent masked rates of joblessness and underemployment in the slums that were several times higher. Labor Secretary Wirtz passed this information along to the president with the ominous warning that, unless something were done to change the situation, "there would be a revolution."[8]

Wirtz's warning turned out to be prophetic when urban riots broke out across the nation in 1967. The War on Poverty may have been partly to blame for this, by raising expectations among the poor that their situation would indeed improve. When it did not, and these expectations were dashed, there was an angry reaction from the ghettos. The Kerner Commission, appointed in response to the disturbances, offered conclusions similar to those of the earlier OEO study:

We recommend a three-year program aimed at creating 250,000 new public service jobs in the first year and a total of one million such jobs over the three-year period. . . . In the public sector a substantial number of such jobs can be provided quickly, particularly by government at the local level, where there are vast unmet needs in education, health, recreation, public safety, sanitation and other municipal services.[9]

Yet another study conducted in the wake of the riots, by the Senate Subcommittee on Poverty, prompted senators Clark and Robert Kennedy to propose an emergency employment bill of 1967. The bill would have granted the Labor Department $2.5 billion over fiscal years 1968 and 1969 for job creation. Pressure from the administration kept the Clark-Kennedy bill from coming to a vote, and a watered-down Republican version was defeated by five votes.

The Johnson administration tried to deflect demands for public jobs by enrolling the support of the National Alliance of Business (NAB) in a voluntary, private sector, job creation effort. The JOBS (Job Opportunities in the Business Sector) program aimed at getting businesses to hire the hard-core unemployed. The program was barely off the ground when the job market began to slacken late in the decade. Business's interest in the program quickly dissipated, and the program fell far short of its projected placements. A report by the National Commission on Employment of Youth, comparing job creation in the public sector with JOBS, stated that "employers in the public sector seem to be achieving their hiring goals more readily than those in the private sector."[10]

The disappointment with JOBS helped confirm a central belief among public employment advocates that the private sector was unable to create sufficient job opportunities for all who needed them. Harold Sheppard of the Upjohn Institute concluded that "even with the best of motives, the best of recruiting, training, on-the-job techniques, etc., the actual numbers of jobs now available for the hard-core unemployed . . . in private industry are limited, or not readily accessible."[11] With the private sector unable to absorb all job seekers, on the one hand, and unfilled vacancies in the public sector (many requiring little or no training), on the other, it seemed common sense to fund jobs in state and local government.

The unimpressive results of the MDTA and EOA training programs also lent support to efforts for a jobs program. Unemployment statistics called attention to the fact that, while the nation as a whole was enjoying unprecedented prosperity during most of the 1960s, poverty and unemployment persisted among urban populations. In the early 1960s the assumption was that there were plenty of jobs available to absorb the unemployed, if only they had the requisite training and placement services at their disposal. The perception grew that the antipoverty effort, and training programs in particular, had failed to bring the disadvantaged into the mainstream of unsubsidized, private employment. This position was defended by showing the unemployment rates for various groups in the workforce. The national unemployment rate stood at a postwar low of 3.4 percent in the fourth quarter of 1968, but comparatively high rates for various groups of the hard-core unemployed persisted. Despite the expansion of manpower programs, the unemployment rate for nonwhites looked little better in 1969 than it did in 1963, and among nonwhite youths there was no change whatsoever.[12]

This prompted Senator Nelson to hold hearings throughout the country in 1969 to discern how well the nation's manpower programs were enabling participants to move into the mainstream of American working life. The findings from city to city showed training programs were generally ineffective, due in large part to the fact that there simply were not adequate supplies of jobs available at decent pay in areas of high unemployment. The committee's hearings also indicated that the demand for public services was far outstripping the fiscal capacities of local governments to provide them. A parade of local officials came forward affirming the dire need for expanded public services.[13] Nelson's subcommittee concluded that the chief shortcoming of employment policy, with its emphasis on training, lay in the insufficient attention paid to the lack of job opportunities for those who had been trained.

Hence, the major premise of the poverty program—that joblessness among the disadvantaged was due to their own deficiencies in skills, work experience, and proper work habits—came under attack. Proponents of the "new" public service employment (PSE) directly challenged the assumption of human capital theory—that poverty was created by insufficient investment in skills training. Sheppard and fellow economist Bennett Harrison, along with William Spring, a staff member of

Nelson's subcommittee, located the problem in the market, instead, and saw the poverty program as part of the problem rather than the solution:

Persistent poverty and underemployment are directly attributable to the conviction—among Democrats and Republicans—that those who cannot "make it" in our labor markets are unable to work at all, or lack the skill, drive and motivation needed to earn an adequate living.

. . . A public service employment program . . . would represent a qualitative shift of emphasis. Part of the "blame" for personal misery, frustration and lack of fulfillment would be shifted from the individual to the economic system, where it belongs.[14]

Advocates of the new PSE were careful to try to avoid identification with the WPA program of the 1930s. The latter was conceived as a temporary work relief program, intended to meet an emergency situation that was expected to pass once economic growth resumed. It was government acting as the employer of last resort. Proponents of the new PSE rejected the negative and inferior status of the old jobs programs. They looked not to Harry Hopkins but to John Kenneth Galbraith, who decried the imbalance between public and private spending that produced "public squalor amidst private affluence."[15] With so many useful public services left unattended because of local fiscal constraints, jobs proponents began to speak in terms of government as the employer of first resort. "There is no connection between this job program and the old WPA of the New Deal days," declared Clark. "These jobs will improve our cities, towns and rural areas, rebuild our blighted neighborhoods, improve the physical environment in which we live, and provide for many of the human services needs that are not now being met."[16] Intellectuals and economists on the left, like Michael Harrington and Frank Reissman, saw PSE as a tool for transforming society: "A quality public service employment program is a major strategy for reorganizing our society, redistributing wealth and services, and shifting resources from the private sector to the development of human services."[17]

PSE drew a wide range of support. It brought liberal and civil rights activists and local officials together. These two groups had been at loggerheads over the community action activities undertaken as a major part of the poverty program. For liberals in Congress, public employment held out the promise of uniting the interests of their liberal constituencies with those of big city mayors who sought greater federal support for local services. Establishment organizations like the National Urban Coalition (NUC) also backed PSE, both as "riot insurance" and as a way to fund needed city services. The NUC was formed by the

U.S. Conference of Mayors and the League of Cities. The NUC's mission was "to awaken the American people to their responsibilities in dealing with the urban crisis . . . and help them in the search for solutions," according to its chairman John W. Gardner.[18] The coalition represented a "remarkable coming together" of elites in American society, including Henry Ford II, David Rockefeller, George Meany, Walter Reuther, Roy Wilkins, Richard Daley, and John Lindsay. The NUC, which had helped finance Sheppard's studies of the number of unfilled jobs in local government, urged the federal government, during the riot-torn summer of 1967, to develop an emergency jobs program.

Funding for PSE also gained advocates within the ranks of manpower experts, who earlier had been interested mainly in training programs. In a letter to President-elect Nixon on the future direction of manpower policy, the National Manpower Advisory Committee (NMAC) recommended enlarging "the role of the federal government in direct job creation" as a "priority policy action."[19] The National Manpower Policy Task Force (NMPTF) took a similar stand, calling for a "substantial federal initiative" in public jobs.[20] There were, however, also differences in the degree of enthusiasm among those who supported public employment. The NMAC and NMPTF were more cautious in their advocacy than those in the new PSE movement. The NMPTF cautioned that "job creation, like training, is a limited instrument" that should "be viewed as one tool of a comprehensive manpower policy."[21] "It should be recognized," the task force report went on to say, "that, although such programs create jobs, they do not automatically create jobs for the disadvantaged. As in the private sector, underwriting services must be tied directly to hiring and training those who would otherwise be unlikely to obtain jobs."[22] From this perspective, any jobs program should be carefully designed to complement the traditional employability objectives of training programs.

Public jobs became more politically attractive as the 1970s began. The catalyst for getting PSE on the agenda was the gradual rise in the national unemployment rate. In the summer of 1969 the jobless rate stood at 3.5 percent, but by the first quarter of 1970 it had increased to 4.3 percent, the highest it had reached in five years. By the fourth quarter of that year, it hit 5.1 percent. It was this trend that turned what had been an ardent commitment to a jobs program that was limited to liberals like Senator Nelson into a more generalized concern throughout Congress. Once higher unemployment began to spread to the general work force, congressmen heretofore unconcerned began to support the idea.

Partly blamed for the rise in unemployment was the Nixon administration's macroeconomic policies. The 1965 tax cut, spending for the Great Society programs, and the Vietnam War had stimulated economic growth. The failure to enact a timely tax increase to offset the increased war spending exacerbated inflationary pressures in the economy. Just at the time when the expansion was wearing off, the new administration came into office declaring that inflation was the major problem confronting the economy. Fiscal and monetary policies turned to restraint. In the spring of 1970 Arthur Okun, who had been chairman of the Council of Economic Advisers under President Johnson, told Congress: "I am . . . deeply concerned that the stringent tight money that was so essential to halt the boom last spring and summer may now be weakening the economy too much."[23]

The rise in unemployment lent a good deal of credibility to the argument that macroeconomic policies could not be depended upon to deal with unemployment, and that in such an environment the most that could be expected of training programs would be to redistribute job opportunities in favor of those trained for the jobs that were in demand. The liberals, who had been able to get little in the way of public employment from Johnson, now redoubled their efforts with Nixon.

The Perspective of the Nixon Administration

The new administration's economists took the same position as had those in the previous two. Temporary shortages of jobs could be treated by expansions of aggregate demand alone until those at the end of the job queue were reached. George Shultz, Nixon's first labor secretary, argued that the economy was basically healthy, providing a good supply of "regular" jobs. But Nixon's opposition to a large-scale program of public service jobs was hardened, unlike his predecessors', in traditional Republican antipathy toward make-work. That is, public employment was not simply unnecessary, expensive, or impractical, it was an inappropriate task for government in a free enterprise economy.

The position of the president and his advisers was congruent with the prevailing view in the Labor Department, which would have no part of an employment policy that included a sizable and permanent jobs program. A massive employment program threatened to eclipse its organizational mission—increasing the employability and earning capacity of individuals through training. The demand for labor was deemed a matter "for broader national action," meaning fiscal and monetary policies. As James Hodgson, Shultz's successor at the Labor Department, explained in this exchange with Senator William Proxmire:

SECRETARY HODGSON: The administration is dedicated to manpower policies that will help the unemployed worker become employed. That is the whole thrust of it.

SENATOR PROXMIRE: Employable or employed?

SECRETARY HODGSON: Employable and employed.

SENATOR PROXMIRE: I am sure about the first; I am not sure about the latter.

SECRETARY HODGSON: From the standpoint of sound manpower policy, it seems to us that putting money in a man's pocket is not enough. We ought to give him some competence, some confidence . . . that he can make it in the real world of work.[24]

Officials in the department were not opposed to a limited public jobs component, however. Funding short stints of employment connected to training opportunities in the public sector was acceptable. Established manpower programs like Operation Mainstream and New Careers were designed for this purpose. The public sector was a rapidly growing sector of the economy, accounting for 15 percent of the total labor force. The department had recently initiated a small experimental program, Public Service Careers, that provided training for jobs in local government. But these jobs were to be one part of an overall comprehensive package of services designed to place individuals on the first rungs of an occupational ladder leading to regular employment in the public or private sector. They were desirable only where they "would serve a function within the overall employability development plans for clients." According to Hodgson,

In our view . . . public employment should be used for the basic purpose of improving the individual's capacity to move into a regular private or public job, because money spent in this way becomes an investment in human potential. So if we want to describe this succinctly, we might say that public employment should serve as a halfway house for the unemployed individual. . . . The work in question should be preparatory for the real world of work, not a substitute for it, and the work should be of limited duration—a bridge to be crossed toward something better, not a permanent subsidized job.[25]

This compromise position, between creating a massive jobs program or creating none at all, was not only a way for the department to reconcile PSE with its manpower development goals, but it was also designed to deflect the pressures building for a massive program. The DOL feared that if spending for jobs got out of control it could transform manpower policy into a fiscal assistance program: "Providing funds to state and local governments to meet their personnel requirements is not the proper function of a manpower program. To do so through manpower legislation would be a disguised form of revenue sharing which, if desirable, should more properly be established through legislation specifically designed for that purpose."[26]

In short, the administration's position was that any PSE program had to be temporary and transitional, leading to "real" jobs in the public or private sector. This did not sit well with those outside the administration who pressed for PSE and who opposed such restrictions. To call a program temporary and transitional seemed like a clever rationale for avoiding a meaningful commitment to federally subsidized public services.

THE FOOT IN THE DOOR:
THE EMERGENCY EMPLOYMENT ACT OF 1971

As discussed in the preceding chapter, the unplanned outpouring of training and work experience programs in the 1960s produced an unwieldy administrative structure, which was partly blamed for their poor performance. For the DOL in particular, administrative reform became imperative, and the Nixon administration targeted the programs as a prime candidate for decentralization under its New Federalism initiative.[27] For congressional liberals, the administrative overhaul provided a golden opportunity to establish public service employment as a major and permanent component of employment policy. Congressman James O'Hara, chairman of the House Employment Subcommittee, introduced a bill that attempted such a fundamental redirection. The heart of the bill was its provision of public employment for anyone unable to find a job in the private sector. Its inspiration was not from the poverty program's emphasis on training discrete categories of disadvantaged individuals but from the 1946 Employment Act's declared goal "to promote maximum employment." Because the O'Hara bill guaranteed employment for "every American who is able and willing to work," it placed no restrictions on eligibility for jobs, training, and other services. "This act does not specify a clientele, because it is not envisaged as meeting only the special needs of a single clientele," stated O'Hara.[28] Reflecting the strong support for public jobs among liberals, O'Hara announced at the hearings:

I deeply believe . . . that we can't have a comprehensive manpower program worthy of the name unless we provide job opportunities for those who are trained for employment. To the extent that the private labor market is unable to provide those opportunities, we must provide them. I think unless we come to grips with that problem, we are sort of ducking the major issue.[29]

As expected, House Republicans viewed the matter quite differently. Putting his finger squarely on the problem that would divide the

Democratic majority and Nixon for the duration of his presidency, Congressman Steiger remarked: "You obviously have a significant ideological problem, if one talks about a massive employer of last resort or guaranteed employment program."[30]

A more incremental approach was chosen in the Senate. No guarantee of a job to anyone who wanted one was promised, merely a specific authorization of $750 million for fiscal year 1971, $1 billion for 1972, and $1.25 for 1973. Senator Nelson pointed out that his bill's authorization "was still far from the Kerner Commission recommendation of 1 million jobs."[31] Nevertheless, this was not intended as a temporary program, or a modest complement to the training activities. Total spending on PSE over the three years would constitute over 50 percent of the employment and training budget.

When it appeared likely that the Senate would pass a reform bill that included the separate jobs title, the president reluctantly gave the DOL permission to accept it only if certain conditions were met. The administration insisted that any jobs program be a temporary stopgap—only for periods when other permanent employment was not available and only as transitional employment, eventually leading to "regular" jobs. The DOL would be authorized to approve plans and monitor prime sponsors to insure that the jobs provided were temporary and transitional. Nelson resisted such changes, however. Nelson feared that the result might be to destroy the program. Under Republican leadership, the DOL might be tempted to discourage local governments, who were to administer the program, from using the money to create jobs by pressuring them to meet unreasonable goals and threatening to terminate funding.

When the bill went to the floor for passage, Republicans tried to drive a wedge between the Senate as a whole and the overwhelmingly liberal committee, where, according to Senator Dominick, "what could almost be called ideological differences" existed. The jobs program constituted "nothing more than a dole," which provided "simply . . . an additional number of federally supported employees."[32] Dominick's amendments, intended to make the jobs program temporary and transitional, were defeated, and the bill passed essentially unaltered.

Dismayed at the outcome, the DOL turned to the House, where it hoped to get a more acceptable bill. Chairman O'Hara had abandoned his original proposal and had joined his counterparts in the Senate in advancing the passage of the more modest jobs bill. The DOL, which badly wanted the programs reformed, struck a bargain with O'Hara and his colleagues: the administration offered to go along with the jobs bill if it met their conditions and if it included the administrative reform the administration sought. A compromise acceptable to both sides was concluded. The bill passed over the objections of several House GOP members, who protested that even with the changes the bill embodied "the philosophy of the Government as employer of last resort."[33]

However, the legislation that emerged from the conference committee between the two chambers clearly reflected the positions of the Senate on PSE. The secretary of labor recommended that the president veto the legislation, whose "most offensive feature" was the PSE provision. The "conference bill," according to Hodgson, "would see the beginning of a decade of federally subsidized state and local employment, which far from being a manpower program would constitute a constant demand on the federal treasury to maintain and expand."[34] The veto message sharply criticized the bill as "WPA-type" legislation. "The conference bill provides that as much as 44 percent of the total funding in the bill will go for dead-end jobs in the public sector. Such a program represents a reversion to the remedies that were tried 35 years ago," argued the president—an inappropriate and ineffective response to the problems of the 1970s."[35] With the conference bill having passed the House with a mere eighteen votes to spare, there was no chance the veto could be overridden.

Undeterred, Nelson introduced a new bill in the following legislative session. The president had left the door open in his veto message by stating that "transitional and short-term public service employment can be a useful component of the nation's manpower policies."[36] The revised bill was presented as "strictly emergency stopgap legislation" and embraced all of the conditions regarding temporary and transitional jobs. The secretary of labor was given authority to conduct "periodic reviews of the employment prospects for each person employed . . . to assure that maximum efforts will be made to assist public service jobholders in locating employment . . . not supported under this legislation."[37] The authorization remained modest, only $750 million.

Unemployment had failed to abate throughout 1971, and when the bill was sent for Nixon's consideration it stood at 6.2 percent. Having already vetoed a public works bill that session, and conceding that the revised bill had met his stipulations, the president decided to give his approval. To veto three such bills within one year, with less than a year to the next election, was perceived as risky. Given the growing support for PSE in Congress, the possibility of a veto override grew as well. It was political pragmatism, not any change in its ideological stance or economic advice, that led to the administration's decision.

A far cry from O'Hara's proposal, the Emergency Employment Act of 1971 (EEA) was by no means a full-employment guarantee or even an attempt to restore unemployment to its prerecession level. It created about 140,000 jobs during fiscal year 1974, amounting to a mere 3.7

percent of those who were unemployed. The EEA provided New York City 2,503 job slots for over 204,000 unemployed persons; and it allotted Boston 569 slots for an estimated 90,000 jobless. According to one study, its impact "on aggregate or local rates of unemployment was indiscernible."[38] Advocates of the "new" PSE had envisioned a large-scale, permanent, federally funded program of regular public service jobs at the local level. Compared to the O'Hara proposal or to those called for in the various government reports, the EEA was, as one disgruntled PSE proponent called it, "a temporary and reluctant expedient."[39]

Despite its puny size, the EEA was not without significance. It was the first program since the Great Depression to create jobs in the public sector for the express reason of relieving unemployment. More importantly, it served as a harbinger of things to come in the 1970s. At long last, liberal advocates of the idea had broken through. After almost forty years, the federal government was back in the business of providing work relief. It marked a watershed in postwar employment policy, denoting the start of a gradual shift in its focus from poverty to unemployment, from training to jobs, and from labor supply to labor demand.

PUBLIC EMPLOYMENT AND CETA

After the 1972 election, relations between Congress and Nixon deteriorated. The confrontation was touched off by the administration's planned budget cuts. The administration judged that the economy would continue the robust expansion that got under way in 1972. A 10 percent cut in the funding of employment programs was planned, to be achieved mainly by phasing out the EEA. In addition, the administration decided to eliminate the Job Corps and the NYC summer youth program. Since the EEA's passage, unemployment had fallen from 6 percent to 5.2 percent in January and was expected to reach 4.5 percent by the end of 1973.[40] According to the administration, the emergency the EEA was intended to treat had ended. With the local fiscal crisis declared over, continuation of subsidized employment would tempt recipient governments to substitute federal funds for their own, leading to no net decrease in the number of unemployed.

The brightened economic picture across the nation as a whole obscured pockets of stagnation that still existed in many urban areas. With strong encouragement from the AFL-CIO and the mayors, the battle over the EEA galvanized Democrats to fight for a two-year extension of the program. In the House, these efforts stalled when Republicans used parliamentary tactics to prevent the bill from coming to a vote. But in the Senate, the bill was passed.[41] The vote sent a clear signal to the administration that, despite its opposition to the bill and an improvement in the economy, a solid majority favored the continuation of federally funded jobs.

At the same time, the Watergate scandal began taking its toll on the Nixon administration's power. The bold combativeness produced by the electoral landslide a few months earlier was now giving way to the first signs of a more conciliatory posture on the part of a beleaguered White House. With John Ehrlichman's departure, the Labor Department seized the initiative with the intention of getting Congress to go along with administrative reform in exchange for continuing public employment. The Labor Department and the Office of Management and Budget (OMB) sent the president a memorandum asking him whether he would be willing to accept "a limited public service employment program" in exchange for a reform bill that essentially met the administration's requirements. The document urged the president to accept the recommendation, arguing that, given the strong support for continuing the jobs program, any refusal to go along would require the president to veto a bill containing the kind of administrative reform that they had sought for over four years.[42] Nixon agreed, leaving only the amount of the PSE appropriation left for negotiation.

By the time the legislation reached the conference committee, another problem loomed on the horizon: the OPEC oil embargo. With increasingly dire predictions of an impending economic emergency, the administration's bargaining position had weakened further. Just before the conference committee met to decide on the PSE funding level, Chairman of the Council of Economic Advisers Herbert Stein told Congress that the administration now supported a public service employment program because it anticipated a rise in joblessness as a result of the energy crisis.[43] A compromise was reached to set the level of funding at $350 million for fiscal year 1975. The Comprehensive Employment and Training Act of 1973 (CETA) decentralized and decategorized most existing employment programs, placing them in the hands of thousands of CETA prime sponsors (local and state governments), and included a separate Title II for public employment.

Public Employment Expansion in a Period of Stagflation

CETA was barely in place when the economy experienced its worst recession since the 1930s. One Senate report described it as "an American employment crisis of intolerable proportions."[44] Real growth declined from the fourth quarter of 1973 to the first quarter of 1975, and unemployment rose from 4.8 percent to 8.7 percent. Throughout the decade and well into the 1980s, the jobless rate would not again approach the pre-1973 level.

The significance of the unemployment crisis of the 1970s for employment policy was reflected in CETA's budget. Spending leaped dramatically from $2.2 billion in fiscal year 1968 to a peak of $9.6 billion in fiscal year 1978, almost a fivefold increase. Just as dramatic was the shift in the composition of the budget. Under CETA, job creation became the dominant component of the program. By 1978, PSE comprised 60 percent of the budget and dipped below 30 percent only in 1981. At the same time, training programs shrank to 16 percent of the budget in 1978 and only once rose above 25 percent. With employment programs counting for fully 80 percent of CETA in its peak year, the T in CETA clearly became a minor theme.[45]

The supply shock of the embargo and the subsequent quadrupling of petroleum prices transferred income from the industrial nations to the oil-producing states, contracting economic activity and increasing unemployment. The recession was accompanied by an inflation that went beyond the one-time increase in the price level. It added momentum to the spiral of inflationary expectations that had begun earlier in the decade. The simultaneous existence of high rates of inflation and unemployment was a novelty in modern economic experience, and a new term was added to the political lexicon: *stagflation.*

Policy makers found themselves on the horns of a dilemma, in which established rules for managing the economy were no longer adequate, and conventional means were rendered obsolete. The dominant notion among economists in the 1960s was that a sufficient expansion of aggregate demand, through a stimulative fiscal policy and an accommodative monetary policy, could bring down unemployment to the 3 to 4 percent level without causing unacceptable rates of inflation. This indeed had occurred in the wake of the 1965 tax cut. But now, any attempt to stimulate the economy through the customary expansion of fiscal and monetary policy would aggravate an inflation rate already headed for double digits. The consumer price index eventually rose to a whopping 15.7 percent for 1974. Like most other countries, the United States chose the cautious course of restraint. Hence, the deep recession of 1974/75 and beyond can be understood as resulting from a drain of economic resources out of the country, followed by a counterinflationary response by policy makers.

At the same time, PSE enjoyed a reputation as a program that both worked well and was useful. The title of the National Manpower Policy Task Force's 1975 policy statement was "The Best Way to Reduce Unemployment Is to Create More Jobs." Acceptance of PSE as a useful policy tool had spread throughout most of the economics profession. Economists as disparate in their views as Walter Heller, John Kenneth Galbraith, Arnold Weber, William Simon, and Arthur Burns gave their endorsements to various PSE proposals. Paul McCracken, who had served on the Council of Economic Advisers of previous Republican presidents, said: "We do need to come back again with an open mind on public service employment programs."[46] Otto Eckstein, in testimony before Congress, pointed to the popularity of the EEA program in Congress: "The reason we are sitting here today with public service employment enjoying as high a standing as it does, with a range of opinion as was present at the [president's economic] summit, sort of rallying to this particular cause, was because it had done fairly well in the last session."[47] William Fellner, a member of President Ford's Council of Economic Advisers, advocated targeted job programs to drive down the unemployment rate as an alternative to using fiscal and monetary stimulation that risked setting off inflationary pressures.[48]

The most important endorsement of an expansion of the PSE program came from Arthur Burns, chairman of the Federal Reserve Board. Like Fellner, he feared an overstimulation of the economy and spoke out against a general tax cut, a spending increase, and especially an easier monetary policy. Burns's concerns were not unfounded. Support for a major tax cut was starting to gather steam in Congress and among several economists.[49] Before the Joint Economic Committee in February, Burns argued that the conventional practice of stimulating economic activity through running a budget deficit would be imprudent. He explained that the current recession was unlike previous downturns in that it was not caused by a general falling off of demand. An economy already experiencing sharp inflationary pressures could not afford the conventional Keynesian prescription. What Burns recommended instead was a tight fiscal policy to moderate inflationary pressures.[50] And then before the House Appropriations Committee Burns said he did not disapprove of "selective measures" like "an expanded public employment program."[51]

In a letter to the president in May, Burns suggested an expansion of PSE in the context of measures to control inflation. The Burns proposal called for an additional expenditure of $4 billion to create 650,000 jobs if the unemployment rate exceeded 6 percent. The program would be triggered on and off as the rate rose and fell. "This particular means of easing especially troublesome situations of unemployment will not add permanently to governmental costs."[52] Burns estimated that the program could reduce unemployment by 0.06 percent, while allowing for the substitution effects of state and local fiscal practices. As the spring and summer wore on, pressures for an expansion continued to grow, though the unemployment rate stayed around the 5.2 percent level. The Burns plan was virtually identical to a bill introduced in early February by Senator Jacob Javits, which would have amended CETA by adding a new PSE title. Burns was a strong supporter of the Javits bill throughout the year, as his warnings of inflation became more urgent and as he vowed to maintain a restrictive monetary policy. He predicted an inevitable rise in unemployment as a result of tightening, and he endorsed PSE as a way to offset the restraint.

Another Federal Reserve member, Andrew Brimmer, conducted a study showing that the largest and most rapid short-run impact on employment would be produced by a new public employment program. Compared to a tax cut or other government spending at the same level, the PSE program would generate "two to three times the number of jobs" as these other alternatives.[53] The endorsement of PSE at such high levels was obviously more than simply concern for the unemployed. It was an admission that existing tools for maintaining acceptable levels of unemployment could not be relied upon, at least for the time being.

Burns's advocacy of PSE was decisive for broadening the attention and support it received. The Federal Reserve chairman had considerable influence within the administration and was not reticent in giving the president advice on a range of economic issues falling outside the confines of monetary policy. Assistant Secretary of Labor Kolberg has placed particular emphasis on Burns's endorsement of PSE, "because of his reputation as a key conservative economist and his powerful position as Chairman of the Federal Reserve Board." His support was "a major policy breakthrough that made PSE a much more 'respectable' subject of attention as one of the measures in a counter-inflationary or counter-recessionary economic strategy." According to Kolberg, "It was the Burns proposal that emboldened key Congressional figures to begin to prepare new PSE programs."[54] In the ensuing months, bankers, businessmen, and conservative politicians lined up to sing the praises of PSE.[55] Virtually every defender of public employment cited Burns's endorsement as critical proof that PSE was a preferred course of action.

As the economy quickly deteriorated after the Ford administration took office, the president responded by approving an immediate increase in the number of PSE jobs from 73,000 to 170,000.[56] He then held a series of public meetings in the fall of 1974 that culminated in an "economic summit conference." Prominent at these meetings were economic advisers from past administrations, both Democratic and Republican. The general view from these meetings was that the maintenance of a restrictive monetary policy, coupled with the administration's insistence on a tighter fiscal policy (in addition to its refusal to impose wage and price controls), would lead to higher unemployment. Even those who supported this policy mix admitted that inflation would likely take some time to subside. Administration economists expected that bringing inflation within reasonable bounds would take two to three years of restraint-induced unemployment. The political as well as the moral implications of having persons who were most vulnerable to joblessness shoulder such a burden were clear. Therefore, there was a general agreement that a PSE program was needed to compensate the victims of the fight against inflation.

With the Ford administration's acceptance of PSE as a tool for fighting the recession, the battle that had raged during the Nixon years appeared to be over. But it was not. The administration's proposal, developed by the CEA and OMB, was much more limited than those introduced in Congress or favored by the Labor Department. First, unemployment insurance (UI) was designated the first line of defense in granting relief from the recession, with PSE playing an ancillary role, essentially as an alternative form of public assistance for only those who had exhausted their benefits. The UI proposal called for an additional thirteen weeks of benefits for those who had exhausted their regular benefits and twenty-six weeks of benefits for those who were not covered by regular unemployment insurance. PSE funding was to be based on graduated triggers, with the dollar amounts triggered smaller and the triggers set higher than contained in the proposals in Congress. The new PSE jobs were to be limited to six-month projects. The money would not be available to all CETA prime sponsors but only to designated "integral labor market areas" that had unemployment rates above 6.5 percent. The wage level for the jobs would be $7,000, well below the $10,000 limit established for PSE under Title II of CETA.

The administration was worried about more than simply the short-term impact on the budget. It wanted to avoid tying any new PSE program too closely to the fiscal interests of local governments, which is what was happening to CETA. If the program became a part of the CETA statute and budget, it would be more difficult to terminate it once the economy recovered. Similarly, the low cap on wages would ensure that these jobs did not become "so good" that they would be treated as permanent, thus draining workers from the private sector.

The proposal received a rude reception on Capitol Hill, not only among Democrats but among most Republicans as well. Under the pressure of the emergency, and with congressional elections just weeks away, a bipartisan consensus developed for the first time over public employment. When Congress returned from its election recess in November, the rapidly worsening situation compelled the White House to make concessions. On December 31 President Ford signed the Emergency Jobs and Unemployment Assistance Act, creating a new Title VI of CETA for countercyclical job creation, to be administered by CETA prime sponsors. The administration failed to shape the PSE program to its liking. Instead of restricting the jobs to labor market areas with 6.5

percent unemployment and for use in six-month projects, aid was available without a trigger to all CETA prime sponsors. Instead of being limited to those who had exhausted their unemployment benefits, it was available to anyone unemployed for fifteen days (Title II required thirty days). The wage limit was set at $10,000.

Yet, the administration did manage to achieve its most basic goal—to keep PSE subsidiary to unemployment insurance in relieving economic distress. The act provided up to thirteen additional weeks of benefits to those already covered by UI, and up to twenty-six weeks for those not covered. Millions of the unemployed were covered by the new expansion of UI benefits, while PSE would benefit merely thousands.[57] "The White House program," remarked Otto Eckstein, "is intended to be a temporary novocaine for the recession, designed as much to avoid the appearance of being callous as to bringing down unemployment." Though the proposals advanced in Congress were more liberal than that of the president, they too were intended less as ambitious programs for putting a large proportion of the unemployed back to work, than as demonstrations of concern on the eve of the November election. "It's really a sop for doing very little," stated Eckstein. "It's not going to be bigger than $2 to $4 billion and the economy needs a stimulus four to five times that."[58]

During the remainder of the Ford administration, the policy debate reverted to the sharp partisan conflict that characterized the Nixon years. A steadily decreasing unemployment rate after May 1975 convinced the administration that there was no longer a need for Title VI jobs. With recovery under way, Republicans argued that continued deficit spending would either spur inflation by overheating the economy or choke off economic recovery by crowding out private investment. Any further stimulus that might be needed should be sought through tax cuts. Continued funding of the "temporary emergency positions" under Title VI would "tend to cause them to be perceived as permanent."[59]

The 1974 elections produced a substantial post-Watergate windfall for the Democrats, who advertised themselves as a "veto-proof" Congress, mistakenly, as it turned out. The ensuing months evidenced the classic confrontation between competing party philosophies. "We feel that jobs can be had and that unemployment can be controlled and ended best by stimulation of the private sector," declared Republican Leader in the House, John Rhodes.[60] But according to Majority Leader Tip O'Neill, "The battle lines are clearly drawn—no other issue divides the ideals of the Democratic and Republican parties. . . . We have an obligation, a duty to those Americans—our constituents—who last fall voted to send us to Washington to defend their interests."[61]

The period was largely one of stalemate, with the Democrats unable to expand Title VI, but with the administration unable to reduce or eliminate it. The recovery from the 1974/75 recession stalled during the second quarter of 1976, with the unemployment rate leveling off at 7.5 percent in May and then rising to 7.9 percent in August. After securing the Republican nomination in a struggle with Ronald Reagan, Ford abandoned his efforts to get rid of Title VI. With the jobless rate rising and the election one month away, he instead approved its continuation by signing the Emergency Jobs Program Extension Act of 1976.

From Recession Relief to Economic Recovery

With the return of the Democrats to the White House, spending on CETA, and PSE in particular, expanded dramatically. President-elect Carter quickly announced his "first priority"—to reduce the rate of joblessness to 6.5 percent by the end of 1977 and to 4–4.5 percent by the end of his first term.[62] Recovery from the recession had stalled under the defeated Republican. As a proportion of the CETA budget, PSE reached a peak of 60 percent in 1978, up from 37 percent in 1975.[63] By fiscal year 1978, the number of PSE jobs had more than doubled, going from 310,000 under Ford to 725,000 under Carter. Through the first three years of the administration, PSE averaged above 40 percent of the budget.[64] The expansion occurred when PSE became part of the new administration's economic recovery program launched during its first year in office. For the first time, spending on jobs was not purely an emergency response to ameliorate a recession but a tool for aggressive fiscal stimulation. Less than a year after the stimulus act had been signed into law, the number of PSE jobs funded by CETA had more than doubled. The full 725,000 level was reached several weeks ahead of the March 1978 target date. During the buildup, the unemployment rate dropped from 8.6 percent to 5.7 percent in June 1978. It stayed within the 5.6 to 5.9 percent range throughout 1978 and 1979, the lowest it had been in four years, since before the 1974/75 recession. The PSE program itself was credited, however, with shaving less than 1 percent off the jobless rate. The rest of the reduction was attributed to macro-economic expansion. With 6.75 million individuals unemployed when the stimulus package was enacted, the increase in the number of PSE jobs to an additional 415,000 accounted for only 6 percent of all those unemployed.[65] Nevertheless, judged according to whether the program helped to reduce unemployment, it had succeeded.

From Recovery to Recession and the End of PSE

By 1978 the administration had decided that PSE was a costly ap-proach to driving the unemployment rate down. Not only was the program expensive, but it was believed that local governments were using a considerable proportion of the money to fund jobs that would otherwise have been funded from their own budgets. The PSE budget would be maintained at present levels, but it would be targeted at those groups still experiencing high unemployment.

Second, with unemployment having fallen, the administration increasingly focused on inflation, which had remained stubbornly above 6 percent since it took office. In 1978 inflation rose to 9 percent. On the other hand, the administration also had committed itself to achieve an unemployment rate of 4 percent under the Humphrey-Hawkins full-employment legislation pending before Congress.[66] Its objective, then, was to drive the unemployment rate down further without exacerbating inflation. With the stimulative effects of CETA having taken effect, the next task was to target PSE jobs on those left behind by the expansion.[67] Its economic team believed that it would not be possible to reach a noninflationary 4 percent rate by relying upon traditional fiscal stimulation.[68] This conclusion rested on evidence that showed the overall unemployment rate to be a poor indicator of the tightness of labor markets. Pursuit of the 4 percent goal through fiscal stimulation may not have been inflationary in the 1960s, but it would be in the 1970s and 1980s, because the labor force now included higher proportions of groups with traditionally high jobless rates—in particular teenagers, blacks, and the disadvantaged. The unemployed in these groups were not "job ready" (because of lack of training) and were not likely to be hired even during periods when the demand for labor was increasing. Teenage unemployment stood at 17 percent, several times higher than the overall rate, and the rate for black teenagers was almost 40 percent. The 4 percent goal could be attained by using a highly targeted PSE program. According to Assistant Secretary of Labor Arnold Packer:

Given the present structure [of labor and product markets], it is unlikely that a 4 percent unemployment rate could be achieved through aggregate demand policies alone without at the same time causing a significant increase in the rate of inflation. Responsible policy, however, requires not that we abandon efforts to reach the [4 percent] 1983 unemployment goal, but that we work steadily to reduce the conflict between unemployment and inflation by developing structural measures to improve the functioning of markets.[69]

The president's *Economic Report* suggested that training and other manpower development programs had been "fairly successful," but that "regular public service employment programs for adults have not focused significantly on the structurally unemployed to the extent that they should. As the overall unemployment rate declines," the report argued, "employment and training programs should be carefully directed demographically and geographically toward this goal."[70]

The 1978 amendments to CETA substantially changed the composition of PSE enrollees in the direction favored by the administration. Nevertheless, not only was the 4 percent unemployment goal not reached, but the jobless rate rose from 5.8 percent at the end of 1978 to 6.2 percent a year later. For 1980 it averaged 7.1 percent. The economy was hit by another round of supply shocks in the form of higher meat prices and, most of all, higher OPEC oil prices that drove inflation into double digits. The administration's response, like the Ford administration's before it, was fiscal and monetary restraint. Included was a proposed cut of $2.6 billion from CETA for fiscal year 1980, which would have eliminated about 100,000 public employment jobs. Although Congress reduced this amount to $0.7 billion, $1.3 billion more was cut from the program in fiscal year 1981.

The tone for budgetary policy was set for the next several years, and in retrospect, these actions signaled the end of the expansion of the social programs of the 1960s and 1970s. As expected, there was a sharp protest from liberal Democrats, mayors, and governors, who labeled them "disastrous." But unlike the Ford years, political support for CETA's PSE program was evaporating rather than building within Congress and among local governments. The program's reputation had suffered, particularly during 1976–1978, from reports of waste, abuse, and fiscal substitution, and from Congress's inability to decide whether the program should provide fiscal assistance to the cities or help the disadvantaged (two goals that turned out to be incompatible). This reputation lingered even after Congress placed major restrictions on how the money could be used in 1978 and even though reports of abuse dropped significantly. The restrictions, in turn, reduced the enthusiasm of local governments for CETA, its most important constituency in Washington. With the program vulnerable and the administration in a budget-cutting mood, the PSE budget shrunk after 1979, even though in 1980 the economy experienced yet another recession.

Under Carter, PSE had fallen from grace almost as quickly as it had risen. Under Reagan, it was quickly eliminated altogether. The new administration was the most ideologically conservative in fifty years. Liberals had struggled to establish and keep such a program under Nixon and Ford. Under Reagan, they stood little chance. The Reagan administration was widely viewed as having a mandate to reverse the kind of "misguided liberal programs" that CETA symbolized so exquisitely. The liquidation of PSE came just prior to the deep recession of 1982. Though that recession was worse than any in the 1970s, the federal government did not respond as it had in the 1970s. PSE was an idea whose time had come and gone.

FULL EMPLOYMENT REVISITED

The public employment programs of the 1970s were largely emergency measures—responses to the unemployment crisis of the period.[71] This was not the only liberal response of the decade, however. A positive, long-term strategy emerged, resurrecting the liberal dream of full employment and coinciding with the thirtieth anniversary of the Employment Act of 1946. In certain respects, the conditions favoring the enactment of full-employment legislation were as good as they had been throughout the entire postwar period. With unemployment levels higher than at any time since the 1930s, joblessness was often a salient issue. Also, the Democratic party was poised to regain the White House after an eight-year absence, and they had enlarged their majorities in Congress in the wake of Watergate.

The Full Employment and Balanced Growth Act of 1978 (known as Humphrey-Hawkins) was initially introduced by Congressman Augustus Hawkins in 1974, whose district was the heavily black Watts section of Los Angeles. A fervent liberal, Hawkins was soon joined by Hubert Humphrey, who sponsored a similar bill in the Senate. Both viewed a job at a "decent" wage as a human right. The bill went through several versions until it was enacted in 1978. The first version, introduced in June 1974 primarily with the objective of mobilizing support for the idea, was broadly similar to the original 1945 Full Employment Bill. It guaranteed a job for all adults able and willing to work at "fair" rates of compensation. Each year the president was required to submit to Congress a plan for stimulating demand to reach full employment, and the Joint Economic Committee was to review the needed appropriations.

There were two major new provisions since the 1945 bill. If demand expansion proved insufficient to stimulate employment in the private sector, the federal government itself would create enough jobs to employ everyone through federally financed job reservoirs. Planning councils in each local community would develop private and public projects to meet community needs. Job seekers were to be referred by Job Guarantee Offices. The most controversial provision was an enforceable, legal right to a job. Individuals denied employment were entitled to sue the government for redress.

The second version was introduced in March 1975, just at the time the unemployment rate was turning sharply upward from 5.2 to 8.7 percent. In the crisis atmosphere, an "interim target" was set at 3 percent, to be achieved within eighteen months. The ultimate goal of "real full employment" was kept as well. In an effort to capture the backing of advocacy groups across a variety of issues, the bill's authors greatly expanded the list of national priorities. Jobs were to be created to meet a variety of social needs, including housing, child care, mass transit, conservation of natural resources, the development of cultural and recreational activities, and education for any who desired it. The strategy failed to work, however, when there was no groundswell of support. In spite of the increase in unemployment, the political climate favoring positive federal action that prevailed in the 1960s had greatly diminished. None of these issues, including full employment itself, reached the political agenda.

With the 1976 presidential election on the horizon, the Democratic leadership decided to make unemployment a major issue. A full-employment bill was to be passed and put on President Ford's desk by the election. With Ford's veto a certainty, the Democratic nominee, who everyone thought at the time would be Humphrey, would be able to use the issue to help get elected. Thus another version of the bill, this time intended to garner broader support, was introduced in March. This version embodied a more elaborate blueprint for economic planning than the earlier versions. It also contained a broader set of policy initiatives, including countercyclical grants and other fiscal assistance to cities and depressed areas, youth employment programs, and anti-inflation tools.

Though more ambitious in means, this version had decidedly more modest objectives. The guaranteed right to employment was diluted by eliminating the right to sue, and the stated goal of 3 percent adult unemployment was left undefined. Even if the 3 percent overall goal was reached, according to some full-employment advocates it could leave substantial pockets of unemployed minorities, youth, and discouraged workers. Moreover, unlike the second version, the 3 percent goal was not an interim, but a final, goal. The bill also placed severe restrictions on the use and size of public jobs as a tool for reaching the 3 percent target. This, some argued, would hurt those groups in the population least likely to gain employment in the private sector through demand expansion. Finally, most of the additional "national priorities" listed in the second version were dropped. Many of the supporters of the earlier versions correctly viewed the new bill as a retreat from the principle of guaranteed employment for everyone who wanted a job.

Despite the bill's softening, it and subsequent versions had a rough political road to travel, and the final legislation enacted in 1978 was a rather pale counterpart of the initial versions. In this essential respect,

Humphrey-Hawkins and the Full Employment Bill of 1945 shared a similar fate, one that was bitterly disappointing for many of its supporters. There were also essential differences between the two stories, however. One of the most crucial difference was the lukewarm or conditional support given to Humphrey-Hawkins by many Democrats. If nothing else, Humphrey-Hawkins revealed a dispirited liberalism. By the mid- to late 1970s, liberals had lost a good deal of confidence in the notion that positive government intervention could effectively address social and economic evils. The ambitious goals of eliminating poverty and rebuilding the cities that were proclaimed in the 1960s raised expectations that were then dashed. Even many who supported full employment, and strong government intervention to achieve it, saw Humphrey-Hawkins as another promise that could be legislated but that, for whatever reasons, would not be kept.

The loss of confidence in liberal efforts to address effectively problems like unemployment was revealed in public opinion polls as well. In chapter 2 it was reported that in 1944, on the eve of the introduction of the first full-employment bill, there was a good measure of bipartisan agreement on the need for full-employment legislation as reflected in the platforms of the two political parties.[72] Likewise, public opinion polls revealed that a healthy majority of the American people agreed that "government should provide jobs for everyone able and willing to work but who cannot get a job in private employment." When asked in October 1944, 68 percent agreed, 25 percent disagreed, and 7 percent had no opinion.[73] By the mid-1970s such support had evaporated. In 1976 Schlozman and Verba asked respondents, "Would you still favor ending unemployment even if it meant that the government would have to hire everybody who was without a job?" The response was the reverse from 1944, with 30 percent favoring such action and 70 percent opposing it.[74] It is important not to exaggerate the turn in public opinion away from liberal positions on how to deal with unemployment, however. At the same time a majority of the public was rejecting a policy of full-employment guarantees, there was overwhelming support for the kinds of public service employment that liberals had successfully pushed in the 1970s. For instance, 89 percent of the public favored "the government putting people who can't find any jobs on the payroll and finding work for them such as helping out in hospitals or cleaning parks."[75]

It is perhaps partly the result of liberalism's lost confidence that debate over Humphrey-Hawkins exhibited much less of the ideological conflict than that which marked deliberations over the 1945 legislation. Conservative opponents had less of a need to wage their battle against the legislation by invoking cultural symbols—"free enterprise" versus "state socialism"—and could instead exploit liberal misgivings by arguing, "on the merits," that Humphrey-Hawkins was misguided.

It was not only experience that had shaken the confidence of many liberals and moderates but also the rude reception that Humphrey-Hawkins received from most of the economics profession, and in particular key economists who were dominant voices within the Democratic party. If any single, direct, and immediate factor created difficulties for the bill, it was this one. The Full Employment Bill of 1945 was both inspired and largely supported by an economics profession converted to a Keynesian policy of high-deficit spending and public investment. The authors of the Humphrey-Hawkins bill, however, faced more opposition than they did support from professional economists. Moreover, by the 1970s economic expertise had become fully institutionalized within government, with top economists holding positions of influence on the Council of Economic Advisers and elsewhere.

Opponents of the Humphrey-Hawkins bill found support for their views among an array of noted economists, including John Kenneth Galbraith, Arthur Okun, Alice Rivlin, Herbert Stein, and Alan Greenspan. Several of them were identified closely with Democratic administrations or Democratic majorities in Congress. The minority report accompanying the bill to the floor of the House pointed to the statements of a "veritable who's who of the economics profession."[76] The most damaging testimony came from Charles Schultze, who had served in the Budget Bureau in the Johnson administration and was chairman of the Council of Economic Advisers under Jimmy Carter. Schultze was known as a "liberal whose views have been tempered by government experience."[77] Schultze's attack on Humphrey-Hawkins in congressional testimony is widely credited with killing the bill during 1976 and with weakening several of its key provisions afterward.[78] According to the *Washington Post,* Schultze's testimony before Congress "has had an unusual impact on the debate over the month since it was delivered."[79] Some suggested that Schultze's criticism of the bill was rooted in his experience in the Budget Bureau during the Johnson years, where he participated in an "effort to conceal" the escalating costs of the Vietnam War, which proved highly inflationary when the president resisted efforts to raise taxes.[80]

Just before becoming chairman of the CEA, Schultze had written that he wanted to see policy debates in Washington move away from being "couched in simplistic, irrelevant, ideological terms," and toward more rational debate "about realistic and useful alternatives."[81] This shift in the intellectual tone of debate turned out to be a boon for conservative opponents of full employment. Specifically, Schultze's views and those of other economists were seen as particularly powerful because they validated, "on the merits," the opposition's major criticism of the Humphrey-Hawkins bill—that it would be inflationary. According to Schultze,

> Every time we push the rate of unemployment toward acceptably low levels, by whatever means, we set off a new inflation. And in turn, both the political and economic consequences of inflation make it impossible to achieve full employment or, once having achieved it, to keep the economy there. . . . Once the overall rate of unemployment edges below 5.5 percent or so, and the rate of adult unemployment gets much below 4.5 percent, inflation will begin to accelerate.[82]

Schultze was particularly critical of the bill's provision to create "last resort" jobs at prevailing wages. By draining away labor from private industry, workers would become scarce in many semiskilled and unskilled occupations. Wages would be bid up and price rises would soon follow. The government job programs would grow rapidly, as workers left lower paying private employment for such jobs.

The intellectual underpinning of this argument was the hypothesized trade-off between unemployment and inflation. According to this thesis, governments must choose between some level of inflation and some level of unemployment, which are inversely related. The idea was first put forth by A. W. Phillips, a British economist, whose data appeared to demonstrate that, as unemployment rose, wages increased less and less rapidly. Phillips had said nothing about prices, but economic textbooks soon extended the thesis so that low rates of unemployment were said to be associated with high rates of inflation, and vice versa. Low unemployment stimulated wage demands, which in turn were passed on in the form of higher prices. As a result, there existed a "natural rate" of unemployment below which inflation would be ignited. Furthermore, the natural rate was believed to have risen during the 1970s for a variety of reasons, chief among them the changing composition of the labor force, which now included more women and youth. In spite of attacks on the Phillips curve thesis throughout the 1970s, it still held sway among many mainstream economists, particularly Keynesians.[83]

As in the debate over structural unemployment in the 1960s, the debate over the Phillips curve and its implications for full employment pitted Keynesians against a more amorphous group of institutional economists. Once again, the differences between the two camps was rooted in the theoretical controversy over whether the wage rate operates in response to the law of supply and demand, as posited by

neoclassical theory.[84] Recall from chapter 2 that Keynesianism was reformulated by American economists in the form of the neoclassical
synthesis. Keynes's approach to macroeconomics was married to micro-
economic principles. Institutionalists argued that the synthesis involved
a basic contradiction, because Keynes explained unemployment and
inflation in terms of systematic rigidities in certain prices (particularly
wages and interest rates), while orthodox theory maintained that the
price mechanism functioned smoothly to allocate economic resources
in the market. Schultze and other American Keynesians continued to
view inflation in neoclassical terms: When the demand for labor exceeds
the supply, wages are driven up, and price inflation follows. When
unemployment is high, supply exceeds demand, and wages are stable
or falling. In theory, inflation should not occur until unemployment
reaches zero. However, unemployment is an imperfect measure of
the gap between supply and demand. There are always some people
between jobs, not all people who want to work are qualified for the
jobs available, and not all people who claim to be unemployed really
want to work. Thus, the natural or noninflationary unemployment rate
is above zero.

The institutionalists argued that the wage rate does not, and cannot,
function the way orthodox theory predicts. Wages are determined not
by supply and demand but by social and institutional factors (e.g.,
custom, occupational status, or trade union strength). Inflation is triggered by external shocks that upset established wage differentials, and
the bulk of it is created when individuals and institutions react to
restore the original differentials. These shocks come from any number of
sources, but in the 1970s they were primarily in the form of higher
energy and food costs. The level of unemployment, on the other hand,
is primarily determined by the level of aggregate demand, and also by
the structure of labor markets. Jobs in the secondary labor market tend
to generate higher rates of unemployment for a variety of institutional
reasons. Such jobs tend to be menial, low-wage jobs that are sensitive
to economic flux. They produce high voluntary turnover and cultivate
groups with marginal attachment to the labor market. Hence, "Wage
determination [and ipso facto the inflationary process] and unemployment are two distinct processes that are largely independent of each
other and must be understood separately."[85]

Proponents of Humphrey-Hawkins argued not only that the Phillips
curve trade-off was mistaken, and therefore that full employment did
not cause inflation, but that even if the trade-off existed, sacrificing full
employment for lower prices was morally indefensible. Maintaining

unemployment in order to control inflation placed the burden dispro-portionately upon those who could least afford it. As Robert Lekachman put it facetiously, this is "a bit hard on those selected to serve their country by losing their jobs, but their patriotic sacrifice is nothing less than a valuable public service."[86] Finally, in the third version of the bill, an entire section was devoted to anti-inflation measures: monitoring of sectoral trends to avert potential inflationary bottlenecks, increasing the supply of goods, services, and labor in tight markets, and strengthening antitrust laws.

Humphrey-Hawkins became part of the Democratic party platform in 1976, but one of its champions, Senator Humphrey, had to drop out of the primary campaign because of failing health. While other liberal candidates enthusiastically endorsed the bill, Jimmy Carter endorsed its goals only reluctantly. Carter demurred because he feared that full employment could not be attained without worsening inflation and making it more difficult to balance the budget.[87] Once in office, Carter and Schultze insisted upon more changes, thus another version was drafted. Unemployment was to be reduced to 3 percent within four years for adults twenty years of age and over. This translated into a 4 percent overall rate. Young people were covered by separate programs, but there was no timetable for reducing their rate. For the first time, an inflation goal was included, a concession long resisted by the bill's advocates because they feared that setting a specific inflation goal would reduce the priority to achieve full employment. In addition, organized labor feared that inclusion of the inflation goal might lead to wage and price controls. Under Nixon, labor felt that wages were controlled better than prices and interest rates. The planning mechanism was weakened, as well as the jobs reservoir. Public jobs were to be a last resort and were to be at lower wage and skill levels, so they would not draw workers from private employment. They were not to be created until two years after the bill's enactment.

Despite all this, the bill got nowhere in Congress until Humphrey and the liberal-labor coalition insisted that it be placed on the agenda. Humphrey's death in 1978 added impetus to get the bill enacted as a tribute to him. But from 1976 to 1978, the recession abated and inflation became a more salient issue. This contributed to the steady drumbeat of attacks on the bill. At each step in the legislative process, the strategy of the bill's opponents was to weaken the bill further by adding amend-ments that multiplied the bill's specific goals. In the Senate, four major amendments were added. Two of these established the goals of inflation at 0 percent and a balanced budget by 1983. Another amendment,

offered by Senator William Proxmire, a Democrat from Wisconsin, set
a goal of limiting the federal budget at 20 percent of gross national
product. A fourth, by Senator John Tower, a Texas Republican, authorized the president to modify the 4 percent unemployment goal in his
first economic message after the bill's passage. Proxmire's amendment
was later modified, and the goal of reducing federal spending was set
at the "lowest level consistent with national needs."

The final legislation was much different from Hawkins's original
proposal. Gone was the absolute guarantee of a job for every American
willing and able to work. Also eliminated were any specific job creation
measures, such as the job reservoir. The law did establish specific goals
for reducing unemployment (3 percent for adults, 4 percent overall,
within five years) and inflation (3 percent by 1983, and 0 percent by
1988). Despite the inflation goals, the primacy of lowering unemployment was preserved in the act's provision that "policies and programs
for reducing inflation shall be so designed so as not to impede achievement of the goal and timetables" on unemployment.

The act also stipulated procedural requirements for making economic policy. The president was required to annually submit, in his
economic report, numerical goals for employment, unemployment,
production, real income, productivity, and prices. Short- and medium-
term goals, of two and three years, were established not only to achieve
full employment but to balance the budget, improve the trade balance,
and lower federal outlays as a percentage of GNP. Congress was given
the opportunity to review, accept, modify, or reject the goals. The
Federal Reserve Board was required to report to Congress twice yearly
on how it planned to pursue monetary policy to reach the unemployment and inflation goals. The act stressed that the legislation could
not be used to control production, employment, wages, prices, or the
allocation of resources. Employment growth should come from growth
in the private sector, and only if the private sector proved inadequate
should federally subsidized jobs be created. The employment reservoir
was the final option, triggered only by the president if he found that
other measures were not working. In addition, any public jobs created
must be in the low wage range so as not to disturb private sector labor
markets.

The mixed success of efforts by full-employment advocates in getting
the kind of legislation they wanted produced differences of opinion as
to whether anything meaningful had been won. Implementation of the
act, however, makes it clear that whatever victory the adoption of
Humphrey-Hawkins represented for its supporters has been a hollow
one. From the start, the act had no apparent impact on economic

policies, and its goals have been ignored with impunity. The ink had hardly been dry in 1979 when the second major OPEC supply shock of the decade prompted the Carter administration to restrain federal spending. CETA and other programs were cut. The president's budget predicted that the unemployment rate would rise from 5.8 percent at the end of 1978 to 6.2 percent by the end of 1979. Such budget cuts, coming from a Democratic administration just months after the Humphrey-Hawkins Act had been signed, was a particularly bitter pill to swallow for the act's supporters. Predictions of an impending recession in 1979 or 1980 fueled the criticism. Hawkins denounced the reductions as a "direct violation" of the act's mandate of 4 percent joblessness and found ten other violations as well.[88] The recession of 1980 pushed the unemployment rate up to 7.1 percent.

With the Reagan administration in power, another recession, the worst since the Great Depression, pushed the unemployment rate to 10.8 percent at the end of 1982. This recession was largely the creation of the federal government itself, specifically the Federal Reserve, which sought to wring out inflation by pursuing a restrictive monetary policy. The Fed's policy, along with the fortuitous collapse of the OPEC cartel, had its intended impact by reducing inflation in the 1980s well below levels experienced in the previous decade. Yet this was accomplished in direct contravention of the Humphrey-Hawkins Act's proviso that policies for reducing inflation "shall be so designed so as not to impede achievement of the [unemployment] goal and timetables." And although the unemployment rate dropped steadily during the decade, it has never reached the full-employment goals mandated by the act.

Although the conservative resurgence under Reagan is often viewed as an ambitious attempt to break the fifty years of growing government involvement in the economy, in this area at least, the resurgence appears more as a continuation of past patterns. At the outset of the postwar era, the rejection of a full-employment policy based upon high levels of public investment and spending on domestic needs was followed by a turn to tax cutting and increased military spending. Likewise, the defeat of the Humphrey-Hawkins Act in the late 1970s was followed by a strategy of large tax cuts and military spending. Thus commercial Keynesianism triumphed a second time, fifteen years after its first success. Although the policy of the 1980s was dressed in a "supply-side" doctrine that rejected much of the theory of Keynes that gave intellectual license to a potentially larger and more positive government, the logic of the strategy was virtually the same as it had been earlier in the period. The president himself acknowledged as much when he presented as a chief argument for the policy that he was merely following the precedent set by John Kennedy and the Democratic Congress. And once again the policy worked. Unemployment fell to politically tolerable levels throughout the 1980s as it had in the 1960s. And just as important, this was accomplished while avoiding the establishment of any "right" to a job, erosion of corporate control over the economy, and increases in domestic federal spending.

CONCLUSION

Liberals' efforts to include public job creation as a key component of employment policy was critically shaped and limited by prevailing intellectual currents and by more long-term ideological cleavages. The ranks of economists and other experts who saw PSE as a feasible and useful policy tool expanded from the early 1960s to the mid-1970s. The apparent failure of both macroeconomic policies and training programs to reduce poverty, and the fiscal incapacity of urban communities to meet the demand for public services, lent credence to the argument that what the poor needed most was not training (or not only training), but federally created jobs. The idea incubated throughout the decade, kept alive by a variety of studies of urban poverty, academic critics of the poverty program, and a handful of liberal members of Congress in the "new" PSE network. With an overall healthy economic climate and with presidential opposition to the idea, however, the consensus did not expand beyond liberal circles. The best opportunity came in 1969, when administrative reform was on the agenda. The most radical proposal, O'Hara's for a guaranteed employment program, failed to incorporate the reforms widely considered necessary, and even the more modest Nelson bill was vetoed by Nixon.

It was not any heightened concern with poverty that eventually led to PSE's adoption and subsequent expansion, but concern with cyclical unemployment in 1970 and stagflation in the years thereafter. The worsening unemployment rate was merely the catalyst for the policy shift, however. The chief underlying cause was the prevailing state of opinion that deemed PSE to be a plausible policy option. No such consensus among experts and reformers had existed during the recessions of the 1950s, nor in the debate over the poverty program in the 1960s, and it would disappear by the recessions of 1980 and 1982. The use of PSE as a tool to ameliorate unemployment under Nixon and Ford, and then as a full-fledged countercyclical instrument under Carter, occurred only when the mainstream of the economics profession gave it its endorsement. The support of the respected and powerful Federal Reserve Chairman Arthur Burns, in particular, legitimized PSE. The simultaneous occurrence of high unemployment and inflation prompted the search for a way to cope with unemployment that would not aggravate inflation. A general expansion of demand through macroeconomic stimulation was no longer effective, and PSE seemed a plausible alternative.

The trend in the state of expert opinion favoring PSE did not translate easily or automatically into public policy, however. It was tempered by conservatives' resistance to the idea, whose antipathy toward make-work was overcome only because the emergency situation demanded that it give way. The ideological divide that PSE had to cross was a wide one, and it turned employment policy into a highly partisan, conflictual arena. It also affected liberal strategies for getting PSE adopted. Far-reaching proposals, such as Congressman O'Hara's for a guaranteed right to employment and massive job creation, were put aside in favor of an incremental strategy of gradual expansion of the program. Republican administrations managed to forestall creating PSE programs as large as most experts, including Burns, had recommended. It was not until the election of a Democratic administration that conservative opposition was effectively removed, allowing PSE to grow substantially.

If the views of economists were congruent with the expansion of PSE, they were incongruent with the adoption and implementation of full-employment legislation. Dominant voices in the profession and in the federal government allowed the opponents of Humphrey-Hawkins to cite influential, authoritative opinions that judged the legislation misguided. These opinions among mainstream economists, many of them Keynesians with ties to the Democratic party, reinforced misgivings among some liberals themselves of achieving a goal that had occupied a central place for thirty years on their unfulfilled agenda. The self-confidence of the early postwar period that unemployment and inflation could be managed simultaneously had evaporated, and the Keynesians were in retreat. No new strategy had taken its place, and a vague sense that positive government intervention had failed was pervasive. The opposition of economists like Charles Schultze opened the door for an evisceration of the act's provisions and made it virtually impossible to pass a bill with strong language. His attacks on the legislation were conceived and presented as a hardheaded and realistic appraisal of the legislation's probable impact, especially on inflation. Precisely because they were clothed in dispassionate analysis, these arguments were at least as powerful as the more simplistic, emotionally charged, symbolic attacks made on the 1945 legislation.

Yet the assessments of Humphrey-Hawkins were based upon theories of the labor market about which there can be fundamental disagreement, both analytically and politically. The policy recommendations of mainstream economists were premised upon the existence of an hypothesized trade-off between inflation and unemployment. This premise assumed, in turn, that the labor market operated much as neoclassical textbooks said it would—with relative wages acting to efficiently allocate economic resources. For most economists, the textbook model is not only an accurate view of reality but also highly desirable, because it promotes efficiency as a value. It is not difficult to see how such a view, once its policy implications are deduced, buttresses conservative beliefs in limited government.

Part II

Institutions

5

Congress, the Executive, and the Problem of State Building

IDEAS AND BELIEFS are translated into public policy through the mediation of political institutions.[1] During the formulation of public policy, institutions shape, filter, and delay proposals for change; and during implementation, they help determine to what extent the government is successful in achieving its objectives. Thus institutional structure and resources are key elements in determining the government's capacity—setting limits on what it can and cannot do. Institutional structures that enhance the government's internal unity and integration allow it to develop and pursue distinctive, coherent strategies and deploy its resources to achieve its objectives. Governments with low capacity share several characteristics. They enjoy little autonomy, their policies being simply driven by groups and classes in society. Rather than take preemptive or anticipatory action, they are capable only of reacting to crises once they develop. They are prone to stalemate and delay in making decisions; have difficulty developing consistent and clear objectives; pursue policies that produce undesirable, unintended consequences; and use inadequate means to attain objectives.

The United States is typically identified as a "weak state," one comparatively lacking in institutional capacity and with fewer resources at its disposal.[2] Public authority is highly fragmented and decentralized, with little integration between various institutional actors and comparatively low levels of administrative and fiscal capacity. The separation of powers, the federal system, weak national party organizations, and the committee system in Congress make policy making easily prone to particularism and resistant to central direction. Because there are few formal mechanisms available for integrating the various actors and providing decisive leadership, temporary and shifting coalitions must painstakingly be built at each stage in the policy-making process. The many points of access permit organized groups and constituencies to gain leverage over the process and to play off one institution (or part of an institution) against another. National politics is thus characterized by protracted struggles between the executive and legislature until a compromise is finally reached. The result is often stalemate, drift, or incremental adjustments to the status quo, and the frequent domination of policy making by subgovernments that quietly run according to their own routines or by less stable and clearly defined issue networks.[3]

This chapter and the two that follow examine the role of institutions in employment policy. Chapter 5 looks at three principal features of national policymaking: (1) the relationship between Congress and the executive; (2) congressional incentives and internal decision-making procedures; and (3) bureaucratic politics within the executive branch and the problem of state building in the Labor Department. Institutions vary in their competencies and incentive structures. Depending upon the institutional context in which they operate, public officials will find it feasible and attractive to become more engaged in certain policy domains and less in others. The institutional arrangements of the federal government have divided policy making between an employment policy subsystem, which deals with relatively narrow programmatic issues, and a broader arena in which major issues of economic policy are resolved. Chapter 6 explores the intergovernmental aspect of employment policy. The search for effective administrative and service delivery arrangements among the federal, state, and local governments has been a constant source of difficulty and has accounted for the repeated need to reform the system. Finally, chapter 7 is devoted to the Comprehensive Employment and Training Act (CETA), the largest employment program of the postwar period and its most visible political failure. CETA's experience is analyzed in terms of the discussion in chapters 5 and 6.

CONGRESS VERSUS THE PRESIDENT

A Division of Labor

Macro economic policy is largely mapped out at the highest levels of the executive branch, while employment policy has been to a much greater degree congressionally centered. Congress is much better equipped to formulate employment policy, within its fragmented decision-making structure, than it is to handle economic policy. And members of Congress have greater incentives to get involved in employment policy than they do in economic management.

Because the president is held accountable to a greater degree than Congress for the performance of the national economy, he has assumed much of the responsibility for formulating macroeconomic policy. Macroeconomic policies are concerned with the manipulation of aggregate levels of taxing, spending, the money supply, and the setting of interest rates. By their very nature, these instruments are best suited to an institutional context where there is a good measure of centralization of decision making. Top decision makers in the executive branch are in a more advantageous position to take the kind of overall, broad picture of total spending and taxation that is needed. Moreover, changes in policy must often be made in a prompt and timely basis to have the intended effect of staving off a recession or cooling down an economy on the brink of overheating.

For its part, Congress has seen fit to devolve upon the executive branch much of the responsibility for initiating fiscal policy and has delegated, in a wholesale manner, monetary policy to the Federal Reserve Board.[4] Congress's slow and deliberative procedures and its fragmented structure do not lend themselves very well to the conduct of economic management.[5] Since 1974, Congress has strived to improve its making of fiscal policy by instituting a budget process and by developing its own expertise. Yet the budget committees of each chamber must share power with revenue and appropriations committees, and their budget resolutions must gain a majority in both houses. Their counterpart in the executive branch, the Office of Management and Budget, is able to exert a much greater degree of control over agency requests for spending and in shaping the president's budget. Moreover, improving Congress's ability to make fiscal policy was only one of the objectives of the 1974 Budget Act. Fiscal policy considerations, and their impact on inflation, unemployment, and growth, must compete with Congress's attempt to use the budget process to establish distributive priorities—defense versus domestic programs, the burden of taxes, and so forth. Distributive issues often loom larger than the impact of fiscal policy on the economy. According to one observer, fiscal policy considerations have definitely been of secondary importance to budget committees: "Fiscal policy has been a derivative concern, and the talk has centered on budget numbers rather than jobs, economic growth, or prices. At no time do the members of the Budget Committees vote on economic policy directly; nor do such votes occur when the budget is debated in the House or Senate."[6]

It is not surprising that the management of fiscal policy is a relatively neglected aspect of congressional policy making. It is difficult for any single member of Congress to take credit for a fiscal policy decision, and any decision is likely to have macroeconomic impacts that are diffuse and less clearly focused on constituency groups than are decisions on particular programs or parts of the budget. The average member of Congress, wishing to claim credit for a particular legislative accomplishment, is likely to concentrate on specific programs rather than on aggregate levels of spending and taxation, whose impacts are much more difficult to attribute to his or her own efforts.

By contrast, the making of employment policy is better suited to Congress. It is easier to make decisions about job creation and training programs within a segmented policy-making context, because these activities are micro in nature, rather than macro. Decision making can be more focused, because these programs do not impinge upon all of the activities conducted by the federal government. Finally, employment policy is more attractive to Congress because its benefits are more particularized and selective, making it easier for legislators to claim credit for their efforts to garner funding for subsidized jobs or a training program in their districts.

Stalemate and Incoherence

The fact that Congress has a greater role in employment policy than in economic management does not mean that it monopolizes control over it. As in other areas, Congress shares power with the president, and this has often been a recipe for conflict and deadlock. The potential for conflict has increased in the postwar era with the greater frequency of the two branches being controlled by different parties. The most egregious example of how this arrangement has led to stalemate and drift was with the Comprehensive Employment and Training Act (CETA). The administrative reforms embodied in CETA were delayed for five years, despite widespread acknowledgment of the dire need to consolidate and decentralize the myriad programs haphazardly established in the 1960s. The Democratic majority in Congress refused to permit reform without assurances that public service employment (PSE) would be a permanent part of CETA. Nixon was adamantly opposed to PSE and insisted upon complete devolution of the programs, with no federal oversight role. The deadlock was resolved only because of the fortuitous occurrence of the Watergate scandal, which gave the pragmatists in the Labor Department a window of opportunity to reach an agreement with Congress. Had Watergate not intervened, the stalemate could have lasted indefinitely. Consequently, when the new administrative structure was finally established, on the eve of the unemployment crisis of 1974/75, valuable time had been lost for institutionalizing and consolidating the new arrangement.

CETA illustrates another major consequence of the separation of powers: the proclivity to produce incoherent policies that have unintended consequences. Because agreement is so difficult to reach, the test of an acceptable public policy becomes simply reaching an agreement, whether or not it is coherent and consistent. Consideration of possible consequences became relegated to considerations of how well the final bargain optimized the interests of the contenders. Public service employment and administrative decentralization, the principal terms upon which the CETA compromise was built, proved highly problematic. CETA's tribulations during implementation and its eventual downfall are directly traceable to the original legislation, which contained a basic contradiction between its administrative design and substantive goals.[7]

Even when both branches are controlled by the same party, there is no assurance that a compromise will be reached, or if reached, that the resultant legislation will prove meaningful or effective. The separation of powers and its corollary—weak party discipline—have made it especially difficult to adopt policies with broad purposes and that promise large-scale change. A classic example is the Full Employment Bill of 1945. The Democratic party platform had called for its enactment, the Democrats were in the majority in Congress, and President Truman favored the bill. Yet it was left to languish in the House Expenditures Committee until its supporters enlisted Truman's assistance to pressure the committee's key southern Democrats to take action. Truman could manage only to get the conservatives to agree to report "some sort of bill," and the president promised that he would not insist upon the original bill, the Senate-passed version which was much like the original, or even a bill with the words "full employment" in it.[8] The committee reported a substitute bill that eviscerated the key provisions of the original bill. When the House and Senate versions went to a conference committee, again Truman pressured Congress to go along with the stronger Senate bill, but to no avail. As Stephen Bailey concluded, "the forces which shaped and modified the legislation were far beyond [Truman's] control, and it is almost certain that if he had vetoed the conference bill he would have got nothing in its place."[9]

When the Humphrey-Hawkins Act was introduced in 1976, again, the leadership of the Democratic party was behind the legislation and the party's platform gave it a clear endorsement. The party, however, could not even insure that its own presidential nominee would support it. By the late 1970s, party reforms had made political parties even weaker institutions for selecting nominees and for governing than they already were. Self-promoted as an outsider running against the Washington establishment, Jimmy Carter was a moderate who was chosen by primary voters rather than anointed by the national party and constituency leadership. Carter was the first Democratic presidential candidate who was not an authentic descendent of Roosevelt's New Deal—his lack of liberal credentials distinguished him from his predecessors. During the primaries, Carter obscured where he stood on issues behind an image of personal trustworthiness and moderation. When not ambiguous or vacillating, his positions were of little comfort to the liberal wing of his party. He failed to support Humphrey-Hawkins until after he was assured of the nomination. Thereafter, his support remained unenthusiastic, and once in office, he insisted upon changes that severely weakened the original proposal.[10]

EMPLOYMENT POLICY IN CONGRESS

Issue Salience and Mobilization

For the average member of Congress, concern with unemployment tends to be episodic. Cyclical downturns in the economy heighten the salience of joblessness as an issue, and conversely, economic recovery lowers its salience. This pattern is reinforced by the tendency of inflationary pressures to increase as economic recovery progresses and the unemployment rate falls. When this happens, joblessness tends to fade as a pressing issue, and Congress becomes more aware of inflation. Thus, it is not surprising that innovations in the domain of employment policy, as well as expansions of existing responses to joblessness, have been preceded by episodes of cyclical unemployment. It was the recessions of the 1950s and 1960/61 that were very much on the mind of Congress when it passed the Manpower Development and Training Act (1962), and the Tax Reduction Act (1964). The recessions of 1970/71 and 1973/74 spurred Congress to pass the Emergency Employment Act (1971), the Emergency Jobs and Unemployment Assistance Act (1974), and the Emergency Jobs Programs Extension Act (1976). The Job Training Partnership Act (1982) was enacted partly in response to the recession of 1982. The only significant pieces of employment legislation not enacted in response to a cyclical downturn were the training programs of the poverty program and the 1977 Economic Stimulus Act, which more than doubled the number of public service employment jobs. Both of these were initiated by the executive branch, not by Congress, and were not ad hoc reactions to an immediate crisis.

As the frequent use of the qualifier *"emergency"* in statutory language indicates, Congress is almost never mobilized to act until an economic crisis is at hand. It has little interest in long-term measures to plan or invest in the economy. Since Congress mobilizes primarily in response to manifest crises, proposals directed toward the long term have been introduced during crisis periods. The full-employment legislation of the 1940s and 1970s are good examples. The problem, however, is that at such times Congress is mainly interested in short-term responses that can provide immediate relief to constituents. And because the legislative process takes so long, the crisis has usually passed before any final action can be taken.

Policy responses to economic trends must be made on a timely basis, often before events actually unfold, if they are to be effective. Yet Congress has resisted virtually every kind of planned intervention—that is, anticipating developments before they occur and having facilities and plans prepared ahead of time to absorb unemployed labor. Congressional decision making is slow and prolonged. The legislative process can take months of testimony, debate, negotiation, and marking up legislation. And there is the still pervasive notion that consideration of certain measures (e.g., creating jobs in the public sector and deficit financing) should be undertaken, if at all, only when there is clear evidence of an impending economic crisis.

Nor does Congress have much interest in encouraging planning within the bureaucracy. Planning requires a prior commitment of funds, automatic triggering mechanisms, and a shift in discretion from the legislative to the executive branch. None of these appeals to an institution that jealously guards its prerogatives. The best example is the Manpower Development and Training Act (MDTA). Title I of the MDTA gave the secretary of labor a broad charter to launch labor market planning. This provision passed more because its main sponsor, Senator Joseph Clark, took a particular interest in the manpower issue than because of any generalized interest or enthusiasm in Congress. Most members of Congress had a limited vision of the role of manpower policy in the economy. The attractiveness of MDTA for most of Congress was simply that it was a response to a perceived crisis, providing money for retraining displaced workers back home. Clark's arguments—that manpower planning and investment were necessary in order for the United States to compete internationally with the Soviet Union and to increase productivity and growth in the economy—were rhetorically appealing, but they were not decisive in Congress's approval. Very few in Congress understood that structural unemployment was a problem of the market's inability to adequately adjust to changes in the structure of the market itself. The idea of most was simply to bring relief to already displaced adult workers, rather than to speed labor market adjustment.

Unemployment that is not generated by cyclical downturns in the national economy tends to be less salient among congressmen generally. Economists label such unemployment *structural*, because it has to do with changes in the structure of the labor market rather than with deficiencies in the demand for labor. Structural unemployment manifests itself in a variety of ways—from inner-city youth without basic skills or geographic mobility to take the jobs that are available, to the southern textile worker whose job has been exported to cheaper labor markets abroad, to the midwestern autoworker who is displaced by automation.

The much higher level of appropriations for programs directed at cyclical unemployment (i.e., countercyclical PSE) than for those directed at structural unemployment (i.e., training, work experience, and noncountercyclical PSE) is an important indicator of the greater salience of the former than the latter. The lower salience of structural unemployment is caused by a number of factors. First, structural unemployment is usually not perceived in the context of a national emergency. Whereas cyclical unemployment is triggered by a sudden and quite visible downturn in the economy, structural changes in the labor market tend to build gradually over time and tend to persist. Because structural unemployment can exist within an economy that is enjoying overall prosperity, it is possible to view it as an aberration. Second, structural unemployment tends to affect discrete demographic groups in particular communities, regions, and sectors of the economy, while cyclical unemployment affects very large numbers of people throughout virtually the entire nation. In a nation as vast and diverse as the United States, it is possible for acute structural problems to exist during times of national economic expansion. Displaced steel and auto workers in Pennsylvania and Indiana are likely to be a major source of concern for legislators from those states, but their plight will be much less visible and urgent to those from other states. Similarly, the long-term problems of disadvantaged youths in the central cities will be highly salient to congressmen from Harlem and Watts, but will be much less so for those representing suburban and rural districts. For most members of Congress, as for most people, the structurally unemployed are so geographically and socially isolated as to be virtually invisible.

Also contributing to the greater salience of cyclical (as opposed to structural) unemployment are the kinds of policy prescriptions that are put forward to cope with each type of problem. Quite often, the salience of an issue depends as much upon what people advocate should be done about it as it does upon the existence of the problem itself. Generally, the more controversial the remedy proposed, the more salient the issue becomes. Proposals to deal with cyclical unemployment include expanding unemployment insurance benefits, creating jobs in the public sector, creating budget deficits, and lowering interest rates. Several of these options are almost guaranteed to create conflict, partly out of fears that they will contribute to inflation, but mainly because they have an ideological property to them.[11] Liberals may view job creation programs and fiscal deficits as perfectly acceptable and necessary methods to fulfill the government's obligation to the jobless. But conservatives are likely to view them as wasteful and, especially in the case of increasing spending for public employment, in direct conflict with their faith in the capacity of the private market to provide sufficient jobs.

This ideological polarization is in sharp contrast to the policy debate over structural unemployment. The conventional remedies for structural unemployment have been training or retraining, education, better placement services, and so forth, which are comparatively noncontroversial kinds of policy instruments.

If structural unemployment is an issue of relatively low salience to most legislators, how is it that Congress mobilizes to respond to it at all? First, while structural unemployment is likely to be a low-salience issue for a majority of congressmen, they may still be moved to action by a determined minority of their colleagues who are deeply concerned about it. Legislators not only pay attention to the needs and concerns of their own constituents but to those of their colleagues in Congress. Second, legislators committed to doing something about structural unemployment have often taken advantage of periods when the general concern about cyclical unemployment has been high—that is, during recessionary periods. Third, at times Congress has been mobilized by a president who has made structural unemployment a priority of his legislative program, the best example being Kennedy's and Johnson's push for the manpower training and work experience programs of the 1960s.

Policy-Making Goals and Orientations

Assuming Congress is mobilized, what are the patterns of policy choice that are typical when responding to unemployment, and what might account for them? David Mayhew has argued that, because the most important goal of congressmen is reelection, they will be attracted to those types of policies that seem to have the greatest promise of an electoral payoff. As a result, there is a "strong tendency to wrap policies in packages that are salable as particularized benefits." According to Mayhew, "On measures lacking particularized benefits the congressman's intrinsic interest in the impact of legislation vanishes."[12] Second, a great deal of legislative activity can be characterized as "symbolic politics"—taking positions on issues (e.g., "poverty is a national disgrace"), without prescribing policies for dealing with them, or prescribing policies without putting them into effect. The reason for this "is that in a large class of legislative undertakings the electoral payment is for positions rather than for effects."[13]

Even a cursory review of major pieces of legislation dealing with unemployment over the past decades reveals a pattern that is fairly consistent with Mayhew's thesis. Employment policies often contain strong elements of either symbolism or particularized benefits, or both. Full-employment legislation (the Employment Act of 1946 and the Humphrey-Hawkins Act) is a classic example of symbolic policies—promises to substantially reduce the unemployment rate—that are subsequently left unfulfilled and largely devoid of any commitment of resources to achieve them. The Manpower Development and Training Act (MDTA) provided retraining and other benefits to local communities to combat structural unemployment. "For senators and congressmen, concerned with particular constituents in particular communities, the structural explanation struck a responsive chord."[14] Similarly, other categorical employment programs of the 1960s delivered particular services to specific constituencies. The Comprehensive Employment and Training Act (CETA) was both symbolic and full of particularized benefits (primarily in the form of public jobs) for local communities. CETA's ostensible objective to provide "aid for the unemployed" was manipulated as a symbolic ruse for funneling federal money to local communities that lobbied for it to relieve their fiscal stress.

By contrast, Congress ignores or rejects proposals that offer neither particularized benefits nor symbols. The localistic orientation of Congress toward manpower programs was clearly evidenced in its rejection of relocation incentives for workers as one component of MDTA.[15] Providing incentives to relocate workers from areas with surplus labor to those with a shortage clashed directly with reelection incentives. In effect, legislators would have been bestowing benefits upon constituents for leaving their states and districts.

Maximizing support for employment programs requires spreading their benefits as diffusely as possible. For instance, manpower experts argue that areas of at least 1 million population are the optimal size to facilitate rational labor market planning. The *politically* rational size of labor market areas for Congress, however, is jurisdictions of much smaller size. To garner a majority coalition in favor of spending on employment measures, Congress has balkanized labor market areas to include many more communities as eligible recipients of funding. In the case of CETA, the figure was as low as 100,000 in population.

Nonelectoral Goals and the Role of Analysis in Policy Making. The electoral connection is by no means a comprehensive explanation of congressional behavior. First, congressmen pursue goals other than reelection, such as making "good" public policy.[16] While members usually perceive a congruence between their reelection goal and what they regard as good policy, the two may come in conflict, and it ought not be assumed that the reelection goal will always take precedence. Given the substantial advantages of incumbency, members are able to satisfy their reelection goal without having it interfere with their ability to formulate considered judgments "on the merits" of policy issues. In fact, as Derthick and Quirk argue, "much of the attraction of serving in

Congress is the opportunity to debate issues, form opinions, and make efficacious judgments on matters of public concern. . . . Exercising a certain amount of political independence and voting on the merits of issues is for such members part of the point of having the job."[17]

Second, policy issues vary in the degree to which they provide incentives and opportunities for basing policy decisions primarily on electoral considerations. Many of the problems that Congress has confronted in the employment policy domain are ones for which any credit that can be claimed does not entail any electoral payoff. I am speaking here of the managerial issues that have increasingly crowded the legislative agenda. More and more attention has been devoted to finding out effective administrative and service delivery arrangements. These problems cannot be addressed by delivering more benefits back home or by manipulating symbols. Indeed, the more the agenda has been dominated by managerial issues, the less time and justification has existed for creating new programs or expanding existing ones. Nor are voters likely to notice, much less reward, incumbents if problems in the design or execution of policy are overcome. Everyone expects that programs will be efficiently and effectively carried out. An employment program reputed to be wasteful and mismanaged offers little in the way of rewards but plenty of embarrassment for those who must deal with the failure.

CETA illustrates both points. CETA's adoption was in response to the proliferation of categorical employment programs that Congress created during the 1960s. Categorical programs appeal to Congress because of the particularized benefits that they provide to specific groups. CETA consolidated these programs, eliminating the specific programs for which individual legislators had taken credit. It is true that CETA delivered tangible benefits to a wide variety of local communities, but those who gained most were elected officials at the local level who were given the discretion to allocate funds to constituents and to provide for a variety of services. It was they who could claim direct credit for the program's accomplishments. It is difficult to see how the reelection thesis can explain why Congress would choose to refashion programs that maximized their ability to claim credit and that particularized benefits into a package that decreased their ability to claim credit and where their potential political rivals at the state and local level gained control over how the programs' resources were used. Congress went along with the reforms because there was widespread recognition that the existing design of the programs was administratively unworkable and that program consolidation and decentralization was necessary. It could no longer ignore the chaos that the categoricals had created, despite their attractiveness from the electoral perspective.

Thus, in trying to decide what to do about unemployment or how to manage employment programs effectively, Congress has been concerned not only with the claims and concerns of constituents, but with the arguments and opinions of experts, administrators, and fellow legislators concerning the substantive merits of policy.

We have seen that policy making has an important intellectual component in which reason, evidence, and analysis are brought to bear upon decisions. Yet we are only beginning to learn about the conditions under which disinterested economic analysis has an impact on policy makers. One of these conditions is the establishment of institutional arrangements that facilitate the bringing of economic advice directly to the center of policy-making deliberations. While such a competence was established under the Employment Act of 1946 with the Council of Economic Advisers in the executive branch, it was not until later in the postwar period that Congress developed most of its formal mechanisms for receiving and generating economic advice.

Another condition is the degree to which economic arguments and evidence are presented to policy makers in a manner that is clear and comprehensible to laymen,[18] and the ease with which policy makers can link them to the common knowledge they derive from their own experiences and those of their colleagues and constituents. For instance, manpower training programs were enacted by Congress earlier than a tax cut (and without a protracted debate) in part because the structural explanation of unemployment had a marked advantage over the theory of deficient aggregate demand. Keynesian economists had the more difficult task of educating Congress and the president on the principles of the "new economics." Members of Congress found it difficult to associate personal misfortune with abstract and arcane Keynesian notions like the inadequacy of aggregate consumption and expenditure flows in the economy. On the other hand, it was much easier to identify those individuals who had lost their jobs to automation, plant closings, or obsolete skills. Likewise, the structuralist prescription to retrain the unemployed had a much more practical and straightforward ring to it than creating deficits to put people back to work.

A final condition is what Derthick and Quirk call "political adaptiveness"—the degree to which analysis is or can be made to suit the political needs of actors. The structural explanation struck a responsive chord with the typical congressman, who saw in manpower training a way to directly address the personal misfortune of unemployed constituents, and with conservatives, who saw training programs as an acceptable alternative to stimulating the economy through deficit creation. Yet what was lost through both the need to translate economic analysis into layman's understanding and to adapt analysis to political goals

was the more abstract and fundamental argument of the structuralists—
that the market mechanism itself was unable to satisfactorily bring labor
supply and demand into balance—a critique that, taken to its ultimate
conclusion, would have justified far-reaching public planning and intervention in the labor market.

Committee Behavior

The House Education and Labor Committee and the Senate Labor
and Public Welfare Committee are the most critical sites for making
employment policy in Congress. According to Richard Fenno, members
of the labor committees, unlike members of most other committees,
"emphasize a strong personal interest in and a concern for the content
of public policy in their committee's subject matter; in short, they want
to help make good public policy."[19] In their subject matter interest and
their commitment to certain broad policy orientations, labor committee
members have a fairly clear idea of their substantive policy goals and
exhibit a high level of satisfaction in making policy. Reelection and
influence within the parent chamber, the two other major goals of
congressmen, are much less important reasons for wanting to gain a
seat on the committee. In fact, Fenno found that a majority of the
members of the labor panel considered their membership "as having
an adverse effect on their re-election."[20] Members also appear to place
comparatively less value upon enhancing their reputations among their
colleagues outside the committee, especially if bettering one's reputation means having to compromise on the policy positions one holds.

The labor committees exhibit the greatest degree of ideological and
partisan conflict of any in Congress. "Prosecuting policy partisanship"
is a key "strategic premise"—or decision rule that guides committee
behavior. Democratic members most likely to be attracted to serve on
the labor committees tend to be more liberal than their brethren in the
Congress as a whole, while Republicans tend to be more conservative,
although there have been some key GOP liberals like Senator Jacob
Javits who have sat on the committee. The issues that the committees
deal with, which fall mostly into the areas of economic and social
policy, naturally lend themselves to deep ideological divisions and a
predisposition to partisanship. These characteristics of the committees'
subject matter reflect the liberal-conservative cleavage that crystallized
around the economic debates that were the hallmark of New Deal
politics.[21] The competing perspectives of liberals and conservatives still
resonate clearly on many matters of social and economic policy. However, not all issues reflect polarization. Some, including manpower
training, vocational education, and aid to higher education, enjoy bipartisan consensus.

Fenno says that a second strategic premise of the committees is "to pursue one's individual policy preferences," which often overrides partisanship if the two do not coincide. The acceptance of "policy individualism," an independent, entrepreneurial style of policy making, works against party discipline and cohesion. Even if they are novices, committee members are expected to fight for their own version of a good public policy, in a free-for-all, every-man-for-himself fashion.[22] As a result, committee proceedings are often tempestuous.

These characteristics of labor committees' members do not win them many admirers in the parent chamber, where their colleagues view them as excessively conflictual and rancorous. The committees' "distinctive aversion to compromise" and the free-wheeling, unrestrained style of members pursuing their own particular policy preferences clash with congressional norms, which stress consensus building, a deference to seniority and specialization, and the crafting of careful legislation. Committee members lack those attributes commonly admired in Congress—unity, stability, an accommodative bargaining style, and regard for majority sentiment in the parent chamber.[23] Also, because of its pronounced liberal leanings, the House Committee on Education and Labor is regarded as unrepresentative of the House as a whole. It rarely presents a unified front to its parent chamber, and seems to worry little about success in getting its legislation approved in the House. Individual members often bicker, offer amendments, and appear confused on the floor of the House. For these reasons, the Education and Labor Committee has historically experienced greater difficulty than most committees in getting its bills passed on the floor.[24] Bills brought to the floor for passage run a relatively high risk of being drastically altered, recommitted for further action, or rejected altogether.

Impacts of Individualism and Fragmentation

One consequence of the absence of strong, programmatic political parties in the United States is that the various tasks involved in making policy—agenda setting, formulating programs, and building a consensus—must be undertaken through the fluid, loose-jointed, interaction of individuals. Because of weak party leadership and the incentives and opportunities that exist for individualism, these tasks have been carried out to a great extent by individual legislative entrepreneurs or small groups of key congressmen on particular committees. The role of the entrepreneur is to publicize issues he or she deems of national significance, advocate a preferred course of action, build a coalition to get the proposal through the legislative process, and protect the program's budget and reputation once it has been established.

Entrepreneurialism emerged as a dominant legislative style in the postwar period with what Sundquist calls new-style members of Congress. Old-style members were socialized into pre-Progressive-party organizations. Their nominations were gained through past service to the party, and in Congress they were socialized to accept the norms of apprenticeship and deference to leaders. Their careers did not depend upon advocacy of issues or legislative brilliance, only on gaining material rewards for their districts, which would increase with seniority and insure renomination. New-style members neither owe their office to party organization nor accept the norms supportive of leadership. Nominations are won through advocacy of issue positions rather than party service, though delivering constituent benefits continues to play an important role in assuring a lengthy career. Impatient, ambitious, and with a sense of mission, new-style members want to make an impact on national policy and are not content to defer to those with greater seniority.[25]

Sundquist marks the 1958 election as the arrival date of the new-style congressman, a year that brought into office a large group of freshmen Democrats. Many came from states where the Democratic party had been traditionally weak but where the Progressive party was strong early in the century. They arrived as individualists or as products of new-style Democratic organizations that inherited the Progressive tradition and took shape after the war. It is interesting to note that the author of the first postwar employment program—the Manpower Development and Training Act of 1962—was among them. Senator Clark came into office in a campaign promising to do something about the high unemployment rate in Pennsylvania, which affected one of nine workers in that state and much higher ratios in some coal counties. Clark was determined to use his chairmanship of the employment and manpower subcommittee as a vehicle for enacting employment legislation that would bear his name.[26]

Almost all of the major pieces of employment legislation have had key legislative entrepreneurs behind their adoption: James Murray (the Employment Act), Paul Douglas (Area Redevelopment Act), Joseph Clark (Manpower Development and Training Act), Hubert Humphrey (the Job Corps and Neighborhood Youth Corps), Gaylord Nelson (Operation Mainstream), James Scheuer (New Careers), Jacob Javits and Robert Kennedy (Special Impact), Joseph Clark and Gaylord Nelson (Public Service Employment under the Emergency Employment Act and the Comprehensive Employment and Training Act), Augustus Hawkins and Hubert Humphrey (Full Employment and Balanced Growth Act), Augustus Hawkins, Dan Quayle, and Edward Kennedy

(Job Training Partnership Act). Each new training, job creation, or work experience program created bore the imprimatur of a congressional sponsor.

The legislative process is especially burdensome for getting far-reaching proposals enacted, such as full-employment initiatives. Majorities must be built and rebuilt at several junctures in the process, without the benefit of party discipline. And because the institution is so fragmented, it offers multiple points of access for determined minorities to block or weaken proposals. For example, though the Full Employment Bill of 1945 passed the Senate largely as it had been introduced, when it moved to the House it was mistakenly sent to the Committee on Expenditures rather than the more liberal House Labor Committee. The Expenditures Committee was heavily weighted with Republicans and southern Democrats. Entrenched on the committee through the benefit of the seniority system, and enjoying the autonomy and discretion accorded committees of Congress, the conservative coalition was able to weaken the bill. The committee produced a substitute bill that rejected the fundamental principles and mechanisms of the Full Employment Bill. The substitute was sent on to the Rules Committee—another strategic point in the process that was dominated by conservatives—which proceeded to grant a rule permitting conservatives on the Expenditure Committee to control the time for debate as well as the procedures for floor voting. The rule made it virtually certain that, if the substitute bill was not passed, nothing would be passed. Through legislative maneuvering on the floor of the House chamber, the original bill's opponents managed to deny the authors of the original bill even a vote on it, thus "sparing the Southern Gentlemen from the wrath of unemployed voters" in the next election.[27] In the end, the substitute passed with a large majority, with supporters of the Full Employment Bill having to accept it or nothing at all. Thus, an emasculated version of the original bill was passed, the Employment Act of 1946.

The attempt to commit the federal government to full employment through the pursuit of a Keynesian fiscal policy based upon high levels of government spending deficits failed. Locally based, conservative elements in Congress were able to use the fragmented decision-making structure and cumbersome procedures of the legislative process to gain leverage to thwart the proponents of a full-employment policy. In the absence of strong central leadership and disciplined, cohesive political parties, policy making fell victim to a legislative process that required that temporary power coalitions be laboriously rebuilt at each point in the policy-making process. This afforded a small group of power brokers, responsible only to the parochial concerns of their local constituencies, the opportunity to have decisive influence over decision making.[28] In the end, these institutional constraints proved too formidable for the proponents of a full-employment policy.

The long, delayed struggle to enact CETA illustrates the same point. Although the main stumbling block to administrative reform was conflict between Congress and the president over public service employment, another impediment for a time was Congress's reluctance to eliminate the existing array of categorical programs and to devolve authority to the states and localities. Individual legislators had a proprietary interest in the specific programs that they had launched and nurtured. Consolidating them into a single block grant and vesting discretion with local officials meant that they might no longer survive, and that the specific client groups served might lose the services. Most members of Congress also viewed block grants as an abdication of the power of the purse. The same government that raised the revenue to fund programs, so the argument went, should take responsibility for seeing how the money was spent.[29]

Finally, the fragmentation of decision making within Congress interferes with better integration of economic and employment policies. Virtually all of the labor committees' attention is focused on the design and implementation of the various programs that come under their jurisdiction. Little attention is paid to broader questions relating to the basic purpose and scope of employment policy or to how employment programs fit into the larger set of policies directed at the economy. Even if the labor committees were inclined to involve themselves in the larger questions of economic policy, their likelihood of gaining influence in economic policy decisions is highly improbable given the relatively narrow jurisdiction they are granted. Congress has only one mechanism for dealing expressly with economic policy, the Joint Economic Committee (JEC). The JEC, on which sit members of both the House and Senate, takes a comprehensive overview of how different policy instruments are related to one another. The JEC is also the only place in Congress where one finds employment programs discussed in the context of economic policy and where some thought has been given to how employment programs have a role to play in the broader concerns of the national economy.[30] Yet the JEC's status is strictly that of an advisory body. It has no power to make policy. It cannot legislate, spend money, or raise revenue. To put it mildly, a committee of Congress without the authority to write laws, to spend, or to tax, is a committee whose influence is likely to be very limited.

EMPLOYMENT POLICY AND THE EXECUTIVE BRANCH

Owing to its unique position as the only public office elected by all the people, and the symbolism attached to it, the presidency is the focal point of national politics. Beginning with Franklin Roosevelt, the president has been held responsible for the economic health of the nation more than any other elected official. Presidents have good reason to be concerned about economic performance, and unemployment in particular. Incumbents who have run for reelection (or their party's nominees to succeed them) have fared poorly at the polls when the unemployment rate has been rising or when recovery has stalled. Richard Nixon in the election of 1960, Gerald Ford in 1976, and Jimmy Carter in 1980 were all defeated, in part, because of voters' dissatisfaction with the performance of the economy, and specifically with the rate of joblessness.[31] Because the unemployment rate is a key indicator of economic performance, and because economic performance is crucial in the president's approval rating, some have suggested that presidents may try to manipulate the policy instruments at their disposal in order to curry favor with the electorate. In the months just prior to the election, so this argument goes, presidents will take actions to expand economic activity, resulting in a falling unemployment rate and a rise in real incomes.[32] Nevertheless, evidence on the existence of political business cycles is mixed.[33]

Presidents have tended to place employment policy within a somewhat broader context than has Congress and have tried to make it a part of grander designs for domestic policy reform. For instance, manpower training was one component of the Johnson administration's War on Poverty. Reforming manpower administration and service delivery under Nixon was part of the much broader series of New Federalism initiatives—an ambitious scheme to restructure domestic policy responsibilities by sorting out the appropriate functions of the three levels of government. Similarly, the Carter administration used CETA as part of its economic stimulus package when it entered office in 1977, and developed plans (none of which came to fruition) to use employment programs as part of its strategy for urban revitalization and reforming the welfare system. Finally, under Reagan, employment programs were among many social programs targeted for draconian fiscal retrenchment, and what remained of the programs was slated for devolution to the states as part of another New Federalism initiative. The approach of Congress, on the other hand, has tended to be more narrowly focused.

The salience of unemployment to the president, and the likelihood that he will actively seek to get programs adopted to reduce it, tend to vary with the party that occupies the White House. Unlike Congress, which has been dominated by Democratic majorities throughout most of the postwar period, the presidency has shifted back and forth between the two major parties. Using econometric estimates, Douglas Hibbs found that macroeconomic performance varied with the incumbent president's partisan affiliation.[34] The unemployment rate during Democratic administrations has tended to be somewhat lower than in Republican administrations immediately preceding them. Spending for employment and training programs (average annual increases adjusted for inflation) has risen faster under Democratic than Republican administrations. The average increase during the Kennedy-Johnson years was 78 percent, and for the Carter years 35 percent; while under Nixon-Ford spending rose by 22 percent, and under Reagan it fell by 14 percent.[35]

Likewise, the major pieces of employment legislation were passed under Democratic administrations. The New Deal work relief programs were created and pushed through Congress by Roosevelt. The Employment Act was passed under Truman. What followed was an eight-year hiatus under Eisenhower, when few measures were passed in Congress, and those that gained legislative approval were blocked by vetoes. Kennedy and Johnson presided over the passage of the Manpower Development and Training Act, the Tax Reduction Act, and the Economic Opportunity Act. Under Nixon, the Emergency Employment Act was pushed by a determined Democratic majority in Congress in the face of the administration's resistance. The measure was first vetoed by Nixon, then accepted only grudgingly in the middle of an election-year recession. The passage of CETA took place under Nixon, but CETA was largely a reorganization of existing programs. After it had passed, Nixon fought hard to reduce spending through the elimination of public service jobs. The Emergency Jobs and Unemployment Assistance Act of 1974 and the Emergency Jobs Program Extension Act of 1976 were passed during Ford's tenure but, as with Nixon, with great reluctance on the part of the president, who was dogged by the Democratic Congress and prodded by a sharp recession. Under Carter, the Economic Stimulus Act was passed, more than doubling the funding for CETA, and the Humphrey-Hawkins full employment bill was enacted along with the Youth Employment Demonstration Projects Act. Finally, under Reagan CETA's budget was substantially cut, eliminating all funding for public employment. The Job Training Partnership Act was passed, but largely because of congressional pressure on the administration.

The Department of Labor and the Economic Policy Agencies

Within the executive branch, there has been little connection, formal or informal, between those agencies responsible for economic policy and the Labor Department, which has authority over employment policy. The Labor Department is not part of the "troika": the Council of Economic Advisers (CEA), the Office of Management and Budget (OMB), and the Treasury Department. Along with the Federal Reserve Board, these are the major actors in the economic policy arena. In the status hierarchy of the executive branch, the Labor Department ranks below all of these agencies. It does not operate within the core of the domestic policy-making apparatus of the American state, and therefore does not enjoy preferred access and close proximity to the president.

One reason for this is the structural differentiation between types of federal agencies. The responsibilities and orientations of the economic policy agencies are broad, diffuse, and functional. The Labor Department (and similarly situated agencies, such as Commerce), on the other hand, have relatively narrow and specific programmatic responsibilities.

Second, because of its close ties, real or imputed, with organized labor, the Department of Labor is a "constituency department." Thus, unlike OMB or CEA, Labor is not considered a "neutral" source of policy advice, because it is viewed as representing a parochial interest. As a result, not only does Labor have limited access to economic policy deliberations, but it must compete with several other second- and third-echelon bureaucratic supplicants for the president's attention and for budget resources. Its requests for new or expanded programs are often regarded by OMB and CEA as particularistic budget claims, which may be inconsistent with general economic policy.

A third reason for the exclusion of Labor has to do with the professional personnel that populates the other agencies. Economists who find their way into the tight circle of agencies responsible for economic policy tend to foster similar outlooks on the substance of policy. The policy advice emanating from agencies like CEA and Treasury are likely to come from macroeconomists, who view the economy in macro terms—conceptualizing economic policy options largely in terms of manipulating aggregate fiscal and monetary measures. Employment policy consists of a set of microinstruments—training the unskilled, providing jobs or wage subsidies to the unemployed or to firms that will hire them, relocating workers, finding jobs for workers, and so forth. These microinstruments have been championed most vigorously by labor and manpower economists, who are most likely to be found in the Labor Department. Thus the Labor Department's approach to unemployment is institutionally subordinated to the macro approach, which predominates among those responsible for making economic policy. One can better appreciate the relationship between the Labor Department and these other agencies by examining the perceptions that individuals from both worlds hold of each other. The commentary below is that of Alan Greenspan, chairman of the CEA in the Ford administration:

INTERVIEWER: I have the impression that over the years the policies of the Labor Department, which are micro, have never been plugged into a larger macro overview. They existed in a limbo—the manpower programs and others—without much thought of their implications for macro policy.
GREENSPAN: It's not to say that all these programs don't have a significant macro effect. The real question you should be asking is, if macro economic policy presumably has a far greater effect on employment and unemployment than all of the micro policies, why aren't they [the Labor Department] key players in the [economic policy-making] system? The major reason is that the Labor Department has a very strong constituency, and, as a consequence, does not produce the non-constituency policy-making output that, for example, CEA does. In other words, we did not have a constituency. In a sense, neither does OMB. The President is our constituency, but I mean somebody behind us pushing. . . . Since the Labor Department felt it should in part at least advocate and support positions of its constituency, it had a certain partisan position, which may or may not have been consistent with the policy of the country as a whole, or of the administration in general. That institutional limitation fundamentally inhibited their ability to deal in macro areas in the same sense that OMB and Treasury and CEA do.[36]

Regardless of the party of the administration in power, the relationship between the Labor Department, on the one side, and the OMB and CEA, on the other, is often contentious and discourages Labor's participation. Take the following reflections of a high-ranking political appointee in the Labor Department during the Carter administration, for instance:

People tend to always get a sense of déjà vu any time an issue comes up . . . you know, we would [say] here comes the Treasury Department again, or here comes OMB again, trying to cut our budget just as they would say, here come those left-wing Commies from the Labor Department attempting to drive up the deficit again, or here they come with their wierd ideas on regulations and social issues and so on. And people tended to see each other as sort of fixed pieces in a military battle after a while. . . . And after you've been in place for a period of time, . . . you start to kind of lose your enthusiasm for the battles, and you start to kind of draw back and be more conservative and say, oh, well, we might as well not suggest that because, you know, [CEA chairman] Charlie Schultze or [Treasury secretaries] Mike Blumenthal or William Miller are going to do us in on the issue.[37]

Not surprisingly, employment programs have been largely left without any important role in managing the economy. For the most part, structural impediments to the Labor Department's participation have kept employment policy out of economic policy deliberations. Any enlargement of the department's role, or change in employment policy's mission from social welfare to positive economic intervention, has been kept off the agenda simply by excluding Labor and by maintaining the definition of economic policy as exclusively a macromanagement task. In addition, macroeconomic policy authorities have been able to control, within rough limits, the level of expenditures for employment programs. The Labor Department's attempt to create a massive public employment program as the centerpiece of the War on Poverty was blocked by the CEA and the Budget Bureau. The same agencies under Johnson, Nixon, and Ford were able to delay the establishment of a PSE program, and when it was finally created, kept the level of appropriations lower than proponents of the program in Congress wished. The expansion of PSE in the 1970s came only after the Federal Reserve Board and macroeconomists in the CEA endorsed the idea. The high point of PSE expansion came when President Carter and his economic advisers decided that direct job creation should be a part of the stimulus package enacted in 1977. When OMB and CEA decided that fiscal restraint was needed in the second half of the Carter term, the PSE budget was cut, and the same agencies eliminated it altogether under Reagan.

There have been opportunities to provide employment policy with greater representation at the highest levels of the executive branch. When manpower policy was on the agenda in the early 1960s, Senator Clark proposed the creation of a Council of Manpower Advisers, patterned after the Council of Economic Advisers and lodged in the Executive Office of the President. Had it been approved, such a council would have given the proponents of a national manpower policy access at the highest level of the executive branch and might have elevated manpower policy in importance and visibility, enabling it to compete for scarce budgetary resources and for a role in economic policy. According to Mangum, "its intent was to exalt manpower considerations in the scheme of economic policy-making." But the idea was rejected by Kennedy's advisers, who argued that "having an employment-oriented economist among the members of the Council of Economic Advisers would be sufficient," and by the Labor Department, because it feared losing its control over training programs.[38]

The Department of Labor and the Problem of State Building

Because presidents are inherently limited in their control over the executive branch, relevant federal agencies usually loom large as key actors in their own right. Stephen Skowronek has characterized the twentieth-century American state as "a hapless administrative giant, a state that could spawn bureaucratic goods and services but that defied authoritative control and direction."[39] Though the Labor Department is hardly an administrative giant compared to other agencies, there are few observations that could encapsulate the role and performance of the Labor Department so aptly as this one. The Department of Labor is at the very center of employment policy in the executive branch, from the formulation of policy to its implementation and evaluation. Yet, its experience with employment policy has been both troublesome and troubling. In this section we trace the historical development of the department and discuss its implications for the federal government's ability to effectively carry out employment policy.

A Legacy of Partisanship and Stagnation. Congress established the Labor Department during a period of rapid state building in America, from the late nineteenth century until World War I. Early patterns of federal administrative growth were related to the conduct of certain core functions of the early American state (i.e., finance, justice, foreign relations, and defense). But many of the new agencies that dotted the landscape of turn-of-the-century Washington reflected a growing clientelism between the state and major sectors of the economy. The labor movement was convinced that the national government was populated by businessmen hostile and insensitive to the plight of the working man. Like agriculture and business, organized labor demanded recognition in the form of a federal agency that could promote its interests and aspirations.[40]

During the same period, Progressive reformers sought to dismantle what Skowronek has labeled the "state of courts and parties" and to replace it with a new institutional order composed of "an independent arm of national administrative action."[41] Both the demands of economic interests for direct representation in the bureaucracy and the Progressive reaction against the established institutional arrangements were prompted by the strains produced in American society during industrialization. While the Progressives were skeptical of powerful economic interests and sought to "take politics out of administration," many of them were also repelled by the exploitation and social dislocation produced by industrialism, and sought to apply the knowledge gained from scientific investigation to the entire range of labor and social problems. Hence, the impetus for establishing the Labor Department was a curious mixture of Progressive reformism and the drive for bureaucratic representation by an increasingly organized sector of the private economy.

Organized labor waged a long struggle in the face of resistance from employers—from 1864 to 1913—to gain representation in the cabinet. The first bureaus of labor, established in several states, mainly served as agencies for the collection of information and statistics on topics related to working conditions. At the federal level, a Bureau of Labor was eventually set up in the Interior Department and then transferred to a new Department of Commerce and Labor. The American Federation of Labor (AFL) complained that labor's concerns were subordinated to those of capital. When labor stepped up its campaign for its own cabinet department, it found an ally in Woodrow Wilson, who promised to go along with the idea in exchange for the AFL's support in his electoral bid for the presidency. With Wilson's victory in 1912, labor's cries for its own cabinet department were finally answered.

From the very beginning, the Department of Labor has been embroiled in an issue that has continued to this day: should the department act as a partisan agency, whose purpose is to serve as the "voice of labor" in the councils of government? Or is it to be an impartial source of analysis and advice on matters of policy? Like the state-level bureaus of labor that preceded it, the Labor Department has always been a mixture of neutral competence and an advocate for the labor movement. The reformist tradition of Progressivism stressed the notion that the collection, analysis, and dissemination of statistics could provide a factual and objective basis for guiding the making of labor policy. Scientific investigation and objective analysis would be combined with reformist zeal to address the problems of inadequate wages, poor working conditions, child labor, labor-management conflict, and so forth. The core of the department's analytic capability is the Bureau of Labor Statistics (BLS), the heir of the original Bureau of Labor started in 1884. As an economic fact finder and gatherer of statistics, the BLS is widely respected for its professional competence and integrity. The BLS has nurtured its reputation by carefully shielding itself from charges of partisanship, in part by distancing itself from the rest of the Labor Department. (BLS autonomy extends to its physical presence, which is in a separate building several blocks away from the Labor Department's headquarters in Washington.)

Nevertheless, partisanship has clearly dominated its image in the eyes of the organizations that make up the department's environment. The department's raison d'être is set down in its charter: "to foster, promote, and develop the welfare of the wage earners of the United States, to improve their working conditions, and to advance their opportunities for profitable employment." Whether the perception of a constituency-oriented agency is valid or not—and there is reason to believe that it is at least partially valid, part of the time—is largely beside the point. The fact that this image exists, and that it provides those in its environment with a convenient interpretation for its views and behavior, presents the department's officials with a conundrum. If the department's legitimacy, not to mention its raw political muscle, rests upon its status as a representative of its labor constituency, this must place constraints upon what the department can do and what it can advocate as a public agency credibly claiming authority to act in furtherance of a more general interest.

Stagnation in a Period of State Expansion. The department's history up until the 1960s was one of stunted growth. Even today, it is the smallest of all cabinet departments in terms of number of personnel. The stagnation that plagued the Labor Department during much of this century comes into sharp focus when one considers that it did not grow at all during the Great Depression and World War II—times of great expansion in the size of the federal government overall. During 1932, the last year of the Hoover administration, appropriations for the department totaled $15 million. The highest appropriation for any of the war years from 1941 to 1944 was $14.1 million. While federal employment soared from 600,000 in 1932 to 3.5 million at the end of the war, the Labor Department's employment actually dropped from 6,000 to 5,230 in the same period.[42]

Virtually every major program and activity dealing with labor undertaken by the New Deal bypassed the Department of Labor (DOL). Most of them fell under independent boards and agencies created for specific purposes. The two main reasons for this were the perception of the department's bias toward labor and the fact that Roosevelt's labor secretary, Frances Perkins, enjoyed little popularity in Congress, with the labor unions, or in the press. Perkins fought to get the National Labor Relations Board and the Social Security Administration under the control of the DOL, but she could not muster sufficient political influence with any of the major sponsors of the legislation in Congress. Nor were any of the New Deal work relief programs, with the exception of the Civilian Conservation Corps, put under Labor Department supervision. The most important was the Works Progress Administration, which remained outside Labor's control. A similar aversion to the department was evidenced during World War II, with the National War Labor Board and the War Manpower Commission—which were in charge of assuring adequate supplies of labor for war production, settling labor-management disputes, and reconverting to peacetime employment—placed out of the purview of the department. Roosevelt considered a centralized manpower program administered by the Labor Department but bowed to public pressure when charges mounted that the agency was too "soft" on labor.[43] In sum, neither war nor a devastating economic crisis—traditionally two of the most familiar catalysts for state building—made any appreciable difference in the development or size of the Labor Department.

In Search of Renewal. By the 1950s the Department of Labor had become a bureaucratic backwater. It was headed by a secretary whose main function was that of representing organized labor's interests at the cabinet table. Labor secretaries, resembling medieval kings, reigned rather than ruled over a scattering of bureaucratic fiefdoms. The various agencies—the Bureau of Employment Security, the Bureau of Apprenticeship and Training, the Bureau of Labor Statistics, and others—jealously guarded their autonomy from the secretary.

President Eisenhower's labor secretary, James Mitchell, appointed an ad hoc committee of consultants to assist him in reevaluating the department's mission and organization. The group included a number of prominent manpower economists, the most noted being Eli Ginzberg, who concluded that the department should change its image and "become the Manpower agency of the Federal Government."[44] As discussed in chapter 3, the manpower issue emerged out of World War II experiences with manpower planning for production and with drafting men into the armed forces. These experiences revealed alarming inadequacies in the areas of health care, basic education, and technical skills among the nation's servicemen. Mitchell seized upon the manpower issue as one that held out the possibility of reinvigorating his stagnant department. Like others who drew attention to the issue, Mitchell sought to build support for a manpower policy by linking it to the broader issue of national security. He warned that "the United States' margin of advantage in the Cold War world is slipping. To prevent this, we must develop and use our skills."[45] Improvements in the preparedness and utilization of manpower were viewed as imperative in a precarious world, where the United States had assumed the major responsibility for checking Communist expansion. Mitchell proceeded to create an Office of Manpower Administration in 1954, headed by an assistant secretary for employment and manpower and staffed by leading labor economists interested in the manpower problem. Mitchell directed them to plan programs to meet the needs of civil defense and war mobilization.

The coming to power of the Kennedy administration set into motion liberal plans for a variety of domestic legislation, manpower among them. Senator Clark introduced his bill, the Vocational Retraining Act, written by the head of the vocational education program in the senator's state of Pennsylvania. As a new title to the Smith-Hughes Act, it would hand manpower retraining over to the Office of Education in HEW and the vocational education establishment at the local level. This set off a struggle between vocational education and the Labor Department over which agency would control the program and what kind of training would be provided—traditional classroom instruction or on-the-job training. Those who saw retraining as an employment issue argued for greater reliance upon on-the-job training. Those who saw it as an education issue regarded it as part of the traditional function of the schools. Vocational education viewed a job as an end, while manpower experts in the Labor Department viewed a job as both the means and the end. Vocational education was under severe attack for relying on archaic classroom methods and not meeting current economic needs with its traditional curricula. It seemed unwise to entrust a major new program to retrain experienced workers to the vocational educators, who, it was argued, were not doing a satisfactory job with the nation's youth, and whose methods were unsuited to retraining adult workers. Reliance on state vocational agencies limited the kind of training offered, since most voced programs operated through public schools. Manpower experts argued that an older worker in need of retraining, but with a limited or unsuccessful school experience, might refuse to participate in classroom training. By allowing the DOL to utilize nonacademic institutions, such as industry on-the-job training and union-run projects, a wider range of training opportunities existed. It offered the possibility of training in a wider variety of occupations, where practical application would benefit workers more than would textbook learning.

The Budget Bureau became a strong proponent of a bill that would place the reins of authority clearly in the hands of the Labor Department. The bureau was a vocal critic of the weaknesses of vocational education and was impressed with the success of on-the-job training in wartime industries and the rehabilitation of veterans under the GI Bill after the war. A DOL program would give the agency the freedom to utilize whatever facilities, either public or private, the DOL found suitable for training purposes, rather than being locked into the traditional voced approach.[46]

A relatively small group, the American Vocational Association, was nevertheless one of the most entrenched and influential lobbies in Washington, with an effective organization in each state and powerful allies on the labor committees in Congress.[47] Having had a major role in drafting the Clark bill, the AVA had a critical stake in its survival. Testifying before Clark's subcommittee, the AVA expressed its fear over any involvement by the Labor Department in what it viewed as a function of the Office of Education. If the DOL got a foothold in training, predicted the AVA, a "dual school system" would be created. Similar arguments came from the Council of Chief State School Officers—an association of state superintendents of public schools—which vigilantly watched against any federal encroachment on state and local control of education. Its power had been enhanced by the Eisenhower administration's program of minimizing federal involvement and protecting local control over education. Lister Hill, chairman of the Labor and Public Welfare Committee, warned Goldberg that any bill opposed by the education groups faced a rough sledding on Capitol Hill.[48] The AVA's influence was particularly strong among southerners, who along with conservative Republicans could block any legislation to come before the House Rules Committee.

The final legislation that was the Manpower Development and Training Act delicately balanced the interests of the Labor Department and those in charge of vocational education in the Department of HEW. Responsibility for MDTA was to be shared between the two agencies. The training program was divided into on-the-job training, for which the secretary of Labor was to have sole responsibility, and classroom training, which would be jointly shared by the secretaries of Labor and HEW. The case for giving DOL the chief responsibility lay in the argument that it was better equipped to handle the new program and that effective pressure could be brought to bear on the vocational education establishment to reform itself.[49] Far from ending the struggle between Labor and the voc ed administrators, the passage of MDTA merely transferred it to the bureaucratic arena.

Building Administrative Capacity. Employment policy (i.e., manpower) gave the Labor Department its stake in the great expansion of bureaucratic goods and services that began during the New Deal and took off in the decades after World War II. The legislative outpouring began with the Manpower Development and Training Act in 1962, followed almost immediately thereafter with numerous other programs under the War on Poverty. Questions related to administrative design and implementation were largely left to the agencies designated to carry out the programs, principally the Department of Labor. Its long-awaited deliverance from stagnation now presented a new hurdle: the department's administrative capacity had not been a problem when it was relegated to limited and peripheral functions, but if the department was going to carry out the activist policies that the federal government launched in the 1960s, it would have to be much more concerned with internal administrative control as well as competition from other agencies.

The quest for a workable administrative structure has been a major theme in the story of employment policy, running like a thread throughout the period looked at in this work. Congress played no positive role in revitalizing the department. Instead, it made the problem more challenging by producing a series of manpower training and work experience programs, giving little thought to how they related to each other and how they were to be implemented. The department faced a complex and formidable task, and still does in important respects. The department's efforts to build such a capacity in the 1960s may be divided into three separate (although related) tasks: (1) centralizing authority within the department, (2) acquiring control over those employment programs that Congress assigned to other federal agencies, and (3) finding organizations that could effectively administer the programs and deliver the services at the local level. The last task is the subject of the next chapter.

When the Manpower Development and Training Act was passed, on-the-job training was given to the Bureau of Apprenticeship and Training (BAT). BAT conducted no apprenticeship programs itself but acted mainly to certify the apprenticeship activities of its political constituency, the building trades unions of the AFL-CIO. Responsibility for classroom training was divided between the United States Employment Service (USES)—which, combined with the Unemployment Insurance System, made up the Bureau of Employment Security (BES)—and the Division of Vocational Education within HEW's Office of Education. Both BAT and BES had their own field offices, and BES had its own political constituency—the Interstate Conference of Employment Security Agencies (ICESA), a confederation representing the separate state employment services that made up USES. Two other bureaus were created in response to MDTA. One was the Office of Manpower, Automation, and Training (OMAT), which was responsible for program evaluation and research, and the Bureau of Work Programs (BWP), which administered the Neighborhood Youth Corps, a program created under the Equal Opportunity Act but assigned to the Labor Department rather than to OEO.

The key to pulling together the operations of BES, BAT, BWP, and OMAT was in building an administration that would be directly accountable to the secretary of labor. Secretary Willard Wirtz took the first step by creating the Manpower Administration in 1963. OMAT, without the benefit of either its own field staff or a political constituency, was quickly brought within the orbit of the Manpower Administration. Wirtz then moved to strengthen the hand of his manpower administrator, Stanley Ruttenberg, by elevating him to assistant secretary and creating a field staff of regional manpower administrators. This strengthened Ruttenberg's hand in dealing with BAT and BES. In 1967, the major ally of BAT and BES on Capitol Hill died, Congressman John Fogarty, chairman of the Labor-HEW Appropriations Subcommittee. Meanwhile, yet another manpower program was created—the Work Incentive Program (WIN), under the 1967 Social Security Act amendments. WIN was not assigned to any of the established bureaus. Wirtz and Ruttenberg then orchestrated a "realignment," where on-the-job training was taken out of BAT and, along with WIN, were put into BWP, which was renamed the Bureau of Work and Training Programs (BWTP). All staff functions were pulled out of the bureaus and put into the Manpower Administration under the decentralized regional structure.

Exerting control over these traditionally autonomous bureaus was especially difficult in the case of BES, which had long been dominated by the state-run U.S. Employment Service. The Employment Service was dominated by the unemployment insurance system (UI), which was financed from proceeds from the Social Security payroll tax on employers, and upon which the Employment Service relied for its budget. Control of the state services was in the hands of the individual state employment service directors, most of whom were recruited through the UI system, and their influential lobby—the Interstate Conference. The ICESA controlled how the money was spent and had a powerful ally in Wilbur Mills of the House Ways and Means Committee. Rooted in its role as administrator of the "work test" to unemployment insurance claimants, and attentive to the placement needs of local businesses (which were staunch opponents of any increases in the payroll tax), the Employment Service was a reluctant partner when it came to administering manpower services for the disadvantaged.[50]

In 1965 Wirtz created an Employment Service Task Force to review the relationship of the Employment Service to manpower policy. Chairman of the task force was George Shultz, Dean of the University of Chicago School of Business, who also had close ties to organized labor. Shultz chose Arnold Weber, a colleague, to act as his vice-chairman. Later, under Nixon, Shultz would become labor secretary and Weber assistant secretary for manpower. The task force stated that "the public Employment Service is in a strategic position to function as a manpower center at the community and labor market levels," discussed the service's shortcomings, and recommended reforms.[51] Cognizant of the power of BES, the ICESA, and their friends in Congress, the task force stopped short of recommending federal takeover of the Employment Service. But it did recommend enhancing the Manpower Administration's control over the agency by separating the Employment Service from the unemployment insurance system and emphasized increased federal leverage through the budget and program review process, as well as nontrust-fund support.

After a couple of attempts, Wirtz managed to get congressional approval, partly by assuring the ICESA that the states would retain control over the unemployment insurance system, and partly because Mills had become disenchanted with the Employment Service's involvement in manpower programs whose disadvantaged clients competed for attention with its traditional constituency, local businesses. But time ran out before the 1968 election, and the ball passed to the new administration. Once in office, Shultz and Weber organized an effective lobbying campaign to get congressional approval of the reorganization. One of their selling points to the ICESA was that the new administration was highly sympathetic to state interests and intended to utilize the Employment Service as "local manpower centers." In return, they asked to "put their own house in order in Washington."[52] In the end, Congress approved. BES and BWTP were combined to form the United States Training and Employment Service, a staff unit within the Manpower Administration.

The second task was to acquire the programs that were controlled by other agencies. Congress chose to divide administrative authority over the employment programs it created in the 1960s among several federal agencies. The Labor Department was the most important agency, but the Bureau of Vocational Education within the Department of Health, Education, and Welfare (HEW) controlled that portion of the MDTA classroom training. Authority was further fractionated when major portions of the manpower programs under the Economic Opportunity Act were handed to the Office of Economic Opportunity (OEO). According to one observer, the attempt by Labor to control these programs and bureaus made manpower "one of the more spectacular bureaucratic battlefields during the decade."[53]

Aggressive lobbying by the Labor Department helped bring many of OEO's programs under its control. It acquired Special Impact, New Careers, and Operation Mainstream, to add to the Neighborhood Youth Corps, which it already administered. Labor's efforts were aided by the controversy stirred by OEO's community action agencies (CAAs). The CAAs were blamed for creating turmoil at the local level, where they often clashed with elected officials and such established manpower providers as the Employment Service. The result was that OEO's bargaining position in Congress was severely weakened. By 1969 OEO was no longer administering any manpower programs directly, although OEO programs delegated to the Labor Department still often operated through the CAAs.

Labor had several advantages over HEW, as well. Manpower programs occupied a much more privileged position in the Labor Department than in HEW. The Manpower Administration was put under an assistant secretary for Manpower in the Department of Labor, but in HEW manpower training was buried as a "bureau within a bureau" of the Office of Education. Vocational education in general is something of an unwanted stepchild within the Office of Education, which has concentrated its resources and attention on general education. The Labor Department also dominated in the budgetary process. The account for MDTA-institutional programs was assigned to Labor, despite joint administration. The Manpower Administration enjoyed a close relationship with the Bureau of the Budget, where manpower examiners shared the on-the-job training perspective of the Labor Department, rather than the classroom approach to training dominant in HEW.

Thus nearly all federal programs had fallen into the hands of DOL's Manpower Administration. According to one observer at the time, "The new structure is designed to reduce the power of categorical program specialists, who had previously been assigned to BES and BWTP," as well as to OEO and HEW. Control was under the Manpower administrator, whose deputy maintained a direct line of authority to the regions. Thus by the late 1960s, the Labor Department was largely successful in achieving the first two objectives listed above.

What have proven to be much more intractable problems are finding an effective agency at the state or local level to plan, to allocate resources, and to administer the programs; and making an appropriate division of responsibilities between Washington, the states, and local governments. Building effective administrative and service delivery mechanisms at the local level has been by far the most problematic and continues to bedevil policy makers in Washington. Local administration and service delivery benefited substantially by the Labor Department getting its house in order and removing HEW and OEO from the picture. But deciding how much discretion at the local level can be afforded without sacrificing national objectives, to whom the discretion should be given, and finding (or creating) dependable organizations that can deliver employment services at the local level—all these questions remain unresolved. These topics, therefore, deserve more extended discussion.

CONCLUSION

Political institutions have had a variety of impacts on employment policy. They have filtered out some kinds of proposals and facilitated the adoption of alternatives. The structure of institutions determines the organizational capacity and incentives for formulating and carrying out certain policies but not others.

First, the chances for passage of far-reaching, large-scale policies have been diminished in favor of more limited, incremental policy changes. The former kind of proposals broaden the scope of conflict within the employment policy arena, making it more likely that opposing interests will mobilize. American political institutions, for instance, have provided a variety of access points for opponents of change to dilute or block altogether full-employment legislation, which would have almost certainly required the federal government to reorder its economic policy priorities and increase spending and public investment to guarantee jobs to anyone unable to find employment in the private sector. When large-scale changes have not been blocked, they have been delayed because fragmentation makes deadlock more likely within Congress and between Congress and the president. CETA is the most relevant example here. As a result, those who have sought to expand the role of the federal government in addressing unemployment have resorted to an incremental strategy. In the 1960s a number of narrow-gauged categorical programs to provide training and work experience were adopted, and in the 1970s public service employment was expanded and administrative reform accomplished in a series of steps. In short, fragmented institutions give to opponents of change, especially large-scale change, the leverage to influence policy that they would not be availed of in a more centralized arrangement.

Second, institutions have greatly increased the incoherence of employment policy. Employment programs proliferated in a haphazard manner during the 1960s, reflecting the segmented approach to policy making through the committee system and the fluid style of legislative entrepreneurs. This pattern was mirrored in the executive branch, where a set of autonomous federal agencies attempted to administer a hopelessly confusing jumble of programs. It is clear that the requisite administrative capacity was not available when the programs emerged, and the Labor Department, an underdeveloped backwater of the federal bureaucracy, spent much of the decade building such a capacity. Rationalization of the system in the 1970s did not put an end to incoherence. Out of the competing objectives of the Nixon administration and the Democrats in Congress came CETA, which decentralized authority over the programs at the same time that it augmented national goals. No longer would employment policy simply train the disadvantaged, but it would give jobs to the cyclically unemployed and provide relief to local governments. These goals were not compatible, particularly in the context of competing goals between national and subnational political authorities.

Third, the structure has contributed to maintaining economic policy exclusively as a macroeconomic management task, preventing the integration of microinstruments with macroinstruments, and consigning employment programs to a separate institutional subsystem. It hardly needs be said that attacking unemployment is one of the major objectives of economic policy. It stands to reason, therefore, that measures to address joblessness belong, if anywhere, within the scheme of interventions concerned with management of the economy. Economic policy is monopolized at the highest levels of the executive branch by macroeconomists, who define policy options almost exclusively in macro terms. The Labor Department lies outside this circle, and its views are often regarded as partisan and particularistic. Proposals to create an institutional mechanism that would elevate employment policy to the highest levels of the executive branch, such as Clark's for a Council of Manpower Advisers, have been rejected. At times, economic policy makers have turned to employment programs on an ad hoc basis, usually during emergency episodes of high unemployment. But the normal practice has been for those who formulate economic policy to ignore job creation, manpower training, and the like, treating them as peripheral to the task of managing the economy. Employment policy is largely the province of the Labor Department and the labor committees in Congress. Within this institutional arena, issues tend to be construed narrowly as problems of administrative control, service delivery, and specific provisions of programs. Thus, beginning with the MDTA, conflict within the employment subsystem has been limited to such issues as whether classroom or on-the-job training is most appropriate.

A fourth consequence is that policies with indirect, long-term benefits are eschewed in favor of granting direct benefits on a short-term basis. There is limited interest in broad policy mandates in which long-range goals are set and the particular distribution of benefits and costs is uncertain, such as full-employment guarantees. There is even less interest in encouraging labor market planning, or commitments to investment in measures that promise long-term payoffs. Reforms in the formulation and implementation of policy offer few rewards and threaten to upset existing power relationships. They are taken only when the system collapses. Measures that directly clash with reelection goals, such as relocation incentives, are rejected. In addition, Congress becomes mobilized most often during times of an immediate economic crisis, specifically during recessions. Measures that attack cyclical unemployment tend to get greater attention than those that address structural unemployment.

6

Employment Policy as an Intergovernmental Dilemma

CERTAIN ACTIVITIES of government require a decentralized administrative structure if they are to be undertaken. Where relevant conditions vary widely across local settings, the intelligence for making decisions is in the field. Thus many programs can be implemented effectively only if subunits have sufficient discretion to respond to variation from area to area. It is vital in such cases that the political and bureaucratic incentives at the local level are congruent with the policy goals articulated at the center.

Those tasks related to employment policy fall squarely into this category. This is especially the case for a positive labor market policy, but it applies as well for the more limited policy that the United States has pursued. Implementing employment programs is a complex task that cannot be adequately managed from the center, because the information needed for making rational decisions by those in Washington is lacking. These limitations are magnified in a nation as large and diverse as the United States.

Three related characteristics of labor market intervention make it essential for there to be administrative capability and effective service delivery at the local level. First, local and regional labor markets vary in the particular problems they experience. In one area there may be an oversupply of available labor, while in others there may be a shortage. The skills demanded by employers in one area may differ from those in another. Demographic and occupational groups each have their own employment problems, and such groups are found in some areas but not in others.

Second, employment programs involve providing multiple services—forecasting trends in supply and demand, evaluating and testing clients, counseling clients, providing remedial education and skill training, and placing clients in jobs. These activities must be integrated in order for unemployed or underemployed individuals to smoothly enter and reenter the labor market. For example, individuals who have been trained will need an effective placement service to secure employment. But a placement service is only effective if individuals graduate from training programs that have good reputations among employers and that teach skills in demand. Thus employment programs consist of a concatenation of interdependent activities.

Because of the need to provide multiple services, employment programs require coordination and communication among several community organizations involved in the labor market, among them schools and colleges, businesses, employment offices, trade unions, and social service agencies. Administrators must know which service deliverers to utilize and which ones to avoid. There is great variation across communities in the competence and responsiveness of different providers. In some localities, the U.S. Employment Service is effective, in others it is not. In some localities, classroom training can best be provided by vocational schools, in others community colleges or opportunity industrial centers (OICs) are preferred. In some communities, local businessmen are committed to the idea of employment programs and have established linkages with schools and government agencies. Participants in employment programs pass in and out of these organizations before, during, and after their participation in the programs. Successful transitions from school to work, or from one job to another, depend upon the forging of effective linkages between the organizations. Administrators at the local level can contribute greatly to effective transition by forging these linkages.

Third, once the need for decentralization is recognized, there is an additional set of problems stemming from the intergovernmental nature of a federal system such as the United States. The challenge here is in insuring that the necessary discretion in planning and management that is vested at the local level leads to outcomes that are consistent with broad national goals established by Congress and the administration in power. These may include serving particular groups in the population, such as those living below the poverty level, or it may mean using resources to achieve certain outcomes, like creating new jobs in the public sector. Policy makers in Washington must be assured that, not only will local administration be conducted competently, but that those at the local level will not pursue administrative or political objectives that may conflict with those established by Congress. There must be a flow of communication and monitoring between the center and the periphery to carry out employment programs effectively so that national policy objectives can be realized within the context of diverse local needs and problems. Decentralization can be successful only where there is integration among public authorities at the different levels of government.

The federal government's traditional response to the need for decentralization has not been to directly administer programs through a network of field offices but, instead, to offer grants-in-aid as inducements to subnational units of government for carrying out its programs. Reliance upon the competence and commitment of state and local governments has been possible, because these governments have been prepared (to some degree at least) to implement the policy objectives that Washington has deemed desirable. In some areas, like aid for elementary and secondary education, state and local administrative capacity already has been in place. Decades of public education at the local level have led to a unified, well-established system of state education agencies, local school boards, and schools.[1] In other areas, the federal government took upon itself the task of building mechanisms at the local level to administer and deliver services. Agriculture is the classic example, where the federal government created the Extension Service, local farm bureaus, and land grant colleges to carry out its farm programs.[2]

Neither of these solutions has succeeded in the area of employment policy, however. No reliable administrative and delivery structures already existed when federal manpower programs began. And efforts by federal officials to build such structures have met with limited success thus far.

THE EMPLOYMENT SERVICE AND THE
PROBLEM OF SERVICE DELIVERY

There is perhaps no public agency at the local level with more important tasks to fulfill in the employment area than the U.S. Employment Service. The service's primary task, aside from administering unemployment insurance benefits, is to fill employment vacancies with qualified workers. As a clearinghouse for employers and prospective employees, it is strategically located at the center of the labor market in each community. A properly functioning service does more than efficiently match employers with people seeking work, however. It also conducts placement-related activities like vocational counseling, testing, and gathering information necessary for forecasting trends in labor supply and demand. It is crucial for vocational educators and those who seek training or retraining to know about the pace and nature of automation in particular occupations, the likelihood of labor surpluses and shortages in various markets and localities, and changes in the skills demanded by employers. The Employment Service needs to know what kind of training is most needed and for what skills, for meeting local demands. It needs to know where vacancies exist and whether relocation to some other area is advisable. It needs to select trainees and, to do so, needs to have knowledge of available workers, their aptitudes, and their experience, and be able to motivate potential trainees. Finally, it needs to know which facilities are available for training, which are tailored to the needs of its clients, and so forth.

The Employment Service in the United States (now called the Job Service) has not played this pivotal role. The service's placement record has been dismal throughout its history. One measure of the effectiveness and importance of the Employment Service is a measure called the penetration rate, which measures the number of job vacancies filled by the Employment Service as a proportion of the total number of vacancies filled in the economy. The penetration rate of the U.S. Employment Service has been quite low—about 10 percent throughout the 1960s and 1970s—a figure far below that of other industrialized nations.[3] Moreover, the jobs handled by the Employment Service are overwhelmingly low-wage positions. The average wage for Employment Service placements in 1980 was $3.99 per hour, not far above the minimum wage rate of $3.10 per hour.[4] The inability of the U.S. Employment Service to penetrate the labor market affects not only placement but how well it conducts its other activities as well.

In comparative perspective, two factors suggest why the U.S. Employment Service has been marginalized. One is the existence of private employment agencies with which the public service must compete, and the other is the absence of mandatory employer listings with the service. With the exception of Britain, all countries of the European Economic Community prohibit the operation of private employment exchanges. Many of them also require employers to notify the employment service of all their job vacancies, and obligate every worker who is looking for a job to register with the service.[5]

Development of the Employment Service, 1900–1960

The poor performance of the U.S. Employment Service is rooted in its historical development. Employment offices were established in those states where Progressive reformers found a hospitable climate for establishing labor exchanges that attempted to rationalize the labor market by more efficiently matching workers with available jobs.[6] Reformers pressed for federal legislation to set up a national network of exchanges but faced concerted opposition from business, labor, and private employment agencies, all of which had their own reasons for resisting federal involvement. A major recommendation of the Progressives was for a federal mechanism to regulate the flow of labor, patterned after the Federal Reserve Board's regulation of credit. Many of them were economists who were aware of developments across the Atlantic, and their idea for a regulatory mechanism bears a striking resemblance to contemporary employment services in many European countries.[7]

World War I accomplished what the Progressives could not. The federal government was forced to set up a nationwide system of employment offices to plan the allocation and utilization of labor for war production, under the aegis of the United States Employment Service (USES). No sooner had the war ended than pressures mounted to dismantle the USES. A common argument of the agency's opponents was that the service was being used as a patronage machine and a device for organized labor to coerce employers. The Labor Department was established to represent and promote the interests of labor in the councils of government. As an agency within the Labor Department, the fledgling USES could hardly avoid its identification with the labor movement.

With the abolition of the USES and the end of the Progressive Era, the network of employment offices quickly decayed. In Europe, on the other hand, the war served to permanently consolidate national control over employment services. Uniform standards replaced local diversity, and private agencies' activities were curtailed or outlawed altogether. The establishment of unemployment insurance schemes in many countries during and after the war greatly contributed to these developments, because the administration of benefits required a national network of employment offices. But in the United States, the retarded development of welfare state provisions, like unemployment benefits, went hand in hand with inaction on the employment office front.

It was not until the height of the Great Depression, with the passage of the Wagner-Peyser Act in 1933, that a new USES was established. To dispel suspicions that what was being created was a powerful, nationally directed service, those who wrote the Wagner-Peyser Act made sure to establish a federal-state system of administration, where the two levels of government would share jointly in the financing and operation of the system.

The service was immediately enlisted to recruit labor for the work relief programs of the New Deal, but its activities were confined to those states without employment services of their own. The passage of the Social Security Act in 1935 brought about the completion of the system of state employment services. In order to comply with Title III, which set up the unemployment insurance program, all states were required to establish agencies capable of paying claims and making referrals under the "suitable work test."

The first year in which benefits were paid under the program was 1938, a year that saw a return to Depression-level joblessness. Under the welter of massive benefit claims, the primary function of the U.S. Employment Service became the administration of the unemployment insurance (UI) program. A critical feature of the system is the way in which the financing of the Employment Service became inextricably tied to the UI program. The Wagner-Peyser Act originally called for Employment Service offices to be supported by federal grants-in-aid on a fifty-fifty matching basis with the states. However, the Depression years placed such a heavy burden on the new service that from the beginning the states could not manage the drain of resources, and funds were tapped from the UI payroll tax. Henceforth, Employment Service operations were paid out of the federal UI tax on employers.

This financial arrangement gave the business community a proprietary interest in the operation of the Employment Service in each state. Since they paid to support the system, they felt it should serve their purposes—and as inexpensively as possible. And since the Employment Service had to operate during a period of low demand for labor, the need to attract employers to use the service became the primary focus of the staff. Local offices tended to refer only the best qualified applicants to fill job orders, in the hope that employers would be encouraged to send more orders. According to one expert, "screening has remained a formidable obstacle to all efforts to shift the emphasis of the employment service in accordance with changing national needs."[8] With its own source of revenues, the payroll tax also gave the Employment Service financial independence from the federal budget and appropriations process, insulating the service from political control in Washington.

During World War II the Employment Service was taken over by the federal government for wartime planning. When the war concluded, the question arose as to whether the service should remain federalized or whether its operation should be returned to the states. Fears of a return to Depression-level unemployment and the conversion to Keynesianism led to efforts to adopt a full-employment policy in 1945. Many full-employment advocates saw the Employment Service as a key mechanism for assuring that available jobs were filled with available workers within a framework of a national full-employment policy. As the Full Employment Bill was debated in Congress, the leadership of the USES contemplated a six-point program for actively participating in carrying out its new mandate. Liberals argued that the preceding years demonstrated that the unemployment problem was national in scope, and that the responsibility for it clearly resided with the only level of government capable of taking the necessary measures, in Washington. If it remained in the grip of the UI system and local businesses, the Employment Service could not be oriented to perform its role in implementing a policy of full employment.

The attempt to keep the Employment Service under federal control, like the full-employment struggle itself, failed. Defeated in their attempt to retain federalization outright, liberals in Congress tried to maintain de facto federal control by strengthening the supervisory provisions of the Wagner-Peyser Act. This effort drew heavy opposition as well, particularly one amendment to permit the secretary of labor to determine "reasonable referral standards." Critics of the state-run service, such as organized labor, complained that the states were using the UI program to depress wage levels by forcing workers to accept low-wage, low-skill jobs under the threat of a loss of benefits. The UI laws in each state stipulated that, under the suitable work test, receipt of benefits was contingent on workers making themselves available for positions comparable in earnings and skill level to their previous records of employment. Critics claimed that unemployed workers were forced to take lower wage jobs, enabling employers to keep wage rates depressed, reducing the costs of UI, and in turn, keeping their UI taxes low.

For these and other reasons, the stakes of business lobbyists in the program were high. They were joined by the Interstate Conference of Employment Security Agencies (ICESA), a group composed of the administrators of the Employment Service in each state. As a pressure group supported by the UI tax, the ICESA proved to be a formidable opponent during the postwar period to any changes in the Employment Service–UI system that might increase federal control and encroach on the autonomy of the state agencies.[9]

In most states, Employment Service functions and UI functions have been jointly administered by a single state body—the employment security agency. The mission and orientations of each staff differs. Employment Service functionaries are engaged in vocational guidance and placement and are more likely protagonists for individuals needing employment assistance. The UI civil servants, on the other hand, are claims examiners and are more likely to see themselves as "guardians and protectors of a financial system" against possible cheating and exploitation. The recessionary environment of the 1950s placed a great burden on the UI system, pulling many Employment Service personnel into UI work. Federalization of the Employment Service during World

War II (which left UI still in the hands of the states) gave UI personnel a seniority advantage, leaving them in command of the postwar employment security system. State administrators, therefore, tended to come from the UI side of the system. Thus the ICESA has been dominated by a seniority system that reflects the dominance of UI throughout the entire state administration.

The next largest group of state administrators come from a background in small business. Together, old-line administrators and employers-turned-public executives form a powerful alliance whose primary interest is in the insurance, rather than the Employment Service, aspect of employment security. Their instinct is for thrift and economy first, and service second. Finally, state administrators are usually tied closely to state politicians, a factor that helps immunize them from Washington. In short, the leadership of the state agencies has tended to be highly conservative. Their primary interest lies in the management of the UI system rather than making improvements in the kinds of labor market services assigned to the Employment Service. One indication of this neglect has been the Employment Service's very low penetration rate, mentioned earlier.

Responsive only to themselves and the local business community, which funded their operations (and whose main interest was to keep the UI tax as low as possible), the ICESA made sure these views were reflected in Washington. It had powerful allies on the House HEW-Labor Appropriations Subcommittee in Congress and also in the Labor Department. The local orientation of the Employment Service's constituent state agencies was reflected in the Labor Department by the Bureau of Employment Security (BES). BES was one of the department's bureaucratic fiefdoms that protected the state services. The USES was under BES supervision. The ICESA and BES had a powerful ally in the House HEW-Labor Appropriations Subcommittee. Subcommittee members were attuned to the bureaucratic and business interests that wanted to keep things as they were. In sum, the entire Employment Service constituted a classic subgovernment—protective of its own bureaucratic and clientele interests and resistant to any outside pressures seeking to challenge the status quo. What was intended under the Wagner-Peyser Act to be a partnership with a strong national orientation had gradually become "a confederacy of autonomous state agencies, each calling its own tune."[10]

The Employment Service Since 1960: A Reluctant Soldier in the War on Poverty

When Congress enacted the Manpower Development and Training Act (MDTA), it left to the secretary of labor to decide who would deliver services and how they would be delivered. As the most ubiquitous labor market organization in the country, the USES was assumed to have a major role in the program. The USES was knighted the "Chosen Instrument of the Manpower Revolution."[11] Through its affiliated state agencies and 1,900 local offices, the service was designated the "presumptive provider of manpower services." Federal agencies were to contract with the service whenever possible. The Employment Service would provide services directly or subcontract to other organizations, such as businesses, to run on-the-job training.

At first, many in the Employment Service welcomed its designation as the presumptive provider under the MDTA. The new program would give it a new lease. In the late 1950s and early 1960s, the service had made a serious effort to improve its capacity for universal service and to prove itself a worthy competitor with private agencies. Offices were relocated where the jobs were, and offices in outlying neighborhoods were closed down. Separate offices were opened for special occupational groupings (e.g., manufacturing, clerical and sales, professional, casual) in areas in easy reach of employers and workers. The language of the Wagner-Peyser Act, "to promote and develop a national system of employment offices for men, women, and juniors" meant that the Employment Service was to be available to all people. These changes made a great deal of sense from the standpoint of universal service and during the persistent recessionary environment of the 1950s. Staff energy was directed at raising the efficiency of the placement function, because it was believed that an improved labor exchange was a significant antirecessionary device.

The early optimism quickly dissipated when it became clear that MDTA, initially designed to serve the needs of workers displaced by automation, was being turned into a poverty program. The response of the Employment Service to its new assignment was more reactionary than revolutionary. Its administrators, who believed that they were going to be working with a population of predominantly white, prime-age, experienced workers, found that they were being pushed to focus their resources on mostly young, disadvantaged, minority clients. The poverty program's emphasis on certain groups went against the mission of providing a universal service. A bureaucracy wedded closely to the status quo could not be exhorted to act as a "catalyst in social change."[12] The service was trying to dispel its image among mainstream workers and employers as an unemployment agency because of its identification with UI claims and its service mainly to the secondary labor market. The stress on the poverty population did not sit well with the service's traditional clients in the business community. They were used to an Employment Service that was anything but a catalyst for social change.

Antipoverty efforts were greeted with suspicion, because they threatened the establishment in each community.

The Labor Department's (DOL) leadership had to reckon with the Employment Service's subgovernment if it hoped to use the service to deliver manpower services to the poor. The DOL spent the 1960s in repeated attempts to get the service under the control of the newly created Manpower Administration. Not only did its traditionally neglected placement, counseling, and labor market information functions need to be strengthened, but it had to develop and initiate training programs tailored to the needs of each locality. Throughout the decade, the Manpower Administration repeatedly sought to exercise control over the service through the budget process, reform of the basic Employment Service legislation, and through the introduction of modern management techniques in planning and budgeting. It was, and is, the failure of the service to adequately adapt to this new role that has served as a major impediment to effective manpower service delivery.

The Manpower Administration's first attempt to redirect the state services came when Congress appropriated additional funds from the UI trust fund to take care of the extra work load expected when the poverty program got under way. To make sure that the funds were used for specialized services to disadvantaged groups, the Manpower Administration insisted that the services come up with detailed plans as to how they would use the money. The services balked and demanded that the money be apportioned across-the-board to all states, using existing apportionment formulas.

The Manpower Administration next tried the legislative route. In 1965 Secretary Wirtz appointed a task force headed by George Shultz, then the dean of the Graduate School of Business at the University of Chicago. The task force recommended that part of the Employment Service's budget be drawn from general revenues. Services performed by the Employment Service related to the national manpower program were to be freed from support through the UI system. It also recommended that the service change its planning and budget procedures to reflect the goals of the program. A bill that embodied the recommendations was emasculated in the Senate and died in the House.

Next, the DOL attempted to modernize the service's planning and budgeting by ending the long-established interdependency between the state services and the Bureau of Employment Security. The Manpower Administration replaced the leadership of the BES with individuals it had selected. This allowed the DOL to gain control in Washington, but it had limited effect at the state level, where the staffs remained inadequate and poorly paid. State civil service rules prevented upgrading salaries and staff qualifications. The effects of low salaries are high turnover and an inability to attract talented individuals. Upgrading the staff by establishing higher qualifications was necessary, especially in the area of counseling. It was also difficult to attract minorities into the service, because of its poor reputation among them. The federal government has gained the authority under the law to set standards for salary levels and job classification. But strict enforcement is not a useful tool, since noncompliance can only be handled by a withdrawal of funds.[13]

While the Labor Department attempted to recruit the Employment Service into the antipoverty effort, Congress created several other training and work experience programs under the control of the Office of Economic Opportunity (OEO). The OEO was established to run the War on Poverty because, at the national level, it was thought that old-line agencies like Labor and HEW were hidebound and unprepared to direct their energies toward helping the poor. It was empowered to establish community action agencies (CAAs) at the local level to carry out its programs. The CAAs were set up to involve the poor and their advocates in mobilizing resources. They too were deliberately created outside established local bureaucracies like the Employment Service, which had a reputation for being unresponsive to the poor. The struggle between the Labor Department and OEO in Washington was reflected in the struggle at the local level between the Employment Service and the CAAs, which repeatedly locked horns in local turf battles. "Both correctly saw manpower as the key to control and power in the urban ghetto areas."[14] The struggle finally ended when the entire community action program ran into trouble in Congress, after it had created considerable political turmoil in several communities. With OEO on the defensive, the Labor Department was able to bring OEO programs under its control. This resolution was more of a loss for the community action agencies than it was a boon to the Employment Service, however, whose reputation in most communities did not improve.

In the late 1960s it became clear that new legislation would be needed to fold the existing categorical grants-in-aid into a block grant that would be administered by officials at the state and local levels. The Nixon administration's original reform proposal reflected the Labor Department's longstanding proprietary interest in its own agency. It appeared that the Employment Service would finally become the "presumptive provider of manpower services." The service would formulate statewide manpower plans and use its facilities to deliver the services or contract with others for their delivery. State manpower plans were required to include programs conducted under the Wagner-Peyser Act. The DOL argued that local governments be required to use the service, because "it is clearly not a desirable management posture for the same agency to support both a public employment service under state aegis and a competitive public employment service under local government aegis."[15]

But when the proposal was sent to Congress, one of the few points of unanimous agreement between virtually all of the witnesses who testified was that the Employment Service should not be given the status of presumptive provider. Opposition to the Employment Service among members of Congress, and especially local groups and agencies, was practically universal. State governors, who took little interest in manpower reform generally, never came to the defense of the state employment agencies. The White House, too, insisted that the service's role be left to the discretion of local governments. Forcing prime sponsors to go through the service would be inconsistent with vesting authority in elected generalists. To provide local officials with maximum flexibility, utilization of the Employment Service was left, therefore, as an option. Local managers of CETA were not required to use the Employment Service, and in effect, the CETA prime-sponsor system established a labor market agency at the local level that duplicated many of the activities of the service. In most localities, satisfactory relationships between CETA operators and the Employment Service were not established. The reputation of the service at the local level among all groups, including business, remains at a low ebb.

In sum, the Employment Service is both a cause and an effect of institutional failure: the service has been unable or unwilling to perform any of the tasks for which it has been called upon (with the exception of administering UI). This, in turn, is a result of the pervasive localism and decentralism in American political life. The tight grip of the state agencies, the attitudes of local business, and Congress's parochialism all conspired against transforming the service into an arm of national administration. Decentralization bred autonomy, and by the 1960s, the service had become the inflexible, distrusted institution that it is today. Little wonder, then, that its role has been marginal in the conduct of employment policy.

THE PROBLEM OF ADMINISTRATIVE DESIGN

From Centralization to Decentralization

When employment programs first came on board in the 1960s, neither Congress nor the executive branch fully appreciated the inherent complexities of implementation. These complexities were compounded by the way Congress designed the programs. Problems in the implementation of MDTA were clear from the start. As early as 1963 a study by Senator Clark's subcommittee highlighted the difficulties of inter-agency coordination.[16] With the addition of several similar programs under the poverty program a couple of years later, the situation became intolerable.

The major problem was overcentralization. Grants were channeled to state agencies, or in some cases directly to local areas. In either case, Washington kept a tight rein, by approving all contracts made with service providers and by maintaining rigid guidelines designating the eligibility criteria for participants, the services to be provided, and who would deliver them. In addition to the sheer burden of approving 50,000 contracts each year, it proved impossible to understand the employment problems of each community—who needed help, what mix of services they most needed, and which service providers were best equipped to deliver them. The specific purposes and rigid guide-lines laid down for each categorical program made it impossible to flexibly tailor programs to local conditions.

Second, programs were administered by different agencies in Wash-ington—the Labor Department, the Office of Economic Opportunity, and the Department of Health, Education, and Welfare—with no coor-dination among them. The programs had grown out of the fragmented, individualistic legislative process in Congress, where little attention was paid to how the programs might overlap and compete with each other. Fragmentation at the top was reflected in chaos below, where the services were delivered.

Despite these problems, it was not until after a prolonged stalemate that a new administrative arrangement, consolidating and decentraliz-ing the programs, was established in 1973. Initial efforts at reform, within the established administrative structure, proved inadequate. New legislation was needed. Most authority for planning and managing the programs devolved to state and local elected officials under the Comprehensive Employment and Training Act.

Administrative Efforts at Reform. One of the Clark subcommittee's recommendations led to the creation of the President's Commission on Manpower (PCOM), established to bring together the heads of various federal agencies with jurisdiction in the area. President Johnson ap-pointed Labor Secretary Wirtz the committee chairman and Garth Man-gum its first executive director.[17] The PCOM sent three-man teams representing the DOL, HEW, and OEO to major metropolitan areas in order to coordinate the jumble of programs. These teams discovered a desperate need for integration, but after limited success they were eventually disbanded.

Another attempt at coordination was made in 1967 with the Concentrated Employment Program (CEP), established at Wirtz's behest, after it was realized that the greatest poverty-related unemployment was in central cities. The CEPs were to concentrate manpower funds in one source in each targeted community, so that the funds could be used flexibly, to suit the community's specific needs and to deliver an uninterrupted sequence of services based upon each enrollee's employability.[18]

The most ambitious attempt to bring order out of chaos was the development of the Cooperative Area Manpower Planning System (CAMPS). The CAMPS experiment focused on coordinating state governments. Unlike CEP, CAMPS worked primarily at the state rather than at the community level. The Labor Department forged an agreement with the other agencies to install CAMPS committees at the state and regional levels, which would operate under DOL guidelines. Local plans were approved by state CAMPS committees, which in turn sent them on to regional committees.

Each of these attempts produced little progress in terms of rationalizing administration. Manpower programs continued to proliferate, and many of the most important programs were left out of these experiments. By 1968, the Job Corps, the Community Action Program, and other OEO programs were not yet under the control of the Labor Department. The CEPs foundered because they were unable to act as single units. Often there were lags between the enrollees' completion of one step and their movement on to the next, precipitating frequent dropouts. More important were the jurisdictional battles that ensued between the Employment Service, which under MDTA and CEP was designated the "presumptive provider of manpower services," and OEO's community action agencies, which regarded themselves as the representatives of the poor. Also left outside of the CEP structure were the classroom training programs of MDTA, which operated under HEW's Office of Education, and the newly created JOBS program (Job Opportunities in the Business Sector), operated by the National Alliance of Business.

CAMPS committees increased communication between the various agencies, but they did not produce any substantial coordination of the various programs. Each program, still under the control of its parent agency, was constrained by its own budget and procedures. CAMPS planning documents were merely compilations of each individual agency's plans. The committees could not alter the flow of federal funds appropriated by Congress. The root of the problem, and that which CAMPS could not grapple with, was that each federal agency retained

authority over decisions involving eligibility criteria, funding allocations, and the kinds of activities that grant recipients were permitted to
undertake.

Many agencies felt the Labor Department tended to dominate
CAMPS. Although each agency was supposed to be equal on the
CAMPS committees, the state committees were chaired by Employment
Service directors, and the regional and national committees by the
Manpower Administration. The DOL was, in addition, the source of
guidelines and economic data upon which the plans were based. It
will be recalled from the previous chapter that the Labor Department
centralized control internally by establishing the Manpower Administration. This allowed it to gain control over its own semiautonomous
bureaus, each of which was responsible for parts of the various training
programs, and to acquire many of the programs that came under the
jurisdiction of OEO and HEW.

Centralizing authority at the top made it easier for the department
to attempt to build a mechanism at the local level to coordinate the
programs. The Labor Department utilized its regional manpower administrators as stepping-stones for devolving manpower planning and
operations to state and local governments. In 1970 and 1971 it granted
its regional offices authority to decide project applications previously
handled in Washington. At the same time, Labor actively moved to
push decisions down to the mayoral level. In 1969 the department had
encouraged mayors to assume leadership of local CAMPS committees,
but few did. Usually the people put in charge were the managers of
manpower programs from the local Employment Service or community
action agency, the very organizations whose authority these actions
were supposed to diminish. But in 1971 the Manpower Administration
began a series of field experiments, using more than $16 million in
grants to local officials to finance their efforts to establish CAMPS
committees.[19] At around the same time, it made block grants available
for pilot programs in seven selected state and local governments across
the nation to plan and implement comprehensive manpower services.
These served as prototypes for a nationwide transition to a the new
administrative structure. The Emergency Employment Act, which specified for the first time in legislation that state and local officials would
be prime sponsors, also helped place local officials at the center of
administering DOL programs. By 1972, the Labor Department was one
of the most highly decentralized of all federal agencies and served as a
model for other departments.[20]

These attempts at administrative rationalization threatened to un-
ravel the linkages between individual federal agencies and their local

clients and service providers. Each federal agency saw consolidation as
a threat to its control over its own programs and viewed with suspicion
efforts to transfer control to elected officials. Providers like the Employment Service and vocational education had cemented relations with
agencies in Washington and feared that their future operations would
be left to the mercy of governors and mayors who might be insensitive
to their interests.

Leaving aside their less than spectacular achievements, CEP,
CAMPS, and the devolution experiments provided the Manpower Administration valuable experience in implementing a system of local
control and helped mobilize local officials behind legislation for a new
administrative arrangement. By the time the Nixon administration took
office in 1969, a bureaucratic environment favorable to reform had been
fostered. According to Levitan and Zickler, "Those who wrote CETA
and drafted its regulations drew heavily on those experiences."[21]

Legislative Efforts at Reform.   The Nixon administration's first proposal, the Manpower Training Act (MTA), placed considerable stress
on the role of the states, rather than local governments. This had been
recommended by manpower experts, and it reflected the planning
structure under CAMPS. Governors were empowered to allocate the
federal dollars appropriated for the programs, designate local prime
sponsors, and establish a comprehensive manpower agency, which
would be headed by each state's employment service. The agency's
tasks were to approve local plans annually, in accordance with a plan
developed for the state as a whole, and to evaluate and monitor local
performance. In order to facilitate planning that encompassed entire
labor markets, local government jurisdictions with 75 percent or more
of the total population in a metropolitan area were automatically designated as the prime sponsors for their areas. Vesting most authority
in the states had several advantages. The states possessed superior
administrative capacity in basic education, job placement, and vocational education. The states also encompassed broader geographic
areas, facilitating planning, which was difficult to accomplish within
balkanized metropolitan areas. Local interests could be protected from
discriminatory state action by promulgating pass-through provisions.

The proposal had no chance in Congress because of its stress on
state governors and the Employment Service. A fairly potent lobby at
the local level materialized opposing the dominant role given to the
states in the MTA. Advocacy groups for the clients joined in an unlikely
alliance with mayors and other local officials, who also disliked the idea
of state control over manpower programs. When Senator Nelson's
employment subcommittee traveled across the country, local witnesses

protested that vesting the states with such power would endanger programs that were now operating effectively in their communities. Part of this distrust was due to the historical dominance of rural interests in many state capitals and their insensitivity to local (and especially urban) problems. But a major source of complaint was over the proposed role for the Employment Service in the MTA. Local groups feared that governors would simply delegate control over the programs to the Employment Service, as they had in the past. Typical was the attitude expressed by the leader of one black organization:

So far as the Employment Service is concerned, its record has been a dismal failure. . . . I have been dealing with the . . . Service for many years . . . and it is really an almost hopeless proposition to try to get much out of that agency. . . . The individuals who need additional training or guidance . . . usually become part of the existing files gathering dust in local offices.[22]

Many congressmen were sympathetic to the local opposition. The Employment Service enjoyed little credibility with Nelson, in particular, who as governor of Wisconsin often found himself at loggerheads with it.[23]

The administration made a costly error in designating the governors as point men in its plan for decentralization. The governors exhibited little interest in manpower reform, and when the Manpower Training Act came under attack, they did not mobilize to defend it. Efforts by the administration to mobilize the National Governors Conference proved fruitless. That the governors had historically been uninvolved in employment and training programs is a likely explanation for their poor show of support. In the CETA legislation that emerged, the states were left with little role. They were designated simply as the prime sponsor for the rural areas not covered by local governments of sufficient size to run their own programs.

The passivity of the states and the mobilization of local governments served to increase the number of political jurisdictions that would directly receive and control federal money. Local officials were lured not only by the prospect of running their own training programs but by the promise of money to create public service jobs, support for which was building in Congress at the time. Members of Congress, too, favored increasing the number of eligible prime sponsors, because it increased the number of communities in their districts that would directly receive benefits.

The Labor Department and manpower experts viewed this development with concern. The use of political jurisdictions as the basis for determining planning and administrative units fragmented metropolitan and regional labor market planning. A balkanized political structure at the local level undermined the possibilities for economic planning and, instead, created another federal subsidy program. "It is desirable to run the program on a labor-market basis," said one Labor Department official; "you are able to orchestrate the supply and demand of jobs more effectively and reduce administrative costs more effectively than you can when each unit of the labor market is operating its own programs."[24] Among the experts, the politically unrealistic minimum of one million population within each jurisdiction was preferred. Mangum told the Congress that a proliferation of prime sponsors would make the new administrative structure as unwieldy as the one then in operation.[25]

But political incentives dictated the size of the populations presided over by eligible prime sponsors at a minimum of 100,000, the figure adopted in CETA. Ironically, it was the department's own mobilization tactics and field experiments, as well as the 75,000 cutoff point adopted for the Emergency Employment Act, that helped to stimulate interest among smaller jurisdictions to run their own programs. Many suburban counties had gained inclusion in the EEA, further strengthening the local governments' position.

From Decentralization to Centralization to Decentralization

CETA soon proved disappointing. Local governments knew precious little about how to run employment and training programs. Regional offices of the Labor Department, which were assigned the role of overseeing the performance of local governments and providing them with technical assistance, performed neither function adequately.[26] With high levels of unemployment prevailing in the 1970s, Congress and the Carter administration mounted a massive effort at countercyclical job creation, straining an already fragile administrative capacity. Congress grew disenchanted when local authorities used their discretion to pursue objectives that diverged from those laid down by Congress and, in some cases, severely mismanaged the program.

Centralized control was reimposed when CETA was reauthorized in 1978. Recentralization achieved a much greater congruence with congressionally mandated policy objectives and eliminated much of the waste and mismanagement that occurred under decentralization. But predictably enough, tightening control over local CETA managers created tremendous administrative burdens at all levels of government. The CETA system included 475 prime sponsors. As a consequence, organized political support for the program among local governments, which was important for maintaining CETA funding, evaporated.

When CETA was terminated in 1982 and replaced by a more modest program, the pendulum swung back once again to a decentralized administrative framework, with much of the planning and control over the program devolving to the states rather than localities. At the time, Senator Dan Quayle was chairman of the Senate Subcommittee on Employment Opportunities. Quayle opened the hearings by posing what had remained, after two decades of federal involvement, a knotty problem: "For me, the overriding issue and the real, the tough nut to crack . . . is one to define the role of Government in this endeavor. What is the role of the Federal Government? . . . The State Government? . . . The local government? . . . Of private business and private industry?"[27]

Quayle's original proposal represented something old and something new. It resurrected the Nixon administration's proposal to funnel the bulk of funds to the states. Governors, subject to review by local governments, were given a wide range of powers: to designate the boundaries of local service delivery areas, allocate the funds to those areas, conduct audits, transfer authority from the CETA prime sponsor to private industry councils (PICs), and to approve the PICs' annual plans. What was new was the idea of incorporating business as a key actor in the process. Through the PICs, local businessmen would replace local public officials as the planning and administrative authorities at the local level. Forging public-private partnerships had become an increasingly popular idea, fueled by organizations like the National Alliance of Business and the Committee for Economic Development.[28] The PICs had the responsibility of drawing up annual plans and also managing the programs if they were judged by the governor to have sufficient administrative capacity. Sixty percent of the seats on each PIC were to be held by representatives of private business, and 10 percent each from local government, educational agencies, organized labor, and community-based organizations. Business representatives were to be nominated by businesses in the area.

Quayle joined Senator Edward Kennedy and worked with Congressman Augustus Hawkins in developing a bipartisan bill. To do this, however, he needed to make certain concessions. Kennedy and Hawkins preferred a less substantial departure from CETA, by maintaining greater involvement of local governments. The final legislation that passed, the Job Training Partnership Act (JTPA), was dubbed "the job training balancing act." Hawkins agreed to let the governors designate the service delivery areas in each state. However, jurisdictions with a minimum 200,000 population (up from 150,000 in the original House bill, and 100,000 under CETA), and consortia with a minimum population of 200,000, automatically qualified as delivery areas. A grandfather clause included in the original House bill—allowing current prime sponsors to qualify as service delivery areas for another five years—was eliminated. Most of the rest of the concessions on the major issues clearly came from the Senate side. Local plans were to be approved by the governor, but this was, in effect, the authority to disapprove only. A governor must approve a plan unless it failed to meet criteria specified in the bill concerning issues of coordination and compliance. Governors would not be able to disapprove plans based simply on their substantive elements. In effect, the design of the programs would be kept firmly under local control. The relationship between PICs and prime sponsors bore a greater resemblance to the House version. PIC members would be appointed by local officials from nominations made by local groups. A majority of PIC members would be business representatives, and local officials would remain distinct from the PIC. Both PICs and local governments would have to agree on procedures for developing plans, on the plans themselves, and on the entity to administer the programs. The PIC, the local government, or some combination of the two could be designated to develop the plans, receive the money, and serve as the administrative entity. The JTPA, in short, was a delicate balance of power between business, the states, and local authorities.

CONCLUSION

The complex array of public responsibilities assumed by the federal government in the postwar period far outstripped the existing administrative capacity to undertake them effectively. A larger government was not a more capable government, but less of one. As Heclo put it, "people increasingly expect[ed] Washington to solve problems but not to get in anyone's way in the process. The result [was] that policy goals [were] piled on top of each other without generating any commitment to the administrative wherewithal to achieve them."[29]

In employment policy, Washington attempted several strategies to build the requisite administrative and service delivery mechanisms. All of these failed. It tried to reorient the Employment Service, an existing agency nominally under Labor Department control, to become the presumptive provider of manpower services. The department had to overcome a formidable set of obstacles: the Employment Service's confederate structure of autonomous state agencies, its inadequate staffing, its legacy as an unemployment insurance agency, its commitment to local businesses' interested in keeping the payroll tax low, and perhaps most of all, its total lack of credibility among local officials and client groups.

Congress also created new entities, such as community action agencies and CETA prime sponsors. The ill-fated community action agencies battled with established public agencies and were ultimately disbanded. CETA prime sponsors had neither the technical nor managerial capacity for delivering comprehensive employment services.

On the administrative front, the centralization of the 1960s proved unworkable. Overcentralization in Washington, in the form of inflexible categorical restrictions, revealed the federal government's incapacity to tailor national policies to the variable circumstances in each part of the country. Devolution of authority to local governments in the 1970s, in turn, ended in disappointment in part because of the mistaken assumption that the goals of local political authorities would be congruent with those of Congress (as best as these could be discerned) and in part because of the CETA prime sponsors' sheer mismanagement of public service employment. As Martha Derthick pointed out, the federal government's control over subnational levels of government is imperfect at best: "The federal government cannot order these [state and local] governments to do anything."[30] State and local authorities retain a substantial degree of autonomy from Washington, and operate under political incentives that often lead them to develop policy objectives that diverge from the center. Recentralization in 1978 cured many of the problems associated with devolution, but was no more administratively feasible than the categorical programs of the 1960s. Like day following night, once again authority was devolved in the 1980s.

The problems of local administration and service delivery are more than strictly administrative in their implications. Improperly designed and operated administration and service delivery arrangements will certainly contribute to an image of waste, mismanagement, and ineffectiveness, which will make the programs politically vulnerable. Second, programs that enjoy stable and well-established administrative and service delivery arrangements tend to develop, over time, strong, supportive constituencies. A well-organized network of local administrators and service deliverers could play a valuable role in maintaining pressure to expand the flow of resources for the programs, or at least in protecting existing resources from the draconian budget cuts that reduced the JTPA to almost an irrelevancy in the 1980s. The existence of such constituencies is particularly critical in the case of programs whose intended beneficiaries—the unemployed and the poor—are largely incapable of mobilizing on their own behalf.

7

The Saga of CETA

In a word, CETA worked!
—*Garth Mangum*

CETA has become a four-letter word.
—*Anonymous congressional aide*

THE COMPREHENSIVE Employment and Training Act (CETA) was hardly in place when the recession of 1974/75 hit. With a sharp increase in joblessness brought about by the energy crisis, Congress responded with Title VI—a new countercyclical public service employment (PSE) component of CETA.[1] The creation of CETA, the recession that followed, and the adoption of Title VI all constituted a baptism by fire for the fledgling administrative arrangement. CETA had begun to show the first signs of pathology, but these were largely eclipsed by the need to use CETA to respond to the crisis. Thus began the expansion of the program that would eventually lead to its downfall.

GROWING PAINS OR FATAL FLAWS?

The 1974 congressional elections produced a substantial post-Watergate windfall for the Democrats. Of the $2.5 billion authorization for Title VI for fiscal year 1975, only $875 million had been appropriated. The additional $1.625 billion had yet to be released by the Appropriations Committee, and nothing had been authorized for fiscal 1976, which was scheduled to begin in July. The Democrats on the Education and Labor Committee in the House considered the $2.5 billion authorization simply a foot in the door. They sought to expand the current level of 310,000 PSE slots to 1 million. However, this initiative was put aside in favor of a proposal brought forward by the Appropriations Committee, whose influence in the House was considerably greater than the Labor

Committee. The Emergency Employment Appropriations Act contained $5.9 billion to immediately create 900,000 more jobs. Of this sum, however, only $1.625 billion—the remainder of the Title VI authorization—was appropriated under CETA's PSE programs. The bulk of the funds were to be spent on public works projects rather than public service employment. Members of the Labor Committee, intent on a substantial expansion of PSE, seemed blithely unaware of what were becoming increasingly visible problems with the PSE program. The appropriations bill indicated a growing disenchantment among many in Congress with the PSE approach to job creation. Even the $1.625 billion figure was more of a commitment to PSE than several members of the Appropriations Committee were inclined to make, including Chairman George Mahon, who said he preferred "more productive types of work." The report accompanying the appropriations bill expressed concern over "the potential for waste, mismanagement, and corruption that exists in public service jobs" and the use of funds by local officials "to enhance local political objectives" and "replace already existing locally funded jobs with federally funded jobs."[2] One observer noted that "the growing abuses in the PSE program were beginning to give the entire concept a bad reputation only six months after Title VI was passed."[3]

Since the Ford administration had agreed to only the $1.6 billion already authorized for PSE, the additional $3.7 billion for work projects was almost certain to produce a veto. What a few months earlier had been a emergency-induced bipartisan attempt to stem the tide of unemployment now reverted to a sharp partisan confrontation. The final version of the bill passed 293 to 109, essentially along party lines, and by a voice vote in the Senate. The House vote was 25 votes more than the two-thirds needed to override a presidential veto, which came as expected. The majority failed in the attempt to override by a mere five votes, 277 to 145. It was a stunning defeat for the Democrats, who had advertised Congress as a veto-proof legislature, and who had appeared to have the strength to override just a few weeks earlier. The Republicans suffered only five defections from party ranks, and in all, 28 GOP members switched sides to vote against the override. Eventually, the balance of the Title VI authorization was appropriated, but any expansion of PSE or public works had been effectively stymied.

Congress had ostensibly intended PSE to augment existing public payrolls, not replace local resources with those from Washington. Fiscal substitution defeated the countercyclical objective of PSE—to create a net number of new jobs in the economy and thus reduce the rate of unemployment. In essence, it was argued that PSE was becoming a glorified form of revenue sharing. The severe recession had simply aggravated the serious and longstanding structural crisis of urban America, which was marked by an erosion of local tax bases and a simultaneous expansion of demand for services. The result was a situation where CETA was supporting a significant proportion of the local payroll, especially in major industrial cities. Substitution was a manifestation of the fiscal dependency that had developed between Washington and local communities in dire fiscal straits. While at no time did the proportion of rehires (rehired laid-off, regular municipal employees with PSE funds) exceed 10 percent of the total program, and the national rate hovered around only 4 or 5 percent, in cities under tremendous fiscal pressure, it reached 50 percent or more. It was reports about these prime sponsors that accounted for the negative publicity.[4]

The CETA statute prohibited using funds to rehire laid-off employees in anticipation of receiving CETA funds. Sponsors could, however, use CETA money to rehire workers legitimately laid off from local public payrolls. In the event, sponsors were required to petition the Labor Department for the right to rehire laid-off county or municipal employees.[5] The key determination was whether the layoff was, or was not, bona fide. Determining permissible hiring and rehiring under CETA, even where it entailed few ambiguities in statutory interpretation, was still subject to political pressures. The Labor Department was often the target of lobbying by big city mayors hoping to use CETA funds to maintain their payrolls.[6] Substitution had become more tempting, because the strain produced by the economic downturn was now affecting public sector employees heretofore untouched by recession. Legitimate layoffs were occurring. From the perspective of city hall, it made little sense to hire the unemployed at a time of retrenchment when regular employees, some of whom were highly trained in public health and safety, were being asked to leave. Moreover, as part of permanent legislation, PSE was no longer viewed as a novel, and possibly temporary, experiment. Local governments could now plan their budgets with the knowledge that federal money for jobs was forthcoming. As a result, substitution had become both more feasible and harder to monitor. Finally, Title VI relaxed whatever safeguards against "paper layoffs" existed under Title II. Instead of thirty days, those hired under Title VI simply needed to be unemployed. The CETA statute allowed rehiring for bona fide, not paper, layoffs, but such distinctions were difficult for the Labor Department to make, particularly when local governments could point to their own emergency fiscal situations.

A second source of trouble was the target group for PSE. Who was supposed to be served by CETA was one of the most confusing aspects of the program. The confusion began in 1971 with the passage of the Emergency Employment Act. The EEA, as we have seen, was passed as a response to the 1970/71 recession, intended broadly for the "unemployed and underemployed" population, regardless of family income or duration of unemployment. On the other hand, the argument of those supporting the EEA was usually couched in terms of assisting the long-term, hard-core unemployed, who were associated with structural rather than cyclical unemployment, a rhetorical posture at least partially designed to calm Republican fears of establishing a WPA-like program. The act's preamble suggested a primary concern with the structurally unemployed. Prime sponsors were required to "give preference" to those handicapped by structural difficulties, such as the low-income unemployed, migrant workers, new entrants into the labor force, veterans, and others. Such groups were to be given "equitable service" by local governments. When Congress enacted CETA, Title II was designated to provide transitional jobs to essentially the same categories of individuals in geographic areas experiencing structural problems with unemployment rates over 6.5 percent. Despite this, participation in Title II was in fact open to a broader group—all persons who were unemployed thirty days or more or who were underemployed. A majority of those enrolled in Title II (like EEA before it) were nondisadvantaged, adult, white males who had been unemployed for relatively short durations. There were no significant differences between the characteristics of those enrolled in the Title II structural PSE program and the Title VI countercyclical program.[7]

At the time, few in Congress were aware of or interested in the neat distinctions between structural and cyclical unemployment. What they were concerned about, however, was that PSE jobs went to those who needed them most, and not to those who were able to compete for jobs in the regular labor market. There was a growing belief that this was not taking place. Title VI was explicitly designed to help victims of the recession. Yet statistics showed that in 1975 only 14.5 percent of those enrolled had been receiving UI benefits, and only 13.7 percent had been on public assistance.[8]

The problem of assisting the right people was directly related to the problem of substitution. The loose eligibility requirements of titles II and VI permitted prime sponsors to ignore those most in need, whether they suffered from structural difficulties or from prolonged layoffs from their regular jobs. Under Title II, individuals had only to be unemployed for thirty days, a brief amount of time whether or not it was a paper layoff. Title VI only required that the individual be unemployed or underemployed, and there was no guarantee that prime sponsors would give "preferred consideration" to those who had exhausted their UI benefits, were not eligible for UI, or who had been unemployed for fifteen weeks or longer, as specified in the law. In addition, municipal public employee unions were strongly opposed to hiring outside workers when their own members faced layoffs. The unions were suspicious that local governments would hire nonunion CETA workers to lower labor costs.

Even where local governments did not engage in rehiring their regular employees, they would be inclined to skim the cream off the eligible population. With funds sufficient for only a fraction of those eligible to participate in the program, local governments were free to choose the most productive workers. Many of the jobs that prime sponsors sought to fill were professional and technical positions beyond the skill and experience of those with the most serious financial and employment problems. In short, there were few incentives for prime sponsors to hire the less qualified workers and many reasons for selecting the more qualified.

These difficulties came less than a year after the enactment of Title VI and, combined with a steadily decreasing jobless rate after May 1975, convinced the Ford administration that the countercyclical PSE program should be terminated. It had originally accepted Title VI only as an expedient to blunt some of the mounting pressure to pursue more expansionist policies during the emergency. More jobs spending would increase the deficit, which, in turn, would either spur inflation by overheating the economy or choke off economic recovery by crowding out private investment—or both. Continued funding of the temporary emergency positions under Title VI, the administration feared, would "tend to cause them to be perceived as 'permanent' public employment positions."[9] The decision was backed by the DOL; it had not accepted the idea of countercyclical PSE as an appropriate objective of CETA, and it believed that PSE threatened to displace Labor's traditional mission of manpower development. The revenue sharing aspects of the program, and the administrative troubles they entailed, confirmed the department's long-standing misgivings. These views were particularly strong under Republican control, when job creation was considered more appropriately the function of the private sector:

If Congress wants to approach the problem of the cities and prime sponsors in trouble, then it ought to approach that problem, but we can't on the one hand, permit a program like this to become "get well" for the cities and on the other hand expect jobs to be created, because it won't happen.

The question has to be raised as to whether it is fair to put the kind of resources necessary to get all of the cities and prime sponsors "well" and permit them to maintain their payroll at the expense of doing better things in the private sector to create jobs.[10]

The perception that CETA was becoming more a fiscal assistance program for local governments than a work and training program for the disadvantaged was making friends of the program in Congress uncomfortable, as well. As Congresswoman Fenwick of New Jersey candidly stated, "We are doing a form of revenue sharing, and it would be better if we admitted it, because I think revenue sharing is good. We cannot just have our taxes rising and rising in our desperate towns. But let us really do it. Let us admit it."[11]

Under conflicting pressures from CETA's prime sponsors, who wanted more flexibility in the use of funds, and from their critics, who called for reforms to make substitution more difficult, the House passed an odd mix of provisions, along a party line vote, that went in both directions. When the bill got nowhere in the Senate, the Democrats passed another bill simply to extend Title VI through January 1977. Senate liberals, however, evidenced greater concern with CETA's reputation as a subsidy for local government that was doing little to help the jobless. In the Budget Committee, senators Kennedy and Cranston unveiled a plan to expand PSE but to target the bulk of the jobs toward the long-term unemployed, welfare recipients, and the working poor. The bill that emerged from the Senate contained the limitations the DOL believed were essential in a revamped Title VI: restrictions in eligibility to low-income workers and to the long-term unemployed, and stipulations that new PSE jobs be created only for one-year projects.

In 1976, an election year, the unemployment rate, having fallen from the height of the recession, leveled off at 7.5 percent then rose to 7.8 percent in July. Even conservatives found themselves in an uncomfortable position. As one southern senator put it:

This . . . is a typical example of the position in which we quite often find ourselves. Many of those from North Carolina who are continually talking about balancing the budget . . . are amongst those continually writing to me and pleading with me to vote for this issue, because if I do not vote for it, this county would lose over 300 persons or that city would lose so many other persons they have on their payroll.[12]

A veto of the Title VI extension would likely result in an override in Congress. To do so only weeks from the election was flirting with trouble. The president agreed to support the bill as long as all new jobs were filled with the long-term unemployed.[13]

The remaining obstacle was with the House version of the Title VI bill, which contained no targeting provisions whatsoever. This matter was taken up in a House-Senate conference. The House conferees were adamantly opposed to targeting all new PSE jobs toward the long-term jobless. Over the past two years, the House Education and Labor Committee had become the pressure point for local governments demanding more, not less, flexibility in the use of PSE money. The American Federation of State, County, and Municipal Employees (AFSCME), fearing that targeted PSE funds would be used to gradually displace its members, demanded that there be no changes that would require only the long-term unemployed to fill jobs where present PSE workers left or were laid off.

The House conferees eventually agreed that any new PSE enrollees above the current level would be limited to persons from the target groups. What they refused, however, was to target any current jobs that would become vacant. The conference remained deadlocked until Senator Javits proposed a compromise where, in cases of attrition, 50 percent of the jobs would be targeted and 50 percent remain under existing Title VI requirements. Finally, Congress passed a continuing resolution for fiscal 1977 that kept the size of the program at its present level. The combination of an impending election and a stalled recovery from the 1974/75 recession weighed heavily on the Ford administration, which was committed to eliminating Title VI. The unemployment rate for August crept upward another one-tenth of a percentage point to 7.9 percent. The president signed the bill quietly on October 1, one month before the election that would bring a new administration and renewed support for enlarging the PSE experiment.

The severe recession of 1974/75, like the much milder one in 1971, pushed the focus of employment policy further in the direction of work relief. Once again an emergency provided liberals, mostly Democrats, with the leverage they needed over a conservative Republican president to accept a measure he would otherwise have blocked.

PROGRAM EXPANSION UNDER THE DEMOCRATS

CETA programs came of age during the Carter administration. The budget expanded dramatically, as programs and objectives proliferated. Attempts were made to link CETA to a variety of related policy fields—welfare reform, economic management, and urban revitalization. Budget outlays for Carter's first budget in fiscal 1978 showed a 70 percent increase from the year before, going from $5.6 billion to $9.6 billion.[14] The last two years of the Carter period saw a drop in outlays to $8.9 billion in 1980 and to $7.6 billion in 1981, but this was still higher than spending in the Nixon or Ford years. The emphasis in this expansion was placed on the PSE component of CETA. As a proportion of the budget, PSE reached a peak of 60 percent in 1978, up from 37 percent in 1975. In terms of the commitment of resources, what had been a gradual expansion of job creation from 1972 to 1977 now leaped forward. By fiscal year 1978, the number of PSE jobs had more than doubled, going from 310,000 under Ford to 725,000 under Carter. Throughout the first three years of the Carter administration, PSE stayed above 40 percent of the budget.

The reason for this expansion was the part CETA was called upon to play in the economic program launched by the new administration during its first year in office. The economy had slowly crawled out of the recession during 1975 and the first half of 1976, but had sputtered before the election. By November, the rate of unemployment was back up to 7.9 percent. It had been decisive in defeating the Republican incumbent. After the election, a continued deterioration in economic performance gave added impetus to calls for aggressive fiscal stimulation. The president elect quickly announced that his "first priority" was to reduce the rate of joblessness to 6.5 percent by the end of 1977 and to 4–4.5 percent by the end of his first term.[15]

Carter came under heavy lobbying by congressional leaders, organized labor, and mayors and governors of northeastern states for a larger and more accelerated stimulus than the one being developed by his advisers. The AFL-CIO, backed by forty-one liberals in the House, proposed a $30 billion program, with $20 billion in spending for job creation in 1977 alone. They argued that spending for PSE jobs and public works would go directly and immediately to those who needed help and would create more jobs per dollar than a tax cut.[16]

PSE had several advantages compared to alternative countercyclical tools. Unlike public works projects, PSE jobs required less lead time for planning and were more labor intensive. Unlike a general spending increase or tax cut, PSE monies could be targeted directly at the unemployed. And unlike a tax cut, part of which would be saved, PSE promised more bang for the buck. A Congressional Budget Office report concluded that, compared to tax cuts or increases in other government spending, PSE was likely to "have the highest employment impact of the measures considered."[17]

The package settled on by the president reflected an attempt to balance the aims of the liberal-labor lobby for job creation and of the administration's fiscal conservatives for tax cuts. The total stimulus amounted to $30 billion, as called for by the liberals, but it was to be spread over two fiscal years. Though half the package was tax cut provisions and half was spending for jobs, the heart of it was clearly in the tax cuts. Much of the spending on jobs was deferred until the second year, allowing enough time to cut spending in 1978 should the economy rebound stronger than anticipated. An important argument,

again, was that jobs programs, particularly public works, required a
long lead time to plan and implement. The decision also was geared to
calm the fears of the administration's fiscal conservatives, who remained wary of launching large-scale spending commitments that they
believed would prove politically difficult to curtail when they were no
longer justified economically.

The AFL-CIO rejected the package as overly cautious and slow.
Democrats in Congress challenged its size and content, in particular
the emphasis on tax cuts as opposed to spending measures. In February
the House and Senate budget committees approved an alternative package that more than doubled the amount of spending in the Carter plan
for the remaining eight months of fiscal 1977.[18]

Throughout these deliberations, the level of funding for CETA's
PSE programs was not a point of contention, however. CETA's weak
administrative structure simply could not support more PSE slots than
those contemplated by the administration's proposal. The president
had originally supported one million PSE slots, the figure long advanced
by PSE advocates in Congress. The new labor secretary, Ray Marshall,
told the president that such an expansion would strain the CETA system. The department maintained that there were "significant questions" about the number of people the PSE program could absorb
"without resorting to leaf-raking" or other abuses. In any event, most
of the pressure in Congress for spending was for public works projects
rather than PSE.

Nevertheless, the number of new PSE slots included in the president's economic stimulus package constituted a significant expansion
of the PSE program. The level would rise from 310,000 to 600,000
slots by the end of fiscal year 1977, and to 725,000 during fiscal 1978.
The split between Titles II and VI for fiscal year 1978 would be
125,000 and 600,000, respectively. This reflected a 133 percent increase
in the number of jobs funded under CETA. There was also an
expansion of other CETA titles for training and work experience
programs, as well as money for a new program to combat youth
unemployment.

The Economic Stimulus Appropriations Act of 1977 passed the
House comfortably on 15 March, even with most Republicans voting in
opposition. In May it was approved by the Senate, even though the
Republicans had launched a concerted attack on the Title VI—PSE
funding provisions. Republicans considered Title VI jobs as a temporary
relief measure, put in place to help cushion the shock of the sharp
recession of 1974/75, which, they argued, had passed. To them, countercyclical PSE was designed for the same purpose as the relief programs

of the 1930s, but the Democrats now viewed PSE as an instrument for helping the economy move toward its full potential.

In previous years, Republicans had objected to PSE on sheer ideological grounds or on the basis that it rested upon faulty economic logic. Now, however, the brunt of their case against PSE was based on the actual performance of the program—the hard fact that the program was a failure. By 1977 a number of evaluation studies had surfaced that called into question the effectiveness of PSE.[19] A report issued by the General Accounting Office, for instance, cited (1) the inability of most of the program's participants to find permanent, unsubsidized employment; (2) maintenance-of-effort violations on the part of prime sponsors, where federal funds were used for jobs that should have been financed with state and local funds; (3) the failure of the Labor Department to monitor those violations due to insufficient time and staff; (4) the funding of questionable make-work projects; and (5) the failure of prime sponsors to verify regularly the eligibility of participants selected.[20]

All of this evidence had a serious flaw, however. Most of the damaging studies focused on the public employment program funded under the Emergency Employment Act of 1971. None of the studies evaluated the 1976 amendment of Title VI, which, argued its supporters, provided targeting provisions that would insure that very few regular public employees would be able to meet its eligibility requirements. More important, the decisive factor that protected PSE from attack was, as it had been in the past, the high rate of joblessness.

To demonstrate CETA's usefulness as a countercyclical instrument required prompt administrative action. Long delays in the implementation of the expansion would not only have risked lending credence to the view that it was futile to use spending measures to make a timely contribution to economic recovery, but would have risked injecting an unwanted stimulus should the economy surge ahead on its own at the time the spending finally took effect. One of the more indisputable achievements of the PSE program was the rapid and smooth buildup during the period from mid-1977 to mid-1978. Less than a year after the stimulus act had been signed into law, the number of PSE jobs funded by CETA had more than doubled. The full 725,000 level was reached several weeks ahead of the March 1978 target date. During the buildup, the unemployment rate dropped from 8.6 percent to 5.7 percent in June 1978. It stayed within the 5.6 to 5.9 percent range throughout 1978 and 1979, the lowest it had been in four years, since before the 1974/75 recession. The PSE program itself was credited, however, with shaving less than 1 percent off the jobless rate. With 6.75 million individuals unemployed when the stimulus package was enacted, the increase in the number of PSE jobs to an additional 415,000 accounted for only 6 percent of all those unemployed. (This calculation, however, does not include any multiplier effects.)

The rapid buildup of 1977/78 transformed CETA from a fairly modest program to one of the most costly and visible grant-in-aid programs the federal government had ever undertaken. It dwarfed the antipoverty programs of the previous decade, which at their peak spent about half as much money and affected far fewer people.[21] CETA workers were increasingly becoming an important part of the fabric of local communities, and of the dependency of those communities on Washington. The expansion greatly magnified CETA's warts and aggravated its weaknesses. Problems cited with the program fell into four familiar areas: (1) fiscal substitution; (2) insufficient participation by the disadvantaged; (3) a low transition rate to unsubsidized employment; and (4) waste, fraud, and abuse. This last problem was by no means least.

Fiscal Substitution

Was CETA successfully creating jobs or mainly acting as a subsidy for local governments? The studies conducted to find this out demonstrated the limited utility of program evaluations for policy making, even when conducted by capable experts. Variations in assumptions, methodology, time frames, and interpretations of data resulted in a wide divergence of conclusions.[22]

One of the studies, conducted by the Brookings Institution, received considerably more attention than the others. It was cited by local governments and other supporters of PSE as evidence that a relatively small proportion (18 percent) of the jobs created were substitutions. Jobs created under the project approach showed an even lower substitution rate of 8 percent. Opponents of PSE, on the other hand, cited a figure of 50 percent from the same study to argue that rampant substitution existed. Why the confusion? A crucial factor in arriving at the 18 percent figure was in the very narrow definition of substitution that was used. What should be counted as substitution? To answer this question, investigators had to first determine what would have happened in the absence of CETA money. In several cities, regular city activities were carried out by CETA workers because local financial constraints would otherwise have meant cutting back these services. The Brookings study did not include under substitution these program maintenance jobs. That is, the Brookings study did not count as substitution the use of CETA funds to support and maintain service levels that otherwise would have been cut. Presumably, in the absence of CETA monies, cities would have been required to cut substantially spending on such personnel as police and firemen. Hence, the low rates of substitution reported by Brookings should be understood as exclusive of those jobs already in existence that local governments would not have been able to support without federal funds. Counted as substitution were only those jobs that CETA money was used to displace, that is, jobs that prime sponsors would have funded anyway, using their own resources.

If one adds the displacement rate of 18 percent to the program maintenance rate, one gets 40 percent of the PSE monies going to purposes other than new (i.e., net) job creation. Looking only at central cities, the rate of program maintenance was 31 percent, bringing the proportion of new jobs created to 49 percent. The combination of jobs actually substituted plus those being maintained meant that a sizable portion of CETA funds were essentially treated as revenue sharing. It is valid to argue, as the Brookings study did, that a job saved is a job created. But it is important to remember that the intent of Congress was to augment, rather than merely maintain, existing levels of local services and the number of jobs available. The program was meant to create new job opportunities, not simply support those already created.

The Brookings study did help to dispel some of the confusion surrounding substitution. And by all accounts, it defused the criticism of substitution. In the Senate, concern over substitution subsided. Like the proverbial glass of water that is half empty or half full, substitution was a problem that varied with perception. It is clear that job creation and fiscal assistance were not completely incompatible objectives. On the other hand, CETA's countercyclical objective—the essence of which was to expand the number of jobs available—was substantially compromised because it was used to maintain jobs already in existence, especially in large cities.

Serving the Disadvantaged

Substitution went hand in hand with another of CETA's perceived problems: creaming the population eligible for PSE jobs. Those who were most attractive to hire were not usually those who most needed the work experience. The original intent of Congress was to design a double-barrelled PSE program, where Title II would provide entry-level jobs for the structurally unemployed in areas of "substantial" unemployment, and where Title VI would be available for those out of work due to fluctuations in the economy. This distinction was reflected in neither the eligibility criteria of the two programs nor in the job placements. Data collected by program evaluators show little difference in the characteristics of Title II and Title VI jobholders.

Maintaining the distinction between titles II and VI was not a terribly important matter in Congress. What was politically important was which groups were getting CETA jobs overall. Despite the 1976 amendments, the cry continued that persons most in need were still underrepresented. This criticism was voiced most regularly by Republicans, who, except during the trough of the 1974/75 recession, opposed the use of PSE for countercyclical purposes. According to them, CETA was intended for those with structural barriers to unemployment and not for individuals who, they were persuaded, could find jobs in the private sector. Congressional reactions to the short term being what they are, it was natural that when the economy improved in 1978 this view gained more adherents. Apparently, the 1976 amendments were indeed having their intended effect on the composition of the participant pool. Fiscal 1978 participant characteristics showed a PSE pool that was less educated, less white, and coming from households with lower income and longer spells of unemployment than for the period immediately before the amendments (fiscal 1976).

Given these improvements, why were CETA's participant characteristics still perceived as a problem during 1978, when CETA's reauthorization became a focal point of debate over the performance of the program? One obvious reason is ignorance. Unlike the studies dealing with substitution, data on participant characteristics were not available at the time. No one knew, or could be certain, whether the 1976 amendments were making the intended improvements. Second, despite changes in participant characteristics, there was still a sizable proportion of PSE participants who did not share all of the characteristics that policy makers associate with being disadvantaged. In fiscal 1978 a majority of PSE workers (Titles II and VI combined) were still white male adults, with at least a high school education, who were not on welfare. Although only 25 percent fell outside the economically disadvantaged category, in the other characteristics there were noticeable differences between PSE participants and those enrolled in CETA training programs.[23] The high education profiles of PSE participants was particularly striking. In fiscal 1978 almost 40 percent of all PSE participants had thirteen or more years of education. Thus, with anecdotal press reports of middle-class graduate students holding down PSE jobs, it is not surprising that CETA began to be perceived by its critics as a program that was not serving those who needed employment the most.[24]

Wage Levels and Distribution Formula

One obstacle to eradicating substitution and hiring more disadvantaged participants was CETA's wage structure. Another obstacle that kept the program from serving more disadvantaged individuals was CETA's distribution formula. The 1976 amendments left both wages and the formula untouched. One of the greatest problems in the program's design was CETA's permissive wage provisions. CETA paid a maximum of $10,000 per job, but local governments were allowed to supplement this wage out of their own resources as much as they wished. Teachers, police, firemen, engineers, and other professional and managerial positions could be supported. Some cities supplemented the wages of employees earning over $20,000.[25]

Hence, the question of where to peg the PSE wage level and whether to permit supplementation were directly related to whether the principal aim of the program was to support municipal services or, alternatively, to provide entry-level jobs and training for the hard to employ. If the former objective was to be realized, the law had to permit prime sponsors to pay wages high enough to attract and maintain personnel who were qualified to perform the most valuable local public services. If the latter was to be the priority, then wage levels had to be set low enough to discourage highly skilled workers from competing with less skilled workers for available CETA positions.

At the same time, however, wage levels needed to be high enough to enable individuals to have access to meaningful employment so they could obtain useful work experience and, second, to take into account the nearly 30 percent inflation that had occurred since 1973. Furthermore, wage levels set too low could violate equal pay for equal work standards, by placing lower wage workers into higher wage classifications, anathema to local public employee unions, which feared displacement of regular employees by "cheap labor." Hence, the issue of wage levels, which was complicated by the range in levels across the country, presented policy makers with a Gordian knot of conflicting program objectives.

Another aspect of the issue of who should be served by the program was the geographical distribution of funds. CETA distributed funds broadly, rather than concentrating on those areas most in need. It was far more distributive than redistributive in nature. Any local political jurisdiction of 100,000 population was eligible for funds. The need to capture and maintain sufficient political support for the programs in Congress produced these broad distributive characteristics. Critics, especially Republicans, complained that the ostensible purpose of CETA—to help the underprivileged—had been lost by spreading benefits so widely.

Transition to Unsubsidized Jobs

By 1978, CETA was four years old, and sufficient time had passed to assess one of the program's central objectives: preparing people to take unsubsidized, permanent jobs. The Labor Department's regulations set a goal, but not a requirement, of a 50 percent annual transition rate. DOL figures showed that 39 percent of Title I participants transferred into unsubsidized jobs, 17.7 percent of Title II, and 34 percent of Title VI. Another report, by the GAO, found that during fiscal year 1977 only 22 percent of Title VI PSE enrollees nationwide were terminated from the program. Of this 22 percent, 43 percent found unsubsidized employment upon leaving CETA, and only 38 percent of this proportion, in turn, found unsubsidized work in the private sector.[26] Critics complained that participants were able to stay in the program indefinitely, going from one CETA program to another, and that they "look upon it as a way of life."[27]

No one knew for certain why transition rates were so low. Obviously, an important factor was simply the shortage of jobs during the prolonged recession. On the other hand, despite unemployment, the private sector economy was creating a large number of new jobs. Critics contended that PSE jobs provided too little training to make participants more employable. Others placed the blame on CETA's lack of involvement with business and industry, on red tape and record-keeping requirements, and on CETA's wage structure, which discouraged workers from taking the lowest paid jobs in the private sector. Still others complained that CETA jobs were most likely to lead to permanent jobs that could only be found in the public sector where skills like firefighting were used.[28]

"Jiving the Masses"

The legitimacy of CETA was seriously eroded by the stream of "bad press" it was receiving—adverse publicity on waste, nepotism, patronage, and corruption. Perhaps nothing contributed more to the loss of confidence and legitimacy in CETA and, ultimately, to its demise. The premium placed on the rapid buildup of PSE jobs in a short period of time took a toll on the management of CETA. It was no coincidence that in 1978, at the height of the buildup, the greatest number of abuses were reported. CETA became a favorite topic for investigative journalists and an irresistible whipping boy for editorial writers. There was hardly a member of Congress who was not familiar with the program, and each, it seemed, had his or her favorite CETA horror story.

Unlike CETA's other problems, scandalous reports of waste, corruption, nepotism, and the like were both highly visible to the public and unambiguous signals of failure. Substitution, low transition rates, and the maldistribution of benefits were problems that could be hidden behind a maze of statistics or justified under CETA's confusing myriad of objectives. Substitution, for instance, could at least be understood, if not justified, as a method of helping localities that were in desperate fiscal straits. And because it relied on some comprehension of intergovernmental financial practices, substitution was hardly as salient an issue as waste and abuse.

Allegations of misuse of funds took several forms and appeared in numerous localities, but cities that seemed especially susceptible were those with political machines. In Chicago, for instance, the Labor Department demanded that the city repay almost $1 million after it was discovered that CETA jobs were doled out by Chicago's Democratic political apparatus, which required applicants to have referral letters from ward committeemen. Applications of those unemployed persons without political connections, many of them disadvantaged minorities, on the other hand, were set aside in unopened mail sacks.[29]

Some of the more colorful examples of abuse were reported (although often unconfirmed) in the *Reader's Digest* and *Time*. One author called CETA a "grotesque Lazy Susan of programs that are rife with waste and mismanagement as funds are dispersed in everything-for-everybody style." The more bizarre examples cited by the *Reader's Digest* article included the following:

In Miami, Florida, CETA dollars paid for a "nude sculpting workshop," in which naked men and women ran hands over one anothers' bodies. "This was to help them discover that they had both male and female qualities." . . . In Atlanta, CETA funds paid the former leader of the Black Panther Party, an avowed Marxist-Leninist, $475 a month to, as he said, "keep an eye on city, county, and state governments and their jiving of the masses." . . . Watergate burglar Bernard Barker held a $10,000-a-year CETA job as a sanitation inspector, which he got on the recommendation of Miami City Commissioner Manolo Reboso. CETA also paid half of his tuition as an engineering student at Florida International University. CETA pays Barker's ex-wife Clara $14,000 a year as a clerk-typist and his present wife Maria $12,500 a year as a city sanitation inspector. Says Barker: "I think it is a wonderful program."[30]

These episodes were not limited to the PSE program but also included CETA's training programs. *Time* reported:

Federal funds account for most of the $1.3 million that is spent each year by Miami's Edison–Little River Council programs for the unemployed and disadvantaged. But when Dade County investigators checked up on how Council President Nathaniel Dean was actually using all that money, they found evidence that he had diverted $22,000 for the use of a gasoline station he owns. He also made an undetermined number of interest-free loans to his various relatives. He employed a staff psychologist at the council who had no degree in psychology and whose home address turned out to be a vacant lot. In addition, Dean spent $300,000 on a farm worker project in which no trainees ever served, and paid for farm machinery that was nowhere to be found. . . . Margarita Ross, whose husband heads a Coral Gables engineering firm, was paid $14,000 a year, largely from CETA funds, as Miami's "cultural experiences coordinator." Mrs. Ross was apparently well connected: she is a former partner in a downtown art gallery with the wife of Miami Mayor Maurice Ferre. Ferre says he sees nothing wrong with politicians helping friends obtain CETA jobs. Says he: "It's just incongruous to conceive that elected officials aren't going to recommend people they have a high regard for." But spokesmen for Miami's poor complain that the program is being turned into a hiring hall for the middle class. Says Urban League Director T. Willard Fair: "The chronic unemployed are being left out of the system." Indeed, Fair's own $189,000 CETA job-training program is being investigated—for spending money on training programs for long-time employees who were already skilled in their jobs.[31]

But the most damaging press accounts dealt with the CETA program that operated directly under the nose of the federal government, in the District of Columbia. A series of articles in the *Washington Star*, detailing abuses taking place in the nation's capital, drew a storm of protest in Congress. Following up on the allegations, the Labor Department found that the District's city council had made extensive use of PSE funds to enlarge the council's staff by hiring friends, relatives, and political supporters of council members. Because CETA permitted the District to supplement PSE salaries using its own funds, many of these employees earned between $10,000 and $20,000—much above the average CETA salary throughout the nation. Numerous other hiring violations were cited.[32]

No one, of course, could know how much abuse and mismanagement was actually taking place. But in terms of their political implications, this hardly seemed to matter. Whatever the frequency of abuse, it was sufficient to do considerable damage to the program's reputation. CETA's defenders, including the Labor Department, acknowledged the problem but argued that press accounts greatly exaggerated occurrences that were not generalized, and that in any event, the funds in question amounted to less than 1 percent of CETA's total funds. Perhaps the best judgment of the situation was made by Senator Nelson when he stated, "Though such abuses have not been pervasive, neither have they been limited to a few isolated instances."[33] What *was* pervasive was the erosion of CETA's political respectability.

REHABILITATING CETA: THE 1978 REAUTHORIZATION

The Carter administration began 1978 fairly optimistic that the economic recovery, which had pushed the unemployment rate to 6.4 percent (its lowest since October 1974) would continue a steady course. Cyclical unemployment now had receded as a priority. The proposed budget reflected a new emphasis on the need to attack inflation and structural unemployment, a topic stressed in the state of the union speech and economic policy messages. The budget called for no increases in the level of PSE funding. The level of 725,000 jobs, expected to be reached in March, would be maintained for fiscal 1979, but thereafter declining need for PSE was projected as the economy improved and as the administration's "private sector initiatives," unveiled at the same time and designed to involve the business community more heavily in CETA, took effect.

According to the president, "As the economy improves, employment and training programs should shift their emphasis from creating jobs in the public sector to providing training and finding jobs in the private sector."[34] By "zeroing in on the pockets of unemployment that are the most difficult to resolve," as one top Labor Department official put it, CETA would begin to be directed back to those groups in the labor market that were the concern of the 1960s—hard-to-employ youth, minorities, and the disadvantaged.[35] A key element of the package was targeting all CETA funds, including all PSE jobs, exclusively on the disadvantaged—defined as those whose family income was no greater than 70 percent of the government's standard for a low-income family budget.

The reaction from the strongest proponents of PSE—urban politicians, labor leaders, congressional liberals, and the Black Caucus—was disappointment. They had hoped for an expansion of up to 1 million slots. How hard and how fast the administration was willing to push down unemployment was becoming a matter of intense debate because of on-going negotiations over the Humphrey-Hawkins full-employment bill.

The major political problem with placing eligibility restrictions on the CETA program, of course, was the dependence of local governments on CETA funds. Local governments wanted to avoid cutting essential services like sanitation, police, and firemen. The administration's plan, ultimately ill fated, was to wean them off CETA by proposing an "urban package," the centerpiece of which was a multibillion-dollar National Development Bank.

Meanwhile, Congress had grown increasingly exasperated with reports of the program's performance in the wake of the PSE buildup. According to Congressman David Obey, CETA had become "the second most unpopular program in the country after welfare."[36] ironically, part of CETA's dilemma was that unemployment had ebbed since 1977, and public opinion polls showed more Americans concerned about the persistence of inflation than about joblessness. The budget-cutting mood was greatly inspired by California's Proposition 13, a grass roots revolt against high taxes with national impact.[37] But CETA was "ripe for a pretty heavy attack," for reasons much more directly related to the program itself. As we have seen, the rapid buildup, coupled with DOL's management of the program seemingly not equal to the task, produced more bad news than good by 1978. Democrats on the House Education and Labor Committee found themselves in the same predicament that they had been in during the preceding few years. They needed to placate their urban constituency, which had grown increasingly dependent on CETA as a flexible source of support. But they also needed to take steps to restore credibility to a program that was rapidly losing support in the parent chamber.

Seeking to maintain flexibility in the use of their allocations, local officials greeted the administration's bill with a storm of protest against any new restrictions. A major concern was with the eighteenth-month limitation on how long a participant could remain in the program. Mayors complained that it was unfair and counterproductive to force people off the program, often to return to unemployment and welfare. Hawkins, chair of the Subcommittee on Employment Opportunities, expressed sympathy but argued that, given that there were many more individuals who needed help than were getting it from the "pathetically under-funded" program, it was only fair to expand the program's participation by restricting the duration of each individual's enrollment. Hawkins also pointed to the budget-cutting mood in Congress.

The CETA reauthorization bills that emerged from the House and Senate Labor Committees were essentially unchanged from the administration's draft. Just days before the House committee's bill was scheduled to be brought to the floor of the House, the scandalous reports of the District of Columbia CETA program were splashed across the pages of Washington newspapers. The anti-CETA fever on Capitol Hill was now at a fever pitch. The House committee's bill was bombarded with a multitude of amendments. Several constituted major alterations. Many members felt that the bill's restrictions on eligibility and abuse were not tight enough and believed the bill was too heavily weighted toward employment rather than training.

The most significant amendment was offered by Congressman Obey, who had become CETA's most influential critic in the House. Obey and a handful of other liberals on the House Appropriations Committee had grown increasingly concerned with the performance of the PSE program, particularly since it had become one of the largest and most visible of all domestic spending programs. Several times over the previous five years, Obey had been called upon to protect CETA's budget by offering amendments on the House floor to replace appropriations that had been cut in his committee. Although a friend of CETA, he realized the program had become more and more difficult to defend.

Obey's amendment was directed at the wage level for PSE jobs. The current law provided a ceiling of $10,000, with $7,000 set as the average wage. "I simply do not want to have any more stories appearing in newspapers, such as the column by Mr. Kilpatrick, which indicates that the Washington City Council hired 56 CETA people at an average wage of $18,000 a year for jobs that paid only $8,500 in other Government agencies," declared Obey.[38] As proposed in the House bill, the $10,000 maximum wage could be supplemented by prime sponsors up to $15,000. Obey called the $15,000-a-year figure "politically indefensible." Republicans complained that setting CETA wages too high made them so attractive that participants were encouraged to stay in them "rather than go out and take their chance in the real world in the private sector."[39] Obey's amendment passed by a 55 vote margin, 230 to 175.[40]

Another amendment, by Congressman James Jeffords, was to cut Title VI by $1 billion and shift half of the amount to CETA's youth programs, an idea that according to the chairman of the Black Caucus would "throw the father out of work in order to hire the son. Look at what that does to family life."[41] With several more amendments still to be considered, and momentum clearly on the side of CETA's attackers, Hawkins abruptly withdrew the bill from further floor action. More restrictive amendments seemed likely to be approved had not debate been terminated.

The aborted attempt to reauthorize CETA came as an embarrassment for the Democratic leadership. Alterations made in the bill were condemned by labor and urban groups. "I think there is a mood in the House to cut back on programs for the poor and lower-middle class," said AFL-CIO lobbyist Kenneth Young. "The members are running scared. They think the more conservative they vote, the better off they are back home." Another union representative attributed the setback to Congress's concern over inflation and its belief that unemployment was down. Detroit mayor Coleman Young called the cuts in PSE funding "unsensitive and irresponsible," a misguided reaction to Proposition 13. Young predicted that the wage limitations would "cause havoc in employment practices in city halls across the country."[42]

Mindful of what had taken place in the House, the sponsors of the Senate bill engaged in weeks of behind-the-scenes negotiations to avoid embarrassment on the Senate floor. As a result, the bill passed by a sixty-six-to-ten vote, with little of the criticism or angry debate that had marked House deliberations. Provisions explicitly prohibited the hiring of a CETA participant when any other person was on layoff from the same or a substantially equivalent position, and required that CETA jobs must be in addition to those that would be funded by a state or municipality. Also adopted was an amendment to further tighten eligibility requirements for PSE jobs.

Lobbying on behalf of the House bill by local and state governments proved fruitless, and it remained in serious trouble after the Labor Day recess. Having retreated once already in their efforts to pass their bill, they were now forced to compromise with CETA's critics if they hoped to get any legislation passed. The final legislation that emerged from the conference committee retained substantially all the major provisions asked for by the administration, including the elimination of 100,000 PSE jobs and strict wage provisions.

After Reauthorization

CETA remained an embattled program during the rest of the Carter administration. No sooner had the reauthorization been passed than OMB proposed cutting $2.6 billion for fiscal year 1980. This cut the number of PSE slots from 600,000 to 500,000. The action set the tone for budgetary policy for the next few years and, in retrospect, signaled the end of the expansion of the social programs of the 1960s and 1970s. As expected, the decision drew a sharp protest from liberal congressional Democrats, mayors, and governors, who labeled the cuts (which were not limited to CETA) as disastrous. Predictions of a recession in 1979 fueled the criticism. The president's budget predicted that the unemployment rate would rise from 5.8 percent at the end of 1978 to 6.2 percent by the end of 1979. What made the announced cutbacks a particularly bitter pill to swallow was that the Full Employment and Balanced Growth Act had been signed just months before in a White House ceremony. Hawkins denounced the reductions as a "direct violation" of the act's mandate of 4 percent joblessness.[43]

Congress was well attuned to public opinion, and despite predictions of higher joblessness later in the year, the public had clearly grown weary of inflation. Every poll on the subject showed that inflation had supplanted unemployment as the number one concern of the general public. At least as important, there was a clear sense that the public had grown more conservative in their attitudes toward taxes and spending. The congressional elections of 1978 saw the unexpected defeat of several liberal incumbents, the Proposition 13 tax revolt, and a campaign for a balanced budget amendment. With many liberals from the West and Midwest up for reelection in 1980, the Democratic majority in the Senate was vulnerable. The 1978 election presaged the more impressive conservative victories of 1980.

The objective economic and political situations did not by themselves account for CETA's vulnerability. Perceptions of the program's performance had not improved. Discretionary programs like CETA are "controllable" parts of the budget, because spending reductions can be achieved through the budget and appropriations process, requiring no changes in the program's authorizing statute. During budget-cutting exercises, discretionary spending is especially vulnerable, and that spending considered wasteful or ineffective is doubly so. Press accounts of CETA's patronage and substitution declined noticeably by the fall of 1979, as the restrictions imposed the year before took effect.

Yet the program's troubled image remained. CETA often seemed to be in a no-win situation because of conflicting criticisms as to how it should be run and what it should be doing. For instance, in the first year following the tighter eligibility restrictions of the recent amendments, enrollments in the PSE program remained low. Within the span of two months, the Labor Department was called on the carpet both for not pushing prime sponsors hard enough to enroll disadvantaged persons and for pushing them too hard. The House Subcommittee on Employment Opportunities wanted to know whether enrollments were low because of administrative negligence or because prime sponsors simply did not like dealing with the hard-core unemployed. At the same time, the Senate Labor-HEW Appropriations Subcommittee chided the DOL for trying to push prime sponsors too fast in building up the PSE program.[44]

One of the criticisms in a series of articles in the *Washington Post* was that over the years CETA had provided jobs but little training for the unemployed. CETA had turned into a complex multititle program that was understood by most people only as a vast job-creating machine at the local level. It was true, of course, that CETA was predominantly a job creation program. But that is exactly what Congress had in mind when they enacted and expanded titles II and VI. Neither title was supposed to provide much training, because it was thought, correctly or not, that it made little sense to train individuals (some of whom suffered from no shortage of skills) when there was a shortage of jobs.

By 1981 it was clear that the 1978 amendments had succeeded in overcoming many of the program's chronic difficulties. Creaming the population (selecting those most likely to succeed rather than those most in need) declined significantly, as did substitution and program abuses. By 1980, low-income persons were 92 percent of the new PSE enrollees and 95 percent of the participants in training programs. This was an improvement of 17 and 22 percentage points, respectively, above the 1978 levels. Larger proportions of welfare recipients, persons with less than a high school education, minority groups members, and especially youth (60 percent) were reported. The reduction in PSE wages had the intended effect of discouraging more qualified persons from competing for jobs with the less qualified, and of discouraging local governments from using CETA workers to replace regular public employees. Unfortunately, these improvements came too late to save CETA.[45]

These positive changes were hardly an unmixed blessing, however. The drift of CETA toward recentralization was accompanied by a sharp increase in the administrative burdens imposed upon prime sponsors, which took the forms of tighter restrictions, more stringent reporting requirements, and increased monitoring. According to Franklin and Ripley,

Administrative complexity increased as requirements and regulations mushroomed and extensive changes in local management systems were imposed on prime sponsors. Funds for administration did not increase, however. Local flexibility, both managerial and programmatic, decreased as options were constrained by nationally imposed limits and mandates. Increasing local fiscal liability helped reduce incentives to innovate. Morale of staff plummeted and frustration soared due to the aggregate effect of the federal interventions, the assumption of guilt implicit in the changes made in the 1978 reauthorization, and the spiraling staff layoffs between 1979 and 1983 as first PSE and then all of CETA were phased out.[46]

Moreover, as red tape increased and discretion decreased, CETA's value to local prime sponsors declined. In turn, the incentive for local governments to pressure Congress to maintain appropriations was greatly reduced. Creaming and substitution could only be eliminated by targeting and by tighter restrictions, but targeting and restrictions were unpopular among those who had been CETA's most vocal, and politically influential, beneficiaries.

CONCLUSION

"We've got to get rid of the name of CETA," Congressman James Jeffords declared flatly when the time came in 1982 to decide what should be done about employment policy.[47] That any new program would have to be called by some other name neatly summarized the political failure of CETA. Judged by the harsh criticism leveled at it, CETA was more than just the name of a program that was perceived to have missed its mark. More than any other domestic program of the 1970s, CETA came to symbolize the exhaustion of the liberal agenda and the corruption of its activities. *Corruption* is used here in the broad sense, to denote the debasement of a sound purpose. Not surprisingly, it became a favorite target in a renewed conservative attack on liberal social activism. CETA's size dwarfed not only the employment programs of the 1960s but the entire War on Poverty effort, a fact that contributed to it becoming a visible symbol of what its opponents argued was the futility and failure of government attempts to solve social and economic problems.[48]

The CETA story is one not so much about the failure of a program as it is about the failure of a set of political institutions. It should not be confused with the notion that CETA failed to achieve, to one degree or another, several of its substantive objectives. While few of its programs were undisputed and overwhelming successes, few were abject failures.[49] The gap between the actual results and the dismal perceptions of performance suggests that the place to look for the sources of CETA's difficulties is not in its statistical evaluations but in its political-institutional framework—not so much in what it produced, but in how it was conceived and conducted. Even if CETA's impact upon unemployment and poverty was less than spectacular, such outcomes were in large part the result of flaws in those institutions that design and carry out public policy.

The seeds of CETA's problems were sown in its original legislation, which contained a basic contradiction between its administrative design and substantive goals. Administrative reform through decentralization and decategorization was intended to shift decisions to the local level in order to provide flexibility to respond to the needs and priorities of each community. These varied considerably across the nation and could not be adequately addressed or managed from Washington. At the same time, Congress added a new kind of program—public service employment—to the established set of training and work experience programs. Throughout most of CETA's existence, job creation was the top priority of Congress. Employment policy was now expected not just to train the hard to employ but to create jobs for them, to help local communities better meet the demands for expanding public services, and (with the addition of Title VI) to create jobs for otherwise self-sufficient persons who were laid off during the recession. In sum, CETA was designed with four principal objectives in mind:

1. A structural objective, to provide training, work experience, and entry-level public employment for the hard to employ, that is, those facing major barriers to employment, many of whom lacked basic education skills and who were economically disadvantaged.
2. A countercyclical objective, to expand the number of jobs during downturns in the national economy, for individuals who were job ready.

3. A quasi-revenue sharing objective, to help local communities support expanding public services.
4. An administrative-reform–local-democracy objective, to provide maximum local flexibility and discretion in running the programs.

All of this assumed that local governments would treat resources for employment programs in the same manner that they treat resources devoted to training programs. To put it more generally, CETA's authors believed that, just because there was likely to be a reasonable congruence between national goals and local goals in the area of training, the same would be the case in the area of job creation. As it turned out, the fourth objective often worked incompatibly with the first three objectives and, the first three often could not be attained simultaneously, at least given the level of appropriations Congress was willing to commit to the program. For local governments under fiscal stress, as many were during the 1970s, it made more sense to use much of their CETA monies to maintain rather than augment existing levels of services. For those governments unwilling or unable to raise taxes, many of them having to lay off regular municipal employees during a decade of persistent recession, it made little sense to use CETA funds to hire unemployed individuals outside of its regular workforce. It made even less sense to hire hard-to-employ individuals who were less productive or unfit to perform jobs for which there were already qualified individuals looking for work.

The first indication that congressional intent and local objectives might not be compatible came before CETA was enacted, under the Emergency Employment Act of 1971. Ostensibly, the EEA was expected to serve the same clientele that participated in the training programs (the disadvantaged, in particular). Hard-to-employ individuals residing in areas of substantial unemployment were to be provided with entry-level employment in local public agencies, with the intention that they would eventually be placed in permanent, unsubsidized jobs. The characteristics of those actually hired under the program, however, revealed that few disadvantaged, hard-to-employ persons were hired. The public employment program under the EEA was eventually incorporated into CETA as Title II (transitional employment for the structurally unemployed). When countercyclical PSE was added in 1974, an exclusively national responsibility—fighting recession—was assigned to a program that was explicitly designed for maximum local discretion. There was no reason to believe that local political incentives, objectives, and practices would be consistent with or conducive to attaining national employment policy objectives. The frustrating results could have been expected.

CETA quickly became a surrogate policy—something of a dumping-ground—for national problems that Washington was incapable of addressing or unwilling to address in some other fashion. Other policy problems spilled over into employment policy. Clearly, the paralysis induced by stagflation and structural dislocation in the economy left policy makers desperately searching for something to pick up the pieces. The expansion of PSE under CETA acted in no small part as a political safety valve for policy makers' recognition of the limits to fiscal and monetary stimulation in this new economic environment. CETA also acted as something of a makeshift urban policy, a feeble attempt to deal with the serious structural problems of American cities, which were exacerbated by the recessionary economy but which have their roots elsewhere in the national and international economy. The use of CETA as a palliative for crises it was hardly equipped to handle, but for which it had been recruited, was illuminated in this exchange between Congressman Hawkins and the mayor of one large city:

MAYOR HOLLAND: I just wish that every Member of Congress could serve his time as mayor of a city . . . We are once daily faced with the people who are unemployed . . . They do not have money. They need a job. They come to the mayor. We have no alternative, but to come to see you. We cannot seek recourse on any real estate tax, for example.

MR. HAWKINS: We had, hopefully, designed revenue sharing to take care of that problem rather than handling it through manpower [employment] programs. Unfortunately, because we have not done a good job of providing you with sufficient revenues despite the fact that this recession was largely the result of national policy and not local policy, we imposed the problem on you and then did not provide you with sufficient means of taking care of the problem, and then we offered a manpower [employment] program that caused you, to some extent, to rely on it for counter-cyclical purposes when it was really not altogether intended for that purpose.[50]

In the absence of any national strategy to transform the cities from economic stagnation to vitality, pressures to get fiscal assistance from the national government are inevitable. Yet Congress is as reluctant to redistribute national income on a scale sufficient to address urban needs as it is incapable of designing an economic strategy. During good economic times, when Congress is more generous, redistribution is possible. But in order to gain sufficient legislative support, grant-in-aid programs invariably become more distributive than redistributive. Simple transfers of income from Washington to the localities is unpopular in part because of insistence on accountability for federal money, and in part because, as representatives of local constituencies, congressmen are wary of local political competitors using federal money to build their own political support. Because income redistribution is so difficult to achieve, it is not surprising that advocates of helping distressed urban communities found employment programs a convenient vehicle for that purpose.

Thus CETA became a kind of ersatz urban policy. CETA's PSE program quickly expanded when it became one of Washington's few available tools for coping with the deteriorating economic conditions of the 1970s and the restrictive economic policies that prevailed. These pressures were keenly felt during the Carter administration, coming as they did from the core constituencies in the Democratic party. "Employment and training" served as a respectable symbolic ruse for achieving an objective for which there was no national consensus. This kind of goal displacement was candidly observed by Congresswoman Millicent Fenwick:

We put into a bill that is popular and has become useful, other things which do not belong in the legislation at all. [CETA] has become the lifeblood of many of our central cities . . . because counter-cyclical funds are not popular and revenue sharing does not seem to be very popular either. So we put the whole thing into a basket that has a good name. . . . If we need to help the cities, we ought to say so. If we want to train young people for employment, we ought to say that and make it our only objective. . . . People are not fooled. They know perfectly well that this is not an employment training act. They know perfectly well what it is. And this contributes to the erosion of confidence in Government."[51]

CETA's enactment was the product of a long struggle between the president and Congress, each under the control of a different party. Each had its own policy objectives and institutional jealousies which were partly independent of partisan considerations. Rather than coherence and consistency, the test of an acceptable public policy became simply reaching some agreement. Consideration of possible consequences became relegated to considerations of how well the final bargain optimized the interests of the contenders. In the end, the president conceded on including job creation and the Congress conceded on allowing decentralization. Expedience became the sine qua non of "good" public policy. A benign perspective on this process is held by William Kolberg: "The legislative 'game' has no inflexible criteria by which to judge the 'winners' and the 'losers.' CETA is no exception. All the people intimately involved in the birth of CETA now believe that they were among the 'winners'—and I am no exception. What a delight to play a 'game' with all winners. Such is the art of legislative compromise."[52]

There is something salutary, even rational, about policy making as portrayed in this glowing description. It insures that no one group, institution, or individual policy maker's synoptic view of how the world should operate dominates all others. It is more cautious, open, and responsive to diverse interests and opinions. Most of the interests that found the original employment proposals threatening could find a sympathetic ear in Congress or the executive branch. Yet it carries disadvantages in terms of political accountability and responsible policy making, because no government of the day, in the sense of a party program or definable legislative majority, could be credited with its success or failure. One can point to no single individual, group, or institution and hold them responsible for CETA. Second, it increases the likelihood that public policy will be incoherent, in the sense that parts of the policy will contradict or clash with others. Coherent public policy may demand something more than the piecing together of various ideas and interests through mutual partisan adjustment. The cost of incoherence is likely to be significant, because the unintended consequences of the separate components of the compromise when taken together may be more damaging than each would be by itself.

Flaws in the design of public programs inevitably lead to failures once they are implemented. CETA was not the first program of its type to experience serious problems during implementation. The fact that they were intergovernmental programs has been cited as a chief source of trouble. Martha Derthick's diagnosis of the New Towns In-Town program is a good example: "Failure resulted mainly from the limited ability of the federal government to influence the actions of local governments and from its tendency to conceive goals in ideal terms. Both of these disabilities are associated with its place as the central government in the American federal system."[53]

A much similar postmortem could be written for CETA. Derthick was speaking of the limits to centralization in federal grant programs. Yet ironically, it was these limits that CETA was supposed to overcome. Congress decentralized the management of the program but insisted on grafting onto this arrangement a set of national objectives for which it demanded federal accountability. There is a crucial difference between devolving authority and decentralizing management. The answer to the problem of Washington's limited ability to administer programs, at least ones like CETA that articulate national interests, should not be handing them over to entities that have their own agenda and cannot be controlled. CETA was as disappointing as New Towns In-Town,

because in both cases the federal government insisted on using politically autonomous third parties to run its programs. The crux of the
problem as Derthick identified it—that "the federal government cannot
order these [lower level] governments to do anything"—remained.
Thus, centralization versus decentralization represents a false dichotomy. Until Washington can develop its own network of competent and
effective field administration, these problems cannot be resolved.

The inherent conflict between devolving authority yet maintaining
federal accountability placed the Labor Department in an impossible
situation. According to Charles Knapp, who was in charge of CETA in
Washington during part of the Carter administration, even

> if you specifically define where the balance [between the responsibilities of
> the three levels of government] lies, the problem is that different people
> have different expectations. The states, the cities—the "prime sponsors"—
> read the rhetoric in the preamble of the bill and say, "we are supposed to
> run this program."
>
> Now, when I go up on [Capitol] Hill and testify, I don't get the sense
> that Congress really thinks that I'll let the prime sponsors run that system.
> It's interesting that they don't hold . . . the District of Columbia responsible
> for their rotten CETA program. But they have not hesitated to beat up [As-
> sistant Secretary] Ernie Green and I when we go up in front of [the Com-
> mittee on] Government Operations on how bad the District's CETA program
> is, and it is not an allowable defense to say, but Senator, this is a decentral-
> ized program. They don't like that.[54]

The Labor Department was not up to the task of monitoring almost
500 prime sponsors and 50,000 subcontractors. The goal of monitoring
each prime sponsor once every two years was not achieved. Any general
unit of local government with 100,000 population was eligible to be a
prime sponsor. Employment experts estimate jurisdictions with at least
1 million residents to be a reasonable size for effective administration
and service delivery. This would have substantially decreased the number of prime sponsors the Labor Department would have had to monitor, and would have sharply reduced the balkanization that makes local
labor market planning so difficult. But coalition building in Congress
depends critically upon satisfying the interests of as many local constituencies as possible, who prefer to run their own "piece of the action."
Fragmentation at the top reinforces fragmentation at the bottom, and
vice versa.

The number of staff was inadequate. "DOL lacked enough well-
qualified, trained staff to carry out its role properly through its regional
offices. It generally found itself in a self-made trap of being so caught

up in daily implementation issues that it lost sight of the broad substantive goals toward which implementation activity was presumably directed."[55] Before CETA came on board, the Manpower Administration included 4,200 civil servants; during CETA the Employment and Training Administration included about 800. True, categorical programs impose greater administrative burdens, but it is also the case that CETA's budget was almost three times larger than that of the pre-CETA programs. Operations were plagued by low salaries, which increased staff turnover and caused the most competent personnel to leave.[56] Salaries were frozen for two and one-half years during the Carter period.

Congress compounded CETA's difficulties by constantly tinkering with it. The administrative environment

was characterized by complex and frequently changing administrative rules, delays, and changes in funding, uncertainty over pending reauthorizations, and additions, modifications, and deletions of programs. DOL was unable to push prime sponsors toward national goal achievement, but [especially after 1978] it very nearly pushed them into administrative gridlock by proliferating administrative requirements.[57]

CETA reflected the multiplicity of objectives various legislative majorities thought desirable at particular times. Programs were added and amended, rules and requirements changed, and expectations shifted in a short-term, crisis-management fashion. These vacillations did not lend stability and continuity to implementation.[58] In its short history from 1973 to 1982, CETA was amended no less than eight times and accumulated numerous separate titles, parts, and subparts. Discontinuity in the design of the program was compounded by instability in its appropriations. In eight fiscal years, there were twenty-six separate appropriations, including the many regular, supplemental, and emergency appropriations, plus numerous continuing resolutions.[59] "The erratic appropriations and allocation cycles," according to one study, "kept CETA administrators on a roller-coaster and frustrated their efforts to conduct an orderly program."[60]

Given that Congress takes a proprietary interest in employment programs, it has long resisted provisions in the law that would make planning easier. Automatic triggers for funding, multiyear appropriations, permanent authorization, and advanced funding are all measures that can lessen uncertainty in implementation. But they would take control over the program, especially its budget, out of the hands of the committees. Those in the executive branch also had their own priorities that adversely affected CETA. As Charles Knapp lamented, "When the President decides he is going to balance the budget, he doesn't say, well, gee, I'm really worried about the Title VI program and the local prime sponsors. Yet, when that direction comes back down and hits the prime sponsor, it's chaos, and you've got the mayor saying, well, what the hell is this, the federal government doesn't know what they're doing again."[61]

These difficulties ultimately led to CETA's demise and a loss of confidence. But this was only the most visible cost of failure. The confusion and abuse that accompanied CETA greatly impeded learning. Understanding what works and what does not, under which set of conditions, and for what group in the eligible population requires a stable administrative atmosphere. As one congressional aide succinctly put it, "We don't seem to be able to get past the question 'are they doing things right?' to ask the more important question, 'are they doing the right things?'"[62]

For instance, evaluation studies of the training programs have shown for some time that on-the-job training is more successful than classroom instruction. The number of enrollees in on-the-job training started out very low in the early 1960s and gradually increased throughout the decade. Once CETA started, however, the proportion enrolled in on-the-job-training declined and continued to do so throughout the 1970s. Why did this happen? Because the administrative structure that existed before CETA was swept away and with it many of the institutional linkages that had been established with the local business community. Instability in administrative and service delivery arrangements has been all too much a part of the history of employment programs:

If anything, the process of decentralization impeded the problem-solving process. Current CETA staff throughout this nation are practitioners without a legacy. The fact that seems to have escaped general attention is that when CETA was decentralized to local governments, the knowledge of past successes and failures was not transmitted with the program. The entire perspective of past employment programs was lost. Program development and implementation was relegated to well-intentioned but untrained novices who based program structure on surface and pragmatic parameters. When some programs proved successful, there was no mechanism for transferral of information—a condition that has only marginally improved after six years of operation.[63]

The significant management challenges posed by a schizophrenic law, where different actors have different expectations and are pulling the system in different directions, and finally without enough people and resources—all these are elements of CETA's troubled saga. They reflect in no small measure the institutions that we have inherited for making and carrying out public policy.

Part III

Interests

8

Organized Interests in the Arenas of Employment Policy

WE TURN OUR attention now to a bottom-up view of the politics of employment policy, by examining the role and influence of organized interests. We have seen that it is useful to conceive of two main employment policy arenas. The first is what we might call the employment policy subsystem, which deals directly and primarily with programmatic issues: whether to provide the unemployed with training, jobs, or other services; the eligibility criteria for participants; which service providers will be used; the administrative arrangements for carrying out the programs; and the level of annual appropriations. The second arena concerns broader issues and public policies that impinge upon the subsystem, setting the parameters for the mission and the scale of employment policy. This arena involves a somewhat different constellation of political actors, patterns of interest formation, and levels of conflict and visibility. Debates over full-employment legislation, the conduct of macroeconomic policies (especially major initiatives in the area of fiscal policy), fall into this category. It is useful to deal with each of these arenas separately.

THE EMPLOYMENT POLICY SUBSYSTEM

To discern the role and influence of interests in employment programs, it is necessary to examine three aspects of interest group politics. The first question deals with group *organization*, the second with their *involvement* in the political arena, and the third looks at the *effectiveness* of groups in the making of employment policy. First, do relevant interests exist that are organized and capable of conflict? That is, are those individuals and organizations with clear stakes in the decisions about employment policy sufficiently organized and able to participate in the political arena? Second, are those interests that are organized and capable of participation actively involved in the making of employment

195

policy? Here we will examine the duration, intensity, and nature of organized interests' involvement. Third, where interests have been both organized and involved, how effective, or influential, have they been in getting their demands and preferences translated into public policy? Two somewhat different criteria can be used to judge effectiveness in this context. Groups can be deemed effective simply by ascertaining whether public policy seems to reflect the preferences of the most organized and involved interests (or some balance among contending interests). In other words, do interests get more or less of what they are seeking from policy decisions? A stricter test of effectiveness has to do with control over policy decisions. That is, are the views and actions of the relevant interests decisive? Do they consistently prevail over decisions dealing with the direction and content of employment policy, the particular objectives of the different programs, and the size of their budgets? Let us deal with each of these three aspects in turn, as they apply to employment policy.

Group Organization

A distinctive feature of the employment policy arena is that the intended beneficiaries of training and jobs programs—namely, the unemployed and impoverished—are among the most politically impotent and inert groups in society. Kay Schlozman and Sidney Verba found that, while joblessness creates a severe personal strain on individuals, it is "not translated into politically meaningful activity." The unemployed "are less likely to vote, less likely to take part in other political activities, less likely to be interested in politics, and less likely to be active participants in voluntary associations."[1] The historical record recounted here clearly supports their finding. There is no evidence of the unemployed themselves engaging in political action in their own behalf.[2] As one might expect, it matters a great deal that the ostensible beneficiaries of employment and training programs are politically inert. Schlozman and Verba found unanimous agreement among influential persons involved in employment policy in Washington that if the unemployed were more vocal it would make a difference. "Most felt that the problem [of unemployment] would have been perceived as being more urgent if the unemployed had dramatized their own plight."[3]

While the lack of organization among the unemployed is significant, it alone does not preclude all possibility of interest group politics. Organized groups with stakes in employment policy clearly exist. Those for whom employment policy is (at least potentially) relevant fall into two broad groups. Following the categorization provided by James Q. Wilson, there are groups motivated by "purposive incentives" and those motivated by "material incentives." The former type of organization "is one that works explicitly for the benefit of some larger public or the society as a whole and not one that works chiefly for the benefit of members, except insofar as members derive a sense of fulfilled commitment . . . from the effort."[4] The latter type exists to attract and distribute material benefits under its control.

Purposive groups include advocacy organizations that seek to represent the interests of particular groups of unemployed individuals who suffer higher rates of unemployment than those experienced by the general population. They are motivated by a sense of social justice and rely mainly upon moral suasion. Civil rights groups act as spokesmen for disadvantaged minorities (e.g., the National Association for the Advancement of Colored People), womens' groups act for women, (e.g., the National Organization for Women), and religious organizations for the poor generally (e.g., the National Council of Churches). While these groups regularly support measures to help the unemployed, they are involved in a substantial range of public policy issues. Unemployment is only one concern, and not usually the most central one. The NAACP has traditionally focused its activities on issues such as voting rights, desegregation, and affirmative action. The National Organization for Women tries to represent the views of women across a wide range of public policy matters. Occasionally these groups have joined together to form a coalition, but these have been very loose alliances without many resources at their disposal.

Groups that have material stakes in employment programs are (1) those that deliver training and other employment services at the local level with whom the federal government has contracts, and (2) the local governments and public agencies that administer programs at the local level, particularly since the establishment of a decentralized administrative system. It is to these groups that the federal employment and training dollars flow. There are numerous organizations that train, test, counsel, and offer placement services to those who participate in employment and training programs. The sheer diversity of service providers makes it difficult for any single organization to represent their views in Washington. Providers do not speak with a united voice when important policy issues are debated. Many of them—schools, businesses, unions, OICs, and others—operate independently of one another at the local level, and behave more as competitors for scarce resources than as allies.[5] For example, local businesses involved with on-the-job training may to have little to do with vocational education schools. Similarly, regular vocational education schools, which often have good reputations in the community, are likely to have little to do with schools funded by programs like CETA, which tend to be those with poorer reputations.[6]

Local government organizations that have managed programs are much better organized. The principal organizations here include the U.S. Conference of Mayors, the National League of Cities, the National Association of Counties, and the Interstate Conference of Employment Service Agencies. Local and state officials planned and administered the programs in their respective communities in the 1970s and currently share management with state governments and local businesses under the Job Training Partnership Act (JTPA).

Labor and business, the two most important economic interests in the private labor market, are motivated both by material and by purposive incentives. Both unions and businesses contract with the government to provide on-the-job training, and public employment programs have supplied municipal unions with federally funded jobs. However, among the largest and best-established labor and business organizations in Washington (e.g., the AFL-CIO, the Chamber of Commerce, and the National Association of Manufacturers), purposive incentives are probably greater than material ones. Given that the eligibility for employment and training programs has more often than not been restricted to the disadvantaged and unemployed, the unions and firms affiliated with these organizations simply do not have tremendous material stakes in them for most of their members.

The extent of business and labor organization should not be exaggerated. Compared to other nations, American employers and employees exhibit relatively low levels of organizational density. Union membership is low in the United States, now standing at less than 20 percent of the nonagricultural work force. And some of the more important unions, such as the Teamsters Union, have not been affiliated with the AFL-CIO. There is no single business federation, but rather several, none of which can properly be said to speak for business as a whole.[7]

In sum, the unemployed themselves are not organized into pressure groups and do not engage in any substantial or on-going political activity. Nevertheless, organized groups do exist that have at least some stake in employment policy. Many of these groups, such as service providers and advocacy organizations, are organizationally fragmented or without great resources. There are others, however, that do have the organizational resources and cohesion to participate extensively in the policy process.

Group Involvement

Rather than examine groups' involvement in the abstract, it is more useful to look at various aspects of their involvement in public policy.

First, there is the matter of the *duration* of involvement. Do interests have a long history of sustained engagement in policy debates and decision making, or do they appear on the scene only intermittently and for discrete periods of time? Second, we can speak of the *intensity* (or level) of involvement. Despite the ebb and flow of interests' involvement, when they do get involved, are they highly active in making their views known and pressing their positions on issues? That is, can we identify instances when organized interests considered their stakes in policy of paramount importance and became intensely engaged in what was going on? Interests that are actively involved must first be attentive to what takes place in the policy arena, and attentiveness depends upon the salience of employment policy for them. If employment policy is not highly salient for any given interest, it means that the policy is relatively low on its list of priorities and where it should invest its scarce resources. We would expect involvement to intensify when the stakes to the group are clear, direct, and substantial.

Finally, there is the question of the *nature* of interests' involvement in the policy-making process. Making public policy does not boil down to a decision or even a set of decisions. Rather, it is a process that involves a variety of interrelated activities: identifying problems, publicizing them, getting them on the government agenda, formulating policy options, building a consensus, and so forth. Interests may be involved at one stage in the policy-making process, but not at others. Likewise, they may focus on certain aspects of a given policy proposal but be indifferent to or incapable of forming positions on others.

Unlike many other areas of domestic policy, the absence of sustained involvement by well-established interest organizations is a distinctive feature of the employment and training subsystem. In agriculture, education, and many other areas, there are well-established national organizations representing producer or client interests that have had a long-standing interest in debates over policy. No national organization comparable in size or reputation to the National Farm Bureau Federation, the American Federation of Teachers, or the National Trucking Association has sustained active participation in employment policy.

If there were any organized interests that one would expect to be continuously involved in the government's efforts to address unemployment, they would be organized labor and business. As the largest and dominant member of the liberal-labor coalition, organized labor has been a vocal proponent of public intervention on behalf of the unemployed since the 1930s. The AFL-CIO backed the War on Poverty in the 1960s and was one of CETA's major supporters throughout the 1970s. Unions also have been sponsors of on-the-job training through their apprenticeship programs. This record notwithstanding, labor's concern with employment measures tends to vary with economic conditions—increasing with rises in the unemployment rate, decreasing during relatively prosperous periods. The AFL-CIO has become intimately involved when the president and Congress are locked in negotiations, such as when the final CETA compromise was hammered out in 1973. More sustained and focused attention has come from specific unions like the American Federation of State, County, and Municipal Employees. Like labor unions generally, its attention has focused essentially on job creation rather than training programs.

The overall low level of organized labor's involvement is particularly puzzling with regard to two pieces of legislation. One might presume that labor would have been particularly interested in structural unemployment, specifically programs to retrain displaced workers. The Manpower Development and Training Act (MDTA) was specifically directed toward helping workers in highly unionized sectors of the economy like mining, textiles, and heavy industry. Yet, aside from labor's March on Washington in 1958, a protest that was more a demonstration of generalized dissatisfaction than of legislative lobbying for specific programs, labor was conspicuous by its lack of visibility. According to Stanley Ruttenberg, the AFL-CIO's spokesman on Capitol Hill at the time,

There wasn't that much interest on the part of the labor movement in developing a piece of legislation that would provide training. . . . The Labor movement's intervention into the Manpower Development and Training Act was rather insignificant and modest until they were well along in the first or second draft of that legislation in '62. I think it is crystal clear that the labor movement didn't originate MDTA . . . didn't originate the idea, and were not enthusiastic about MDTA when it was first proposed.[8]

Why would a group with an ostensibly vital interest in a program remain so aloof? Ruttenberg points to two reasons. First, labor found the Keynesian analysis of unemployment more compelling than the structural argument:

They [the labor movement] were still thinking within the general terms that the way to stimulate the economy was not through structural changes such as changes in the ability of people to perform their work, but were more concerned about national economic efforts. . . . So it was aggregate demand versus structural change. The labor movement was strongly on the side of aggregate demand, a stimulative economy, monetary policy, budget expenditures, tax reductions. . . . The labor movement was not strong on the structural side. They were strong on the aggregate demand side.[9]

Second, there was a defensiveness on the part of particular unions that perceived MDTA as a threat to their organizational interests:

I think that in those days there was a feeling on the part of the building trades unions obviously that . . . any kind of government training program would interfere with their apprenticeship program and that wouldn't be good. . . . There [also] was a feeling on the part of some of the other unions like the needletrades, that their problem was that any kind of a training program would turn out to be a subsidy to run-away employers—that therefore, training in the needletrades serving machine operators and so forth, had to be prohibited.[10]

Labor's lack of enthusiasm for the program did not hinder its passage, but it did deny MDTA what should have been its most important organized constituency. This would not prove favorable in the long run, especially when the program had to compete with other budget priorities.

As a second example, take the displaced worker retraining program, established under Title II of the current JTPA. If ever there were intended to be a program of direct benefit to rank-and-file union members it would have to be retraining for displaced workers. Title II attempted to address the dislocations left in the wake of the many structural transitions in the economy: the shift from "smokestack" to "high-tech" and service industries, international competition, automation, and relocation of domestic industries from the "rust belt" to the "sun belt." The clientele for the program was not the traditional groups served by the training programs—the disadvantaged, youth, and so forth—but skilled, blue collar, union members who had been rendered obsolete and were in need of retraining.

Yet organized labor was conspicuously absent throughout the process of getting the displaced worker issue on the political agenda and into legislation. As one Senate staffer put it:

Basically what they [the labor unions] did was not say anything. It is very hard to say what they really think. They didn't come in and oppose it, but when asked "why don't you help us work on this thing?" they would say "no thank you" or "we're busy this week." We called the auto workers, we had a day of hearings on unemployment problems in the auto industry . . . we had a hard time getting the UAW to even send a witness. They finally sent their director of resources, a very knowledgeable guy who gave us lots of statistics, but he is not the guy who speaks on policy and legislation. He didn't really say "here is what we should do about it."[11]

Business involvement has been more sporadic than that of labor. It began in the late 1960s when President Johnson called upon the private sector to hire and train disadvantaged workers. The Job Opportunities in the Business Sector (JOBS) initiative was created along with the National Alliance of Business (NAB), but interest waned in the 1970s once the labor market slackened and few jobs existed for which to train the disadvantaged. Business involvement revived in 1978 during the Carter administration, and continues under the JTPA, where private industry councils are assigned a major role in the program.

Similarly, local governments exhibited sporadic involvement. Mayors and county executives did not get involved until the 1970s when, under CETA, decentralization and the promise of public employment jobs spurred them to do so. When local discretion was substantially reduced in 1978, their participation virtually ended. Those organizations that deliver employment and training services (other than labor unions and businesses) always show up at congressional committee hearings and are regularly consulted when there are attempts to change policy. But the involvement of those service providers that are best organized at the national level has declined considerably since the 1960s. The American Vocational Education Association (AVA) was a serious participant in the early 1960s (mainly in its unsuccessful attempt to become the sole provider of remedial training) but lost interest as control over manpower programs gradually shifted out of HEW's Office of Education and into the Labor Department. The interest of the state-run employment services has waned since 1973, when the CETA legislation granted to local prime sponsors the discretion of whether or not to use the U.S. Employment Service. Community-based organizations like the opportunity industrial centers and community action agencies do not have very resourceful national organizations.

The few instances of intense group involvement in employment programs stand out. One was the AVA's (ultimately unsuccessful) attempt to incorporate MDTA within its existing programs. The AVA wrote the bill introduced in Congress by Senator Clark and lobbied heavily for it during deliberations. A second example was the persistent lobbying by local governments who pressed for maintenance of public service employment (PSE) in the 1970s within a decentralized administrative framework.

Did group involvement manifest itself during critical stages in the policy process? Two of the most critical stages are agenda setting and policy formulation. It is difficult to think of many instances where interest groups initiated some change in public policy by pushing an issue onto the political agenda. Organized labor's March on Washington in 1958, to demand action on unemployment after the Democrats had taken control of the Senate, is one such instance. It led Senate majority leader Johnson to form the Special Committee on Unemployment Problems, chaired by Senator Eugene McCarthy, which traveled around the nation publicizing the problem of structural unemployment. Usually, groups reacted to issues and policy proposals that were already on the agenda and had been initiated by other political actors. The general pattern has been noninvolvement. "What is striking," Eli Ginzberg said, "has been the minor involvement of business and labor in the [employment] programs, from planning to implementation."[12]

What about group involvement in policy formulation—developing new ideas about the nature of unemployment, deciding what steps ought to be taken to combat it, and translating these ideas into concrete proposals? Again, there are scattered instances of interest group involvement, but no overall pattern. William Cooper of the AVA drafted the bill that Senator Clark first introduced in Congress to establish the nation's first manpower program. Although the final legislative product (MDTA) was not simply an expansion of the responsibilities of vocational education that the AVA had demanded, it did incorporate much of Cooper's initial proposal.

Oftentimes when groups got involved in some aspect of employment programs, their involvement was not spontaneous or self-generated. Demands, rather than bubbling up from the groups themselves, were often stimulated from above. Groups rarely became involved on their own. Instead they were induced to become active—drawn in by policy makers searching for a constituency to support some initiative or an effective agency to manage the programs at the local level.

Organized labor became involved in support of the MDTA at the behest of the Labor Department. The Labor Department under the Johnson and Nixon administrations in the mid- to late-1960s also actively sought the involvement of state, and then local, governments in the planning and administration of the programs. Through initiatives like the Concentrated Employment Program (CEP) and the Cooperative Area Manpower Planning System (CAMPS), the Labor Department tried to devolve greater responsibility on these lower levels of government. The Nixon administration sought support of the states for its proposal to reform the programs of the 1960s, and when it was not forthcoming, the administration turned to local governments. The many local mechanisms that have been created or recruited to plan and operate the programs have all been created from above: CAMPS, CEP, community action agencies, CETA prime sponsors, private industry councils.

Business involvement, too, was prodded by the government. President Johnson galvanized the business community into active (although as it turned out, short-lived) participation in manpower training when he formed the National Alliance of Business and set up the JOBS program. Similarly, the Carter administration sought business support with its Private Sector Initiative Program in 1978, which served as the seed for business involvement in today's JTPA. In short, the generation of constituency support for the programs usually has come from above, part and parcel of the quest for an effective institutional mechanism at the local level.

A prerequisite for involvement in the policy process is a cohesive national organization. Some groups, like those organizations that provide training and employment services, lack organizational unity. Schools, unions, businesses, the employment service, OICs, and other organizations all contract with the government to train, counsel, evaluate, and place those who participate in the programs. The sheer number and diversity of local service providers make it difficult for them to speak with a single voice on policy issues or concentrate their resources to maximize their influence on decision makers. They are organizationally fragmented and compete at the local level for contracts.

Second, not only do the providers as a whole lack unity, but each provider is internally divided. Because each locality has had discretion in selecting their own providers, participation in the programs for any particular provider varies from locality to locality. This has made it difficult to develop organizational cohesion at the national level. Vocational education schools may provide classroom training to CETA participants in one area, but not in another; the Employment Service may be used in one community, but be left out in another; local chapters of the National Alliance of Business may be heavily involved in one city but not in the next.

Finally, the best organized providers—traditionally the vocational educators and the state Employment Services—were established long before employment and training programs came on board. The client groups that support these providers are not the disadvantaged unemployed, who have been the primary population that the training and work experience programs have sought to help. Vocational education is more concerned about federal funding for the regular vocational education budget and about serving its nondisadvantaged clientele. Similarly, the Employment Service is still heavily involved in administering unemployment insurance and has always viewed employment programs as not fitting in with its traditional functions and clienteles. The result has been little involvement of service providers on questions of national employment policy.

We have seen that there do exist interests that have national organizations and that do get involved, to some degree at least, in the policy process. The reason some of these groups, such as business, labor, and civil rights organizations, fail to get more involved is that employment and training programs are not a top priority on their legislative agendas. Organizations like the AFL-CIO, the Chamber of Commerce, and the NAACP take positions and lobby for a wide range of causes and programs. Employment and training programs must compete for their attention and resources with much larger programs (e.g., Social Security and Medicare) and programs that are viewed as having a much more direct and vital impact on their organizational and members' interests. For organized labor, for instance, unemployment and medical insurance, old age pensions, and labor law reform have a direct and tangible impact on the interests of the rank and file and the unions' organizational survival. The NAACP and National Organization for Women are concerned with unemployment and poverty, but their main focus has traditionally been in the area of gaining and protecting equal rights for the members of the groups they represent. Employment and training programs are simply not perceived as being as critical as voting rights, job or housing discrimination, abortion rights, and so forth. It is not surprising that Verba and Schlozman described the liberal-labor coalition's concern with measures intended to address the plight of the poor and unemployed as "sincere but not paramount," motivated mainly by a sense of "social justice" rather than any overriding direct stake in the programs.[13]

Organized business has never seriously considered these programs as playing a central role in making the labor market work more efficiently. Unlike the business community in some other nations, few American businesses have shown an interest in how programs can be used to stabilize the business cycle, achieve a more favorable trade-off between unemployment and inflation, or speed adaptation to structural changes in the market. Business's interest in training programs has come only of late–in the 1980s under the JTPA. The JOBS program of the late 1960s was a modest endeavor, and businesses' interest in it soon waned. Planning and implementation of both efforts enjoyed the active participation of the NAB. Yet, the NAB represents only a particular segment of American businessmen—mainly retired heads of medium-sized firms located in urban areas. Whether genuinely interested in the plight of the "have nots" in society or more cynically motivated to prevent social disorder, business certainly does not view these programs as having a critical role in serving its broader economic interests or in maintaining a healthy economy.

Employment programs are a low priority for most groups because of the size and design of the programs themselves. Eligibility for many of them has been restricted to the disadvantaged (who are not members of any of these organizations), and their budgets have been low relative to many other domestic programs. Most interests fail to become intensely involved simply because they see the stakes for themselves as limited, as in fact they are. Taking this point a step further, it is apt to say that organized interests have probably had less impact on employment policy than the other way around. It is the design and purposes of the programs that have resulted in the relative lack of involvement on the part of organized interests.

Groups have failed to get involved even when the programs promised very direct, tangible benefits for their members. Again, the most puzzling example is the noninvolvement of organized labor in programs to retrain dislocated workers. Labor's role in getting issues on the agenda, in fashioning policy proposals, and in supporting their adoption has been negligible. There is no simple explanation for labor's curious position on an issue so seemingly vital to its interests. One Senate staffer interviewed cited labor's fears that a retraining program would serve as a "cost-cutting measure," as a ruse for taking away unemployment compensation benefits under existing trade adjustment programs. The unions' ambivalence toward retraining also stems from their perception that the immediate interests of their organizations will be threatened:

If you look at it in very parochial terms, it is very clear [that] if you are going to retrain steel workers you're not going to retrain them to be steel workers. They are going to belong to some other union, or no union at all. [If you advocate retraining], you're showing the membership that you are not protecting their jobs . . . and you will reduce the dues-paying members.[14]

Labor's defense of the status quo may be due to its declining organizational resources and political strength throughout the postwar period. Labor initially looked upon the MDTA, an initiative arising out of structural problems in the labor market broadly similar to those experienced today, as a threat to the building trades unions' control over apprenticeship. When labor decided to back the idea, it did so more as a show of support for the Labor Department in its struggle with the Bureau of Vocational Education than as support for retraining itself.

Unlike many of their European counterparts, American trade unions are internally unsuited for wholesale involvement in economic and social policy. Barbash identifies several factors to account for this: the relatively narrow base of union membership; the absence for many years of important unions in the AFL-CIO; the decentralization of collective bargaining authority; the lack of a strong trade-union–political-party link; the insufficiency of union technical and research staff; and employer resistance to the recognition of unions as partners in economic policy.[15]

The major exception to what has been said so far about the lack of group involvement are the local governments that managed CETA programs at the local level. Decentralization and decategorization of the programs in the early 1970s struck a responsive chord with state and local officials, who formed a natural constituency in support of the concepts. By 1970, lower levels of government were fiscally dependent on Washington. With dependency came increased administrative burdens, a skewing of state and local fiscal priorities, and federal intrusion into affairs formerly under the exclusive control of state and local officials. The growth of federal-state-local entanglements produced a well-organized intergovernmental lobby that included the National Governors Conference, National League of Cities, the U.S. Conference of Mayors, and the National Association of Counties. These groups were a major source of support for the Nixon administration in its fight with Congress for decentralization.

The involvement of these groups was clearly tied to the provision of public service jobs, initially with few restrictions on their use. However, local officials were much less interested in lobbying on behalf of training programs. Jobs, not training, were what spurred local interests to stay involved in CETA. Money for jobs helped ease local fiscal burdens, but training programs served only groups (usually the young, the disadvantaged, and minority group members) with little political influence. As the Labor Department tightened restrictions on the use of PSE throughout the 1970s, local discretion was eroded. And as CETA dollars dried up after 1978, so did the primary incentive for the prime sponsors' interest in, and support for, the program. Once the discretion and dollars disappeared, so did local government support.

The inability to maintain a permanent stake in programs like CETA among local program administrators certainly has been an important reason for the low level of interest group involvement. The recurrent search to find an institution at the subnational level to effectively run the programs has proved fruitless. With no organizational structure having taken permanent root at the state or local level, there is little opportunity for a strong political interest based on such an organization to develop. Again and again, dissatisfaction with how the programs have been managed has led Congress to replace one set of authorities at the local level with another and to reshuffle administrative arrangements between the federal government and the subnational units of government.

Group Effectiveness

As defined at the beginning of the chapter, effectiveness of organized interests in public policy has two similar, though not identical, meanings: (1) that public policy simply reflects the interests of the most organized and resourceful groups, or (2) that organized interests control the agenda and decisions that are made. In one sense it is patently obvious that employment policy has reflected the preferences of those groups that have been the most highly organized around the issues of unemployment and poverty. Virtually all of these groups (labor, urban interests, service providers, liberal advocates, etc.) have been in favor of federal employment and training efforts. Although organized business has been opposed to PSE, they too have supported training programs. Policy outputs, then, seem to match the overall positions taken by many of the relevant groups.

However, the congruence between the preferences of supportive interests and policy outputs is limited. Most of these groups have asked for higher levels of spending than have been appropriated. Even when sympathetic congressional majorities and presidents have been in power, appropriations for job creation programs have always been lower than those called for by the liberal-labor groups. Moreover, while support from such groups has been constant over time, there has been great change and volatility in the kinds of programs provided and in the levels of appropriations. Perhaps most importantly, the coalition of liberal-labor groups, urban mayors, and other interests has not achieved one of its most fundamental aims: a genuine commitment to a policy of full employment, a topic covered later in the chapter.

Is there any evidence to suggest that organized interests exert control over decisions? If the argument of the previous section is valid—that the attention paid by interests to employment policy has been limited, and that their participation in the policy arena has been modest—it is unlikely that they have been able to exert any kind of sustained control over employment policy. There is the possibility, however, that even though groups do not exert control over policy making in any ongoing, detailed fashion, they do have control intermittently—at critical decision-making junctures, or when unemployment is at crisis levels. At such times, groups might be aroused and mobilized and bring their influence to bear decisively on the outcome. A few such episodes stand out as clear examples of this kind of control. Organized labor's influence was critical in maintaining PSE at particular junctures in the 1970s, most clearly when the final CETA compromise was hammered out in 1973. Of course, there are at least as many instances when group pressure resulted in no action by policy makers (e.g., organized labor's 1958 March on Washington), or when groups simply were defeated in their effort to prevent some undesired action (e.g., the termination of CETA jobs.)

One reason it is so difficult to discern whether interest groups have made a decisive impact on policy decisions is that episodes of heightened group pressure that resulted in securing some favorable legislation usually coincided with periods when policy makers were already predisposed to take the action that the groups favored. These periods include recessions when unemployment was on the rise, or the coming to power of a new administration, or periods of generalized recognition that new legislation was needed to reform employment and training programs. The ability of liberals to enact and then expand PSE throughout the 1970s, for instance, was due at least as much to the broader economic and political climate (high unemployment, the desire of Nixon for administrative reform, the election of Carter, etc.) than to direct pressures from organized groups.

The litmus test for ascertaining just how much control organized groups exercised over policy decisions are those instances where groups were highly mobilized and took clear positions that were contrary to majority opinion in Congress or to the position of the administration. In the early 1960s the American Vocational Education Association, reputed to be one of the most influential lobbies in Washington at the time, made a major effort to gain control over manpower training. But in the face of opposition from the Labor Department and Bureau of the Budget, the AVA was forced to compromise on the design of the MDTA. By the mid-1960s it was clear that a separate system of remedial training, stressing on-the-job rather than classroom instruction, had developed outside of the vocational education framework. Similar defeats were suffered by the state agencies and local service providers that wished to retain the categorical grant-in-aid manpower programs that had proliferated in the decade. The categorical programs were swept away with the passage of CETA, and those who had run the programs and delivered the services had to accept a consolidated, decentralized system. Implementation of the programs was handed over to local and state governments, and in particular to the elected officials who headed them.

CETA's prime sponsors fared little better than their predecessors in capturing the employment and training arena. In 1976, only two years after CETA had been implemented, the Labor Department (encouraged by congressional concerns with fiscal substitution and reports of mismanagement) began reasserting managerial control. With CETA's reauthorization in 1978, local officials lost a great deal of their discretion in the use of CETA funds. Despite pressures from the officials to maintain the funding and discretion that was granted in the original CETA legislation, Congress and the Carter administration were able to drastically curtail funding for PSE after 1978, and placed numerous restrictions on how PSE monies could be used. And the program was entirely eliminated under the Reagan administration, despite the fact that many of the organized recipients were highly dependent on the program. When there was a return to decentralized management in 1983 with the JTPA, local prime sponsors were forced to share authority with state governments and private industry. In sum, there is scant evidence of organized interests exerting any kind of sustained control over the employment policy subsystem.

Finally, it is possible that business interests have consciously contrived (or at least permitted) employment programs to exist as part of a strategy for buying social peace, or as a way to preempt public policies that might be more threatening to the prerogatives of business. This would be consistent with the "corporate liberal" thesis, which posits the existence of an enlightened business elite that directs the state to enact policies to save the capitalist system.[16] The NAB's involvement in JOBS and JTPA reflected concern that frustration and alienation among disadvantaged groups might result in social disruption, much as it did in the late 1960s. But given the modest size of both programs, there is little indication that business considered these programs as important instruments for maintaining social control. Moreover, in both cases it was not business people but public officials who took the initiative in getting business involved. When we turn to the largest program, CETA, the facts hardly accord with the corporate liberal thesis. CETA, and in particular PSE, came under consistent attack as wasteful and ineffective make-work by organizations like the Chamber of Commerce when they testified before Congress. If American capitalists favored CETA out of enlightened self-interest, they certainly kept it a secret. There is little evidence of direct capitalist domination of employment programs as posited by many class theorists. Corporate liberalism provides no persuasive argument for understanding how these programs developed, why they operated the way they did, and what forces were responsible for shaping and maintaining them.[17]

While the involvement and effectiveness of organized groups have been limited and sporadic, groups have not been inconsequential. Their primary contribution has been the political support they have provided policy makers seeking to achieve a change in policy or the expansion of a program. Employment and training programs have consistently drawn support from the liberal-labor groups. This coalition has been the bedrock of electoral support for the national Democratic party.

The coalition's success depended upon Democratic party control of the White House. Democrats held majorities in both houses of Congress from 1958–1980, but control of the executive branch shifted between the two political parties. The demands of the coalition for employment programs received a greater measure of acceptance in Democratic than in GOP administrations. Under the former, more new programs were introduced and existing ones were expanded faster. Under Republican chief executives, legislative breakthroughs were less frequent and expansions more modest. Eisenhower blocked area redevelopment legislation dealing with structural unemployment and resisted the adoption of Keynesian techniques for stimulating the economy. The Kennedy administration saw the enactment of the Area Redevelopment Act (predecessor to the Economic Development Administration) and MDTA. Under Johnson a series of poverty-related training and work experience programs were enacted, along with the Tax Reduction Act of 1964. Under Nixon the only program created was the public service employment program under the Emergency Employment Act of 1971, foisted upon a Republican president who vigorously resisted it until the recession of that year. CETA was primarily a reorganization of existing programs. The same is true of Ford's reluctant acceptance of Title VI, the countercyclical component of CETA during the unemployment crisis of 1974/75. When the Democrats returned to office in 1977, Carter doubled the size of CETA's budget by using the program as part of his economic stimulus package. Under GOP administrations, public service employment was under virtually constant threat of elimination. With Reagan's election in 1980, public service employment was eliminated, and the total budget was substantially reduced. Budget outlays for PSE, in particular, fared much better when both branches of government were controlled by Democrats.

One place where organized interests have had a special impact is on the allocation of resources. First, while CETA dollars were tilted toward areas with high rates of unemployment and poverty, because any general unit of local government with a population above 100,000 was designated as eligible for funding, the program's resources were dispersed across virtually the entire nation. Thus, CETA was more distributive than redistributive, particularly when compared to the pre-CETA programs. According to Ripley and Franklin, "the clients receiving benefits are governmental units—states, cities, counties—rather than a class of persons—the economically disadvantaged. The choices about who gets what at the expense of whom (the essence of a redistributive program) are made unclear by the use of a formula to allocate funds and by the stress on local control."[18] Rural and suburban communities, lobbying through the National Association of Counties, were designated as prime sponsors even though many of these communities were relatively prosperous. The association was especially effective during the CETA reauthorization of 1978, when Congress made a conscious effort to target the money to those most in need. Attempts by

Congressman Hawkins and other urban liberals to concentrate CETA money in areas with the greatest need were defeated by rural Democrats and Republican members from relatively better-off suburban communities.

Budget outlays for training programs tend to be lower and more stable than those for job programs, which get more money but have more volatile annual budgets. In part this may be simply because more people are unemployed during recessions, when there is a job shortage, than are unemployed at any time because of inadequate training and other structural labor market problems. In part it may be because cyclical unemployment is the result of sharp downturns that are felt nationwide, while structural unemployment builds gradually over time, persists, and is more concentrated among particular individuals and areas of the nation (and is therefore less visible). What impelled the introduction and expansion of PSE were the recurrent episodes of cyclical unemployment in the 1970s, not poverty or other kinds of long-term structural unemployment.

Until the CETA amendments of 1978, it was mainly the nondisadvantaged, cyclically unemployed, who during good economic times enjoy stable employment, who benefited most from public employment. The cyclically unemployed tend to be adult, skilled, blue or white collar workers, with long histories of stable employment. Training, on the other hand, serves primarily those who have difficulty finding and keeping jobs even in good times. They often suffer from long spells of joblessness, many are young, from disadvantaged backgrounds, and lack basic skills and work experience. Those who suffer from cyclical unemployment are more likely to be politically attentive and to participate in politics. It is not surprising, then, that training programs have meager budgets. No significant organized or attentive constituency exists that demands more spending. If such support existed, or if it could be built, presumably the fiscal commitment would be greater.

Congress's willingness to spend more on jobs than on training also reflects the intense and vocal lobbying for programs like the Emergency Employment Act and CETA by organizations representing local governments (i.e., the U.S. Conference of Mayors, the National League of Cities, and the National Association of Counties) that sought public service jobs to relieve their fiscal constraints. "Jobs for the unemployed" became a powerful slogan to maintain congressional support for fiscal assistance, which would have been harder to maintain if these governments had simply based their appeals on the need for a subsidy to provide local public services. Because money for training programs does not have the fungible quality that money for jobs does, the former does not stimulate the kinds of intense lobbying efforts that the latter does. Given that a sizable proportion of these jobs simply replaced ones that already existed on municipal payrolls (because of substitution effects), the number of new jobs created for the unemployed was less than the number of jobs funded. Even in cases where new positions were created, it was skilled, experienced workers who were likely to get CETA jobs, not those with the most serious employment problems.

It is remarkable, at least from the point of view of group theory, that training programs exist at all. According to a Senate Labor and Public Welfare Committee staffer, "For many of these social programs that don't affect anybody's 'real economic interests' . . . the amount of [interest group] support you need is remarkably little. . . . It doesn't take a lot of support for a program such as this."[19] Perhaps, but without much active support outside of Congress, a program that is perceived as not affecting anyone's "real economic interests" has little chance to make much of an impact on the problem it is intended to address.

The major lesson to be drawn from this is not a very happy one for the unemployed. Higher levels of spending are associated with the mobilization of an organized interest and the degree of salience of unemployment among voters. Yet the very participation of groups like local governments in garnering larger budgets increases the distributive elements in the programs and reduces their redistributive potential. There is no guarantee that the interests of the unemployed, and especially the disadvantaged, long-term jobless, will be compatible with those of the constituency groups that seek program benefits. Thus, without strong, active organizations of their own, the poor and unemployed can look forward to either small-budget programs designed just for them, or programs with larger budgets from which they get limited benefits.

It is important not to lose sight of a broader point when discussing the role of interests as stimulators of public resources. Even at their peak of funding, employment programs never have been able to serve more than a fraction of those who could benefit from their services. In fiscal 1977/78, when spending on CETA was at its highest, spending amounted to only 3.2 percent of the federal budget and 0.7 percent of gross national product. By comparative standards, these figures are low. Comparison with other nations also strongly suggests that the active support and involvement of organized business and labor is crucial for generating high levels of public funding for employment programs. In Sweden, for instance, business and labor have been brought in as key participants in formulating and implementing them. As one observer of the Swedish experience explains, "this kind of [labor and business] involvement produces strong internal stimuli within the system for constantly improving standards, and equally important, an alliance which can be effective in securing large flows of public funds to the purpose of developing active labor market policies."[20]

THE BROADER CONTEXT OF EMPLOYMENT POLICY

The argument up to this point has been that organized interests have had only limited involvement in, and influence on, decisions in the employment policy subsystem. By looking only at the role that interests have played directly in decisions over employment programs themselves, we may be missing influence that has been indirect and more subtle. It could be that, although organized interests have not been of central importance in the employment subsystem, they have played a key role in structuring the broader context in which the basic parameters of employment policy are fixed.

We have seen that the failure to adopt full-employment legislation and the pursuit of a commercial Keynesian strategy of macroeconomic management have affected critically the mission and scale of employment programs. In 1946 and 1978 proponents of full employment were defeated, and subsequently, in both cases, the United States resorted to tax cutting rather than spending increases to stimulate economic growth. The impact on employment and training programs was to truncate their purpose and size. Even at their highest levels in the 1970s, expenditures on CETA could assist only a small fraction of all those who were unemployed.[21] In the 1960s, the programs were absorbed into the poverty program, relegated to a peripheral social welfare mission, with budgets too low to reduce unemployment appreciably.[22] Under CETA in the 1970s the welfare orientation persisted, even though it was the cyclically unemployed and fiscally strapped cities, rather than the disadvantaged, who were the main beneficiaries.

In addition, throughout most of the postwar period, fiscal and monetary policies have not been sufficiently stimulative to maintain an unemployment rate below the full-employment level. For most of the postwar period, economists assumed that there was a rough balance between jobs and job seekers if the unemployment rate was 4 percent or lower. In the 1970s many economists argued that the natural rate of unemployment had risen to 5 percent because of the growing proportion of women and young people in the workforce. If we use the 5 percent level, in only fourteen of the forty years from 1950 through 1989 was unemployment not excessive. If we use the 4 percent figure, we find that in only seven of the forty years did the jobless rate meet the standard, those years when the United States was heavily involved in the Korean and Vietnam wars.[23]

In a comparative study of spending, taxes, and deficits among twenty industrial democracies, David Cameron found that in both the level and the rate of increase in public spending (as a proportion of gross domestic product) the United States has lagged well behind most other industrial nations. And although the United States falls somewhere in the middle range of other industrialized democracies in the size of its budget deficits, it is one of only two nations in which the magnitude of its deficit decreased between the mid-1960s and the late 1970s.[24]

The conduct of monetary policy reveals a similar pattern. Monetary policy is crucial for its direct impacts not only on the economy but on fiscal policy. If the Federal Reserve Board fails to accommodate a fiscal deficit by expanding the money supply, the employment-producing stimulation of the economy is effectively counteracted. Douglas Hibbs found that from 1960 to 1980 monetary authorities in the United States pursued a tighter money policy than all of the other six major advanced industrial democracies included in his comparative study. Looking only at the years 1973–1975, a period of historically high unemployment in all seven nations, he found an inverse relationship between unemployment and monetary expansion, with the United States pursuing the most restrictive monetary policy and making the least progress in reducing the rate of joblessness.[25] Likewise, in 1976 with seven million Americans officially out of work, one observer concluded that "labor markets were being held ransom to fears of an inflation to which they had not contributed."[26] The restrictiveness of macroeconomic policy has probably more than offset whatever reductions in joblessness programs like CETA have accomplished.

Before examining what role, if any, organized interests have had in all this, note that patterns of interest formation in the employment policy arena vary with the kinds of proposals and issues that are on the agenda. Once the social welfare mission of employment policy was established, debate in what we have called the employment policy subsystem focused on relatively narrow programmatic concerns, such as, the eligibility criteria for participating in the programs, the specific services to be provided, the service providers to be used, administrative arrangements establishing how the programs are to be implemented, and annual appropriations levels. Organized interests representing specific constituencies bargain and lobby for benefits that can be easily disaggregated and that are distributive or mildly redistributive for particular client groups. The main institutional actors are the Labor Department, and the labor committees in Congress.

Other issues and proposals fall outside the policy subsystem and involve different patterns of conflict and interest formation. These are proposals that embody full-employment guarantees, that call for using employment programs as part of national economic policy, and that involve major initiatives in macroeconomic policy. Because they raise basic issues about the role of government in the economy and have the potential for shifting substantial economic power and resources between labor and business, they involve clear winners and losers. These issues tend to be more visible and conflictual than those issues that occupy the subsystem's agenda. Because the benefits they provide are more diffuse and less immediate and tangible, they do not encourage the distributive-client politics that often characterizes the employment policy subsystem. Instead, they are redistributive policies. The interests that mobilize form more encompassing, majoritarian coalitions around class and ideological divisions, with labor and liberal activists on one side and business and conservative groups on the other. The main institutional actors are political parties, top leaders of the executive branch, and Congress as a whole.

This contrast can be seen, for example, in the politics of CETA versus the politics of the Humphrey-Hawkins Full Employment and Balanced Growth Act. CETA provided direct, concentrated benefits to specific interests and was the object of intense lobbying by local officials, municipal unions, and particular client groups. No clear pattern of interest group opposition to these groups manifested itself. Humphrey-Hawkins, on the other hand, promised more diffuse, intangible benefits (i.e., a right to employment and procedures for economic planning), involving potential winners and losers. As a result, compared to CETA, Humphrey-Hawkins created a more visible and an expanded scope of conflict, attracting a broad coalition of labor, liberal, and advocacy groups which were adamantly opposed by business and conservative groups. In an analysis of testimony before Congress on the two legislative measures, Schlozman and Verba found greater polarization in the positions taken among organized interests in the case of Humphrey-Hawkins than in the case of CETA. While few spokesmen for the liberal-labor or business-conservative coalitions registered unequivocal support or opposition to CETA (but merely suggested changes in the program), most in the liberal-labor coalition indicated unequivocal support for Humphrey-Hawkins, and most in the business-conservative coalition were unequivocally opposed to the legislation.[27]

Now, to what extent and in what sense can the policy outcomes that fall outside the employment subsystem be attributed to the balance of power between class coalitions? Do they reflect a dominant influence of business elites (and a concomitant weakness of labor) in the American political process? If so, how did such dominance manifest itself? We will be able to give a clearer answer to these questions in the next chapter. For now, however, let us map the extent of business influence over the broader context of employment policy.

Labor's Weakness

Labor in the United States is organizationally weak and has grown steadily weaker over the postwar period.[28] It comes as no surprise, therefore, that the liberal-labor coalition's influence has been minimal in the struggle for full employment. Bailey found that the coalition was not initially excited about full-employment legislation and had no impact on the substance of the original Full Employment Bill introduced by Senator Murray in 1945 nor on the watered-down substitute bill that became the Employment Act of 1946. Once it rallied to the cause, the coalition did work assiduously for its passage, led by the Union for Democratic Action. However, Bailey concluded,

It would be difficult to prove that the direct pressures of the lib-lab lobby changed a single Congressional mind. By and large, the members of Congress who listened with any semblance of receptivity were friends of the liberal cause to begin with. Most of those against [the Full Employment bill] had little or nothing to fear from the lib-lab lobbyists, whose power was largely confined to the urban-industrial centers of America.[29]

In the fight for Humphrey-Hawkins, virtually the same coalition emerged as in 1945—labor, civil rights groups, religious groups like the National Council of Churches, women's groups, and other liberal-oriented public interest organizations—under the loose leadership of the Full Employment Action Council. Others who have studied this episode have concluded that the coalition was weakened by a lack of enthusiastic interest. Attempts to mobilize the rank and file of these organizations (particularly the constituent unions of the AFL-CIO), much less a wider mass public, ended largely in failure. This is consistent with the public opinion data reported in chapter 4, which showed that between the mid-1940s and mid-1970s majority support for employment guarantees had turned to majority opposition. Those who did champion the cause were mainly in the activist and leadership strata of the liberal-labor organizations. And at those levels, support was mainly based upon a moral, ideological commitment to social justice. Full employment was not viewed as a top priority for the organizations in the coalition. More parochial issues, that bore directly and immediately on their memberships and organizations (e.g., labor law reform in the case of the AFL-CIO) were of greater concern. The absence of mobilization among the unemployed, the strains between groups such

as unions and blacks on other issues, and a declining unemployment
rate from 1976 to 1978 that probably enhanced the perception that full-
employment legislation would be of little relevance to the vast majority
of workers with jobs, made it difficult to organize the kind of mass
movement that would have been needed to enact strong full-employment legislation.[30]

Even if the liberal-labor lobby had been a stronger political force, it
is not clear that it would have made an appreciable difference in these
outcomes. Would it have had any leverage over a committee system in
Congress that was dominated in 1945 by conservatives? Could it have
controlled the Democratic party's nominating process that produced a
president who had serious reservations about Humphrey-Hawkins?
Could it have countered the damaging critiques of economists, like
Charles Schultze, who were connected to the party and influential in
Washington? Could it have overcome business opposition to both bills
and an increasingly conservative public opinion emerging in the late
1970s? We can conclude only that the chances for passage of meaningful
full-employment legislation would have increased with a more potent
liberal-labor lobby, but we cannot say with any certainty that it would
have made all the difference.

Business Influence

Business opposition to full-employment proposals has been strong
and united. Large-scale lobbying campaigns were mounted, and business made its objections known. The mobilization of business groups
like the National Association of Manufacturers and the Chamber of
Commerce helped the conservative coalition of southern Democrats
and Republicans defeat the Full Employment Bill in Congress in 1945.
The House Committee on Expenditures, which had jurisdiction over
the bill, purged it of its most important provisions and called upon Dr.
George Terborgh of the Machinery and Allied Products Institute to
craft a substitute. It was the business-inspired substitute bill, a pale
counterpart to the one originally introduced, that became the largely
symbolic Employment Act of 1946.[31] But the most important aspect of
business influence was neither its direct lobbying activities nor its shaping the content of the legislation. Instead, this influence was the result
of a hospitable ideological climate in America that nurtured a provincial
conservatism friendly to business and hostile to government. Take
Bailey's characterization of one of the congressional opponents to the
Full Employment Bill, for example:

To suggest that Buck as a Senator [from Delaware] was a "tool" of the
DuPonts is to misrepresent the nature of what Lynd has called "the

business-class control system." It was not the pressure of DuPont *on* Buck but the pressure of DuPont *in* Buck which was at work. . . . The [fate of the] Full Employment Bill was in no small measure shaped by forces and culture symbols in Greenwood, Mississippi, Allegan, Michigan, Pocatello, Idaho, Wilmington, Delaware, and Temple, New Hampshire.[32]

We saw in chapter 2 that in the aftermath of the defeat of the Full Employment Bill, business influenced the reformulation and introduction of Keynesianism. The Committee for Economic Development, an enlightened business elite, laid much of the foundation for shifting economic thinking from spending deficits to tax cuts as the preferred instrument for economic management. There is little doubt that the CED, owing largely to the creativity of Beardsley Ruml, played a leading role in the development of commercial Keynesianism. And business support was crucial to getting Kennedy to propose a tax cut and getting conservatives in Congress to go along. The result was an economic policy based on increasing private, rather than public, consumption and on automatic stabilizers rather than discretionary spending, avoiding an erosion of corporate control over the economy. Once the tax cut route was chosen, there was little practical reason or political support in favor of the kind of spending on jobs and training programs that would have been a prerequisite for greatly expanding the programs of the 1960s and 1970s. The development of commercial Keynesianism was a watershed in American economic policy, a successful attempt to reshape Keynes to make him compatible with the values and interests of capitalism that are widely held in America. Robert Collins concluded that

The dynamism of American business organizations and leaders . . . was manifested in . . . the emergence of a cadre of business leaders who combined a talent for organizational innovation with a keen appreciation of the uses of expert knowledge and who were able to incorporate their political ideology into cogent policy recommendations. . . . Such influence reflected both the essential conservatism of American political life and the dynamism of American business. The primacy of capitalist values in American culture . . . has contributed greatly to, and been reenforced by, a political mainstream unusual in its depth and stability but striking in its narrowness.[33]

Business was not as directly active in shaping the content of Humphrey-Hawkins, as it had been earlier in the period. By the 1970s professional economists had much greater access to policy makers, and it was they who reshaped the legislation in ways that were close to the position taken by business.[34] Nor did overt appeals to pro-free-enterprise, antistatist beliefs have as large a role as they did earlier in the period. Instead, through their dominant role in the policy debate, economists transformed the full-employment issue from one fought out on the plane of ideology to one judged upon "the merits" according to dispassionate, "rational" economic analysis. It was the threat of inflation, a traditional cornerstone of business's argument against full-employment legislation, that the economic experts stressed in their opposition to Humphrey-Hawkins. Viewed as a political phenomenon, there is ample evidence that inflation reflects, in no small measure, a distributive struggle between business and labor for shares of national income.[35] If business's fears that full employment would strengthen labor's wage demands and intensify the struggle, then it is clear that economists' opposition to the legislation benefited business interests.

Finally, we turn to business influence in monetary policy. John Woolley's careful study of the Federal Reserve Board provided a number of valuable insights on the conduct of monetary policy and the nature of that influence. In terms of the Federal Reserve's decision-making processes, Woolley noted that the agency's conduct of policy in highly technical terms and its formal structure of independence and non-partisanship were "precisely [those] characteristics [that] insulate it effectively . . . to perform its functions of regulating the economy . . . that permits it to behave with relative autonomy from societal groups." Second, he noted that those who occupy important posts on the Federal Reserve Board are drawn overwhelmingly from "mainstream financial networks" and a narrow, upper-middle-class social milieu that produces "outlooks" that "have been very similar," and "that compared to other private sector groups, bankers enjoy unusually good access to the Federal Reserve." Business elites, however, need not "exercise constant, detailed oversight of ongoing decisions," because "officials are selected who are naturally very concerned about the continued health of American capitalism." It is inflation that causes the financial community to lose confidence, and "it will be financial confidence above all else that sets the parameters of Federal Reserve behavior."[36]

CONCLUSION

The involvement and influence of organized interests in the employment policy subsystem are limited. Employment and training programs cannot be said to have resulted in any overall sense from the activities of interest groups or the demands they pressed. Although one finds organized groups as players in the arena, a critical group—the unemployed themselves—are not politically active. Organized interests have been more noted for their lack of involvement than their active participation. With the exception of local governments who ran CETA in the

1970s, there have been no strong, cohesive, interest organizations in Washington for which employment and training programs can be identified as a top priority and that get involved in policy decisions on anything more than an informal and sporadic basis. Groups were rarely anything more than secondary in such critical tasks as getting issues on the agenda, formulating and publicizing the need for adopting concrete proposals, building coalitions, and so forth. Quite often, groups reacted to the initiatives and decisions of other actors in the policy process.

Nor have groups been especially effective in wielding influence. While the interests that have mobilized have supported the programs because of the benefits they hoped to get from them, this does not necessarily mean that their lobbying has been the controlling factor in the programs' existence. They have consistently asked for more spending than they have received, and more importantly they have not been able to sustain the status quo when they have wanted to. When Congress or the administration have been determined to change policy, even in the face of opposition of the most mobilized interests, it has succeeded in doing so. This was clearly evident in the inability of those interests organized around the categorical programs of the 1960s to prevent the CETA reorganization and then again, in the failure of CETA prime sponsors and other pro-CETA lobbies to prevent the federal government from reimposing restrictions on the use of funds and the eventual termination of PSE. In other words, there is no indication of any kind of long-term capture of employment policy by organized beneficiaries.

The overall lack of involvement and influence on the part of organized interests is both a cause and effect of employment policy itself. Because the design and scale of the programs offer most groups few benefits and impose few costs, there are few incentives for organized interests to get involved. This is especially the case for the two most important interests in the labor market—organized labor and business. Conversely, the fact that organized interests have historically failed to get involved partly explains why the programs have had a limited mission and relatively low budgets.

The role of organized interests in the subsystem is not an inconsequential one, however. They do provide a constituency, mainly for jobs programs rather than training. And they can be called upon to testify that a real need for the programs exists. The evidence suggests that organized groups, especially those that lobby heavily, have influence on how the employment and training budget is allocated. There is a tendency for these interests, especially those representing local communities, to make the programs more distributive and less redistributive. An organized constituency for the programs seems to help stimulate higher spending, especially for job creation. However, the interests of organized claimants are not necessarily compatible with those of the unemployed, especially the disadvantaged.

When we turn to those issues and policies that establish the broad constraints in which the employment policy subsystem operates, that critically impinge upon the mission and scope of its activities, we find a somewhat different story. Business has not sought to dominate the employment policy subsystem directly but, instead, has been a key actor in limiting the parameters of employment policy so that a less-than-full-employment, social welfare mission was the only path of development left for it. It has effectively contained and thwarted the development of an economic policy strategy that would use employment and training programs to guarantee full employment, control the business cycle, and restructure labor markets. Through its defeat of more radical policy proposals, its reshaping of the techniques of modern economic management in a direction that is fundamentally compatible with private economic discretion, and its influence over the "commanding heights" of macroeconomic regulation (i.e., fiscal and monetary policies), business exerts an indirect, albeit critical, influence over employment policy.

The failed attempts to enact full-employment legislation, the development of a conservative brand of Keynesian economic management, and the conduct of monetary policy owe in some part to the influence of business in American politics and the weakness of the liberal-labor coalition. Without a history of clearly articulated class divisions or class consciousness, with low levels of union membership, and the absence of a genuine labor party, the United States has lacked a vehicle that would be necessary (though perhaps not sufficient) to push for the adoption of something more than the less-than-full-employment, social-welfare-oriented employment policy that exists.

Business influence stems not only from the lack of political strength on the part of its opponents but from the variety of positive actions it has taken and the structural advantages it possesses. Probably the least important has been the direct control over policy makers that is usually associated with both interest group theory and simple class theories that view the state as a tool manipulated by capitalists. The most direct and palpable kind of influence was intellectual—the concrete policy innovations that business fashioned in shaping legislation like the Employment Act of 1946 and the Tax Reduction Act of 1965. These ideas were especially influential because they were closely congruent with business interests and American beliefs in free enterprise and limited government.

Finally, business has been able to influence economic policy in general because of the critical functions it performs within the structure of the political economy. Business and finance capital require confidence that the economic climate will remain stable and hospitable to profit making. If such confidence can be maintained only by checking inflation through a restrictive monetary policy, cutting taxes, avoiding any commitment to full employment that might shift economic resources and power away from private enterprise, and other such actions, then those in government who control the economic policy levers (whose own power rests in no small measure on maintaining economic prosperity) can be relied upon to accommodate business interests without the necessity for any overt political pressure on the part of business itself. Thus business influence over nonsubsystem issues and proposals reflects a capacity for intellectual innovation, ideological hegemony, and its inherent structural advantages in a capitalist economy.

9

Class Interests and U.S. Employment Policy in Comparative Perspective

COMPARATIVE ANALYSIS lets us probe further into the role and importance of organized interests in employment policy. The most widely accepted explanation for cross-national variation in the extent of full-employment, welfare state development is the degree of political strength and influence attained by the working class.[1] According to the working class strength thesis, the United States has failed to adopt extensive full-employment, welfare state guarantees because, compared to nations like Sweden, the American labor movement has been too weak to challenge business elites. The United States and Sweden stand at virtually opposite poles both in implementing policies to eliminate unemployment and in their levels of working-class organization and political strength. Swedish employment policy is based upon a firm commitment to full employment as a priority goal and is oriented toward achieving national economic policy objectives. It is widely recognized as the most innovative and successful attempt to integrate micropolicy instruments with conventional macroeconomic measures in what is called an "active labor market policy." How and why the Swedes have been able and willing to pursue such a course should shed further light on why the United States has not and, instead, has chosen to pursue a less-than-full-employment, social-welfare-oriented policy. This chapter evaluates the argument that the balance of class power in the two nations is what accounts for differences in the objectives, scope, and scale of Swedish and American policies.[2]

SWEDISH AND AMERICAN EMPLOYMENT POLICIES COMPARED

In every essential respect, the mission and scope of Swedish employment policy has contrasted with that found in the United States. Swedish programs have evolved as a comprehensive and coordinated pack-

224

age of measures that give primacy to the aims of economic policy and only incidentally to the aims of social policy. "Labor market policy," as it became known, developed as "the heart of Swedish economic policy"[3] in the decades following Depression and World War II. In America, as we have seen, the orientation of employment policy has been just the reverse—social welfare or relief objectives have always been paramount. While the emphasis of American policy has been on remedying and alleviating employment problems, the Swedish emphasis has been on anticipating and preventing them. And where U.S. policy has been a reactive effort to assist those individuals who, for whatever reasons, have been left out of the mainstream, Swedish policy has been actively engaged in the fullest employment of human resources. Instead of being confined to the periphery of the economy, the Swedes have assigned employment programs a positive role at the very center of its strategy to sustain economic stability and growth.

One assumption of the Swedish approach is that the best way to assist the poor and unemployed is through the maintenance of a dynamic and growing economy. Those who are employable can find stable employment only when there is a high demand for labor, and this can happen only when swings in the business cycle are stabilized and when structural adjustment in the economy takes place unimpeded. And for those who cannot work, assistance is financially and politically feasible only in a growing economy. Thus the needs of the disadvantaged are best addressed epiphenomenally—along with, and as a result of, full employment. Full employment, in turn, can be sustained only when it does not create intolerable levels of inflation and when the economy is constantly keeping pace with structural changes—when resources are shifted to those places where they can be most efficiently used.

A second assumption is that, if left on its own, the labor market is incapable of maintaining stability and sustaining high rates of growth. The market has no mechanism that automatically prevents fluctuations in the business cycle or that can rapidly correct imbalances in the labor market. Swedish policy stresses restructuring labor markets, not simply assisting the unemployed or semiemployable population, and it does this by increasing primary sector jobs and decreasing jobs in the secondary sector. The primary sector is composed of growing, productive industries that are able to offer stable, high-paying employment, while the secondary sector tends to comprise stagnant, unproductive industries that cannot offer stable, high-paying jobs.

Third, Swedish policy instrumentation is comprehensive and highly sophisticated. Fiscal and monetary policies are inadequate by themselves and are integrated with a variety of microemployment policy instruments that can more directly and selectively intervene in the labor market. These measures include labor market forecasting, training and retraining, targeted job creation, relocation allowances, placement services, and investment reserves that exempt from taxation that portion of business profits set aside for release during the first signs of a downturn in the economy.

Finally, employment programs can contribute to the attainment of economic policy goals only if they are carried out by an administrative apparatus with sufficient resources at its disposal and if it has the ability to intervene flexibly in the labor market.

It follows that Swedish policy contemplates a qualitatively different role for government in the labor market than does American policy. In the case of the latter, public authorities have been called upon to play a residual role—essentially offsetting developments taking place in the private sector but never trying to directly affect decisions made by private economic agents. The government's responsibility has been to address the human and social costs of economic decay and development, without appreciably interfering with the economic structure itself. In the Swedish case, government has deliberately set its sights on altering the structure and improving the operation of the market. It has assumed the role of a purposive economic agent, a player in the market, not simply a deus ex machina that tries to offset private decisions in an effort to redress the market's undesirable impacts.

Sweden's adoption of an employment policy that is an integral part of a strategy to accomplish national economic objectives is reflected in the status and importance of the agency established to carry out the policy—the Labor Market Board—and the size of its budget. The board occupies pride of place among those agencies involved with economic policy. Its importance brings into sharper focus the peripheral role of the Labor Department in the United States. Writing at the end of the 1960s, one observer just back from Sweden drew a vivid contrast between "manpower" policy in the United States and "labor market policy" in Sweden, and how these determined the very different positions of the bureaucracies charged with implementing policy in their respective nations:

When it is well understood . . . that Congress and the Administration have authorized, and the leading manpower program administrators have accepted, the mission to concentrate their attention on the disadvantaged unemployed, those concerned with fiscal, monetary, trade, investment, income, urban and regional development, and military policies may be excused for saying, "What significance does manpower policy have for our task?" I am not aware of any statement from such sources as bold and icy as that. But in conversations with some of them, I sense an assessment of the utility, for their purposes, of close collaboration with the manpower authorities as about equivalent to close collaboration with the Salvation Army.

How different is the status of the Labour Market Board in Sweden where, in spite of some well-suppressed resentment that the Board has been given a privileged position among the agencies concerned with overall economic policy, few moves are taken without considering and giving decisive weight to the evaluation of the labor market impacts of those moves by the Board, and without the synchronization of each economic policy move with the responsive or compensatory activities to be undertaken by the Board.[4]

The contrast in the importance accorded employment policy between the two nations is reflected, as well, in the level of budgetary resources committed to employment measures. In fiscal 1977/78, for instance, while the Swedes spent 9 percent of their budget (or 3 percent of GNP) on employment programs, the United States spent 3.2 percent of its budget (or 0.7 percent of GNP).[5] Swedish spending as a percentage of total government expenditures from 1965 to 1982 was 5.4 percent.[6] Enrollment levels in job creation programs paint a similar portrait. In 1978 in the United States, 6 million individuals were officially jobless; in Sweden there were 95,000. The Swedes created 45 jobs for each 100 unemployed persons. The United States created a total of 725,000, but would have had to create 2.7 million to create as large a proportion as did the Swedes.[7] And 1978 was a year in which U.S. expenditures reached their highest level. U.S. budget figures have fluctuated a great deal more than those in Sweden, which have seen a continuity in spending levels. In most years, CETA funding as a proportion of GNP was half or less than it was in 1978.[8]

THE BALANCE OF CLASS INTERESTS AND RESPONSE TO UNEMPLOYMENT

The working class strength thesis is premised on the notion that policies reflect the balance of class power in society. Swedish working class solidarity translated into high levels of unionization, which in turn provided the basis for powerful trade union and party organizations. These have been the vehicles with which the Swedish working class has been able to win elections for several decades, enabling it to legislate in its own interests. Sweden exhibits the highest level of trade union membership among advanced industrial nations; the United States is at or near the bottom. While Swedish unions have grown over the postwar period—from 62 percent of all wage earners in 1950 to 92 percent in 1980—American union membership has steadily declined, from a high of 33 percent to less than 20 percent over the same period.[9]

While the Swedish Social Democrats (SAP) constitute Sweden's largest political party, a genuine party of the working class does not even exist in the United States. The SAP enjoyed an extended period of rule from 1932 to 1976, most of that time as the majority in government facing a splintered opposition. The United States has no such political vehicle for the expression of working class interests. The national Democratic party consists of a loose coalition of interest groups and regional factions, among which organized labor is a single (albeit important) constituency. The Democratic rank and file is heterogenous, consisting of a substantial proportion of middle-class identifiers. Its philosophical and programmatic commitments, while left of center along the spectrum of American politics, are centrist in the European context. Without the challenge of a solidaristic and politically potent working class, American business has been able to dominate American politics partly by default, and partly by actively blocking far-reaching proposals that would benefit the working class and poor. As Andrew Martin put it:

Business elites have been dominant in the American economic policy-making arena for a long time something like the same degree that labor elites have been dominant in the Swedish economic policy-making arena in recent decades. . . . It is probably a large part of the explanation of why the patterns of economic policy in the United States and Sweden are at or near the opposite ends of the range of variation in the extent to which the full employment welfare state is approximated.[10]

Response to the Depression

During the Depression, Sweden led other industrial-capitalist countries in the use of fiscal policy as a tool of economic recovery. The Swedes began using the budget for recovery in 1932. Large grants and loans were approved for public works projects paying union wages, as well as loans and price supports for agriculture.[11] By 1937 the Riksdag (the Swedith parliament) had officially abandoned the goal of balancing the budget annually.[12] Unlike the United States, where deficits of a more modest size were created primarily for humanitarian purposes and where the New Deal did not break with balanced budgets until late in the decade, the Swedes were firmly converted to the idea of deliberately using the budget to restore economic health in 1932. Ernst Wigforss, a key Social Democratic politician, formulated the SAP's recovery program that stressed deficit creation through spending on public works projects, for which workers would be hired at prevailing wages. Four years before Keynes laid out his theory of the multiplier effect, Wigforss told the Riksdag, "If I want to start jobs for 100 persons, it is not necessary that I put all of the 100 to work."[13]

The Social Democrats' economic policies became immensely popular and enabled them to consolidate the electoral coalition they had forged between urban workers and farmers with a decisive victory in 1936. Thus began an extended period of Social Democratic electoral predominance, which provided the continuity in office that enabled the party to launch a full-employment welfare state. The popularity of the Social Democratic recovery program was not limited to working class and rural interests. According to Esping-Andersen, "within large sections of the business community, the Social Democrats' ability to revitalize Swedish capitalism helped establish social democracy as the best guarantor of economic prosperity and effective government."[14] With its policies enjoying universal political acclaim, and with the SAP abandoning the goal of public ownership and acceptance of the rights of private property, Swedish labor and business were able to conclude the 1938 Saltsjobaden Agreement. The "historic compromise" put an end to chronic industrial conflict and opened the way for the kind of corporatist bargaining over economic and social policies that became a hallmark of postwar Swedish politics.[15] Business acceptance, both of an expanded role for the state in the economy and of the labor movement as a coequal partner in the political economy, never materialized in the United States during the New Deal and afterward.[16] Then in 1944 the Social Democrats adopted the Twenty-seven Points, a program that formally committed the SAP to the pursuit of a full-employment policy.[17] Thus the Swedes pledged themselves to a Keynesian policy of high public spending and investment just at the time when the very same measures, embodied in the Full Employment Bill of 1945, were being dealt a defeat in the U.S. Congress.[18]

The Postwar Period

It was not long after the postwar period began that the Swedes' "simple Keynesian" policy of stimulative fiscal and monetary policies reached an impasse. It became apparent that sustaining full employment over a long period of time produced intolerable inflationary pressures. The question now became how to moderate inflation without, in the process, sacrificing the full employment that had been achieved.

At the center of intellectual efforts to search for a new policy was the Swedish Labor Federation, or LO. The LO became the chief architect of a "post-Keynesian" policy that replaced the simple Keynesian formula of the 1930s and 1940s. One of the LO's top economists, Gosta Rehn, argued that an "active labor market policy" could play a decisive role in dealing with the new postwar challenges. Labor market policy had two basic objectives.[19] The first, economic stabilization, entailed reconciling full employment with price stability. For a variety of institutional reasons—free collective bargaining, monopoly pricing, and segmented labor and commodity markets—it is difficult for industrial economies to reach full employment without first exacerbating inflation. The labor market consists not of one, but of several markets. It is heterogenous and segmented, divided into various geographical areas and industrial sectors of the economy. At any given time, some areas and sectors are characterized by labor surpluses, others by shortages. General or aggregate demand management is inadequate in such an economy. To expand fiscal and monetary policies when the deficiency of demand was a general one, as in the 1930s, was all that was sufficient. But in the postwar era there was no such deficiency. A general expansion tended to generate inflation in tight labor markets, already at (or near) full employment, before reaching the pockets of unemployment in those markets that remained slack. In tight markets, wages would be bid up, supply shortages would appear, and price inflation would soon follow. Clearly, one of the two goals—full employment or price stability—would have to be sacrificed or some alternative policy would have to be adopted to reconcile the two of them. An active labor market policy was introduced as the solution.

The key feature of labor market policy is the selectivity of its instruments. The management of aggregate demand is disaggregated and then is applied to particular problem areas that do not respond to across-the-board stimulation of the demand for labor. This aspect of post-Keynesianism combined moderately restrictive fiscal and monetary policies to dampen the general demand for labor, supplemented by selective intervention. Selectively creating jobs in slack markets and regions creates demand for labor where excess supply exists, while stimulating mobility and expanding training channels it to where the demand for labor is greatest.

The second objective of the active labor market policy was to sustain economic growth by speeding the market's adjustment to a number of structural changes (e.g., technology, international competition, consumer tastes). Change is endemic to a dynamic economy, but it can also create dislocations and inefficiency. Left alone, economic actors may resist change, may adjust too slowly, or may create social and economic costs that could be avoided. Rehn called for speeding structural change and the adjustment to it by combining labor market programs with a "solidaristic wage policy." The wage agreement, negotiated nationally, was designed to raise minimum wages faster than average wages, with the effect of equalizing wages across industries and regions. Besides contributing to labor solidarity and a more equal distribution of national income, the wage policy rewarded firms that were efficient and that therefore could afford to pay the wage standard. At the same time, less profitable and efficient firms, which were unable to competitively pay such wages, went out of business. The latter tended to be stagnant industries, incapable or unwilling to keep pace with structural change. Labor market policy was aimed at reemploying workers displaced through this restructuring. Retraining, counseling, relocation, and placement helped to reabsorb them into the expanding sectors of the economy.

Rehn's proposals did not immediately gain widespread support. Many in Sweden, including politicians in the SAP, instead favored attacking inflation through wage restraint. But this idea was soundly rejected by the LO and its unions for several reasons: (1) it would weaken the unions' primary mission—to bargain with employers; (2) employers would be enticed to redistribute income from wages to profits; (3) wage discipline would weaken labor solidarity by increasing inequality, as the strongest unions could more easily take advantage of wage drift in concluding separate agreements with their own firms; (4) once the controls were lifted, a wage explosion would be unleashed; and finally, (5) controls would allow efficient firms to reap unacceptably high profits and, at the same time, protect inefficient and unprofitable ones. In sum, wage restraint would hurt the LO's organizational and class interests.

The LO's ability to persuade the party to shelve the wage ceiling proposal rested decisively on its ability to offer in its stead Rehn's proposal for an active labor market policy. This event, according to Esping-Andersen, was "without a doubt a turning point for Swedish Social Democracy," because the Swedes had found a politically acceptable way of avoiding inflation while maintaining full employment and growth. And, rather than impeding growth by defending its jobs against readjustment, Swedish labor became a positive economic actor by accepting part of the burden of readjustment in exchange for publicly provided retraining and relocation. "The SAP would otherwise in all likelihood have fallen victim to the chronic political paralysis experienced by the British Labour Party."[20]

Rehn's proposals were adopted by the LO in 1951, but it was not until later that the LO could persuade the SAP that it should endorse them as well. Even if the SAP's leadership had been immediately convinced of the soundness of Rehn's proposals, the political conditions of the 1950s were not hospitable to its approval. The SAP had seen its electoral margins dwindle throughout the decade as a result of inflation and balance-of-payments problems. Until 1957 the SAP was compelled to enlist the Agrarian party in a coalition government, which refused to approve the increase in spending needed to fund the labor market policy. Only after the SAP had won a clear majority in 1958 did the budget for labor market programs grow significantly.

Business Dominance in the United States

We have seen in chapter 8 that the mobilization of business groups helped defeat the Full Employment Bill in Congress and substituted the Employment Act of 1946.[21] By not adopting a simple Keynesianism of fiscal expansion as called for in the Full Employment Bill, it was unlikely that the United States would graduate to a post-Keynesian policy centered around active labor market measures. In the absence of a commitment to full-employment Keynesianism, the U.S. economy remained slack from the 1950s to the mid-1960s. Unemployment was high, but inflation was low. As long as low inflation could be traded off for comparatively high rates of unemployment, there was no incentive to adopt selective employment measures designed to reconcile full employment with reasonable price stability, as occurred in Sweden.

It will be recalled from chapter 2 that the full-employment debacle left a vacuum into which stepped the architects of a new brand of Keynesianism, quite different from the brand that informed the authors of the Full Employment Bill. The effort to conservatize Keynes in the United States was led by a small group of business intellectuals, mainly in the Committee for Economic Development (CED). They accepted the basic logic of the Keynesian prescription—abandoning balanced budgets in favor of stabilizing deficits—and the high-employment objective. Despite the defeat of the full-employment bill, they foresaw the adoption of some form of Keynesianism. It would be wiser for the business community to put itself at the forefront of efforts to shape policy options that were congruent with its own interests than be forced into a defensive fight against an unwanted alternative. This reshaping involved replacing spending deficits and discretionary budget measures with what Robert Lekachman has dubbed commercial Keynesianism— a combination of tax cuts and automatic stabilizers as the preferred instruments for fiscal management. Such a formula was more palatable to business and conservatives because it preserved private sector control over resources and stimulated private consumption, rather than enlarging government spending and discretion.

Primary credit for the new policy thinking must go to the CED, which had become a leading voice in the business community on matters of public policy. As its research director stated in 1944, "it is of vital concern to all who are interested in keeping a system of private enterprise and large personal freedom, that ways be found to counter the tendencies toward boom and depressions without resorting to great expansion of detailed state controls or . . . state employment. We hope our studies will be a significant contribution to this end."[22] The prescriptions put forward by CED economists recast American Keynesianism in three important ways: (1) by changing the definition of the problem from one of a permanent, secular economic stagnation to one of periodic fluctuations in economic activity; (2) by replacing spending increases with tax cuts in prescribing deficit creation; and (3) by shifting from discretionary to automatic fiscal management. Led by Beardsley Ruml, the CED popularized concepts like the high employment budget, an automatic stabilizer, built-in flexibility, as well as the system of current payment, which served as the basis for reforming income tax collection. The CED's activities were not limited to developing new ideas, but they popularized them as well. Working with like-minded reformers in the Chamber of Commerce, the CED helped win over other important segments of the business community to the tenets of commercial Keynesianism.

By the time the Kennedy administration came to power, a new generation of business leaders had been educated in the use of Keynesian fiscal policy and weaned away from fiscal orthodoxy. A decisive factor in Kennedy's decision to finally take the plunge in sending a proposal to Congress was the business community's receptivity to the idea and, specifically, the recommendation for it that he had received from the CED and the Chamber of Commerce.[23] Acutely aware of the sentiment in the business community that made tax cuts, instead of spending increases, politically acceptable, most of Kennedy's economic advisers stressed the former course rather than the latter one. Chairman of the Council of Economic Advisers Walter Heller capitalized on the political significance of business support by keeping the president apprised of the support of the CED and the chamber.

The CED's push in the direction of a Keynesian logic of economic management reflected a belief that the maintenance of high employment and economic growth was possible under an economic system in which the major control over economic resources would be exercised by private business, and that such a shift in public policy would be necessary for that system to survive. Tax cuts and automatic stabilizers were an ingenious formula for accommodating private enterprise to demands for the maintenance of economic growth and employment opportunities.

The delayed introduction of Keynesian techniques, and then the turn to commercial Keynesianism, made it very unlikely that the United States would eventually adopt a Swedish-style active labor market policy. The decision to cut taxes rather than increase spending adversely affected the budget for employment and training programs.[24] As a result, the level of funding for such measures was kept well below that which would have been needed for them to play a significant role in economic management. Once the Kennedy (later Johnson) administration committed itself to a tax cut, it balked at any initiatives designed to attack unemployment through massive spending upon jobs and training. This was apparent during deliberations over the War on Poverty. Officials in the Department of Labor and liberals in Congress argued that the centerpiece of the antipoverty effort should be a large-scale spending program to create jobs financed by raising the cigarette tax. Johnson and his economic advisers explicitly rejected this proposal, maintaining that it would be politically impossible to ask Congress to increase taxes in a year in which the president was already asking it to enact a tax cut.[25] The poverty program remained modestly funded. Training and job creation measures, which occupied pride of place in the Swedish economic policy strategy, were relegated to a peripheral social welfare function and remained outside the locus of economic policy making.

Summary

Thus, the policies adopted in each nation reflected the compromise that the dominant class could enforce given the balance of class power. In Sweden, the rise to power of the Social Democrats during the 1930s resulted in a compromise in which labor received full employment and welfare state expansion, business retained control of investment and the production process, and both agreed on the desirability of growth and a more accommodating industrial relations climate. By the postwar period, full employment had become an accomplished fact, and the challenge confronting Swedish labor was maintaining reasonable price stability, while at the same time not sacrificing full employment, not increasing inequality among workers, and not redistributing national income in favor of business. The Swedes were also compelled to devise policies to deal with structural obstacles to growth by promoting adaptation to economic change. This involved getting their workers to cooperate in readjustment schemes that required sacrifices from those employed in uncompetitive firms, industries, or regions that jeopardized overall growth rates.

The benefits of Keynesian demand management, labor market programs, and other instruments for sustaining growth and reducing unemployment were distributed throughout society. The result was a broad, interclass political consensus on the question of economic governance. Workers understood that full employment could be sustained only if it did not entail creating inflation or impeding structural readjustment. For its part, business accepted full employment and understood that it did not entail an end to price stability or profits. A sign of the Social Democrats' success in building a broad consensus has been the longstanding cooperation and support of the business community for the active labor market policy. Perhaps the most vivid confirmation of this support was the increase in the budget for labor market measures when the "bourgeois coalition" was in power from 1976 to 1982.[26]

In the United States, a class compromise developed implicitly and was, of course, on terms much more favored by business. The absence of a social democratic movement, plus the mobilization of business against the Full Employment Bill, blocked a Swedish-style Keynesian economic program and limited welfare state development. Without a prolonged peacetime period of full employment, moderating inflation in a full-employment economy was not the focus of concern. Rather, the problem was how to avoid a repeat of the economic failure of the 1930s (with the possibility of another New Deal), and how to exploit the enormous growth-producing potential of Keynesian techniques, while at the same time minimizing an erosion of corporate discretion and the expansion of positive state action. The key task in each country, then, was to protect the interests of the politically dominant class but in ways that took into account the broader interests of society and the managerial imperatives of a mature industrial economy.

POLITICAL LEARNING AND POLICY INNOVATION

The working-class strength thesis is not so much wrong as it is incomplete as an explanation for the divergent paths that public policy took in the two nations. First, while the balance of class power affected the broad range of policy alternatives, it does not explain the particular alternative that the dominant class chose to insist upon. The important contributions made by the Swedish labor movement and the American business community to postwar economic policy rested significantly upon their capacity to engage in the kind of political learning that is crucial to the development of new ideas that became the basis for new policies.[27] Swedish and U.S. policies resulted from the exertion of political muscle and from the expression of class preferences, which were duly registered by government; but they also resulted from a distinctive capacity to examine the deficiencies of existing policies as they relate to new problems and then to develop prescriptions to rectify those deficiencies.

Swedish labor leaders and American business elites not only needed

to engage effectively in political battle and gain access to public authority. They also needed to translate the objectives of the classes they
represented into concrete courses of action. In Sweden, a large and
cohesive labor movement tied to a political party able to capture and
retain the reins of government were necessary conditions, but not
sufficient ones, for putting in place a policy of fiscal restraint, active
labor market measures, and solidaristic wages designed to reconcile full
employment with price stability and to speed adaptation to structural
change. Similarly, while organized labor was a relatively weak force in
the American polity, and while American business enjoyed the existence of two major parties that were fundamentally pro free enterprise,
these conditions only begin to explain why the nature and scope of the
U.S. response to unemployment took a course that was thoroughly
distinct from that of Sweden. In short, votes and political organization
were important in determining the timing and general direction of
policy, perhaps, but the capacity to engage in policy innovation was
the decisive factor that allowed labor and business to shape what the
nature of the policy response would be.

Second, it is important to avoid formulations of the working-class
power thesis that make the fashioning of politically feasible policies too
automatic, when in fact they are contingent outcomes. The promotion
of economic interests was very much dependent upon the evolution of
policy thinking in the two nations. It should not be assumed that
working-class or business elites automatically fashion compromises and
pursue policies that match the interests and ideologies of their constituencies and that also gain widespread acceptance in the larger political
community. How political elites are able to do this must be fully examined. The working-class power explanation jumps too directly from the
constellation of political power in each nation to the policies that were
pursued. It treats policy simply as a reflection of the balance of power
among contending classes in society, without paying much attention
to how that power was translated into (and sustained by) a set of
adaptive responses to changing economic conditions. The intellectual
process of actually creating and choosing policy is left untouched by
the analysis. The reason for this, in part, is that what is conceived
as political in much political analysis reflects virtually an exclusive
preoccupation with the distribution and exercise of power.

The analysis presented here moves in a less determinist direction,
taking up where Andrew Martin left off. Martin argued that, once they
have attained power, social democratic parties must "use the public
authority at their disposal in ways that are effective in redirecting the
economic process in accordance with the purposes collectively defined
through the political process."[28] Martin thus pointed to the critical role

of political learning in policy innovation, arguing that working-class parties face a number of options once in power, and whether they choose policies that represent genuine efforts to realize working-class objectives "depends critically on their capacity for solving the whole range of complex policy problems involved in redirecting the capitalist economic process."[29]

Without the organizational capacity of the LO and CED to engage in political learning, neither labor elites in Sweden nor their big business counterparts in the United States could have shaped the content of public policy so decisively. Obviously, the LO and the CED helped to shape policies that were radically different and that reflected the very palpable differences in the ideological commitments and material interests of their constituencies. Yet the contributions made by each organization to the policies of their respective nations cannot be fully understood by viewing these two organizations as merely reflections of their different socioeconomic bases of support. Their role must be seen as centers of political learning, whose impact on the substance of policy was the result of their capacity to creatively search for responses to the complex problems of modern economic life that combined political feasibility with technical soundness.

The two organizations have shared certain orientations that supported such a capacity. Both have rejected a zero-sum view of class relations and have embraced the notion of a common national interest. A political organization that was primarily or exclusively oriented toward defending the ideological and material commitments of its membership was unlikely to be suited for engaging in political learning. A broader, less parochial approach was needed that took account of the interdependencies inherent in industrial capitalism and that recognized the claims of other actors in the political economy. The LO has been prototypical of the integrated trade union movement, pursuing working-class interests in ways that does not create winners and losers. Instead of simply pursuing its own particular interests, it has emphasized enlarging "the area of congruence between its own protective interests and the more general interest."[30]

Similarly, the notion that there can exist genuine harmony between economic classes has been particularly strong within the CED. According to Collins, the CED "took an organic view of American society and denied the legitimacy of class or group conflict, believing instead in the existence of a 'general interest.' "[31] This non–zero-sum view of class relations inclined the LO and CED to search for options that policy makers in both nations found most appealing—ones that could bring about desired economic goals without exacerbating whatever class divisions did exist.

Both the LO and CED also have evidenced a belief in the necessity and desirability of public-private collaboration in guiding economic outcomes. Maintaining the posture that the two spheres ought to remain autonomous, or that one should completely dominate the other, impedes learning. It limits the number of acceptable policy alternatives either to those where the state's role is confined to a limited set of functions on the periphery of the private economy or to those where the state's functions are so expansive as to eliminate most discretion of private economic actors. A belief in public-private collaboration, on the other hand, opens up numerous possibilities for adapting public authority to societal change. What is special about the Swedish LO compared to trade union organizations in many other nations is not, of course, that labor has sought greater state involvement per se in the economy but that it has sought to use the state as an instrument for promoting the "creative destruction" so intrinsic to market capitalism. The state has been used to amplify the market's dynamism, while socializing the costs of readjustment for workers. Thus the LO's policy proposals have reflected a subtle blending of public direction and planning with the basic logic of the market. Likewise, the CED has continually promoted public-private integration by championing various forms of economic planning in which the actions of business, labor, and government are coordinated through partnerships. According to one CED publication, "The United States is not simply a set of economic arrangements governed by a market system, much as that may be implied in popular ideology. The integration of business power and capabilities with those of government is indispensable for achievement of both government and private goals."[32]

Perhaps most importantly, both organizations have stressed an analytic, problem-solving orientation toward the resolution of policy issues. Policy innovation is as much an exercise in analysis, information gathering, and clarification as it is of striking bargains between conflicting interests. As the technical and organizational complexities involved in managing industrial economies increases, the role of analysis in policy making increases as well. Complexity and specialization beget expertise, which becomes an indispensable ingredient in making policy. Professionally trained economists and other experts play a key role in defining problems and evaluating the effectiveness of alternative options for dealing with them. With the Keynesian revolution, the linkages between political elites, on the one hand, and economics and other policy sciences, on the other, grew even stronger. The LO and the CED were able to draw upon the expertise and inventiveness of in-house intellectuals in framing policy alternatives. Individuals like Gosta Rehn and Beardsley Ruml were at the very center of the postwar intellectual ferment that shaped the terms of debate over economic policy. Ruml served as the CED's chief economist and was the organization's intellectual guru in much the way that Rehn was for the LO. By fusing the ideas and analytical resources at their disposal with the political vision of the organizations with which they were affiliated, these individuals produced policy options that were technically and politically feasible.

But quite apart from their own organizational capacity to engage in political learning, the course chosen in each country was critically affected by differences in the prevailing state of expert opinion. These differences were striking. First, conceptions of the economy and definitions of economic problems were affected by the reigning paradigms and theories in the economics discipline of each nation, particularly in its adherence to neoclassical thinking. Swedish economists most influential in setting the terms of discussion at the outset of Sweden's postwar deliberations over economic policy adhered to a conception of the labor market (and of the importance of labor market measures) that in the United States remained marginalized within the profession by the tiny group of structural economists.[33] Structuralists in the United States shared Swedish economists' notion of a labor market that was segmented and heterogeneous and the belief that market forces could not automatically, and with sufficient speed, bring into equilibrium the supply of and demand for labor. But the majority of the most prestigious economists in the United States still adhered in the final analysis to the neoclassical assumption of a self-regulating labor market, a conception of economic management in almost exclusively macro terms, and called for solutions that relied upon aggregate measures.

Second, manpower experts in the United States largely embraced the social policy orientation that directed employment programs toward an exclusive emphasis on serving the poor and rejected any notion that they should be included in a broader economic policy strategy. By contrast, Swedish authorities like Gosta Rehn explicitly rejected this orientation as myopic, one that would at best simply displace low-income people at the lowest rungs of the occupational ladder with other low-income people.[34]

Finally, assessments of the relationship between the balance of class power in a nation, on the one hand, and the policies that nation pursues, on the other, must view the power of class actors as a result, not simply a cause, of the policies pursued and of success or failure of these policies in solving problems. The capacity to engage in learning on the part of the dominant partner makes it more likely that a balance of class power will be sustained over a long period of time. The political hegemony of the Swedish Social Democrats through most of the postwar period was as much a result as a cause of the innovative policies they pursued. The policies greatly enhanced labor's organizational strength and solidarity. Similarly, the success of American business in shaping policies that precluded the outbreak of another depression helped to halt the significant organizational gains that American labor achieved in the 1930s and 1940s.

To reinforce our argument that the capacity to engage in political learning is crucial for understanding the evolution of policy, let us look briefly at a case where such a capacity has been absent. There have been three postwar British governments headed by the Labour party, 1945–1951, 1964–1970, and 1974–1979. In all three cases, the government fell from power because it was unable to sustain a viable economic policy. As in Sweden, the British Labour party was committed to maintaining full employment. And as in Sweden, the commitment was jeopardized by inflation and balance-of-payments problems. Unlike Sweden, however, even though British Labour had ample electoral opportunities for forging policies with long-term political and economic viability, they did not. Labour governments continually relied upon deflation and wage restraint for dealing with inflation. Each attempt at wage restraint ended in failure, for the same reasons that the Swedish LO rejected the option in the early 1950s. Leaders of the Trades Union Congress (TUC), the British counterpart to the Swedish LO, continually found themselves in the untenable position of either accepting wage restraint or contributing to the demise of Labour governments. Despite the TUC's loyalty to the party and the party's significant role in union affairs, wage restraint threatened the stability of the trade unions and their legitimacy as organizations committed to working-class interests. This was especially the case in Britain, where unions are noted for their decentralization and fragmented structure. The power of the unions was strong enough to resist the government's policy but unable to substantially influence government in a positive way.[35]

A key aspect of the recurrent paralysis of postwar British economic policy is to be found in the disjuncture between the Labour party, which strived to be an integrative, national party representing the well-being of all classes, and the union movement, which maintained its role as a working-class organization in a capitalist society.[36] Neither the unions nor the party were able to find a way to protect the interests of their class constituency and, at the same time, govern the national economy. One important reason is the inability of British labor organizations to engage in the kind of learning that leads to creative policy innovation. British labor's lack of innovative orientation is longstanding. The Labour party failed to cooperate with Lloyd George and the Liberals in the 1930s to introduce a Keynesian economic recovery program, while the Swedish Social Democrats readily embraced the new economic doctrine.[37] Likewise, after the war, while the Swedes evolved from a simple Keynesian to a post-Keynesian strategy, British labor responded with proposals for the nationalization of industry, the most traditional of all socialist policies. Not surprisingly, British unions have lacked an essential characteristic associated with policy innovation—an analytical, problem-solving orientation to policy making. According to Barbash, "the expert does not occupy a favored place in the trade union conception of the policy-making process. . . . Statistical and factual analysis is not highly valued in the British unions. The research departments 'often have little importance in the trade union hierarchy.' "[38]

The failure of British labor to engage in political learning led to a significant alteration in the balance of class forces during the past decade. While the success of Swedish policy innovations enhanced labor's political strength and solidarity, in Britain unsuccessful Labour government policies over time eroded its strength and solidarity. Rising militancy within the union movement, the defection of moderates from the Labour party, and the rise to power of a Conservative government committed to free market ideology have polarized British politics, leaving labor at a definite disadvantage, particularly when compared to its much stronger position at the outset of the postwar period.

INSTITUTIONS AND POLICY INNOVATION

If Swedish and American policies reflected the interests of class actors and the innovations developed by their organizations, they were critically affected by the prevailing institutional arrangements in the two nations as well. Institutions facilitated the development of certain policies and made it difficult to adopt and carry out others.

Response to the Depression

In trying to explain Swedish and American responses to the Great Depression, Margaret Weir and Theda Skocpol stressed differences in institutions (what they call "state structures") and the possibilities these held out for bringing together economic experts with party leaders. "Much of the answer to why the Swedish Social Democrats launched a deficit-financed recovery strategy in 1932–34 lies in the history of the Swedish state from pre-industrial times and its long-established mechanisms for bringing experts, bureaucrats, and political representatives together for sustained planning of public policies."[39]

Ever since the monarchical period, the Swedish state developed administrative boards headed by royally appointed regional officials charged with governing the country. These royal investigatory commissions have had a strong influence, occupying a central place in the process of policy formulation. The investigatory commissions have remained separate from regular administrative departments engaged in policy implementation, which has enabled them to take an exclusive interest in the long-term study of problems and planning of policy options. The commissions have deliberated regularly on the most important national issues, not as ad hoc panels set up to respond to immediate problems but as ongoing bodies engaged in extended analysis.

Modern-day commissions are designed in the mold of corporatist decision-making arenas. The commissions not only harness the expertise of the social sciences, but also bring into the process representatives of the political parties and major social groups who participate directly in policy formulation jointly with public officials. By integrating all of the relevant actors in a centralized forum, the commissions are able to go beyond mere fact finding and analysis to actually build a political consensus on the resolution of issues.

The key role of the commissions in deliberation and consensus building has eclipsed the Swedish parliament to a great degree as the focal point of policy making. The Riksdag's involvement in policy is quite limited as compared to that of the U.S. Congress. Investigatory commissions are appointed by senior civil servants, mainly those in the Department of Finance. They give the commissions their directives and guidance, decide what issues ought to be the subject for study and investigation, and choose which individuals will serve as members. Parliamentary deputies occasionally request that a commission be established, but compared to the bureaucracy, the Riksdag's resources are very limited for engaging in the kind of thorough intellectual sifting and deliberation that is considered necessary. The independent role of individual parliamentary deputies in policy making is also limited by party discipline, which party leaders sitting in the cabinet have the power to enforce.[40]

According to one observer, these institutional arrangements reflect Sweden's "deliberative," "rationalistic," "open," and "consensual" political culture.[41] Long periods of time are given to serious study of the nature and causes of current policy problems. Great efforts are made to develop the fullest possible information and analysis of a given problem as well as a full range of possible alternatives. Openness is encouraged by allowing all interested parties to participate in decisions and by promoting an atmosphere where agreement of all parties to the decision is sought. The first two traits account for the high degree of respect accorded to professional experts, especially economists, in Sweden. Deference to expert opinion, along with the strategic importance of the study commissions, has given economists institutionalized access to the very center of the Swedish policy-making apparatus. During the 1930s, at the birth of the managed economy in modern Sweden, one British observer wrote that members of the economics discipline held "an honoured place in the scheme of things in marked contrast to the scepticism or the polite indifference with which he is regarded in this country or the United States."[42]

How did these specific institutional features of the Swedish state increase the likelihood of a bold Keynesian-type response to the Great Depression? As Skocpol and Weir argued, it was "the unique institutional mechanism of the state-sponsored investigatory commission [that] allowed economic experts, Social Democratic politicians, and officials to ponder together—for several years before the depression crisis—how it might be politically and administratively feasible and intellectually justifiable to devise public policies to combat mass unemployment."[43] During a brief interlude in the 1920s when the Social Democrats were in power, they appointed a Committee of Inquiry into Unemployment and charged it with investigating the causes of unemployment and alternative remedies for it.[44] The commission "engaged the research energies of practically all of Sweden's handful of young economists," who would later come to be known as the Stockholm School. Members of the Stockholm School had concluded before Keynes published *The General Theory* that the private economy did not necessarily operate at full employment. The group, which included Dag Hammarskjold, Alf Johansson, Gunnar Myrdal, and Bertil Ohlin, produced a series of monographs completed under the commission's auspices.[45]

With the country mired deep in the Depression, elections were held in 1932 in Sweden. The Social Democratic party proposed to expand public expenditures to increase purchasing power and put people back to work. The election victory returned the Social Democrats to power in a coalition with the Agrarian party. A new Commission on Unemployment was created, which continued the cooperation between party leaders and the innovative group of Swedish economists that had begun under the previous commission. Its directors were the leading figures of the Stockholm School. In formulating the Social Democrats' strategy for economic recovery, Finance Minister Wigforss cooperated closely with this team of economists and relied on their accumulated studies and ideas.

Weir and Skocpol have argued that the possibility of a Keynesian program of economic recovery was not out of the question during the New Deal period in the United States. At critical historical conjunctures in the 1930s and 1940s, political room for maneuver and favorable intellectual currents did exist, but they could not produce an outcome similar to that which took place in Sweden because of differences in the possibilities afforded by the institutional structure of the state. The relief programs begun in the early New Deal boosted Democratic popularity and swelled the party's majorities in Congress in 1934 and 1936. Even though much intellectual and political capital of the first Roosevelt administration was dissipated on the ill-fated National Industrial Recovery Act, the later New Deal held out a real possibility for a Social Democratic-type response to the Depression based upon Keynesian deficit creation. Between 1936 and 1939, class-oriented politics in the United States reached a high-water mark, and alliances were formed between liberal and labor constituencies. Industrial unionism expanded rapidly. A variety of federal programs and agencies existed, like the Works Progress Administration, that might have served as the basis for such a response. While neither the WPA nor any of the other work relief spending programs were conceived in terms of a framework through which an explicitly countercyclical strategy could be pursued, within the Roosevelt administration there were several influential individuals—Marriner Eccles, Lauchlin Currie, Harry Hopkins, and Henry Wallace—who sooner or later came over to the idea.

As noted in chapter 2, the sharp economic downturn of 1937 led to Roosevelt's break with balanced budget orthodoxy and his conversion to the idea of deficit spending as a solution to the Depression. This change occurred just at the time when Keynes's arguments were starting to make a great impression on academic thinking. Stagnationist prescriptions, which called for institutionalizing Keynesian macroeconomic management based on a permanent expansion of federal expenditures for public investment and social services, had come to the fore. Led by Alvin Hansen and other leading economists, the stagnationists had made inroads in prestigious academic circles as well as in Washington bureaucracies and planning bodies.

But these developments were not enough to lead to a Keynesian program of economic recovery based upon spending deficits. The United States did not have the long tradition of centralized administration or disciplined parliamentary parties through which to bring together the intellectual resources and political leadership to implement such a program. The rapid growth of federal administrative agencies took place in a haphazard and uncontrolled manner. Advocates of the new economic wisdom were scattered about, their various spending programs competing with one another for money. Nor were Roosevelt's reorganization proposals, to set up a centralized administration to plan and control the various pieces of the New Deal fiscal programs, successful once Congress interpreted it as an attempt to augment the power of the executive branch at its expense.

Immediately after World War II the United States directly faced the question of whether to adopt a Keynesian program of full employment based upon deficit spending. But the fragmented state structure left advocates of the Full Employment Bill of 1945 with a formidable task of building a coalition in favor of the bill. It also proved a boon to conservative opponents of the bill, who were able to take advantage of the separation of powers, a weak national party system, and most of all, Congress's decentralized authority and localistic orientations, to defeat the effort of full-employment advocates.

In sum, the bold and decisive initiatives undertaken in Sweden in the thirties and forties, to deal with unemployment, and the lack of them in the United States, are closely related to the respective policy-making institutions in each nation. That the Democratic party in America did not serve as the vehicle for expressing working class demands, as the Swedish Social Democratic party did, is an important, albeit partial, explanation.[46]

The Postwar Period

The starting point for Sweden's postwar economic policy debate was not the LO and Gosta Rehn but, instead, the Myrdal Commission of the 1940s.[47] The commission's contributions to the development of Swedish policy were threefold. First, its recommendations were an affirmation of the consensus that developed in the 1930s among experts and political elites across the political spectrum on the soundness of Keynesian analysis and prescription. Second, it reconceptualized the main purpose for using Keynesian demand management techniques in the post-Depression era. Where the focus of the crisis policy of the Depression was on recovery—getting the economy out of a deep trough—the 1940s saw a shift in the basic objective of economic intervention to sustaining full employment. The centerpiece of the commission's reports, of which there were thirteen, was the idea of maintaining aggregate demand in order to sustain economic expansion and, consequently, full employment. The commission argued that demand could be maintained through increased purchasing power and more investment. Where the Unemployment Commission of the 1930s placed a greater reliance on purchasing power, the Myrdal Commission took the view that investment occupied "a central place in employment policy." Public investment, it argued, should be counter-cyclical and planned in detail.

The Myrdal Commission initiated Sweden's first "investment reserves," which sought to get private employers to put aside part of their profits during boom times in order to use them to step up investment during downturns. The commission felt that labor should be employed whenever possible in its ordinary work, and only as a second resort should public works be launched. The Myrdal Commission's report, and in particular its recommendation to pursue a powerfully expansionist economic policy, found its way into the Social Democrats' Twenty-seven Points, a blueprint for a full-employment, welfare-state program. The kind of steps stressed in the commission's report bore a close resemblance to the prescriptions advocated by the stagnationists in the United States that were embodied in the Full Employment Bill.

The Myrdal Commission's report is significant for a third reason: it laid much of the intellectual foundation for developments in Swedish economic policy that would unfold in the postwar decades. Although the centerpiece of the Myrdal Commission's report was Keynesian in that it called for a powerfully expansionary fiscal policy, it had much more to say about labor markets and labor market policy than did Keynes. One of the commission's key arguments was that the labor market is heterogenous and divided into various submarkets. The commission also showed how different employment measures could have a selective impact on the labor market, and how the application of different combinations of them could provide public authorities with a great deal more flexibility for intervening in the market than simply relying upon aggregate policy instruments. As already mentioned, to stabilize the business cycle, the commission put forth the idea of investment reserves in order to iron out fluctuations in private investment. The commission also saw a role for labor market policy in eliminating structural obstacles to growth, such as geographical imbalances in supply and demand for labor, as well as the need to avoid preserving a given structure of production after it was no longer efficient to do so. Toward that end, it stressed the need for "mobility" and a "capacity to adapt" the work force.

Thus in what it had to say about the nature of labor markets and the role of labor market policy, the Myrdal Commission was remarkably prescient. While the commission did not regard labor market policy as a strategic part of economic policy for the 1940s, when its report was issued it did hold a positive attitude toward labor market policy and a clear understanding of the need for one. In its reports one sees an emerging post-Keynesian economic policy, which was actually a refinement of and an elaboration upon the basic Keynesian approach. By anticipating the necessity to go beyond the "simple aggregates" of the 1930s and 1940s and move toward selective, disaggregated intervention, the commission's reports bore the intellectual seeds of the "active labor market policy" that would come to full fruition fifteen years later.

Building Administrative Capacity

During the years in which the Myrdal Commission occupied center stage in the debate over economic policy, the Swedes also launched two other less-publicized investigations, whose importance bore even more directly upon the possibilities for adopting a labor market policy. The first was the Employment Service Enquiry of 1950, which looked into what should be done about the Employment Service, which had expanded during the war. The second investigation was conducted under the auspices of the Labor Market Commission—a crisis body set up initially to deal with any wartime manpower emergencies that might arise. The Labor Market Commission began a rather complicated process of investigation and study, which resulted in a set of substantive proposals that were, like those of the Myrdal Commission, positive toward the use of labor market measures in economic policy. The Labor Market Commission argued that labor market policy was relevant not only during times of high unemployment, but that it also had a role to play when the economy was performing well by helping to accelerate the pace of structural adjustment in the economy.

The most important proposals to emerge from the Labor Market Commission and the Employment Service Enquiry were (1) to set up a permanent administrative organization to oversee labor market policy, and (2) to nationalize the employment service. The comments written by the unions' most influential economists placed particular emphasis on the need for strengthening the Employment Service so that it could be redirected away from the relief-oriented tasks of administering unemployment insurance and the work test and toward a capability of undertaking more positive employment measures. The cabinet and the Riksdag approved the commission's report, putting the Labor Market Board on a permanent footing and nationalizing the operations of the Employment Service.

The organization of the National Labor Market Board (and the Employment Service, which serves as an arm of the board) reflect several distinctive features of Swedish public administration, dating back to the monarchical period. It was set up as an autonomous agency, one of a network of independent boards and agencies that are largely free of parliamentary and ministerial supervision. Cabinet ministries are relatively small and exercise no direct authority over the implementation of policy, which is in the hands of independent boards and agencies. The independent administrative boards evolved from the collegial administrative councils established in the seventeenth century. Theoretically, the boards are accountable only to the king-in-council rather than to cabinet ministers. In other respects, the administrative boards resemble most other modern bureaucracies—hierarchically organized, dedicated to achieving scientific, rational goals, and operating according to orderly procedures. Each is headed by a director-general, who supervises a staff of professional civil servants, most of whom are recruited from the upper and middle classes. The senior civil service enjoys considerable social prestige and possesses a reputation for efficient, dedicated service.[48]

The Labor Market Board's organization also follows the corporatist pattern that, as already noted, is a ubiquitous feature of Swedish politics and administration. At the top sits the National Labor Market Board, a tripartite body consisting of representatives of business, labor, and the state.[49] Labor has a plurality of votes and is usually the most active participant, but nearly all decisions of the board are unanimous. The tripartite arrangement has several advantages. In terms of planning and implementation of policy, it brings together all of the major groups in the labor market, promoting communication and reducing uncertainty in the labor market. The government is kept informed of the problems and intentions of labor and business so that appropriate adjustments in policy can be made, and the parties in the private sector can rely upon public authorities to keep them up to date on trends in labor demand and supply. Tripartite administration has important political consequences, as well. By devolving much of the responsibility for implementation upon business and labor, these groups develop a serious commitment to seeing that administrative standards are improved and that a steady flow of public funds is generated for conducting labor market policy.

As noted in chapter 6, effective implementation of employment programs is critically dependent upon a decentralized administrative structure. Because employment problems vary widely from one local (and regional) labor market to another, local authorities must have a great deal of control over planning and implementation. We have seen that Swedish policy formulation is highly centralized at the national level but that Swedish policy implementation has a tradition of decentralization. Local governments have a long history of working with the national government to implement policy, and functional decentralization of administration among local authorities dates back to the seventeenth century. The National Labor Market Board supervises twenty-four county labor market boards, as well as the Employment Service, with its 220 local offices. All of these have tripartite working groups as well. There is a constant flow of information transmitted both horizontally (among the private and public representatives), and vertically (up and down the administrative hierarchy). Policies can be tailored to meet the needs of local communities without losing sight of overall, national policy objectives.

The importance of setting in place this administrative machinery cannot be exaggerated. It meant that the requisite institutional capacity was already in place before a full-fledged labor market policy was adopted. And it reflected a recognition of the need to set up an agency outside the regular cabinet ministries that was devoted solely to proposing policies and anticipating developments in the labor market. If the notion of an active labor market policy means anything, it surely means having the capability to engage in labor market forecasting in order to anticipate problems in the labor market before they reach a crisis, maintaining a dialogue on the state of the labor market between public authorities and the private sector, and then planning public policy accordingly. Thus centuries of experience in state building in Sweden made it possible to fashion a special administrative apparatus expressly to carry out labor market policy and to retain the expansion of the employment services that had evolved during the war and put them under the control of a national administration.

Administrative developments in the United States were quite different. Wartime planning bodies were quickly dismantled after World War II. No efforts were made to create a special administrative mechanism exclusively responsible for employment policy nor were any efforts made to draw the major actors in the labor market into the carrying out of policy. Instead, manpower policy was placed under the control of the Labor Department—an agency that was atrophied and internally fragmented, noted mainly for its politically charged mission of representing one side of the labor-business equation. Moreover, the failure to nationalize the United States Employment Service after World War II meant that the Labor Department was left without a vital administrative arm for carrying out employment programs at the local level.[50]

It is difficult to see how Swedish labor would have been successful in getting its policies formulated, adopted, and effectively carried out without a set of institutions that facilitated and promoted bold policy innovations. Likewise, it would have been extremely difficult, perhaps impossible, for a powerful American working class to overcome the institutional constraints that militated against radical policy innovations to extend the role of the state in the private economy. Thus part of the explanation for the different policy outcomes in the two nations is the very different institutional arrangements that existed for formulating responses to unemployment.

First, in Sweden centralized policy-making institutions, integrating party leaders, civil servants, economists, and group representatives, provided the capacity for continually reconstituting a broad consensus over the extension of the role of the state in the market. They facilitated a sequence of responses, each response modifying the previous one. Each response introduced a policy innovation that built upon or modified existing policy to take account of changing economic realities. The deficits created in the 1930s in response to the Depression were a rudimentary form of Keynesianism that crystallized into a powerful expansionary tool for maintaining levels of full employment after the war. This simple Keynesian strategy eventually reached its limits, when it became apparent that sustaining full employment over long periods of time led to inflationary pressures. The search for a new response led to a post-Keynesian policy, in which the management of aggregate demand was disaggregated with the use of selective labor market programs. Selective instruments were used in conjunction with conventional macroeconomic policies in order to absorb pockets of unemployed labor while avoiding the inflationary consequences that a general expansion of demand would cause. The Swedes also recognized that selective employment programs sped the process of economic readjustment and, as a result, prevented the occurrence of unemployment due to structural change.

Investigatory commissions were at the center of this process. They were the mechanism the Swedes used to engage in the kind of deliberative, analytical policy making that permitted policy to evolve in an orderly succession of stages. The commissions of the 1920s and 1930s brought economists and politicians together to launch the Keynesian recovery program of the Depression. Similarly, the Myrdal Commission of the 1940s laid an important intellectual foundation for the eventual adoption of an active labor market policy of the 1950s and 1960s and introduced such specific innovations as planned investment reserves. Finally, the commissions were the major mechanisms used for building a specialized administrative organization, the Labor Market Board, and for integrating the Employment Service within the domain of labor market intervention.

Disciplined party government made it possible for there to be a working majority in the Riksdag, which could adopt and implement bold policy innovations. A strong, programmatic party system gave leaders in government the capacity to map out and get adopted coherent policy strategies that went beyond ad hoc crisis management. The active labor market policy was an integral part of a broader strategy, which included solidaristic wages and high spending on social services.

In the United States, on the other hand, the possibility of getting a Swedish-style policy response was precluded by the structure of the policy-making process and particularly by the absence of institutions capable of providing the necessary integration among the various actors and centralized leadership. The Full Employment Bill embodied a set of policy prescriptions similar to those put in place in Sweden, calling for a growing share of GNP taken up in public spending and investment in order to maintain employment-producing growth. That bill's defeat in 1946 at the hands of a powerful legislative minority, which was able to take advantage of the fragmented congressional structure and was free from the discipline of a strong national party leadership, constituted a major setback in the march toward a Keynesian response to unemployment that had begun to manifest itself during the New Deal. It was not until almost two decades later that political conditions again afforded the opportunity to adopt the new economics of Keynes. As we have seen, this delay permitted proponents of a more conservative version of Keynesianism to build a consensus in favor of tax cuts and temporary deficits, which in turn precluded the possibility for launching an active labor market policy in the 1960s, by keeping the lid on expenditures for employment and training measures.

By not adopting a simple Keynesianism of fiscal expansion, as called for in the Full Employment Bill, the United States was unlikely to graduate to a post-Keynesian policy based upon active labor market measures. In the absence of a commitment to full-employment Keynesianism, the U.S. economy remained slack from the 1950s to the mid-1960s. Unemployment was high, but inflation was low. As long as low inflation could be traded off for comparatively high rates of unemployment, there was no incentive to adopt selective employment measures designed to reconcile full employment with reasonable price stability, as was the case in Sweden.

Furthermore, had the commitment been made to pursue expansionary policies throughout the Truman, Eisenhower years, and into the Kennedy years, the Keynesian-structuralist controversy may very well have been avoided. By maintaining sufficient stimulus in the economy, any remaining unemployment would presumably be due to structural causes. Instead, a great deal of confusion and uncertainty was created in the 1950s and early 1960s by the competing Keynesian and structural explanations for the high unemployment that existed. Keynesians, both for intellectual and political reasons, felt inclined to discredit structural explanations and to exclude manpower programs from the conduct of economic policy. Structuralists, who began by discrediting the Keynesians' arguments, did not clarify their position until later: that both demand deficiency and structural imbalances existed in the labor market, calling for both a demand stimulus and manpower measures. The incoherent and haphazard structure of American policy-making institutions did nothing to resolve this confusion in expert thinking. Instead, Congress adopted manpower training two years before it adopted the Keynesian fiscal stimulus. From the Swedish (i.e., post-Keynesian) perspective, putting in place selective measures before having first pursued demand expansion was putting the cart before the horse.

Second, national policy-making institutions in the United States segmented and compartmentalized policy formulation, allowing economic policy to be developed and conducted separately from employment policies. Economic policy was mapped out at the highest levels of the executive branch. This policy was dominated by economists who, unlike their counterparts in Sweden, insisted that full employment could be reached by exclusive reliance upon macro measures, without producing inflationary pressures. They rejected the idea of structural unemployment by clinging to the neoclassical belief in the ability of the private market to automatically bring into balance the supply and demand for labor. By occupying the commanding heights of economic policy making in the United States, American Keynesians in the CEA were able to define economic management exclusively as a macro-economic, tax-cutting exercise. Efforts to create a Council of Manpower Advisers, which would have brought manpower policy considerations into the upper reaches of the executive branch, were rejected, and the Labor Department, which was the chief proponent of selective employment and training measures, was largely left out of deliberations over economic policy.

The notion that macroeconomic instruments could get the economy to full employment without the need for manpower training left training programs with no role to play outside of helping the disadvantaged population, which was the target of the poverty program. The Labor Department shifted the focus of its programs to the poor. The absorption of manpower training into the poverty program had an important implication for the kind of political support employment policy enjoyed. By limiting the objectives and narrowing the constituency of the manpower programs, organized political support for them became essentially nonexistent. In fact, by the late 1960s a backlash developed among white, middle-class taxpayers who felt they were footing the bill for "welfare programs" that afforded them little in the way of benefits. This was exactly the opposite of the Swedish experience, where broad policy objectives and universal eligibility to participate in labor market programs gave rise to a broad-based constituency composed of the most important organized economic interests.

With the economists in the CEA showing little interest in incorporating either jobs or manpower training into either economic management or the War on Poverty, employment policy remained largely in the hands of Congress and the Labor Department. As for manpower policy, its adoption depended upon the commitment of a single individual, Senator Clark. The Manpower Development and Training Act was shown little interest by the political parties or by the major economic interests—business and labor. The debate in Congress revolved around the narrower issues of who would control service delivery, what kinds of training would be provided, and what would be the role of relevant agencies in Washington. While the Kennedy administration accepted the Manpower Development and Training Act, neither liberals in Congress nor officials in the Labor Department could overcome the resistance of President Johnson and his economic advisers to launching a Swedish-style employment creation strategy for the War on Poverty, once the administration had committed itself to cutting taxes.

Finally, economists in Sweden were in a much more institutionally advantageous position to get their ideas translated into public policy in a clear and cogent fashion, than were economists in the United States. Swedish economic experts worked within a centralized state structure, which gave them the opportunity to dominate a relatively insulated policy arena that included a close-knit, relatively limited number of decision makers who sat on key investigatory commissions and in the cabinet. Parliamentary acquiescence in the decisions was essentially assured. Moreover, the investigatory commissions served as ongoing mechanisms, where economists could over time affect the thinking of public officials. Finally, Swedish policy-making orientations that traditionally stressed the importance of analysis and rational deliberation provided a hospitable atmosphere for experts to dominate policy deliberations.

Economists in the United States enjoyed none of these advantages, and as a result, their prescriptions were sometimes defeated, sometimes adopted only after delay, and at other times distorted or watered down. We have already mentioned the defeat of the Full Employment Bill in Congress, which ended the influence of stagnationist-Keynesian ideas in the United States. Kennedy's advisers had different, although no less difficult, institutional constraints to overcome. When the Kennedy advisers came to Washington, they had to essentially start from scratch in their tutoring of top officials, without the benefit of a mechanism that was already espousing Keynesian ideas. In order to get the government to adopt fiscal deficits, the Keynesians had to contend with a Federal Reserve Board hostile to expansionary fiscal policies and with a president and Congress that were for a long time skeptical of the idea of creating deficits. Only after a long campaign of education and persuasion were the Keynesians' views adopted.

The structuralists and human resource economists had a different problem, which was that those in authority tended to grasp (intentionally or unintentionally) only part of what they were arguing. The structuralists' diagnosis of unemployment, as a failure of the market to adjust to structural change on its own, was ignored or misunderstood by most congressmen. Rather than seeing structural unemployment as a problem of the economy, and manpower policy as an exercise in national economic planning, they viewed the problem largely as one of particular groups of individual workers deficient in the right skills, and manpower policy merely as a retraining program to assist them. Congress thus subtly, but profoundly, transformed the full meaning of the structural diagnosis and prescription. Congress's redefinition of the problem was partly due to conservatives who embraced retraining as a substitute for fiscal deficits, which they defined as the antimarket, liberal alternative. It also stemmed from a much more basic fact about the nature of Congress and its orientations to complex economic problems. The typical congressman's understanding of unemployment was in terms of the economic and social plight of constituents without jobs and incomes, not of the structural impediments to the adjustment of labor supply and demand. His conception of manpower policy was as an emergency measure to assist individuals in trouble, rather than an effort to engage in labor market planning and long-term investment.

CONCLUSION

The forces that shaped American employment policy are brought into sharper focus when viewed from a comparative perspective. Political conditions and intellectual currents in other industrialized countries differed markedly from those in the United States, and they consequently led to an entirely different set of outcomes. Sweden's adoption of a full-employment policy that included an active labor market policy oriented toward the attainment of broad economic policy objectives was possible because of the dominant role of Swedish working-class organizations not only at the polls and in parliament but also in developing concrete policy innovations. The capacity to engage in political learning that led to the innovations sustained the Social Democrats' political dominance during the postwar period. In addition, the opinions of professional economists plus a set of centralized, integrated, and administratively competent policy-making institutions facilitated the development of policies that accorded with working-class interests. In the United States, business elites, which helped defeat efforts to move policy in a Swedish direction, possessed a similar capacity to engage in policy innovation. The result was a refashioning of the tools of modern economic management in ways that were compatible with the economic interests of business. And as in Sweden, government institutions and the reigning ideas of professional economists pushed policy in the direction preferred by the dominant class and blocked opportunities that could have enlarged the role of employment policy.

Part IV

The Political Failure of Employment Policy

10

Summary and Conclusions

LIKE THE Progressive social reformers and the New Dealers before them, liberals in the postwar period focused a good deal of their energy on one of industrial capitalism's most enduring problems—unemployed labor. Building upon the widely perceived success of the New Deal, liberals set their sights beyond merely ameliorating the pain of joblessness to preventing it. By the 1980s this experiment had ended largely in political failure, notwithstanding whatever positive accomplishments it may have produced in reducing joblessness. Political failure at the outset was defined as the inability to sustain a broad consensus on policy objectives and the means for achieving them, or the ability to sustain a consensus only on the most limited objectives and means. In this chapter we distill from the previous ones how the failure manifested itself concretely along three dimensions. We then go on to show how these dimensions of failure are rooted in the ideas, institutions, and interests that shaped and constrained employment policy in the postwar decades, by summarizing the influence of each factor and discussing the linkages between them.

Inherent in the question Why the failure? are the questions Why the policy? and Why not another? Given the broad scope and multiple dimensions of the failure, it should not be surprising that more than one or two factors account for the kind of policy and programs that were pursued during the postwar decades. An adequate explanation of the policy record requires a combination of the three categories of analysis. None of the three is adequate alone, and the three analytic factors are linked throughout the historical record. In identifying the impact of each factor it is useful to distinguish between various aspects of public policy. Each explanatory variable played a dominant role in shaping a different aspect of employment policy. Ideas are most critical for understanding the direction and content of employment policy, institutions appear as key determinants of how employment policy was designed and conducted, and interests are important for under-standing the level and distribution of benefits.

The detailed historical account in the previous chapters shows that the causal relationship between interests, institutions, and ideas, on the one hand, and employment policy, on the other, is a complex and contingent one. First, the three determinants were not so constraining as to keep options that were incongruent with them off the agenda. Second, policy choices and performance themselves shaped the nature of interest group involvement and the structure of the institutional arena that were established. Finally, policies are not simply reflections of political and institutional power. They are intellectual creations as well. The distinctive American response to unemployment is to be understood on its own terms, as the search for feasible courses of action to a collective problem at particular points in time. Policy makers' choices reflected what they knew, or thought they knew, about unemployment and poverty and their experience with previous policy choices. If the explanation seems inelegant and complex, it is because the subject matter itself—the evolution of a major public policy over the course of some forty years—is inelegant, complex, and changeable.

THREE DIMENSIONS OF FAILURE

There are at least three dimensions of the political failure of employment policy. First, we may speak of its *unfulfilled agenda and truncated mission.* Its agenda was unfulfilled because efforts to establish a commitment to the goal of full employment fell short. Its mission was truncated because it never developed an orientation or a size that would have allowed it to play a critical role in economic management. As a result of the adoption of a less-than-full-employment, social-welfare-oriented mis-sion, the policy played a residual role in efforts to combat unemploy-ment. A commitment to full employment would have given employ-ment and training programs the legally mandated, overarching purpose these programs have always lacked. As a consequence, program bud-gets were inadequate to significantly reduce joblessness. Expenditure levels rose and fell according to transient political and economic circum-stances; they rose in the midst of an economic emergency, or when liberals could muster sufficient votes in Congress, or when a Democrat occupied the White House, or when local governments lobbied hard. These conditions often obtained when the jobless rate was well above what was considered the full-employment level. Without the full-employment commitment, employment programs were also vulnerable to the kind of goal displacement that took place under CETA, when reducing unemployment was partially eclipsed by efforts to use the program to relieve local fiscal stress.

Even if a genuine commitment to full employment had been faithfully pursued, it would have been necessary simultaneously to orient the programs toward economic (rather than social) policy objectives. A full-employment policy that was not directed toward achieving economic stabilization and growth simply would have produced another CETA, writ larger. As a tool of economic policy, decisions could have been made based upon the requirements of the economy, rather than simply assisting categories of individuals or subsidizing local governments. The stress would have been on preventing recessions (rather than relieving distress); on improving the trade-off between unemployment and inflation by targeting jobs, training, and relocation incentives; on adapting the work force to structural economic change (rather than cushioning its effects). The appropriate model here is monetary policy. Can anyone seriously contemplate a monetary policy almost exclusively devoted to subsidizing marginal financial institutions and firms, while ignoring the regulation of credit, interest, and exchange rates? So an employment policy oriented toward economic stabilization and growth would have required labor market forecasting, the planning of investment reserves, targeted job creation, and large expenditures on retraining and relocation. Yet this was impossible given the nearly exclusive emphasis in economic policy on regulating aggregate demand, a reliance on tax cuts and tax incentives rather than spending on employment measures, and the absorption of employment and training measures into the poverty program and eventually into revenue sharing for the cities.

Perhaps the most important consequence of the adoption of a less-than-full-employment, social-welfare orientation is that it narrowed constituency support for employment policy. Because the consensus among policy makers extended only to a policy of limited vision and commitment, that policy failed to capture the imagination of the major interests in society or of the public at large. The adage that "programs for the poor are poor programs" is apt here. It applies whether the poor are individuals living in poverty or are cities struggling with a shrinking tax base and rising service demands. If the major actors in the labor market—business and labor—see that employment policy has little relevance to their interests, they will have little incentive to push for expanding or protecting its budget.

Second, employment policy foundered because of *confused and conflicting objectives*. While there was agreement that its basic mission should be assisting those who are in trouble, it has been difficult to sustain a consensus over time on what this means concretely. The focus of the programs vacillated repeatedly—between job training and job creation, between structural unemployment and cyclical unemployment, between creating new jobs and relieving local fiscal burdens, and between helping the long-term, hard-core disadvantaged and helping those who have had stable employment experience. In part, this pattern reflects ad hoc reactions to whatever problem was most salient at the time. In part it was the result of Congress's and the administration's apparent inability to decide what kind of employment policy they wanted. Multiple and constantly shifting objectives adversely affected the programs' performance. Objectives and the means for attaining them piled on top of one another and shifted over and over again from one set of concerns to another, creating confusion at the local level, where the programs were implemented.

Finally, there was a *breakdown in performance*, or the way in which the policy was carried out. Administrative and service delivery arrangements were fashioned and refashioned, yet always led to unintended consequences that in turn led to a loss of faith in the programs' effectiveness. Poor performance resulted in a loss of political credibility. Repeated efforts to reform the system disrupted whatever management capacity and constituency support was taking root at the local level. Waste, mismanagement, confusion, and the press reports that they generated validated conservative criticisms that federal programs were ineffective and created more problems than they solved. Without a mechanism at the local level that was both capable of managing the programs effectively and responsive to the objectives intended by Congress, the administrative structure swung back and forth between centralization and decentralization, in an unending quest for an effective intergovernmental relationship.

The three dimensions are interconnected. Without the establishment of full employment as a clear and paramount goal, it was more likely that program objectives would easily shift and proliferate, that reducing unemployment would be displaced by other objectives, and that there would be no agreed-upon standard for judging the adequacy of budgets. Confusing and conflicting objectives, in turn, were the chief reasons for breakdowns in performance. And because poor performance led to declining political support for the programs, it became more difficult to credibly argue that the unfulfilled agenda of employment policy should be completed and its mission reoriented.

INTERESTS

The impact of social groups and classes on employment policy has been largely negative. Domestic programs without an organized constituency committed to their long-term survival and growth are likely to remain modestly funded and politically vulnerable. Because the unemployed themselves are not capable of political mobilization, they depend upon surrogates—liberal advocacy groups, labor, and businessmen with a sense of social responsibility—to push for spending on training and job creation. For these groups, the plight of the unemployed is a sincere, but not paramount, concern of their organizations and memberships. Without interest and involvement among such critical actors in the economy as business and labor, the mission and size of the programs remains limited. Both have demonstrated little enthusiasm for transforming policy into something more central to their interests. Labor leaders, for instance, have greeted retraining programs for workers in highly unionized industries with skepticism as to their impact on the maintenance of their organizations.

While lack of constituency group involvement helps account for the limited role and size of the programs, it also appears that when a constituency mobilized, spending did increase. While those who provide employment and training services at the local level have not been highly mobilized in Washington, local governments that served as prime sponsors under CETA lobbied intensively for public service jobs, the highest funded program. While it would be misleading to view local governments as having captured CETA (after all, Washington imposed severe limits on their activity in 1978 and then eliminated public service jobs in 1981), it is more than coincidental that during the period of heavy lobbying by local governments CETA's budget grew dramatically. Yet because of both real and perceived failures of implementation, local governments were not able to establish themselves as a permanently entrenched constituency.

Clearly, job programs have greater value as distributive benefits than do training programs, which partly explains the greater lobbying for the former than for the latter, and in turn, the higher spending on jobs. This is one reason why the cyclically unemployed (who need jobs) are at a greater advantage than the structurally unemployed (who need training and related services), many of whom come from disadvantaged backgrounds and have little or no history of stable employment. But it is not the only reason. The cyclically unemployed are a more visible group and a more attentive constituency. Their misfortune is highly salient in the public mind, coming at it does during times of nationwide downturns in the economy. They are neither geographically and socially isolated nor is their unemployment likely to be viewed as the result of personal defects or intractable cultural problems, which is often believed of those living in poverty.

Where interests have had their most far-reaching impact is not on employment programs, per se, but on the broader policy context in which the programs operate. The political weakness of the American working class, and of the liberal-labor coalition as a whole, is a chief reason it has not been possible to establish full employment as the top priority of economic policy. More generally, it means that there has been little in the way of a countervailing power vis-à-vis business. We cannot reduce the defeat of full-employment legislation or the conduct of fiscal and monetary policies exclusively to business influence, and especially to a simplistic notion of direct pressure and control of the state by capitalists. Nevertheless, such influence has been a major factor in constraining the role of the state in the labor market.

More important than business's direct lobbying activities are the less visible ways in which business's political influence is felt. First, preservation of business's prerogatives and material interests rest in part on its legitimacy, which is reflected in widespread support for markets, property rights, and individual liberty. Liberal beliefs and values are at the center of America's national character and underpin the lack of class consciousness among the working class. The defeat of the Full Employment Bill of 1945 is perhaps the clearest example of how probusiness values figured in the story of employment policy, but it also has been apparent in the ready acceptance among policy makers of tax cutting as the preferred method of deficit creation (as compared to spending increases) and in the denigration of programs giving the unemployed jobs in the public sector. Second, business has great structural advantages as a key actor in the economy. Policy makers have felt they must create a hospitable climate for business investment. In the defeat of full-employment legislation and the conduct of monetary and fiscal policy, policy makers have implicitly recognized that fears of inflation and higher taxes lower business confidence.

INSTITUTIONS

Institutions filtered, modified, and delayed proposals that clashed with widely shared values, the interests of influential organized groups, and the goals of institutional actors themselves. The institutional structure made it very difficult to adopt comprehensive and far-reaching approaches to the problem of unemployment and facilitated the proliferation of incremental, specific programs. Proposals for large-scale change are more likely to threaten entrenched interests and societal values and are more difficult to build and sustain a majority around. With its fragmented decision-making structure and weak central authorities, American institutions present formidable obstacles to proponents of major policy changes and ample points of access for opponents to block or weaken them. Such was the case with full-employment proposals that contemplated a major alteration in the governance of the political economy. Conservative-business elites were able to defeat the Full Employment Bill of 1945 by gaining leverage over the process through the seniority system and committee autonomy in Congress. Neither the Democratic majority nor the Democratic president at the time could save the bill. Humphrey-Hawkins was affected in a similar way. Despite Democratic control of both branches of government when the legislation was under consideration, despite the party's pledge in its 1976 platform statement to get it adopted as written, and despite major constituency support, the party's own presidential candidate and members of Congress succeeded in seriously weakening the bill through amendments— and ignored it after it became law.

Because large-scale change has been so difficult to accomplish, proponents of federal action on behalf of the unemployed turned to an incremental strategy in the early 1960s. Starting with the Manpower Development and Training Act, they enacted a series of modest programs that identified the employment problems of particular groups and prescribed specific measures to address them. It was not only easier to secure passage of a series of separate categorical programs, each of which was relatively small and noncontroversial, it was also more politically attractive. Because of their specificity as to the target population and their particularized benefits, they served as convenient mechanisms for congressmen to claim credit for legislative accomplishments.

The drawback, of course, was that the jerry-built structure of categorical programs was impossible to implement effectively. The pursuit of individualized credit-claiming within a fragmented policy-making process produced a haphazard, uncoordinated set of programs. By the late 1960s, comprehensive policy change was not a matter of political choice (as it had been with full employment) so much as a matter of administrative necessity. Even though there was widespread recognition early on that change was badly needed, it took over four long years to adopt the reforms that culminated in CETA. Congress initially balked at consolidation and decentralization, which would sweep away existing categoricals and put in their place a single block grant, because discretion for choosing which groups would be eligible to participate, the specific services to be rendered, and who would provide them would shift from Congress to potential political rivals at the local level. The ability to claim credit for delivering particularized benefits would diminish. Congress would also be giving up its institutional prerogative to determine how the revenue it raised would be spent.

However, the major impediment to achieving reform was the separation of powers. A Democratic Congress was pitted against a Republican chief executive, with the former insisting that some of the money support public service jobs as a condition for approving the administrative reforms desired by the executive branch. It was only the fortuitous intervention of the Watergate fiasco that afforded political maneuverability to end the stalemate. The delay and final compromise had a deleterious impact on CETA. The four years locked in stalemate robbed local governments of valuable time and experience that could have been spent developing the institutional capability to carry out their new responsibilities. Instead, as soon as CETA had been launched the economy fell into a deep recession, and local prime sponsors were thrust into administering a rapidly growing, countercyclical job creation program. At the same time that authority over the programs was being decentralized, Congress intended that the disadvantaged clients of the existing programs continue to be served, and it also established a new objective, countercyclical job creation. The new administrative arrangement was only partly compatible with congressional objectives. Incentives at the local level primarily dictated using CETA to support existing levels of public services. Local governments wanted to fill positions with already skilled, experienced workers, not disadvantaged clients; and they often preferred to substitute federally subsidized positions for existing positions rather than create new ones.

Third, the organization of the legislative and executive branches of the federal government institutionalized the separation of employment programs from economic policy, reinforcing the subordination of selective (micro) instruments to macro tools for addressing unemployment. Employment programs are formulated within a subsystem of the policymaking process that tends to define issues in relatively narrow programmatic terms, hiving them off from debate about broad economic policy issues. They are the province of the Labor Department and the labor committees in Congress. Institutional incentives in Congress and the background of most lawmakers lead them to view labor market problems in terms of the needs of individual constituents rather than as more abstract dysfunctions in the structure of the economy and the workings of the market. Programs tend to be seen as responses to immediate, short-term crises and as tangible benefits to be distributed or redistributed, rather than as long-term investments in higher growth and productivity, whose benefits are less immediate and direct.

Neither the Labor Department nor congressional labor committees have gained much access to the highest levels of the executive branch, where economic policy is planned. Economists who occupy key posts in agencies like the Council of Economic Advisers and the Federal Reserve Board tend to conceive of economic intervention as almost exclusively a macromanagement task. Labor economists and manpower experts, who viewed unemployment as much as a structural problem as one of insufficient aggregate demand, have had access mainly through the Labor Department, whose status as a partisan constituency department places it at a disadvantage within the executive establishment. At the critical formative period of employment policy, economists in the Council of Economic Advisers rejected the structural explanation of unemployment (and with it the need for labor market planning and large spending on retraining). They also were instrumental in rejecting a massive job creation strategy as a way of combating poverty. Instead, tax cuts were championed as the preferred strategy for reducing the unemployment rate. Hence, it has been difficult to achieve integration between micro and macro measures, and this lack of integration contributed to the development of employment policy as a social policy and revenue-sharing measure.

Finally, where institutions have had their most visible and troublesome impact is on the performance of employment programs. The programs were lodged in the Labor Department, historically among the least developed agencies in administrative capacity. Its leadership spent several years centralizing authority over its own bureaus, especially the United States Employment Service, which was ill suited for carrying out the department's new tasks, and over employment programs under the control of other federal agencies. These efforts were only partially successful. In the unending quest for an effective federal-state-local partnership, the administrative structure has swung back and forth between centralization and decentralization. Without a mechanism at the local level both capable of managing the programs effectively and responsive to the objectives intended by Congress, the Labor Department had to either impose extensive controls from Washington or hope that local and state governments had objectives consistent with those of Congress. Neither solution has worked.

While out of necessity Congress has paid greater attention to administrative problems after the 1960s, it has not sought to build a federal administrative capacity either in Washington or in the field. The Labor Department has not been given the resources and independent authority to shield it from the conflicting political pressures emanating from Congress and local officials. It has not been permitted to develop the neutral competence of other federal agencies. This is in part out of a fear within Congress that it would lose control over the programs to the bureaucracy and in part because there are few political rewards for building such a capacity. For example, Congress has resisted even the most modest steps that would rationalize how the programs are implemented. Because it would lose discretion over spending, Congress has resisted the use of triggers, with which spending on programs would rise and fall according to the unemployment rate in each community and nationwide. Another example is the diffuse distribution of funding across virtually all legislative districts in order to build majorities to support the programs, rather than targeting the bulk of funding on those with the greatest employment problems. For the same reason, Congress has balkanized local labor market areas by permitting small jurisdictions of 150,000 to operate their own programs, even though the optimal size of local labor market areas for planning programs is least one million.

One can surmise what might have happened if the United States had institutions similar to those found in other Western nations. It is almost certain that the Full Employment Bill would have passed under a system of disciplined parties and parliamentary government. The stalemate between the legislative and executive branches over whether public service employment should be part of CETA would have surely been avoided. There might have been greater integration of employment measures with economic policy. And if nations like Sweden are any guide, the administrative difficulties that have had such an negative impact on the political reputation of these programs likely would have been mitigated.

IDEAS

Of the three factors (interests, institutions, and ideas), none had a more substantial and direct impact on charting the direction and framing the content of employment policy than ideas. Change and continuity in policy objectives and instruments were influenced by beliefs in the appropriate role of government in the economy, understandings of what causes unemployment and of how the labor market functions, and the alternatives considered by experts as feasible and effective means for reducing joblessness. Institutions may have blocked certain alternatives, shaped the packaging of programs, influenced the timing of changes, and led to implementation failures. The political activities of organized interests (or the lack of them) may have influenced the level and distribution of program benefits and circumscribed the role of employment programs in the economy. But it was the subjective predispositions that policy makers brought to their task and their receptivity to the ideas of experts and reformers that had the greatest influence on the substance of policy.

Employment policy developed largely within the limits established by the values and general beliefs widely accepted in American society. These are grounded in the history and culture of the nation and are transmitted through agents of socialization. Struggles over employment policy are fundamentally about where to draw the line demarcating the appropriate role of government in the economy and its obligations toward individual citizens. The American structure of values and beliefs reveals a tension between democracy and equality, on the one hand, and capitalism and individualism on the other.[1] This tension manifests itself clearly in economic issues. Decisions about what to do (or not to do) about unemployment tests the limits of compatibility between the two sets of values and beliefs, and must often be resolved in ways perceived to expand or maintain one set of values at the expense of the other.

Employment policy has been justified on the grounds of expanding equality of opportunity. The entire record of debate is replete with references to this principle. At least in theory, it accommodates equality with an economic order premised upon private enterprise and individual achievement. Policy prescriptions perceived as moving beyond equality of opportunity, and as coming in conflict with values like "free enterprise" and "limited government," either failed to gain adoption (e.g., full-employment legislation), or if adopted failed to be implemented (e.g., manpower planning), or did not survive over the long term (e.g., public service employment).

Training programs engender the least ideological conflict because they are unambiguously consistent with expanding equality of opportunity. Public job creation creates substantially more conflict and thus produces protracted political struggles to get them adopted. Once adopted, during the exigency of recession, their elimination is almost immediately the object of conservatives' efforts. Public provision of employment goes beyond merely providing greater opportunity; its aim is to provide a result. It also substitutes public employment creation for private employment creation, thus threatening to drain resources from the private labor market. Full-employment proposals are the most conflict-ridden of all because they are perceived as presenting fundamental challenges to the existing economic order. The role of the state in resource allocation and spending would have to expand significantly. Enhancing opportunities to compete in the market would be superseded by enlarging democratic rights to include guarantees of employment. The notion of a right to a job clashes directly with the belief that individuals, not society, have the primary responsibility for achieving economic success. Material rewards are supposed to be "earned" through ambition and risk taking in the market; they are not to be bestowed as an entitlement of citizenship. Full-employment legislation breaches the wall of separation in American thinking between the political-legal realm (in which equal citizenship rights are the axial principle) and the economic realm (in which unequal rewards are legitimated through market forces and differences in individual talent and ambition).

As powerful as ideas, institutions, and interests have been, it would be far too simplistic to understand the evolution of employment policy as strictly determined by them. First, at key historical junctures, there were opportunities to breach the constraints and change the course of policy in fundamental ways. Policy options that clashed with dominant cultural values, that were incongruent with institutional structure and incentives, and that met with opposition in the business community, nevertheless did reach the agenda. In 1945/46 and again in 1976/78, legislation guaranteeing a right to employment and proposing a significant enlargement in the scope of public management of the economy was seriously debated. In 1961 the Kennedy administration's proposal for the first manpower program would have provided universal eligibility for all workers and training allowances without a means test. In 1964 and 1968 proposals were advanced to redirect the War on Poverty away from simply training the severely disadvantaged toward a large-scale job creation program for the unemployed generally. In addition, some programs were adopted, despite what one might have expected, such as the Manpower Development and Training Act, with its potential for forecasting and planning the nation's labor market. And despite considerable resistance, public service jobs became the major component of employment policy for a decade.

Second, choices about the mission of employment policy, the design of specific programs, and their administration, shaped the constellation of interests, the institutional context, and political beliefs as much as they were shaped by them. The causal relationship worked in both directions. Because policy was oriented toward limited social policy and revenue sharing goals, and because programs were limited to serving discrete (usually disadvantaged) populations, key actors in the labor market such as trade unions and the business community treated employment policy as peripheral to their concerns. The choices of goals and program design virtually guaranteed that constituency support would come exclusively from advocacy groups for the disadvantaged or from local governments whose main interest was in utilizing the programs as a fiscal subsidy. Likewise, the absence of any notion that employment policy should be geared positively toward economic growth and stabilization strategies virtually insured that it would be relegated to an institutional subsystem in which participants defined issues as distributive conflicts over relative shares of program funds or redistributive debates about the obligation of society to the poor. The choice of administrative arrangements led to implementation failures, resulting in a series of readjustments that continually disrupted institutional development at the local level and made it impossible to sustain constituency support. Finally, widespread dissatisfaction with the performance of programs like CETA undermined support for positive government involvement in the labor market. Although at the start of the postwar period there was widespread elite and mass support for a policy of guaranteed full employment, by the late 1970s much of it had evaporated.

Third, while institutional structure, dominant beliefs, and the balance of power among interests may have set boundaries for what were and were not considered acceptable alternatives, they did not dictate the distinctive American response to postwar unemployment. The content, direction, and timing of policy innovation was in good measure the product of collective puzzlement, of learning about the nature of unemployment as a problem of industrial capitalism, and of devising feasible courses of action to address it. If policy reflects the influence of particular interests, the distribution of authority within institutions, or the pervasiveness of a belief system, it is not because these sources of power are automatically translated into policy. Policies are contingent outcomes because policy making is an intrinsically creative, intellectual enterprise in which policy makers attempt, successfully or not, to apply new ideas and learn from the past.

In the vanguard of this learning process were experts, especially professional economists. Policies contain theories—causal statements of how the world works. Conditions in society become public problems only with the development of knowledge that government can do something about them. Employment policy reflected the state of opinion among economists as to the causes of unemployment, the workings of the labor market, and the measures that could be applied. Had there been no Keynesian analysis and prescription, there would have been no policies to address unemployment, beyond humanitarian efforts to relieve distress. It was Keynes's explanation of unemployment, grounded in a bold critique of laissez-faire, and his prescription for economic recovery that intellectually legitimated using fiscal policy to prevent and eliminate unemployment. Keynes's ideas fired the imagination of a generation of American economists and bore the seeds of the Employment Act of 1946, the Tax Reduction Act of 1964, and the conduct of macroeconomic management generally.

In the aftermath of the defeat of the Full Employment Bill, economic policy could have developed in three directions. Liberals could have attempted to adopt it at a more propitious time, such as the 1960s; Keynesian economic management could have been rejected altogether;

or an alternative Keynesian policy could have been formulated and pursued. Policy evolved along the third path. Temporary fluctuations in demand (rather than permanent secular stagnation) came to be seen as the postwar economic problem, and tax cuts and automatic stabilizers (rather than large spending deficits and the planning of investment) developed as the solution. A Keynesian policy congruent with probusiness values was very much a preemptive response to any renewed attempt by liberals to resurrect a policy that would be more threatening to business prerogatives. It was born of a recognition that purposeful economic management had great growth-producing potential and would be needed to avoid periods of crisis, to which capitalism was prone. Even so, it required reeducating business and governmental elites, introducing innovations in the tax system, and abandoning the balanced budget principle. Tax cuts and automatic stabilizers were an ingenious formula that accommodated the growth-producing potential of Keynesian techniques with business's interests in maintaining private consumption and control over the bulk of economic resources and with conservative's fears of a larger government. It was the capacity of business elites to engage in political learning, and not simply their lobbying activities or their structural power in the economy, that changed policy at this key historical juncture.

As professional economists' access to policy makers increased over the postwar period, two changes were evident. First, the ideological tenor of debate declined. Arguments over the Full Employment Bill of 1945 were based upon simplistic, yet emotionally charged, shibboleths: that the legislation represented state socialism and an end to free enterprise. By 1978 overt appeals to traditional symbols were muted in favor of reasoned argument grounded in dispassionate economic analysis. It was not provincial conservatives in Congress who were chiefly responsible for the evisceration of the Humphrey-Hawkins legislation (as they had been with the 1945 Murray bill), but respected economists at the highest levels of the executive branch and in prestigious centers of learning.

Second, as economists' participation increased so too has their opposition to major pieces of legislation designed to increase the role of government in the economy. In 1945 the dominant voices in the profession adhered to a brand of Keynesian analysis (secular stagnation) that called for extensive public planning of investment and large spending deficits. Soon afterward, American Keynesianism was reformulated in a direction that precluded large spending increases on training and job creation. The neoclassical synthesis grafted that part of Keynes's analysis that related to the management of the macroeconomy onto neoclassical theory's microconception of a market governed by the price mechanism. In clinging to the essence of neoclassical theory, most economists denied the existence of structural unemployment well into the 1960s, which had been the basis for supporting training programs. And in the 1970s, this same theory of the labor market underpinned the hypothesized trade-off between unemployment and inflation. This, in turn, led mainstream economists to oppose unemployment rate targets in Humphrey-Hawkins because of their ostensible impact on inflation. In sum, professional knowledge began the postwar period as a radical challenge to the existing economic order, but as it gained a greater voice in the councils of government, it accommodated itself to the reality of an economic system in which private enterprise enjoys widespread legitimacy and structural power.

Economists and other experts were responsible for putting employment programs on the agenda and for defining their purpose. Structural unemployment and deficiencies in the nation's manpower preparedness turned Congress's attention to the need for a federal training program and underlay the Manpower Development and Training Act. Yet those who advocated the structural explanation were institutional labor economists, a small minority in their profession. Keynesians, who still clung to neoclassical conceptions of the labor market, advanced the rival thesis that joblessness was the result of a demand deficiency. The Keynesians' denial of the structural thesis did not block the enactment of training programs, but it did make it much more likely that such programs would develop in isolation from economic policies and would be far too small. Likewise, the failure to establish a Council of Manpower Advisers signaled an unwillingness to elevate employment policy to the highest levels of the executive branch and to give it the status of macroeconomic policies.

Meanwhile, the discovery of poverty by Robert Lampman and its publicizing by Michael Harrington brought the issue to the attention of the Kennedy administration. Structural unemployment came to be seen more as a problem of the disadvantaged rather than of experienced adult workers in the throes of technological displacement. MDTA was absorbed into the poverty program, and its broad charter to plan the labor market in anticipation of structural economic change was ignored. Buttressed by a series of estimates of the return on investment in education and training, the theory of human capital provided a powerful rationale for training and work experience programs in the War on Poverty. The notion of community action developed by New York–based reformers and social workers captured the imagination of policy intellectuals in government and became the heart of the poverty program. The alternative, a massive jobs program, was explicitly rejected in light of the administration's commitment to create a deficit through tax cutting rather than through spending increases. All of these intellectual currents served to push employment policy toward a limited, supply-side, social policy orientation during the critical formative years of its development.

Job creation programs were introduced after a disappointing experience with training and education as strategies for reducing poverty and during rising unemployment, when the economy contracted in 1970–1971. The idea incubated throughout the 1960s, kept alive by liberal members of Congress, and found its way into the recommendations of a variety of legislative committees, executive agencies, and task forces. Those who pushed the proposal were impressed by critiques of existing policies, primarily the exclusive emphasis on training as a way to lift people out of poverty, and also by the failure of fiscal and monetary policies to create sufficient job opportunities for all those seeking employment. Among advocates of the "new" public service employment, spending on jobs was also viewed as a means to provide needed urban services, which liberals had urged ever since Galbraith's disparagement of "public squalor amid private affluence."

Employment programs were permitted to play a role in the nation's economic policy only when influential macroeconomists deemed it desirable. Public service employment expanded after Arthur Burns championed a countercyclical component of CETA (Title VI) as an alternative to relying solely upon expanding aggregate demand during the stagflation of the 1970s. With the endorsement of President Carter's economic advisers, Title VI expanded further when it was used as part of the 1977 stimulus package. By the 1980s public job creation was no longer recognized as a necessary or desirable tool for addressing unemployment (even though the jobless rate was as high or higher in the early years of the decade than it had been in the 1970s), and efforts to launch public employment once again failed.

Experts were also at the center of efforts to reform administrative arrangements. Antedating the Nixon administration's involvement, a consensus emerged within the community of manpower experts and administrators in favor of reform embodying decategorization, consolidation, and local control. The Labor Department experimented with coordinating bodies whose experiences pointed in the general direction change should take. The crisis in employment programs was cast at the outset, not by conservative proponents of the New Federalism, but by experts in the field who were concerned with good administrative practice. The call for reform by many of those closest to the problems contributed to the pervasive perception in Congress that reform was a pressing need. This consensus was difficult to ignore, regardless of congressional suspicions about Nixon's agenda. Subsequent shifts back to centralization, and then to a new decentralized structure centered on state governments and local industry councils, also came about in the ongoing search for a workable administrative arrangement.

We have noted many examples of the constraints on learning posed by the structure of U.S. governing institutions, a belief system that presumes a limited role for the state, and the lack of interest group involvement in employment policy. On the other hand, public and private organizations often served as centers of learning and policy innovation, bringing together experts, reformers, and policy makers. Economists within the Committee for Economic Development made the chief intellectual contributions to the development of commercial Keynesianism. Congressional committees, executive agencies, and a variety of public and quasi-public task forces and planning bodies brought together experts and reformers inside and outside of government to gather information, analyze and discuss problems, and frame policy options. Institutions served as hosts for many of the intellectuals who put forward ideas that were translated into concrete initiatives.

As a focal point for Keynesian analysis during and just after World War II, the National Resource Planning Board formulated a "new bill of rights" that included a right to employment. Crucial provisions of the Full Employment Bill, such as the National Production and Employment Budget, were authored by Senator James Murray, the passionate liberal chairman of the War Contracts Subcommittee, his staff director Bertram Gross, and a collection of civil servants who shared an interest in postwar employment problems and in Keynes's compensatory fiscal ideas. Will Whittington and other conservatives on the House Expenditures Committee used their links to business economists opposed to the Murray bill to write a substitute bill, which became the Employment Act of 1946, and included provisions for the Council of Economic Advisers and the *Economic Report of the President.*

The Senate Special Committee on Unemployment Problems, set up to conduct field hearings around the country in the wake of the 1958 election, confirmed that there were structural imbalances in the labor market. It was the first public body to recommended a nationwide training program. Joseph Clark, Charles Killingsworth, and other labor economists first became sensitized to manpower deficiencies when they served on the War Labor Board and in the armed services. Much of the intellectual ferment that culminated in the enactment of manpower programs in the 1960s took place in the National Manpower Council and the Conservation of Human Resources Project at Columbia University.

The President's Commission on Juvenile Delinquency and the Shriver Task Force imported the idea of community action from the academic community and fashioned it into the centerpiece of the poverty program. A string of studies by legislative committees, task forces, and blue ribbon panels during the 1960s (e.g., the Commission on Automation and Technology, the Labor Department, and the Kerner Commission) concluded that there was a shortage of jobs in the economy, that the growth in demand for local public services had outstripped local governments' fiscal capacity to provide them, and that existing training and macroeconomic policies had failed to put all Americans back to work. These opinions provided rationales for the first federal jobs program since the 1930s.

Under the auspices of the National Manpower Advisory Committee and the National Manpower Policy Task Force, Sar Levitan and Garth Mangum put forward decentralization, decategorization, and consolidation as concepts guiding the overhaul of categorical employment programs. The Labor Department applied these concepts in its CEP and CAMPS experiments, and they were eventually embodied in CETA. Studies and experiments conducted by the Committee for Economic Development and the National Alliance of Business contributed to the growing consensus by the late 1970s that a successful transition from training to a job required direct participation by local businesses in program planning. Other examples could be cited.

A FUTURE FOR EMPLOYMENT POLICY?

Several developments have combined to keep employment policy off the political agenda since the early 1980s. After the resumption of economic growth in 1983, the unemployment rate steadily declined. An explosion in job growth for over a decade absorbed the large influx of new entrants into the labor force, mainly women and young people. The Reagan and Bush administrations, and the huge budget deficits created during these years, forestalled launching new domestic programs and the expansion of existing ones.

In addition, some economists have argued that unemployment is no longer the problem it once was. This view minimizes the level, duration, and consequences of joblessness. Most unemployment lasts for short spells and is attributed to the "voluntary" behavior of those who quit their jobs, to workers waiting to be called back to work, or to government programs that provide incentives to delay or extend job search activity.[2] But more recent research has cast doubt on this view.[3] Furthermore, most unemployment is prolonged.[4] Paul Osterman argues that there are three major problems with the performance of the contemporary U.S. labor market. First, unemployment rates have remained high. Throughout the postwar period the rate has risen steadily, ending each business cycle at a higher level than before. Even after controlling for the changing composition of the labor force and the reduced stimulus from fears of inflation, there is a long-term trend of worsening unemployment. Much unemployment is a problem of labor market adjustment rather than demand deficiency. Second, for many workers the loss of jobs has had long-term, adverse consequences. While the growth of employment has absorbed most new entrants, the labor market has not effectively reabsorbed experienced, dislocated workers. Third, many of the employed have persistently low earnings, inadequate to support them and their families.[5]

If these analyses are correct, that there still exist problems that require public intervention, then the time for reconstituting employment policy may already be upon us. The political success of such efforts will demand that a new generation of liberal activists and reformers learn from the past and that they confront the myriad challenges to positive government intervention explored in the preceding chapters. The policy record of the 1960s and 1970s exacted tremendous costs in public and official confidence in government's ability to deal effectively with problems of economic dislocation and decay. The future of employment policy—whether there is to be one, what it will look like, and whether it will succeed—rests upon more than identifying needs and devising specific programs. It depends upon our ability to learn how to address the political, institutional, and ideological constraints that in the past have led to failure.

Notes

Index

Notes

CHAPTER 1. *Employment Policy and Liberal Failure*

1. From 1963 to 1982, the federal government spent almost $77 billion providing jobs, training, and related employment measures, excluding the costs of unemployment insurance and the employment service. Of this, about $47 billion, or 61 percent, was spent on CETA. The budget in 1978 was about four times that of a decade earlier in constant dollars. Janet Wegner Johnston, "An Overview of U.S. Federal Employment and Training Programmes," in *Unemployment: Policy Responses of Western Democracies*, ed. Jeremy Richardson and Roger Henning (Beverly Hills: Sage, 1985), 58.

2. Unemployment insurance is another policy tool designed to ameliorate unemployment, by replacing some proportion of the lost income of those who lose their jobs. We shall not be concerned with unemployment insurance, because it is largely unrelated to employment and training programs, our central concern.

3. On the scope, visibility, and intensity of conflict, see E. E. Schattschneider, *The Semi-Sovereign People* (New York: Holt, Rinehart, and Winston, 1960).

4. Hugh Heclo, *Modern Social Politics in Britain and Sweden* (New Haven: Yale University Press, 1975), 305–06.

5. See James Q. Wilson, *American Government: Institutions and Policies*, 3d ed. (Lexington: Health, 1986), 128–29.

6. Kay Lehman Schlozman and Sidney Verba, *Injury to Insult: Unemployment, Class, and Political Response* (Cambridge: Harvard University Press, 1979), 202, 375.

7. Gallup Organization, cited in Hazel Erskine, "The Polls: Government Role in Welfare," *Public Opinion Quarterly* 39 (Summer 1975): 266; see also Albert H. Cantril and Susan Davis Cantril, *Unemployment, Government and the American People: A National Opinion Survey* (Washington, D.C.: Public Research, 1978), 79–98.

8. CBS News/*New York Times* survey, cited in Seymour Martin Lipset, "The Economy, Elections, and Public Opinion," *Tocqueville Review* 5 (Fall/Winter 1983): 444–49.

9. *Time*/Yankelovich, Clancey, Shulman poll, 17–18 Feb., 1987, cited in Everett Carll Ladd, *The American Policy*, 3d ed. (New York: Norton, 1989), 334; and Roper Organization Surveys, cited in Susan Welch et al., *American Government* (St. Paul: West, 1986), 219.

10. See Lloyd A. Free and Hadley Cantril, *The Political Beliefs of Americans* (New Brunswick: Rutgers University Press, 1967); Walter Dean Burnham, "American Politics in the 1980s," *Dissent* 27 (Spring 1980): 151; a survey that notes that increasing liberalism during the postwar period leveled off after 1973 is contained in Tom W. Smith, "Atop a Liberal Plateau? A Summary of Trends Since World War II," *Research in Urban Policy* 1 (1985): 245–57.

11. See Free and Cantril, *Political Beliefs of Americans*; Herbert McClosky and John Zaller, *The American Ethos: Public Attitudes toward Capitalism and Democracy* (Cambridge: Harvard University Press, 1984).

12. Michael E. Borus, "Assessing the Impact of Training Programs," in *Employing the Unemployed*, ed. Eli Ginzberg (New York: Basic Books, 1980), 25–40.

13. James L. Sundquist, *Politics and Policy: The Eisenhower, Kennedy, and Johnson Years* (Washington, D.C.: Brookings, 1968), 91; Jon H. Goldstein, *The Effectiveness of Manpower Training Programs: A Review of Research on the Impact on the Poor*, prepared for the Joint Economic Committee (Washington, D.C.: Government Printing Office, 1972), 2–3, 29–41; Charles R. Perry et al., *The Impact of Government Manpower Programs* (Philadelphia: Wharton School, 1975), 157–80; Steve L. Barsby, *Cost-Benefit Analysis and Manpower Programs* (Lexington: Heath, 1972); Garth L. Mangum and R. Thayne Robson, *Metropolitan Impact of Manpower Programs: A Four-City Comparison* (Salt Lake City: Olympus, 1973).

14. William Mirengoff and Lester Rindler, *CETA: Manpower Programs Under Local Control* (Washington, D.C.: National Academy of Sciences, 1978); see also testimony of Garth L. Mangum in *Employment and Training Policy*, hearings before the Senate Subcommittee on Employment and Productivity and the House Subcommittee on Employment Opportunities, 97 Cong. 2 sess. (Washington, D.C.: GPO, 1982), pt. 1, 346–69; excellent reviews of the evaluation literature are contained in R. Taggart, *A Fisherman's Guide: An Assessment of Training and Remediation Strategies* (Kalamazoo: Upjohn Institute for Employment Policy Research, 1981), 283; Grace A. Franklin and Randall B. Ripley, *CETA: Politics and Policy, 1973–1982* (Knoxville: University of Tennessee Press, 1984), chap. 7; Congressional Budget Office, *CETA Training Programs; Do They Work for Adults?* (Washington, D.C.; CBO, 1982); Ilona Rashkow, *Comprehensive Employment and Training Act*, Congressional Research Service Report 81–56 (Washington, D.C.: CRS, 1981); Johnston, "Overview"; Eli Ginzberg, "Overview: The $64 Billion Experiment," in *Employing the Unemployed*, ed. Eli Ginzberg (New York: Basic Books, 1980), 3–24; Borus, "Assessing the Impact."

15. *Employment and Training Reporter*, 16 May 1979, 621.

16. Laura L. Morlock et al., *Long-term Follow-Up of Public Service Employment Participants: The Baltimore SMSA Experience During the 1970s* (Baltimore: Johns Hopkins Health Services Research and Development Center, 1981).

17. It is plausible that the programs would have had greater results in

promoting employability if not for the deficiencies in policy formulation and implementation. This is not the concern of this study, however.

18. For an exploration of these topics, see Thomas Ferguson and Joel Rogers, *Right Turn: The Decline of the Democrats and the Future of American Politics* (New York: Hill and Wang, 1986); and Kenneth M. Dolbeare and Linda J. Medcalf, *American Ideologies Today: From Neopolitics to New Ideas* (New York: Random House, 1988), 49–66.

19. See, for example, Samuel P. Huntington, "The Visions of the Democratic Party," *Public Interest* 79 (Spring 1985): 63–78. For an examination and critique of this position, see Ferguson and Rogers, *Right Turn.*

20. John E. Schwarz, *America's Hidden Success: A Reassessment of Twenty Years of Public Policy* (New York: Norton, 1983).

CHAPTER 2. *Constrained Origins: Ideology, Economic Doctrine, and the Debate over Postwar Unemployment*

1. On the notion of economic intervention used as an offset, see Robert Solo, "The Economist and the Economic Roles," in *Stress and Contradiction in Modern Capitalism,* ed. Leon N. Lindberg et al. (Lexington: Health, 1975), 101–05.

2. As we shall see in our discussion of Sweden in chapter 9, certain other features of positive intervention follow from the ones just discussed. Employment and training measures (microintervention) must be integrated with macroeconomic measures. Employment and training programs must be made available to all and not limited in eligibility solely to the disadvantaged or those who are already in trouble. There must also be a significant commitment of resources to such measures if they are to play an appreciable role in contributing to the kind of economic growth and stability that is a prerequisite for full employment.

3. E. Wight Bakke, *The Mission of Manpower Policy* (Kalamazoo: Upjohn Institute for Employment Policy Research, 1969), v.

4. Ibid., 4.

5. Testimony of Peter B. Doeringer in *The Effects of Structural Employment and Training Programs on Inflation and Unemployment.* Hearings before the Joint Economic Committee, 96 Cong. 1 sess. (Washington, D.C.: GPO, 1979), 98.

6. Roosevelt's New Deal—however traditional it may have been in extending nonmarket controls already in existence or however conservative in terms of its attempts to salvage rather than replace capitalism—marked a watershed if only because of the sheer scale of reform it achieved. See Jonathan R. T. Hughes, *The Governmental Habit* (New York: Basic Books, 1977), 146–98; William E. Leuchtenburg, *Franklin D. Roosevelt and the New Deal, 1932–1940* (New York: Harper/Torch, 1963); R. G. Tugwell, *The Brains Trust* (New York: Viking, 1968).

7. William Haber and Daniel H. Kruger, *The Role of the United States Employment Service in a Changing Economy* (Kalamazoo: Upjohn Institute for Employment Policy Research, 1964), 25–29; Ewan Clague, *Manpower Policies and Programs: A Review, 1935–75* (Kalamazoo: Upjohn Institute for Employment Policy Research, 1976), 1–5.

8. Robert M. Collins, *The Business Response to Keynes, 1929–1964* (New York: Columbia University Press, 1981), 4.

9. Ibid., 2.

10. William H. Beveridge, *The Pillars of Security* (London: Allen and Unwin, 1943), 51.

11. Collins, *Business Response to Keynes*, 10.

12. Alan Sweezy, "The Keynesians and Government Policy: 1933–39," *American Economic Review* 62 (1972): 116–24.

13. Stephen K. Bailey, *Congress Makes a Law: The Story Behind the Employment Act of 1946* (New York: Columbia University Press, 1951), 43.

14. Reported in Herbert Stein, *The Fiscal Revolution in America* (Chicago: University of Chicago Press, 1968), 174.

15. Bailey, *Congress Makes a Law*, 178.

16. Ibid., 132, 148.

17. Stein, *Fiscal Revolution*, 177.

18. Sweezy, "Keynesians and Government Policy," 121.

19. Quoted in Collins, *Business Response to Keynes*, 183.

20. Stein, *Fiscal Revolution*, 178–79.

21. Collins, *Business Response to Keynes*, 151.

22. Stein, *Fiscal Revolution*, 186.

23. Collins, *Business Response to Keynes*, 189.

24. Ibid., 135.

25. James Sundquist, *Politics and Policy: The Eisenhower, Kennedy, and Johnson Years* (Washington, D.C.: Brookings, 1968), 36.

26. Collins, *Business Response to Keynes*, chap. 7.

27. Sundquist, *Politics and Policy*, 47–48.

28. John Kenneth Galbraith, *Economics and the Art of Controversy* (New York: Vintage, 1959), 55–56.

29. Sundquist, *Politics and Policy*, 443–44.

30. Stein, *Fiscal Revolution*, 449–50.

31. See chap. 5 for a discussion of Congress and economic policy.

32. This is a summary of the thesis of the most prominent structuralist, Charles Killingsworth, from Richard G. Lipsey, "Structural and Deficient-Demand Unemployment Reconsidered," in *Employment Policy and the Labor Market*, ed. Arthur M. Ross (Berkeley and Los Angeles: University of California Press, 1965), 242.

33. See Charles K. Wilber and Kenneth P. Jameson, *An Inquiry into the Poverty of Economics* (Notre Dame: University of Notre Dame Press, 1983); Richard Seckler, *Thorstein Veblen and the Institutionalists* (Boulder: Associated Press, 1975); Charles K. Wilber and Robert S. Harrison, "The Methodological Basis of Institutional Economics: Pattern Model, Storytelling, and Holism," *Journal of Economic Issues* 12 (Mar. 1978): 61–89; K. William Knapp, "The Nature and Significance of Institutional Economics," *Kyklos* 29 (1976): 209–30.

34. See Michael J. Piore's introduction and Eileen Appelbaum, "Labor Market in Post-Keynesian Theory," in *Unemployment and Inflation: Institutionalist and Structuralist Views*, ed. Michael J. Piore (White Plains: Sharpe, 1979), xi–xxx, 33–45.

35. Paul A. Samuelson, *The Foundations of Economic Analysis* (Cambridge: Harvard University Press, 1947).

36. Paul A. Samuelson, *Economics* (New York: McGraw-Hill, 1948).

37. See Alan Coddington, *Keynesian Economics: The Search for First Principles* (London: Allen and Unwin, 1983), chap. 6.

38. Michael J. Piore, ed., *Unemployment and Inflation: Institutionalist and Structuralist Views* (White Plains: Sharpe, 1979), xvi.

39. Charles C. Killingsworth, "The Fall and Rise of the Idea of Structural Unemployment," *Proceedings of the Thirty-first Annual Meeting of the Industrial Relations Research Association Series 1978,* 4.

40. *Economic Report of the President, 1963,* app. A, 181; emphasis added.

41. Quoted in the National Commission on Technology, Automation and Economic Progress, *Technology and the American Economy* (Washington, D.C., GPO, 1966), 23; emphasis added.

42. James Tobin, *The New Economics One Decade Older* (Princeton: Princeton University Press, 1972), 167.

43. Lloyd Ulman, "The Uses and Abuses of Manpower Policy," *Public Interest* 34 (1973): 83.

44. Eleanor G. Gilpatrick, *Structural Unemployment and Aggregate Demand: A Study of Employment and Unemployment in the United States, 1948–1964* (Baltimore: Johns Hopkins Press, 1966), 11.

45. See R. A. Gordon, "Has Structural Unemployment Worsened?" *Industrial Relations* 3 (May 1964): 53–57. Gordon cites the following: Edward Kalachek and James Knowles, ed., *Higher Unemployment Rates 1957–60: Structural Transformation or Inadequate Demand,* (Washington, D.C.: GPO, 87 Cong., 1961); Walter Heller, "The Administration's Fiscal Policy," and Otto Eckstein, "Aggregate Demand and the Current Unemployment Problem," in *Unemployment and the American Economy,* ed. A. M. Ross (New York: Wiley, 1964); 93–115, 116–34; L. E. Galloway, "Labor Mobility, Resource Allocation and Structural Unemployment," *American Economic Review* (1963): 694–716; and *Economic Report of the President, 1963,* app. A.

46. See Lipsey, "Structural and Deficient-Demand Unemployment," 252.

47. Testimony of Charles Killingsworth in *The Nation's Manpower Revolution,* Hearings before the Senate Committee on Labor and Public Welfare (Washington, D.C.: GPO, 1963), pt. 5, 1475, 1479.

48. Sundquist, *Politics and Policy,* 59.

49. Gilpatrick, *Structural Unemployment and Aggregate Demand,* 204.

50. Ibid., 13.

51. Sundquist, *Politics and Policy,* 86.

52. Quoted in ibid., 86.

53. Julius Duscha, "Retraining the Unemployed: Little, Late, and Limping," *Reporter,* 27 Sept. 1962, 35.

54. Henry J. Aaron, *Politics and the Professors: The Great Society in Perspective* (Washington, D.C.: Brookings, 1978), 117.

55. Gilpatrick, *Structural Unemployment and Aggregate Demand,* 216, 218; emphasis added.

56. Ibid., 218.

57. "Oral history interview with Stanley Ruttenberg, 19 July 1974," 22–23, Historian's Office, Department of Labor.

58. Richard A. Lester, *Manpower Planning in a Free Society* (Princeton: Princeton University Press, 1966), 131–32.

59. Anthony King, "Ideas, Institutions and the Policies of Governments: A Comparative Analysis, Part III," *British Journal of Political Science* 3 (1973): 418; see also Andrew Shonfield, *Modern Capitalism* (Oxford: Oxford University Press, 1965), 298–312.

CHAPTER 3. *Manpower Training, the War on Poverty, and Administrative Reform*

1. Joseph H. Ball, "The Implementation of Federal Manpower Policy, 1961–1971: A Study in Bureaucratic Competition and Intergovernmental Relations," Ph.D. diss., Columbia University, 1972, 90.

2. Eli Ginzberg, *Human Resources: The Wealth of a Nation* (New York: Simon and Schuster, 1958), 15.

3. Ibid., 23.

4. Richard A. Lester, *Manpower Planning in a Free Society* (Princeton: Princeton University Press, 1966); Henry David, *Manpower Policies for a Democratic Society: The Final Statement of the National Manpower Council* (New York: Columbia University Press, 1965).

5. David, *Manpower Policies*, 10.

6. Quoted in Gladys Kremen, "The Origins of the Manpower Development and Training Act of 1962," 13, Historian's Office, Department of Labor.

7. Joseph P. Clark, introduction, in "American Civilization and Its Leadership Needs, 1960–1990," *Annals of the American Academy of Political and Social Science* 325 (Sept. 1959): x.

8. Michel Crozier, *The Trouble with America* (Berkeley and Los Angeles: University of California Press, 1984), 38–39.

9. Daniel P. Moynihan, *Maximum Feasible Misunderstanding: Community Action in the War on Poverty* (New York: Free Press, 1969), 23.

10. Ibid., 31.

11. Ginzberg, *Human Resources*, 11.

12. Ibid., 12.

13. National Manpower Council, *Improving the Work Skills of the Nation: Proceedings of a Conference on Skilled Manpower* (New York: Columbia University Press, 1955); the council's other reports include *Student Deferment and National Manpower Policy* (1952), *A Policy for Scientific and Professional Manpower* (1953), *Proceedings of a Conference on the Utilization of Scientific and Professional Manpower* (1954), and David, *Manpower Policies*.

14. Kremen, "Origins of the Manpower Development and Training Act," 30.

15. Garth L. Mangum, *MDTA: Foundation of Federal Manpower Policy* (Baltimore: Johns Hopkins University Press, 1968), 12.

16. The recommendations are summarized in *Report of the Special Committee on Unemployment Problems*, S. Rept. 1206, 1960.

17. James L. Sundquist, *Politics and Policy: The Eisenhower, Kennedy, and Johnson Years* (Washington, D.C.: Brookings, 1968), 85.

18. Part of the text follows:

The Congress finds that there is a critical need for more and better trained personnel in many vital occupational categories . . . that even in periods of high unemployment, many employment opportunities remain unfilled because of the shortages of qualified personnel. . . . That it is in the national interest that current and prospective manpower shortages be identified and that persons who can be qualified for these positions through education and training be sought out and trained as quickly and reasonably as possible, in order that the Nation may meet the staffing requirements of the struggle for freedom. . . . The Congress further finds the skills of many persons have been rendered obsolete by dislocations in the economy arising from automation or technological developments, foreign competition, relocation of industry, shifts in market demands, and other changes in the structure of the economy. . . . That Government leadership is necessary to insure that the benefits of automation do not become burdens of widespread unemployment. . . . That the problem of assuring sufficient employment opportunities will be compounded by the extraordinary rapid growth of the labor force in the next decade, particularly by the entrance of young people into the labor force, that improved planning and expanded efforts . . . to meet shifting employment needs. . . . That many persons now unemployed and underemployed . . . must be assisted in providing themselves with skills which are or will be in demand. . . . That it is in the national interest that the opportunity to acquire new skills be afforded to these people with the least delay in order to alleviate the hardships of unemployment, reduce the costs of unemployment compensation and public assistance, and to increase the Nation's productivity and its capacity to meet the requirements of the space age. (*Manpower Development and Training Act of 1962*, as amended, 42 U.S.C. 2571–620.

19. Sundquist, *Politics and Policy*, 112.

20. Michael Harrington, *The Other America* (New York: Macmillan, 1962); Leon H. Keyserling, *Poverty and Deprivation in the United States* (Washington, D.C.: Conference on Economic Progress, 1962); John Kenneth Galbraith, *The Affluent Society* (New York: Houghton Mifflin, 1958).

21. Arthur Schlesinger, Jr., *A Thousand Days* (New York: Houghton Mifflin, 1965), 1009.

22. Sundquist, *Politics and Policy*, 141.

23. Quoted in Moynihan, *Maximum Feasible Misunderstanding*, 84.

24. Ibid., 99.

25. Sundquist, *Politics and Policy*, 154.

26. Michael Harrington, *The New American Poverty* (New York: Holt, Rinehart, and Winston, 1984), 21–22.

27. Lester Thurow, "Raising Incomes Through Manpower Training Programs," in *Contributions to the Analysis of Urban Problems*, ed. Anthony H. Pascal (Santa Monica: Rand, 1968), 91–92.

28. Thomas I. Ribich, *Education and Poverty* (Washington, D.C.: Brookings, 1968), 1.

29. See Jacob Mincer, "Investment in Human Capital and Personal Income Distribution," *Journal of Political Economy* 66 (Aug. 1958): 281–302; Gary S. Becker, *Human Capital: A Theoretical and Empirical Analysis, with Special Reference to Education* (New York: Columbia University Press for the National Bureau of Economic Research, 1964). For a general review of economic literature on human capital, see Jacob Mincer, "The Distribution of Labor Incomes: A Survey with Special Reference to the Human Capital Approach," *Journal of Economic Literature* 8 (Mar. 1970): 1–26; Theodore Schultz, "Reflections on Investment in Man," *Journal of Political Economy* 70 (Oct. 1962 supplement): 1–8.

30. Henry J. Aaron, *Politics and the Professors: The Great Society in Perspective* (Washington, D.C.: Brookings, 1978), 67; see also Gary S. Becker and Barry R. Cheswick, "Education and the Distribution of Earnings," *American Economic Review* 56 (May 1966, *Papers and Proceedings, 1965*): 358–69; and Barry Cheswick, *Income Inequality: Regional Analyses within a Human Capital Framework* (New York: Columbia University Press for the National Bureau of Economic Research, 1974).

31. Aaron, *Politics and the Professors*, 67.

32. Kremen, "Origins of Manpower Development," 45.

33. Mangum, *MDTA: Foundation*, 20.

34. Stanley H. Ruttenberg, *Manpower Challenge of the 1970s: Institutions and Social Change* (Baltimore: Johns Hopkins University Press, 1970), 12–13.

35. Mangum, *MDTA: Foundation*, 6.

36. Ruttenberg, *Manpower Challenge*, 12.

37. Sar A. Levitan, "Development of a National Manpower Policy," in *Manpower Policy: Perspectives and Prospects*, ed. Seymour Wolfbein (Philadelphia: Temple University Press, 1973), 33–34.

38. Gosta Rehn, "Manpower Policy as an Instrument of National Economic Policy," in *Manpower Policy: Perspectives and Prospects*, ed. Seymour Wolfbein (Philadelphia: Temple University Press), 175.

39. We shall see in chapter 9 that the Swedish approach has been to use training programs in conjunction with other policies to restructure the labor market, by shifting employment out of secondary employment and into more stable employment in the primary sectors of the economy, and to relieve inflation-inducing skill shortages.

40. Harold Wilensky, *The Welfare State and Equality* (Berkeley and Los Angeles: University of California Press, 1975), 6.

41. Paul E. Peterson and Barry G. Rabe, "Urban Vocational Education and Managing the Transition from School to Work: A Review of a Series of Case Studies of Vocational Education Programs in Four Cities," paper commissioned by the National Institute of Education, 1984; photocopy.

42. The center's studies are quoted extensively in *Congressional Record*, 1970, S37669.

43. Martha Derthick, *Uncontrollable Spending for Social Service Grants* (Washington, D.C.: Brookings, 1975), 27.

44. See Lawrence D. Brown, *New Policies, New Politics: Government's Response to Government's Growth* (Washington, D.C.: Brookings, 1983).

45. James L. Sundquist, *Making Federalism Work* (Washington, D.C.: Brookings, 1969), 249–50.

46. *Manpower Act of 1969*, Hearings before the House Committee on Education and Labor, 91 Cong. 2 sess. (Washington, D.C.: GPO, 1970), 439–54; see also National Manpower Policy Task Force, *Improving the Nation's Manpower Effort* (Washington, D.C.: Department of Labor, 1970), 13.

47. Sar A. Levitan and Garth L. Mangum, *Making Sense of Federal Manpower Policy* (Ann Arbor: Institute of Labor and Industrial Relations, University of Michigan and Wayne State University, and National Manpower Policy Task Force, 1967); National Manpower Policy Task Force, *The Nation's Manpower Programs*, Position Paper (Washington, D.C.: Department of Labor, 1969); National Manpower Policy Task Force, *Improving the Nation's Manpower Efforts*, Position Paper (Washington, D.C.: Department of Labor, 1970); Center for Manpower Policy Studies, "State Manpower Organization," Research Report, George Washington University, Washington, D.C., 1970.

48. Garth L. Mangum, "The Governor's Role in Federal Manpower Programs for the Disadvantaged," report prepared for the Executive Committee and Manpower and Labor Relations Committee of the National Governors' Conference, 1968; photocopy.

49. National Manpower Policy Task Force, *Nation's Manpower Programs*, 12–13, 28.

50. National Manpower Policy Task Force, *Improving Manpower Efforts*, 13.

51. Levitan and Mangum, *Making Sense*, 30.

52. Ibid., 31.

53. National Manpower Policy Task Force, *Improving Manpower Efforts*, 13; see also *Manpower Act of 1969*, 439–54.

54. Levitan and Mangum, *Making Sense*, 30–31.

55. *National Journal Reports*, 16 Dec. 1972, 1916.

56. "Special Message to the Congress on Special Revenue Sharing for Manpower," *Public Papers of the Presidents of the United States: Richard M. Nixon, 1971* (Washington, D.C.: GPO, 1972), 379–85.

57. David B. Walker, *Toward a Functioning Federalism* (Cambridge: Winthrop, 1981), 102–07.

58. "Special Message to the Congress," 381.

59. Richard M. Nixon, *RN: Memoirs of Richard Nixon* (New York: Grosset and Dunlap, 1978), 352.

60. Roger H. Davidson, *The Politics of Comprehensive Manpower Legislation* (Baltimore: Johns Hopkins University Press, 1972), 13–14.

61. Grant McConnell, *Private Power and American Democracy* (New York: Knopf, 1966), 32.

62. Lawrence D. Brown, "The Politics of Devolution in Nixon's 'New Federalism,' " in *The Changing Politics of Federal Grants*, ed. Lawrence D. Brown, James W. Fossett, and Kenneth Palmer (Washington, D.C.: Brookings, 1984),

54–107; see also Timothy J. Conlan, "The Politics of Federal Block Grants: From Nixon to Reagan," *Political Science Quarterly* 99 (Summer 1984): 247–70.

CHAPTER 4. *Public Job Creation and Full Employment Revisited*

1. Work experience programs provided short-term or part-time employment with a public employer or private nonprofit organization, employment that was intended to enhance the employability of individuals through the development of good work habits and basic work skills.

2. William J. Spring, "Congress and Public Service Employment," in *The Political Economy of Public Service Employment,* ed. Harold Sheppard et al. (Lexington: Lexington Books, 1972), 135.

3. *Manpower Act of 1969,* Hearings before the House Committee on Education and Labor, 91 Cong., 2 sess. (Washington, D.C.: GPO, 1970), 126.

4. See Senator Gaylord Nelson's extensive citation of this literature upon introducing S. 3867, *Congressional Record,* 1970, 32157–162.

5. *Toward Full Employment,* Committee Print, Senate Committee on Labor and Public Welfare, 88 Cong., 2 sess. (Washington, D.C.: GPO, 1964), 35.

6. National Commission on Technology, Automation, and Economic Progress, "Creating an Environment for Adjustment to Change: Employment and Income," in *Technology and the American Economy,* pt. 2 (Washington, D.C.: GPO, 1966), chap. 3.

7. Ibid., 101–02.

8. Labor Secretary Willard Wirtz to President Lyndon Johnson, "A Sharper Look at Unemployment," 8 Nov. 1966; and "A Report on Employment and Unemployment in Urban Slums and Ghettoes," 23 Dec. 1966. Papers of Secretary Wirtz, National Archives, Washington, D.C.

9. National Advisory Commission on Civil Disorders (Kerner Commission), *Report* (Washington, D.C.: GPO, 1968).

10. National Commission on Employment of Youth, "Summer Jobs for Youth," 29 July 1968, 8; photocopy.

11. Harold L. Sheppard, "The Nature of the Job Problem and the Role of a New Public Service Employment," in *The Political Economy of Public Sector Employment,* ed. Harold L. Sheppard et al. (Kalamazoo: Upjohn Institute for Employment Policy Research, 1969), 13–39.

12. See statement of Professor Robert A. Gordon in *Comprehensive Manpower Reform,* Hearings before the Senate Committee on Labor and Public Welfare, 92 Cong. 2 sess. (Washington, D.C.: GPO, 1972), pt. 5, 1536–47.

13. Gaylord Nelson, preface, in *The Political Economy of Public Service Employment,* ed. Harold L. Sheppard et al. (Kalamazoo: Upjohn Institute for Employment Policy Research, 1969), xviii.

14. Bennett Harrison, Harold L. Sheppard, and William J. Spring, "Government as the Employer of First Resort—Public Jobs, Public Needs," *New Republic,* 4 Nov. 1972, 18, 21.

15. John Kenneth Galbraith, *The Affluent Society* (New York: Houghton Mifflin, 1958).

16. *Employment and Training Legislation*, Hearings before the Senate Committee on Labor and Public Welfare, 90 Cong. 2 sess. (Washington, D.C.: GPO, 1968), 2. See also Alan Gartner, Russell A. Nixon, and Frank Reissman, *PSE: An Analysis of Its History, Problems, and Prospects* (New York: Praeger, 1973).

17. Gartner, Nixon, and Reissman, *PSE: An Analysis*.

18. Ibid., p. 160.

19. National Manpower Advisory Committee to President Elect Richard M. Nixon, "Manpower Advice for Government, Letters to the Secretaries of Labor and of Health, Education, and Welfare, 1962–1971," 25 Nov. 1968, 169–70 (Washington, D.C.: Historian's Office, Department of Labor).

20. National Manpower Policy Task Force, *Improving the Nation's Manpower Efforts*, Position Paper (Washington, D.C.: Department of Labor, 1970), 14.

21. National Manpower Policy Task Force, *The Nation's Manpower Programs*, Position Paper (Washington, D.C.: Department of Labor, 1969), 19.

22. Ibid., 18.

23. *Manpower Act of 1969*, 455.

24. *The 1971 Economic Report of the President*, Hearings before the 92 Cong., 1 sess. (Washington, D.C.: GPO, 1971), pt. 2, 425.

25. Ibid.

26. "Department of Labor Position on Public Service Employment, 1971," Papers of Assistant Secretary of Labor Malcolm Lovell, Historian's Office, Department of Labor.

27. The story of administrative reform is covered in chapters 3 and 6.

28. *Congressional Record*, 1969, H11230.

29. *Manpower Act of 1969*, 120.

30. Ibid., 126.

31. *Congressional Record*, 1970, S32160.

32. Ibid., 32431–433.

33. Ibid., 37694.

34. "Secretary of Labor to the President, 12 Dec. 1970," Papers of Assistant Secretary of Labor Malcolm Lovell, Historian's Office, Department of Labor.

35. "Veto of the Employment and Manpower Bill, 16 Dec. 1970," *Public Papers of the Presidents of the United States: Richard M. Nixon* (Washington, D.C.: GPO, 1971), 1141–42.

36. Ibid., 1140–42.

37. "Report on the *Emergency Employment Act of 1971*," *Congressional Record*, 1971, 9319.

38. Roger H. Davidson, *The Politics of Comprehensive Manpower Legislation* (Baltimore: Johns Hopkins University Press, 1972), 95.

39. Sar A. Levitan and Robert Taggart, eds., *Emergency Employment Act* (Salt Lake City: Olympus, 1974), 14.

40. *National Journal Reports*, 7 Apr. 1973, 491–92.

41. For the recorded votes, see *Congressional Record*, 1973, S26848–849, 26862.

42. "Office of Management and Budget, Director of the Office of Management and Budget, and the Secretary of Labor to the President, 12 Sept. 1973," Papers of Peter Brennan National Archives, Washington, D.C.

43. *New York Times*, 12 Dec. 1973.

44. *Special Employment Assistance Act of 1974*, S. Rept. 93–1327 (Washington, D.C.: GPO, 1974), 3.

45. William Mirengoff et al., *CETA: Accomplishments, Problems, Solutions* (Kalamazoo: Upjohn Institute for Employment Policy Research, 1982), 81.

46. *The Emergency Jobs Act of 1974*, Hearings before the House Committee on Education and Labor, 93 Cong., 2 sess. (Washington, D.C.: GPO, 1974), 31.

47. Ibid., 103–04.

48. *Comprehensive Manpower Reform*, Hearings before the Senate Committee on Labor and Public Welfare, 92 Cong., 2 sess., pt. 5, 1548–62 (Washington, D.C.: GPO, 1972).

49. *New York Times*, 25 Mar. 1974.

50. *New York Times*, 22 Feb. 1974.

51. Ibid.

52. *New York Times*, 27 May 1974.

53. Ibid.

54. William H. Kolberg, *Developing Manpower Legislation: A Personal Chronicle* (Washington, D.C.: National Academy of Sciences, 1978), 53.

55. *New York Times*, 9 Sept. 1974, sec. 4.

56. *New York Times*, 12 Sept. 1974.

57. Robert J. Samuelson, "Public Jobs: Commonsense or Nonsense?" extensions of remarks, *Congressional Record*, 1974, 42073.

58. Remarks of Otto Eckstein, quoted in ibid.

59. See the testimony of Assistant Secretary of Labor William Kolberg before the Senate Committee on Labor and Public Welfare, *Emergency Jobs and Unemployment Assistance Amendments, 1975–1976*, 94 Cong., 2 sess., 1976, pt. 2, 62.

60. *Congressional Quarterly Weekly Report*, 7 June 1975, 1159.

61. *New York Times*, 5 June 1975.

62. *New York Times*, 16 Nov. and 24 Nov. 1976.

63. Mirengoff, *CETA: Accomplishments*, 81.

64. Ibid.

65. This calculation, however, does not include any multiplier effects.

66. Christopher Conte, "Carter Advisers See Inflation Risk in Efforts to Cut Unemployment," *Congressional Quarterly Weekly Report*, 4 Feb. 1978, 275.

67. Testimony of Arnold Packer, quoted in *Congressional Record*, 1978, S27240.

68. *Employment and Training Reporter*, 29 Mar. 1978, 526.

69. Conte, "Carter Advisers See Inflation Risk," 275; see also President Carter's economic message to Congress, *Congressional Quarterly Weekly Report*, 28 Jan. 1978, 219.

70. *Employment and Training Reporter*, 29 Mar. 1978, 275.

71. This section draws substantially upon the accounts provided in Helen Ginsburg, *Full Employment and Public Policy: The United States and Sweden* (Lexington: Heath, 1983), 63–84; and Harvey L. Schantz and Richard H. Schmidt, "Politics and Policy: The Humphrey-Hawkins Story," in *Employment and Labor*

Relations Policy, ed. Charles Bulmer and John L. Carmichael, Jr. (Lexington: Heath, 1980), 25–39.

72. Stephen K. Bailey, *Congress Makes a Law: The Story Behind the Employment Act of 1946* (New York: Columbia University Press, 1951), 43.

73. Reported in Herbert Stein, *The Fiscal Revolution in America* (Chicago: University of Chicago Press, 1968), 174.

74. Kay Lehman Schlozman and Sidney Verba, *Injury to Insult: Unemployment, Class, and Political Response* (Cambridge: Harvard University Press, 1979), 202, 375. Similar results come from the University of Michigan National Election Study of 1978. It asked respondents whether they agreed, disagreed, or were neutral regarding the statement: "Some people feel that the government in Washington should see to it that every person has a job and a good standard of living. Others think the government should just let each person get ahead on his own. And, of course, other people have opinions somewhere in between." Only 21 percent agreed the government should guarantee jobs, 23 percent were neutral, and 53 percent felt that individuals should be left on their own. Reported in Herbert McClosky and John Zaller, *The American Ethos: Public Attitudes toward Capitalism and Democracy* (Cambridge: Harvard University Press, 1984), 271.

75. Gallup poll results cited in Hazel Erskine, "The Polls: Government Role in Welfare," *Public Opinion Quarterly* 39 (Summer 1975): 266.

76. "Minority Views," in pt. 1, *Full Employment and Balanced Growth Act of 1978*, H. Rept. 95–895 (Washington, D.C.: GPO, 1978), 37.

77. Paul Lewis, "Charles Schultze of the C.E.A.," *New York Times*, 9 Jan. 1977, Business section.

78. Helen Ginsburg, "Congressional Will-o'-the-Wisp," *Nation*, 5 Feb. 1977, 141.

79. "Jobs and the Jobless," *Washington Post* editorial, 7 June 1976.

80. Lewis, "Charles Schultze," 7.

81. Henry Owen and Charles L. Schultze, introduction, in *Setting National Priorities*, ed. Henry Owen and Charles L. Schultze (Washington, D.C.: Brookings, 1976), 12.

82. Charles L. Schultze, "Unemployment and Inflation," *Washington Post*, 7 June 1976.

83. See Thomas M. Humphrey, "Some Recent Developments in Phillips Curve Analysis," *Economic Review* (Jan./Feb. 1978): 15–23. Other critiques are found in Muriel Humphrey and Augustus F. Hawkins, *Goals for Full Employment and How to Achieve Them under the Full Employment and Balanced Growth Act of 1978* (Washington, D.C.: GPO, Feb. 1978), 35–38, 48, 49.

84. See Michael J. Piore, "Unemployment and Inflation: An Alternative View," in *Unemployment and Inflation: Institutionalist and Structuralist Views*, ed. Michael J. Piore (White Plains: Sharpe, 1979), 5–16.

85. Michael J. Piore, ed., *Unemployment and Inflation: Institutionalist and Structuralist Views* (White Plains: Sharpe, 1979), xii.

86. Robert Lekachman, "The Specter of Full Employment," *Harpers*, Feb. 1977: 36.

87. *New York Times,* 2 Apr. 1976.
88. *Employment and Training Reporter,* 3 Jan. 1979, 243.

CHAPTER 5. *Congress, the Executive, and the Problem of State Building*

1. Institutions may be broadly defined as stable and valued patterns of interaction, but here they will refer to the specific organizational structure and resources of the state. Organizational structure includes the overall configuration of the government—whether authority is centralized or decentralized and whether its units are fragmented or integrated. It also includes the internal decision-making processes, distribution of authority, collective norms, and incentives within institutions. Resources include the financial, administrative, and technical means at the government's disposal. While empirical research has frequently pointed to the importance of institutions in policy making, recently there has been a renewed focus on institutions and on developing a better theoretical understanding of their role in political life. See, for example, James G. March and Johan P. Olsen, "The New Institutionalism: Organizational Factors in Political Life," *American Political Science Review* 78 (Sept. 1984): 734–63. One avenue these efforts have taken is in comparative-historical studies that "bring the state back" into political analysis. For reviews of and contributions to this literature, see Stephen Krasner, *Defending the National Interest* (Princeton: Princeton University Press, 1978); Peter Katzenstein, "Conclusion: Domestic Structures and Strategies of Foreign Economic Policy," in *Between Power and Plenty,* ed. Peter Katzenstein (Madison: University of Wisconsin Press, 1978: 295–331); Peter Evans, Dietrich Rueschemeyer, and Theda Skocpol, eds., *Bringing the State Back In* (Cambridge: Cambridge University Press, 1984).

2. Krasner, *Defending the National Interest,* 55–85.

3. On subgovernments, see Douglas Cater, *Power in Washington* (New York: Random House, 1964); Roger Davidson, "Breaking Up Those 'Cozy Triangles': An Impossible Dream?" in *Legislative Reform and Public Policy,* ed. Susan Welch and J. G. Peters (New York: Praeger, 1977: 30–53); J. L. Freeman, *The Political Process,* rev. ed. (New York: Random House, 1965); Randall B. Ripley and Grace A. Franklin, *Congress, the Bureaucracy, and Public Policy,* 4th ed. (Chicago: Dorsey, 1987); on the decline of subgovernments and the rise of issue networks, see Hugh Heclo "Issue Networks and the Executive Establishment," in *The New American Political System,* ed. Anthony King (Washington, D.C.: American Enterprise, 1978), 87–124; Thomas L. Gais, Mark A. Peterson, and Jack L. Walker, "Interest Groups, Iron Triangles and Representative Institutions in American National Government," *British Journal of Political Science* 14 (1984): 161–85.

4. Congressmen perceive little political payoff from conducting sustained oversight of the Federal Reserve Board. Whatever political benefits might be derived are outweighed by the obstacles to conducting oversight and the costs that must be incurred. The Federal Reserve is an "independent" agency, which is supposed to be off limits to political considerations. In addition, its deliberations are conducted in secret and discussed in a technical language that is all

but incomprehensible to the average legislator. See John Woolley, *Monetary Politics* (New York: Cambridge University Press, 1984), 131–53.

5. See the discussion in James L. Sundquist, *The Decline and Resurgence of Congress* (Washington, D.C.: Brookings, 1981), 61–90.

6. Allen Schick, *Congress and Money* (Washington, D.C.: Urban Institute, 1980), 112. See also, Allen Schick, ed., *Making Economic Policy in Congress* (Washington, D.C.: American Enterprise, 1983).

7. See chap. 7.

8. Stephen K. Bailey, *Congress Makes a Law: The Story Behind the Employment Act of 1946* (New York: Columbia University Press, 1951), 162.

9. Ibid., 237.

10. See chap. 4.

11. See chap. 4.

12. David Mayhew, *Congress: The Electoral Connection* (New Haven: Yale University Press, 1974), 127, 122.

13. Ibid., 132. On politics and symbolism, see Murray Edelman, *The Symbolic Uses of Politics* (Urbana: University of Illinois Press, 1967).

14. Garth L. Mangum, *MDTA: Foundation of Federal Manpower Policy* (Baltimore: Johns Hopkins University Press, 1968), 9.

15. Gladys Roth Kremen, "The Origins of the Manpower Development and Training Act of 1962," 1974, 48, Historian's Office, Department of Labor.

16. Richard Fenno, *Congressmen in Committees* (Boston: Little, Brown, 1973).

17. See Martha Derthick and Paul J. Quirk, *The Politics of Deregulation* (Washington, D.C.: Brookings, 1985), 143.

18. Ibid., 120, 246.

19. Fenno, *Congressmen in Committees*, 9.

20. Ibid.

21. Ibid., 77–79.

22. Ibid., 76–79, 86–88.

23. Since Fenno's study, these norms have been deteriorating throughout Congress. Members of Congress as a whole have become more individualistic in their orientations and entrepreneurial in their style. See Jack L. Walker, "Setting the Agenda in the U.S. Senate: A Theory of Problem Selection," *British Journal of Political Science* 7 (July 1977): 423–45; Bruce I. Oppenheimer, "Policy Effects of U.S. House Reform: Decentralization and the Capacity to Resolve Energy Issues," *Legislative Studies Quarterly* 5 (Feb. 1980): 5–29.

24. Fenno, *Congressmen in Committees*, 74–79, 226–42.

25. Sundquist, *Decline and Resurgence*, 370–72.

26. James L. Sundquist, *Politics and Policy: The Eisenhower, Kennedy, and Johnson Years* (Washington, D.C.: Brookings, 1968), 85.

27. Quoted in Bailey, *Congress Makes a Law*, 177.

28. Ibid., 236–37.

29. On employment programs, see hearings before the House Committee on Education and Labor, *Emergency Employment Act Amendments of 1973*, 93 Cong. 1 sess., 1973, 49; Hearings before the Senate Committee on Labor and Public Welfare, *Manpower Development and Training Legislation*, 91 Cong. 1 and 2 sess., 1969, pt. 1, 101–03, 117; on Congress's skepticism generally toward

block grants, see Michael D. Reagan, *The New Federalism* (New York: Oxford University Press, 1972), 75–76; Philip Monypenny, "Federal Grants-in-Aid to State Governments: A Political Analysis," *National Tax Journal* (Mar. 1960): 1–16; Paul R. Dommel, *The Politics of Revenue Sharing* (Bloomington: Indiana University Press, 1974), 117–21.

30. See for example, hearings before the Joint Economic Committee, *The Effects of Structural Employment and Training Programs on Inflation and Unemployment*, 96 Cong. 1 sess., 1979.

31. Note that I am arguing that it is the direction in which the unemployment rate is headed, up or down, that is the important part of the matter, rather than the rate itself. The unemployment rate during Ronald Reagan's bid for reelection in 1984 was as high, or in many cases higher, than it had been in previous election years. Reagan was fortunate to have the unemployment rate falling throughout 1984, despite that it was falling from a rate of over 10 percent at one point in his first term, the highest it had reached since the 1930s.

32. Edward R. Tufte, *Political Control of the Economy* (Princeton: Princeton University Press, 1978).

33. See James E. Alt and K. Alec Crystal, *Political Economics* (Berkeley and Los Angeles: University of California Press, 1980), chap. 5; Gerald H. Kramer, "The Ecological Fallacy Revisited: Aggregate versus Individual-level Findings on Economics and Elections and Sociotropic Voting," *American Political Science Review* 77 (1983): 92–111; Roderick D. Kiewiet, *Macroeconomics and Micropolitics* (Chicago: University of Chicago Press, 1983); John R. Hibbing and John A. Alford, "The Electoral Impact of Economic Conditions: Who Is Held Responsible?" *American Journal of Political Science* 25 (May 1981): 423–39; M. Stephen Weatherford, "Economic Voting and the 'Symbolic Politics' Argument," *American Political Science Review* 77 (1983): 158–74.

34. Douglas Hibbs, "Political Parties and Macroeconomic Outcomes," *American Political Science Review* 71 (Dec. 1977): 1467–87.

35. Calculated from budget figures for the U.S. Department of Labor, Employment and Training Administration. See U.S. Office of Management and Budget, *Budget of the United States Government*, Appendix, (Washington, D.C.: GPO, various years); for consumer price index see U.S. Department of Commerce, *Statistical Abstract of the United States* (Washington, D.C.: GPO, various years).

36. Erwin C. Hargrove and Samuel A. Morley, *The President and the Council of Economic Advisers: Interviews with CEA Chairmen* (Boulder: Westview, 1984), 434–35.

37. "Oral history interview with Assistant Secretary of Labor Charles Knapp, 13 Jan. 1981," 26–28, Historian's Office, Department of Labor.

38. Mangum, *MDTA: Foundation*, 14; see also Kremen, "Origins," 34.

39. Stephen Skowronek, *Building a New American State: The Expansion of National Administrative Capacities, 1877–1920* (Cambridge: Cambridge University Press, 1982), 290.

40. James Q. Wilson, "The Rise of the Bureaucratic State," *Public Interest* 41 (Fall 1975): 77–103.

41. Skowronek, *Building a New American State,* 286.

42. Jonathan Grossman, *The Department of Labor* (New York: Praeger, 1973), 59.

43. Ibid., 55.

44. Eli Ginzberg, "Employment Service—Chosen Instrument of the Manpower Revolution," *Employment Service Review* (Mar./Apr. 1967):7.

45. Quoted in Kremen, "Origins of the Manpower and Training Act," 13.

46. Ibid., 39–40.

47. Sundquist, *Politics and Policy,* 88.

48. Ibid.; Kremen, "Origins of the Manpower and Training Act," 41.

49. Stanley H. Ruttenberg, *Manpower Challenge of the 1970s: Institutions and Social Change* (Baltimore: Johns Hopkins University Press, 1970), 18.

50. Stanley H. Ruttenberg and Jocelyn Gutchess, *The Federal-State Employment Service: A Critique* (Baltimore: Johns Hopkins University Press, 1970).

51. Employment Service Task Force Report, 29 Dec. 1965, "A Comprehensive Manpower Services Center," *Employment Service Review* 3 (Feb. 1966).

52. Joseph H. Ball, *The Implementation of Federal Manpower Policy, 1961–1971: A Study in Bureaucratic Competition and Intergovernmental Relations* (Springfield: National Technical Information Service, 1972), 182.

53. Ibid., 54–55; see also Sar A. Levitan and Joyce Zickler, *The Quest for a Federal Manpower Partnership* (Cambridge: Harvard University Press, 1974).

CHAPTER 6. *Employment Policy as an Intergovernmental Dilemma*

1. Even here there have been problems with relying upon local authorities with different objectives from those of Congress with regard to how federal aid should be used. See Jerome T. Murphy, "The Education Bureaucracies Implement Novel Policies: The Politics of Title I of ESEA, 1965–72," in *Policy and Politics in America,* ed. Alan P. Sindler (Boston: Little, Brown, 1973), 161–98.

2. Grant McConnell, *Private Power and American Democracy* (New York: Knopf, 1966).

3. See Department of Labor, *Employment and Training Report of the President;* and *Budget of the United States Government,* (Washington, D.C.: GPO, various years).

4. Helen Ginsburg, *Full Employment and Public Policy: The United States and Sweden* (Lexington: D.C. Heath, 1983), 137.

5. Santosh Mukherjee, "Governments and Labour Markets: Aspects of Policies in Britain, France, Germany, Netherlands and Italy," *Political and Economic Planning* 42 (November 1976): 18–44.

6. See William Haber and Daniel H. Kruger, *The Role of the United States Employment Service in a Changing Economy* (Kalamazoo: Upjohn Institute for Employment Research, 1964), 21–40; William M. Leiserson, "The Movement for Public Labor Exchanges," *Journal of Political Economy* 23 (July 1915): 707–16; William M. Leiserson, "The Theory of Public Employment Offices and the

Principles of Their Practical Administration," *Political Science Quarterly* 29 (March 1914): 29–30.

7. William M. Leiserson, "A Federal Labor Reserve Board for the Unemployed," *Annals of the American Academy of Political and Social Science* 59 (January 1917): 103–17.

8. Stanley H. Ruttenberg and Jocelyn Gutchess, *The Federal-State Employment Service: A Critique* (Baltimore: Johns Hopkins University Press, 1970), 6.

9. Ibid., 52–57.

10. Ibid., 7.

11. Eli Ginzberg, "Employment Service—Chosen Instrument of the Manpower Revolution," *Employment Service Review* (Mar./Apr. 1967), 7–9.

12. Ruttenberg and Gutchess, *Federal-State Employment Service*, 2.

13. Ibid., 43–47.

14. Stanley H. Ruttenberg, *Manpower Challenge of the 1970s: Institutions and Social Change* (Baltimore: Johns Hopkins University Press, 1970), 54–55.

15. William H. Kolberg, *Developing Manpower Legislation: A Personal Chronicle* (Washington: National Academy of Sciences, 1978), 13.

16. Hearing before the Senate Committee on Labor and Public Welfare, *The Nation's Manpower Revolution*, 88 Cong., 1 and 2 sess., 1963–1964.

17. U.S. President, "Establishing the President's Committee on Manpower," *Federal Register*, 17 Apr. 1964, 5271.

18. Sar A. Levitan and Joyce Zickler, *The Quest for a Federal Manpower Partnership* (Cambridge: Harvard University Press, 1974), 83.

19. *National Journal Reports*, 7 Apr. 1973, 492.

20. *National Journal Reports*, 16 Dec. 1972, 1934–35.

21. Levitan and Zickler, *Quest*, 109.

22. Hearings before the House Committee on Education and Labor, *The Manpower Act of 1969*, 91 Cong., 2 sess., 1970, 409.

23. William Kolberg, former assistant secretary of Labor for Employment and Training, interview with author, Nov. 1983.

24. *National Journal Reports*, 7 Apr. 1973, 494.

25. Hearings before the Senate Committee on Labor and Public Welfare, *The Employment and Manpower Act of 1972*, 223–24.

26. Donald Baumer and Carl Van Horn, *The Politics of Unemployment* (Washington, D.C.: CQ Press, 1981).

27. Senate Committee on Labor and Public Welfare, *Employment and Training Programs in the United States*, 97 Cong., 1 sess., 1981, pt. 2, 1.

28. Committee for Economic Development, "New Directions for a Public-Private Partnership," a statement by the Research and Policy Committee of the Committee for Economic Development, New York, 1978; David Robison, "Training and Jobs Programs in Action," Committee for Economic Development, Work in America Institute, Inc., 1978.

29. Hugh Heclo, "Issue Networks and the Executive Establishment," in *The New American Political System*, ed. Anthony King et al. (Washington, D.C.: American Enterprise, 1976), 93.

30. Martha Derthick, *New Towns In-Town: Why a Federal Program Failed* (Washington: Urban Institute, 1972), 84.

CHAPTER 7. *The Saga of CETA*

1. See the discussion of efforts to create and expand public service employment in chap. 4.

2. *Congressional Record*, 1975, H16875–876.

3. William H. Kolberg, *Developing Manpower Legislation: A Personal Chronicle* (Washington, D.C.: National Academy of Sciences, 1978), 75.

4. The same was true about other kinds of abuses: waste, maladministration, nepotism, and the use of funds for political patronage.

5. See the testimony of William Hewitt, associate manpower administrator for Policy, Evaluation and Research, *Authorization of Appropriations for Fiscal Year 1976 for Carrying Out Title VI of CETA*, Hearings before the House Committee on Education and Labor, 94 Cong., 1 sess. (Washington, D.C.: GPO, 1975), 251–52.

6. See the testimony of William H. Kolberg, assistant secretary of Labor for Employment and Training, *Emergency Jobs and Unemployment Assistance Amendments, 1975–1976*, Hearings before the Senate Committee on Labor and Public Welfare, 94 Cong., 2 sess. (Washington, D.C.: GPO, 1976), pt. 2, 64–65.

7. William Mirengoff et al., *CETA: Accomplishments, Problems, Solutions* (Kalamazoo: Upjohn Institute for Employment Policy Research, 1982), table 32.

8. *Congressional Record*, 1976, H2951; Mirengoff et al., *CETA: Accomplishments*.

9. Testimony of Kolberg, *Emergency Jobs*, pt. 2, 62.

10. Testimony of Richard Schubert, undersecretary of Labor, *Authorization of Appropriations*, 252–53.

11. *Congressional Record*, 1976, H2960.

12. Ibid., 26622.

13. Kolberg, *Developing Manpower Legislation*, 86.

14. CETA statistics in this paragraph from Mirengoff et al., *CETA: Accomplishments*, table 7.

15. *New York Times*, 16 Nov. and 24 Nov. 1976.

16. Robert Samuelson, "Carter's Early Economic Choices," *National Journal* 8 Jan. 1977, 59–65.

17. *Congressional Record*, 1977, S13097.

18. *Congressional Quarterly Weekly Report*, 5 Feb. 1977, 244; *Congressional Quarterly Weekly Report*, 12 Feb. 1977, 252.

19. These studies are cited in *Congressional Record*, 1977, H13095; Congressional Budget Office, *Public Employment and Training Assistance: Alternative Fiscal Approaches*, and *Short-run Measures to Stimulate the Economy* (Washington, D.C.: GPO, 1977); George E. Johnson and James D. Tomola, "The Fiscal Substitution Effect of Alternative Approaches to Public Service Employment Policy," *Journal of Human Resources* 12 (Winter 1977): 3–26; National Planning Association, *An Evaluation of the Economic Impact Project of the Public Employment Program, Final Report* (Washington, D.C.: National Planning Association, 1974); Congressional Research Service, *Report on CETA* (Washington, D.C.: CRS, 1976).

20. General Accounting Office, *More Benefits to Jobless Can Be Attained in Public Service Employment* (Washington, D.C.: GPO, 1977).

21. _New York Times,_ 14 May 1978.

22. Michael E. Borus and Daniel S. Hammermesh, "Study of the Net Employment Effects of Public Service Employment—Econometric Analyses," in _Job Creation Through Public Service Employment,_ an interim report to the National Commission for Manpower Policy 1978), vol. 3, 89–149; Richard P. Nathan et al., _Public Service Employment: A Field Evaluation_ (Washington, D.C.: Brookings, 1981). National Academy of Sciences, _CETA: Local Control of Manpower Programs_ (Washington, D.C.: National Academy of Sciences, 1978).

23. Mirengoff et al., _CETA: Accomplishments,_ table 13.

24. William Mirengoff et al., _The New CETA: Effect on Public Service Employment Programs, final report_ (Washington, D.C.: National Academy Press, 1980), table 9.

25. _Congressional Record,_ 1978, H25232.

26. Ibid., 25175; see General Accounting Office, _Information on the Buildup in Public Service Jobs_ (Washington, D.C.: GPO, 1978).

27. Hearings before the House Committee on Education and Labor, _Comprehensive Employment and Training Act Amendments of 1978,_ 95 Cong., 2 sess. (Washington, D.C.: GPO, 1978), 436.

28. _Congressional Quarterly Weekly Report,_ 1 Apr. 1978, 805–06.

29. Lance Gay, "Is Job Program a Boondoggle?" _Washington Star,_ 31 July 1978.

30. Ralph Kinney Bennett, "CETA: $11 Billion Boondoggle," _Reader's Digest,_ Aug. 1978, 72–76.

31. "Psst—Wanna Good Job?" _Time,_ 24 July 1978, 18–19.

32. See for instance, "A Leaking CETA," _Washington Star,_ 13 Mar. 1978; Michael Kiernan, "Abuse of Job Funds Paid to Council," _Washington Star,_ 17 July 1978.

33. _Congressional Record,_ 1978, S27223.

34. "President Carter's message to Congress requesting extension of CETA, 22 Feb. 1978," _Congressional Quarterly Weekly Report,_ 4 Mar. 1978, 592.

35. Harrison H. Donnelly, "Carter Proposes $2 Billion Increase in Labor Spending," _Congressional Quarterly Weekly Report,_ 28 Jan. 1978, 161.

36. _Congressional Quarterly Weekly Report,_ 4 Nov. 1978, 3185.

37. _Congressional Quarterly Weekly Report,_ 29 July 1978, 1924.

38. _Congressional Record,_ 1978, H25232.

39. Ibid.

40. Ibid., 25233.

41. Ibid., 25236.

42. _New York Times,_ 11 Aug. 1978.

43. _Employment and Training Reporter,_ 3 Jan. 1979, 243.

44. _Employment and Training Reporter,_ 14 Mar. 1979, 449; ibid., 16 May 1979, 621.

45. Mirengoff et al., _CETA: Accomplishments._

46. Grace A. Franklin and Randall B. Ripley, _CETA: Politics and Policy, 1973–1982_ (Knoxville: University of Tennessee Press, 1984), 178; on the implementation of the 1978 reforms, see also Donald C. Baumer and Carl E. Van Horn, _The Politics of Unemployment_ (Washington, D.C.: CQ Press, 1985), 125–56.

Pitt Series in Policy and Institutional Studies
Bert A. Rockman, Editor

47. Harrison Donnelly, "New, Smaller Job Training Program Emerging to Help the Hard-Core Unemployed," *Congressional Quarterly Weekly Report*, 6 Mar. 1982, 517.

48. See George Gilder, *Wealth and Poverty* (New York: Basic Books, 1980), 111, 153, 156–59, 161–63, 167–69; Charles Murray, *Losing Ground: American Social Policy 1950–80* (New York: Basic Books, 1984), chaps. 4 and 5.

49. For a review of the literature on evaluation of employment programs, see chapter 1.

50. *Amendments of 1978*, 179.

51. Kolberg, *Developing Manpower Legislation*, 44.

52. *Congressional Record*, 1978, H25183–184.

53. Martha Derthick, *New Towns In-Town: Why a Federal Program Failed* (Washington, D.C.: Urban Institute, 1972), 83.

54. "Oral history interview with Assistant Secretary of Labor Charles Knapp, 13 Jan. 1981," 39–40, Historian's Office, Department of Labor.

55. Franklin and Ripley, *CETA: Politics and Policy*, 172.

56. Knapp, oral history interview, 32–33.

57. Franklin and Ripley, *CETA: Politics and Policy*, 172–73.

58. Many of these conclusions echo those of others who have studied CETA:

The behavior of Congress and DOL in administering CETA appears, when viewed in the aggregate and with the advantage of hindsight, to have been inconsistent and to have lacked continuity. Congress frequently altered its own legislative priorities—from categorical to decentralized, decategorized programs from comprehensive programs to recategorized programs—and DOL of necessity followed suit. DOL's actions were inconsistent because the legislation had multiple and conflicting goals and because both DOL and Congress emphasized different goals at different times. (Franklin and Ripley, *CETA: Politics and Policy*, 164)

"There was inherent competition and inconsistency among different goals, with the result that actions taken to promote one would impede achievement of another," ibid., 172; according to Baumer and Van Horn, "national policy makers transformed an effort at modest policy reform into an enormous program with clear but conflicting objectives," *Politics of Unemployment*, 118; see also Mirengoff et al., *New CETA*, 5.

59. Robert Guttman, "Job Training Partnership Act: New Help for the Unemployed," *Monthly Labor Review* (Mar. 1983): 3.

60. Mirengoff et al., *CETA: Accomplishments*, xiv.

61. Knapp, oral history interview, 36.

62. "Why CETA Is in Trouble," *Business Week*, 2 Oct. 1978, 124.

63. John L. Mori, "May CETA Rest in Peace," *Adherent* (Sept. 1980): 60.

CHAPTER 8. *Organized Interests in the Arenas of Employment Policy*

1. Kay Lehman Schlozman and Sidney Verba, *Injury to Insult: Unemployment, Class, and Political Response* (Cambridge: Harvard University Press, 1979), 332

and 254. They attribute this not to the unemployed condition of the jobless but to the fact that the unemployed tend to have those social characteristics that are associated with low levels of political interest, information, and activity. Another reason frequently given for the acquiescence of the unemployed and poor is that they have been led to believe, especially in America, that individuals deserve their lot in life and are primarily responsible for bettering themselves. See Frances Fox Piven and Richard A. Cloward, *Poor People's Movements* (New York: Pantheon, 1977), 6–7; and Murray Edelman, *Politics as Symbolic Action* (New Haven: Yale University Press, 1971), 56.

2. Neither the organizations associated with the civil rights movement of the 1950s and 1960s (i.e., the Southern Christian Leadership Conference, the Student Nonviolent Coordinating Committee, and the Congress on Racial Equality) nor those connected to the welfare rights movement (i.e., the National Welfare Rights Organization) qualifies as organizations of and for the unemployed. In terms of their membership composition, the civil rights groups attracted mainly blacks, students, and middle-class activists. While the welfare rights organizations were composed of the poor, many of the poor are not unemployed and many of the unemployed are not officially counted as poor. Second, in terms of their objectives, the civil rights movement was primarily interested in securing voting rights and ending discrimination in housing, education, and other areas of social life. The dominant objective of welfare rights organizations was in liberalizing and expanding income maintenance programs like Aid to Families with Dependent Children. Third, these organizations focused their activities mainly at the state and local level (especially in the South), not in Washington, where employment policy is made. These groups rarely, if at all, testified before Congress in the postwar period during hearings on employment and training programs. On these movements, see Piven and Cloward, *Poor People's Movements*.

3. Schlozman and Verba, *Injury to Insult*, 345.

4. James Q. Wilson, *Political Organizations* (New York: Basic Books, 1973), 46.

5. OICs are opportunity industrial centers, nonprofit community-based organizations founded by the Reverend Leon Sullivan, that provide training and remedial education.

6. Paul E. Peterson and Barry G. Rabe, "Urban Vocational Education and Managing the Transition from School to Work: A Review of a Series of Case Studies of Vocational Educational Programs in Four Cities," 1984, photocopy.

7. Graham Wilson, *Business and Politics: A Comparative Introduction* (Chatham: Chatham House, 1985), 22–43.

8. "Interview with Stanley Ruttenberg, 19 July 1974," 2–3, 8, Historian's Office, Department of Labor.

9. Ibid., 13–14.

10. Ibid., 4.

11. Robert Guttman, Senate Committee on Labor and Human Resources, interview with author 27 Aug. 1984.

12. Eli Ginzberg, "Overview: The $64 Billion Innovation," in *Employing the Unemployed*, ed. Eli Ginzberg (New York: Basic Books), 13.

13. Schlozman and Verba, *Injury to Insult*, 340.

14. Interview with Guttman.

15. Jack Barbash, *Trade Unions and National Economic Policy* (Baltimore: Johns Hopkins University Press, 1972), 194.

16. See, for example, James Weinstein, *The Corporate Ideal in the Liberal State, 1900–1918* (Boston: Beacon, 1968).

17. A structural class analysis would posit that business does not need to pressure or control the state to dominate. Instead, the state is relatively autonomous from social classes and can be depended upon to maintain conditions hospitable to capitalism. For a review of this literature, see Robert R. Alford and Roger Friedland, *Powers of Theory: Capitalism, the State and Democracy* (Cambridge: Cambridge: University Press, 1985), 274. James O'Connor argues that it is one of the functions of the state to underwrite certain activities (such as manpower training) as part of its "social investment expenditures" in order to increase the productivity of labor. It underwrites other activities (such as welfare payments) not to help rationalize capitalism but to absorb the social costs of capitalism and maintain social peace; see *The Fiscal Crisis of the State* (New York: St. Martin's, 1973). At one level it is patently obvious that the federal government has established employment and training programs to help maintain the capitalist system. (Because of the welfarist orientation of the programs in the United States, the stress has been on the latter rather than on the former objective.) There are two problems with this, however. Short of proposals to eliminate capitalism, it is impossible to falsify the structural thesis. As long as the basic features of a capitalist economy exist in the United States, and the system's existence is not an issue on the agenda, it must be assumed that any employment policy exists to maintain capitalism. To argue that the purpose of public policy is to maintain a prosperous capitalist system and to compensate for the costs of capitalism is to state a truism. The structural thesis is formulated at too abstract a level of analysis to be useful in explaining why policy makers pursue certain policies but not others.

18. See Randall Ripley and Grace A. Franklin, *Congress, the Bureaucracy and Public Policy* (Homewood: Dorsey, 1984), 189.

19. Interview with Guttman.

20. Santosh Mukherjee, "Making Labour Markets Work: A Comparison of the Swedish and U.K. Systems," *Political and Economic Planning Broadsheet* 532 (1972): x.

21. Helen Ginsburg, *Full Employment and Public Policy: The United States and Sweden* (Lexington: Heath, 1983), 131.

22. See chap. 3.

23. See Eli Ginzberg, *Good Jobs, Bad Jobs, No Jobs* (Cambridge: Harvard University Press, 1979), 35. Data for the 1980s calculated by the author.

24. David Cameron, "Does Government Cause Inflation? Taxes, Spending, and Deficits," in *The Politics of Inflation and Economic Stagnation*, ed. Leon N. Lindberg and Charles S. Maier (Washington, D.C.: Brookings, 1985), 232, 251.

25. Douglas A. Hibbs, Jr., "Inflation, Political Support, and Macroeconomic Policy," in *The Politics of Inflation and Economic Stagnation*, ed. Leon N. Lindberg and Charles S. Maier (Washington, D.C.: Brookings, 1985), 175–95.

26. Garth L. Mangum, *Employability, Employment and Income: A Reassessment of Manpower Policy* (Salt Lake City: Olympus, 1976), 113.

27. Schlozman and Verba, *Injury to Insult*, 343.

28. See chap. 9.

29. Stephen K. Bailey, *Congress Makes a Law* (New York: Columbia University Press, 1951), 97.

30. See Schlozman and Verba, *Injury to Insult*, 338–44; and Ginsburg, *Full Employment*, 76–80.

31. Bailey, *Congress Makes a Law*, chaps. 7, 8.

32. Ibid., 192 and 218; emphasis in original.

33. Robert M. Collins, *The Business Response to Keynes, 1929–1964* (New York: Columbia University Press, 1981), 200.

34. See chap. 4.

35. See Fred Hirsch and John Goldthorpe, eds., *The Political Economy of Inflation* (Cambridge: Harvard University Press, 1978); Colin Crouch, "Conditions for Trade Union Wage Restraint," in *The Politics of Inflation and Economic Stagnation*, ed. Leon N. Lindberg and Charles S. Maier (Washington, D.C.: Brookings, 1985), 105–39.

36. John T. Woolley, *Monetary Politics: The Federal Reserve and the Politics of Monetary Policy* (Cambridge: Cambridge University Press, 1984), 85–87, 188–89.

CHAPTER 9. *Class Interests and U.S. Employment Policy in Comparative Perspective*

1. John D. Stephens, *The Transition from Capitalism to Socialism* (Atlantic Highlands: Humanities Press, 1980); Michael Shalev, "The Social Democratic Model and Beyond: Two Generations of Comparative Research on the Welfare State," *Comparative Social Research* 4 (1983): 316–54; Gosta Esping-Anderson, *Social Class, Social Democracy, and State Policy* (Copenhagen: New Social Science Monographs, 1980); Walter Korpi and Michael Shalev, "Strikes, Power, and Politics in the Western Nations, 1900–1976," in *Political Power and Social Theory*, ed. Maurice Zeitlin (Greenwich: JAI, 1980), 301–34; Andrew Martin, "The Politics of Economic Policy in the United States: A Tentative View from a Comparative Perspective," in *Comparative Politics Series*, ed. Harry Eckstein et al. (Beverly Hills: Sage, 1973); Walter Korpi, *The Working Class and Welfare Capitalism: Work, Unions, and Politics in Sweden* (London: Routledge and Kegan Paul, 1977).

2. It may be argued that, because the United States is so much larger and more socially heterogeneous than Sweden, any comparison cannot be very instructive. It must be kept in mind that the purpose of the comparison is largely analytical, rather than prescriptive. While any effort to adopt a Swedish employment policy would need to take account of differences in size and diversity between the two nations, I argue that these factors are less crucial and directly relevant when trying to explain what accounts for the differences in the policies that were adopted.

3. Andrew Shonfield, *Modern Capitalism: The Changing Balance of Public and Private Power* (London: Oxford University Press, 1963), 201.

4. E. Wight Bakke, *The Mission of Manpower Policy* (Kalamazoo: Upjohn Institute for Employment Policy Research, 1969), 85.

5. Helen Ginsburg, *Full Employment and Public Policy: The United States and Sweden* (Lexington: Heath, 1983), 155.

6. Roger Henning, "Industrial Policy or Employment Policy? Sweden's Response to Unemployment," in *Unemployment Policy Responses of Western Democracies*, ed. Jeremy Richardson and Roger Henning (Beverly Hills: Sage, 1985), 198–99.

7. Ginsburg, *Full Employment*, 131.

8. Ibid., 53; see also Janet Wegner Johnson, "An Overview of U.S. Federal Employment and Training Programs," in *Unemployment: Policy Responses, of Western Democracies*, ed. Jeremy Richardson and Roger Henning (Beverly Hills: Sage, 1985), 57–115.

9. Michael Goldfield, *The Decline of Organized Labor in the United States* (Chicago: University of Chicago Press, 1987); Henry Farber, "The Extent of Unionization in the U.S.," in *Challenges and Choices Facing American Labor*, ed. Thomas Kochan (Cambridge: MIT Press 1985), 16. There is a large literature examining why the American working class never developed the levels of class consciousness and political organization found elsewhere; see Werner Sombart, "American Capitalism's Economic Rewards," 599, and Stephen Thernstrom, "Socialism and Social Mobility," 408–26, in *Failure of a Dream?* ed. John Laslett and Seymour Martin Lipset (Garden City: Doubleday Anchor, 1974); David Potter, *People of Plenty* (Chicago: University of Chicago Press, 1954); Frederick Jackson Turner, *The Frontier in American History* (New York: Henry Holt, 1920); Stanley Aronowitz, *False Promises: The Shaping of American Working Class Consciousness* (New York: McGraw-Hill, 1973); Louis Hartz, *The Liberal Tradition in America* (New York: Harcourt, Brace, 1955); Daniel Boorstin, *The Americans*, 3 vols. (New York: Random House, 1958–1973); Michael Kammen, *People of Paradox* (New York: Vintage, 1973); Ira Katznelson, *City Trenches, Urban Politics and the Patterning of Class in the United States* (Chicago: University of Chicago Press, 1981).

10. Martin, "Politics of Economic Policy," 53–54.

11. Sweden also came out of the Depression before most other countries. However, most analysts today would probably agree that the early revival of Swedish exports, rather than the deficits created by the Social Democrats, was the single most important cause of Sweden's relatively rapid recovery. See Assar Lindbeck, *Swedish Economic Policy* (Berkeley and Los Angeles: University of California Press, 1974), 23.

12. Ginsburg, *Full Employment*, 112.

13. Quoted in Korpi, *Working Class in Welfare Capitalism*, 80.

14. Gosta Esping-Andersen, *Politics Against Markets: The Social Democratic Road to Power* (Princeton: Princeton University Press, 1985), 107.

15. Ibid., 87, 107.

16. See Donald Brand, *Corporatism and the Rule of Law: A Study of the National Recovery Administration* (Ithaca: Cornell University Press, 1988).

17. Timothy Tilton and Norman Furniss, *The Case for the Welfare State: From Social Security to Social Equality* (Bloomington: Indiana University Press, 1977), 126.

18. See chaps. 2 and 5.

19. Berndt Ohman, *LO and Labour Market Policy* (Stockholm: Prisma, 1973), 20–45.

20. Esping-Andersen, *Politics Against Markets*, 107–108.

21. Stephen K. Bailey, *Congress Makes a Law: The Story Behind the Employment Act of 1946* (New York: Columbia University Press, 1951), chaps. 7, 8.

22. Quoted in Robert M. Collins, *The Business Response to Keynes: 1929–1964* (New York: Columbia University Press, 1981), 138.

23. Ibid., 180–91.

24. See chap. 2.

25. Daniel P. Moynihan, *Maximum Feasible Misunderstanding: Community Action in the War on Poverty* (New York: Free Press, 1969), 99.

26. Henning, "Industrial Policy or Employment Policy?" 194–95.

27. For a discussion of political learning, see chap. 1; and Hugh Heclo, *Modern Social Politics in Britain and Sweden* (New Haven: Yale University Press, 1974), chap. 6.

28. Andrew Martin, "Is Democratic Control of Capitalist Economies Possible?" in *Stress and Contradiction in Modern Capitalism*, ed. Leon N. Lindberg et al. (Lexington: Heath, 1975), 22.

29. Ibid.

30. Jack Barbash, *Trade Unions and National Economic Policy* (Baltimore: Johns Hopkins University Press, 1975), 32.

31. Collins, *Business Response to Keynes*, 205.

32. Alfred Neal, *Business Power and Public Policy* (New York: Praeger, 1981), 150–51.

33. See chap. 2.

34. See chap. 3. For contrasting views, also see Sar A. Levitan, "Development of a National Manpower Policy," and Gosta Rehn, "Manpower Policy as an Instrument of National Economic Policy," in *Manpower Policy: Perspectives and Prospects,* ed. Seymour Wolfbein (Philadelphia: Temple University Press, 1973), 33–34, 175.

35. Gerald A. Dorfman, *Wage Politics in Britain 1945–1967: Government vs. the TUC* (Ames: Iowa State University Press, 1973); Leo Panitch, *Social Democracy and Industrial Militancy* (Cambridge: Cambridge University Press, 1976).

36. See Leo Panitch, *Working-Class Politics in Crisis* (London: Verso, 1986), 56–77; This was by no means the only reason for Britain's economic problems. The dominance of the Sterling lobby in British government led to currency manipulations that are widely credited with damaging the productive capacity of the economy. See Stephen Blank, *Industry and Government in Britain: The Federation of British Industries in Politics, 1945–65* (Lexington: Heath, 1973).

37. Martin, "Is Democratic Control . . . Possible?" 22–23.

38. Barbash, *Trade Unions*, 143; Derek Robinson, "Implementing an Incomes Policy," *Industrial Relations* (Oct. 1968): 83.

39. Margaret Weir and Theda Skocpol, "State Structures and the Possibilities for 'Keynesian' Responses to the Great Depression," in *Bringing the State Back In*, ed. Peter B. Evans, Dietrich Rueschemeyer, and Theda Skocpol (New York: Cambridge University Press, 1985), 129.

40. Hans Meijer, "Bureaucracy and Policy Formation in Sweden," in *Scandinavian Political Studies,* ed. Olof Ruin (New York: Columbia University Press, 1969), vol. 4, 103–16.

41. Thomas Anton, "Policy-making and Political Culture in Sweden," in *Scandinavian Political Studies,* ed. Olof Ruin (New York: Columbia University Press, 1969), vol. 4, 94.

42. Brinley, Thomas, *Monetary Policy and Crisis: A Study of Swedish Experience* (London: Routledge, 1936), xix–xx.

43. Weir and Skocpol, "State Structures," 132.

44. The following account of prewar developments in Sweden is a summary of ibid., 130–32.

45. C. G. Uhr, "Economists and Policymaking 1930–36: Sweden's Experience," *History of Political Economy* 9 (1977): 92.

46. Skocpol and Weir point out that the Labour party in Great Britain, which was in power for part of the 1930s, did not break from the orthodoxy of the balanced budget to adopt a Keynesian economic recovery program.

47. From Ohman, *LO and Labour Market Policy,* chap. 1.

48. M. Donald Hancock, *Sweden: The Politics of Post-Industrial Change* (Hinsdale: Dryden, 1972), 205–07.

49. Three of its fifteen members come from the LO; two from the federation of white collar employees, one each from organizations representing professionals, government employees, agriculture, and women; three from the federation of Swedish employers; and three civil servants from the staff and directorate of the board.

50. See chap. 6.

CHAPTER 10. *Summary and Conclusions*

1. See Herbert McClosky and John Zaller, *The American Ethos: Public Attitudes Toward Capitalism and Democracy* (Cambridge: Harvard University Press, 1984), chap. 6.

2. Mary Corcoran and Martha S. Hill, "Reoccurrence of Unemployment Among Adult Men," *Journal of Human Resources* 20 (Spring 1985): 168; Martin S. Feldstein, *Lowering the Permanent Rate of Unemployment,* prepared for the Joint Economic Committee (Washington, D.C.: GPO, 1973).

3. Carl Rosenfeld, "Job Search Among the Unemployed," *Monthly Labor Review* 100 (Nov. 1977): 39–42; James Tobin, "Inflation and Unemployment," *American Economic Review* (Mar. 1972): 1–18.

4. George Akerloff and Brian Main, "An Experience-Weighted Measure of Employment and Unemployment Durations," *American Economic Review* 71 (Dec. 1981): 1003–11; Hal Sider, "Unemployment Duration and Incidence: 1968–82," *American Economic Review* 75 (June 1985): 461–72; Lawrence Summers, "Why Is the Unemployment Rate So Very High Near Full Employment?" *Brookings Papers on Economic Activity* 2 (1982): 339–96.

5. Paul Osterman, *Employment Futures: Reorganization, Dislocation, and Public Policy* (New York: Oxford University Press, 1988), 17–35.

Index